Mastering
Turbo Pascal 5

Mastering Turbo Pascal 5®

Second Edition

Douglas Hergert

San Francisco • Paris • Düsseldorf • London

Acquisitions Editor: Dianne King
Supervising Editor: Joanne Cuthbertson
Copy and Technical Editor: Brad Hess
Word Processor: Chris Mockel
Pasteup and Chapter Art: Lucie Živny
Typesetter: Elizabeth Newman
Proofreader: Lisa Jaffe
Indexer: Ted Laux

Cover Designer: Thomas Ingalls + Associates
Cover Photographer: David Bishop
Screen reproductions produced by XenoFont

Library of Congress Card Number: 89-62754
ISBN 0-89588-647-2

Manufactured in the United States of America
10 9 8 7 6 5 4 3 2 1

ACKNOWLEDGMENTS

My sincere thanks to Scott Palmer for his time in preparing this revision. I would also like to thank Nan Borreson of Borland International for supplying timely information with copies of beta software.

CONTENTS AT A GLANCE

Introduction		*xvii*
PART I:	***The Turbo Pascal Environment***	***1***
Chapter 1:	An Introduction to Turbo Pascal	3
Chapter 2:	The Menu System and the Editor	55
Chapter 3:	Using Units in Turbo Pascal Programs	117
PART II:	***A Turbo Pascal Language Tutorial***	***141***
Chapter 4:	Fundamentals of Turbo Pascal Programming	143
Chapter 5:	Decisions and Loops	195
Chapter 6:	Records and Arrays	235
Chapter 7:	Other Data Types and Data Structures	277
Chapter 8:	Pointers, Dynamic Variables, and Linked Lists	313
Chapter 9:	Numeric Functions and Procedures	357
Chapter 10:	String Functions and Procedures	385
Chapter 11:	Sequential-Access Data File Programming	419
Chapter 12:	Random-Access Data File Programming	447
PART III:	***Advanced Programming Techniques***	***489***
Chapter 13:	Graphics	491
Chapter 14:	Date-Arithmetic Procedures	521
Chapter 15:	Recursion	555
Chapter 16:	Object-Oriented Programming	567
Appendix A:	Summary of Turbo Pascal Editor Commands	594
Appendix B:	Summary of Reserved Words	598
Index		*611*

TABLE OF CONTENTS

INTRODUCTION   *xvii*

____*PART I:*   *THE TURBO PASCAL ENVIRONMENT*_____

CHAPTER 1:   *AN INTRODUCTION TO TURBO PASCAL*   *3*

The Elements of Turbo Pascal   5
   The Edit Window   7
   The Output Window   9
   The Watch Window   10
   The Main Menu   10
   Techniques for Using Menus   14
   The Help Facility   16
The Pascal Language   18
An Introductory Programming Exercise: The *Today* Program   20
   The Listing of the *Today* Program   23
Working with the Turbo Pascal Editor   31
   The Save-and-Continue Operation   32
   Essential Editing Commands   33
Compiling a Program   39
   Compiling to Memory   39
   Correcting Compile-Time Errors   40
A Trial Run of the *Today* Program   41
   Run-Time Errors   42
Using the Built-In Debugger   45
   An Exercise with the Debugger   45

Generating an Executable Program File	50
Summary	52
CHAPTER 2: **THE MENU SYSTEM AND THE EDITOR**	**55**
The File Menu	56
The Load Command	57
The Pick Command	59
The New Command	59
The Save Command	60
The *Write to* Command	61
The Directory Command	61
The *Change dir* Command	62
The *OS shell* Command	62
The Quit Command	63
The Run Menu	63
The Run Command	64
The *Program Reset* Command	64
The *Go To Cursor* Command	66
The *Trace Into* Command	66
The *Step Over* Command	67
The *User Screen* Command	67
The Compile Menu	67
The Compile Command	68
The *Primary file* Command	68
The Make Command	70
The Build Command	70
The Destination Command	70
The *Find error* Command	71
The *Get info* Command	72
The Options Menu	73
The Compiler Options	74

The Linker Options	88
The Environment Command	89
The Directories Options	91
The Parameters Command	92
The Configuration File Commands	93
The Debug Menu	94
The Evaluate Command	95
The *Call Stack* Command	97
The *Find Function* Command	99
The *Integrated Debugging* Command	99
The *Standalone Debugging* Command	100
The *Display Swapping* Command	100
The *Refresh Display* Command	101
The Break/Watch Menu	101
The *Add Watch* Command	102
The *Delete Watch* Command	102
The *Edit Watch* Command	102
The *Remove All Watches* Command	103
The *Toggle Breakpoint* Command	103
The *Clear All Breakpoints* Command	103
The *View Next Breakpoint* Command	103
A Second Look at the Editor	104
Block Operations in the Editor	104
Using Include Files in Turbo Pascal	105
Find and Replace Operations	108
Customizing the Editor	112
Summary	113
CHAPTER 3: **USING UNITS IN TURBO PASCAL PROGRAMS**	**117**
Creating a Unit	118
The USES Statement	122

Using Standard Units 124

The *ChrnUnit* Unit 126

Program Example: The *Hours* Program 129

    Running the Program 129

    The Program Listing 132

Summary 138

PART II: A TURBO PASCAL LANGUAGE TUTORIAL

CHAPTER 4:   *FUNDAMENTALS OF TURBO PASCAL PROGRAMMING*   *143*

Turbo Pascal Program Structure 144

    User-Defined Identifiers 147

    CONST Declarations 151

    TYPE Declarations 152

    VAR Declarations 152

Introduction to Standard Data Types 153

    General Characteristics of the Numeric Types 154

    Integer Types 155

    Real Number Types 156

    Characters and Strings 157

    Boolean Values 159

    Assignment Statements 159

Procedures and Functions in Turbo Pascal 160

    Parameter Lists 162

    Procedure Calls and Function Calls 163

    Global versus Local Declarations 165

    Value Parameters and Variable Parameters 167

Operations 170

    Numeric Operations 171

    String Operations 173

Screen Output and Keyboard Input 176

  Screen Output: The WRITE and WRITELN Statements 176

  Keyboard Input: The READ and READLN Statements 180

Sample Program: Generating Printed Reports from Account Files 182

  The Listing of the *BillTime* Program 186

Summary 193

CHAPTER 5:   **DECISIONS AND LOOPS**   *195*

The *CliList* Program 197

Logical Values and Expressions 200

  Relational Operations 200

  Logical Operations 201

The IF Decision Structure 206

The CASE Decision Structure 208

FOR Loops 212

WHILE Loops and REPEAT UNTIL Loops 217

  The WHILE Loop Structure 217

  The REPEAT UNTIL Loop Structure 219

Adding New Functions to *StrUnit* 221

The Listing of the *CliList* Program 224

  The *SortClientFiles* Procedure 230

Summary 232

CHAPTER 6:   **RECORDS AND ARRAYS**   *235*

The *CliAddr* Program 236

Record Structures 240

  Defining Record Types and Declaring Record Variables 241

  Working with Field Values 243

  Variant Fields 245

Arrays	249
Defining Array Types and Declaring Array Variables	249
Passing Arrays as Arguments	254
New Input Routines for the *CliAddr* Program	256
The Listing of the *CliAddr* Program	258
Working with an Array of Records	267
Type Casting	271
Version 5.5: Object Structures	272
Summary	275
CHAPTER 7: OTHER DATA TYPES AND DATA STRUCTURES	**277**
The *CliMenu* Program	278
Sets	280
Set Operations	282
Enumerated Types	288
Ordinal Functions and Type Casting	290
Subrange Types	293
Typed Constants	294
The Listing of the *CliMenu* Program	297
The *InitializeMenu* Procedure	303
The *GetSelection* Procedure	305
Advanced Use of the READKEY Function	307
The EXEC Procedure	310
Summary	311
CHAPTER 8: POINTERS, DYNAMIC VARIABLES, AND LINKED LISTS	**313**
Introduction to Pointers and Lists	314
Declaring a Pointer Variable	318
Creating a Dynamic Variable	320

Building a Linked List 322

Accessing Values from a Linked List 327

The *PtrAddr* Program 340

Inside the *PtrAddr* Program 342

Inserting New Records into the List 344

Moving through the List 348

Using the DISPOSE Procedure 350

Version 5.5: Dynamic Allocation with Objects 352

Summary 354

CHAPTER 9:   NUMERIC FUNCTIONS AND PROCEDURES   357

Numeric Functions by Categories 358

The EXP and LN Functions 358

The Trigonometric Functions 364

The Integer Functions 364

Arithmetic Functions 365

Type Casting and Numeric Conversions 366

The RANDOM Function 368

The Functions of *RandUnit* 369

The *RandAddr* Program 372

Inside the *RandAddr* Program 380

Summary 382

CHAPTER 10:   STRING FUNCTIONS AND PROCEDURES   385

String Functions 386

Substring Functions 387

Alphabetic Case Functions 391

Routines That Change Strings 392

Repeating-Character Functions 394

Information Functions	395
Type Conversion Functions	396
Programming for Command-Line Parameters	397
Designing Stand-Alone Programs	397
Using PARAMSTR and PARAMCOUNT	399
The *AddrCom* Program	401
Inside the *AddrCom* Program	412
The *CheckArguments* Function	413
The *DoCommand* Procedure	415
Summary	416

CHAPTER 11: SEQUENTIAL-ACCESS DATA FILE PROGRAMMING — **419**

The *CliChart* Program	421
Working with Sequential Files	423
Establishing a TEXT File Variable	425
Opening the File	426
Writing Data to a TEXT File	427
Reading Data from a TEXT File	429
Closing a TEXT File	431
Inside the *CliChart* Program	431
Untyped Files	439
Summary	443

CHAPTER 12: RANDOM-ACCESS DATA FILE PROGRAMMING — **447**

Managing a Client-Profile Database	450
Random-Access File Management	456
Defining and Opening a Typed File	457
Using the SEEK Procedure	459
Writing a Record to a Typed File	460
Reading a Record from a Typed File	462

Inside the *CliProf* Program   464

    Appending a New Record   482

    Revising an Existing Record   484

Summary   485

___*PART III:* *ADVANCED PROGRAMMING TECHNIQUES*_____

CHAPTER 13: **GRAPHICS**   *491*

Procedures and Functions in the GRAPH Unit   493

    Initializing a Graphics Mode   498

    Plotting Points and Drawing Lines   503

    Displaying Text on the Graphics Screen   505

    Drawing Circles   508

    Drawing Pie Charts   509

    Creating Bar Charts   513

    Drawing Miscellaneous Shapes on the Screen   515

Summary   517

CHAPTER 14: **DATE-ARITHMETIC PROCEDURES**   *521*

A Library of Date Routines   524

    A Date Input Routine: The *InDate* Function   533

    Inside the *InDate* Function   534

    A Scalar-Date Conversion Routine: The *ScalarDate* Function   537

    The Current Date: The *TodaysDate* Function   538

    A Date Display Routine: The *ScalarToString* Function   539

    Inside the *ScalarToString* Function   540

    The *DayOfWeek* Function   542

Printing Late-Payment Notices: The *LateCli* Program   543

     Inside the *LateCli* Program   549

Summary   552

CHAPTER 15:   **RECURSION**   *555*

Demonstrating the Quick Sort: The *ShowOff* Program   556

     Recursion in the *QuickSort* Procedure   560

Summary   563

CHAPTER 16:   **OBJECT-ORIENTED PROGRAMMING**   *567*

Turbo Pascal Objects   569

     Creating Objects and Object Types   570

     Objects and Encapsulation   574

The *CliBil_1* Program   574

Virtual Methods and Late Binding   581

Dynamic Allocation with Objects   590

Object-Oriented Debugging in Turbo Pascal   592

Summary   592

APPENDIX A: **SUMMARY OF TURBO PASCAL EDITOR COMMANDS**   *594*

APPENDIX B: **SUMMARY OF RESERVED WORDS**   *598*

INDEX   *611*

covering the menu system and the process of developing, compiling, and debugging a Turbo Pascal program.

Chapter 1, "An Introduction to Turbo Pascal," presents a first hands-on programming exercise, designed to give you an overview of the Turbo Pascal system and to prepare you for a more systematic study of the environment and the language.

Chapter 2, "The Menu System and the Editor," describes the Turbo Pascal menu system in detail and completes your tour of the built-in debugger and editor.

Chapter 3, "Using Units in Turbo Pascal Programs," shows you how to use *units* to develop Turbo Pascal programs consisting of separately compiled parts.

Support for units is an important feature of version 5.0. Throughout this book you will find a useful collection of units that you can incorporate into your own library of general-purpose Pascal procedures and functions. These include: *ChrnUnit*, a library of chronological and date functions; *InUnit*, a collection of special input routines; *RandUnit*, a group of functions that supply randomly generated data values; and *StrUnit*, a collection of string routines. Some of these units are developed over the course of several chapters.

Part II, "A Turbo Pascal Language Tutorial," is a topical introduction to the compiler language itself, focussing on structured program design.

Chapter 4, "Fundamentals of Turbo Pascal Programming," discusses a variety of introductory subjects, including Turbo Pascal's two basic program modules—procedures and functions; elementary data types available in the language; numeric and string operations; and essential input and output procedures.

Chapter 5, "Decisions and Loops," shows you how to use Turbo Pascal's rich variety of control structures for implementing decisions and repetition loops in programs.

Chapter 6, "Records and Arrays," is an introduction to user-defined data structures in Turbo Pascal.

Chapter 7, "Other Data Types and Data Structures," describes Pascal's additional user-defined data types and data structures, including sets, enumerated types, subranges, and typed constants.

Chapter 8, "Pointers, Dynamic Variables, and Linked Lists," explains the use of dynamic variables and shows you how to create linked lists of data in Turbo Pascal.

INTRODUCTIO

Mastering Turbo Pascal is an introduction to versions 5.0 an
of Borland International's Pascal compiler. This compiler, desi
for IBM Personal Computers and compatibles, supplies a fast
powerful version of the Pascal programming language. Also incl
in the Turbo Pascal package are a built-in editor, a built-in debu
and a menu-driven development environment designed to help
create, compile, and test your own Pascal programs.

This book will help you master both the development environ
and the essential elements of the Turbo Pascal language. The pace
level of the book are planned especially for readers who have had s
programming experience—with a previous version of Pascal
example, or perhaps with an interpreted or compiled version of the l
language. At the same time, the book presents challenging exercises
range of readers, from ambitious beginners to intermediate-level
grammers who wish to sharpen and expand their algorithmic skills.

The book is divided into three parts. Part I offers a com
description of the Turbo Pascal environment. Part II is an intro
tory Pascal-language tutorial, and Part III presents a short selec
of advanced programming topics. As with many other comp
skills, the best way to master Turbo Pascal is to study examples of
grams written in the language. For this reason, all of the chapte
this book contain complete sample programs for you to study, ex
ment with, and incorporate into your own programming proj
These program examples are designed to accomplish three main g

- To help you improve your own programming skills

- To teach you a variety of new programming techniques

- To demonstrate the style and techniques of structured
  gramming in Pascal

Here is a brief description of the topics covered in each cha
Part I, "The Turbo Pascal Environment," contains three chap

Chapter 9, "Numeric Functions and Procedures," looks at Turbo Pascal's library of numeric routines, including exponential, logarithmic, trigonometric, integer, arithmetic, and conversion functions, and Turbo Pascal's random-number generator.

Chapter 10, "String Functions and Procedures," discusses Turbo Pascal's library of string routines, and introduces the PARAMSTR function, designed to return strings of parameters from the DOS command line.

Chapter 11, "Sequential-Access Data File Programming," discusses text files and illustrates the techniques of sequential file programming.

Chapter 12, "Random-Access Data File Programming," explores the characteristics of typed files, and shows you how to use Turbo Pascal structures and procedures to define work with random-access files.

The programs presented in Chapters 3 through 12 all revolve around a single business application. This application is designed for maintaining records of work hours billable to particular projects or clients, and for producing printed reports from those records. The application is developed and then fine-tuned throughout the course of Parts I, II, and III. Here are the various programs included in this application:

- *Hours* (Chapter 3) maintains chronological records of billable work hours for a given client.

- *BillTime* (Chapter 4) reads a client account file (created by the *Hours* program) and prints a billing report that details dates and amounts due for the account.

- *CliList* (Chapter 5) prepares a printed list of all client files stored in the current directory, and shows the total number of billable hours currently recorded in each file.

- *CliAddr* (Chapter 6) creates and manages a file of client addresses, and allows you to sort and print address lists and phone lists from the data. (Several variations of this program appear in subsequent chapters.)

- *CliMenu* (Chapter 7) effectively combines all the billable-time applications presented in previous chapters into a single menu-driven program.

- *PtrAddr* (Chapter 8) illustrates the use of dynamic variables and linked lists in an enhanced version of the *CliAddr* program.

- *RandAddr* (Chapter 9) creates randomly simulated data to test the algorithms of the *PtrAddr* application.

- *AddrCom* (Chapter 10) performs the same operations as the *CliAddr* program, but is designed to be executed directly from DOS, and to accept option choices as parameters from the DOS command line.

- *CliChart* (Chapter 11) creates simple horizontal bar charts depicting the relative number of billable hours recorded in sets of client files.

- *CliProf* (Chapter 12) manages an indexed database of client profiles, and allows the user to add new records to the file, examine records stored in the file, and to revise records.

- *LateCli* (Chapter 14) uses date arithmetic routines to plan the content of late-payment notices to clients who have not paid their bills.

Part III, "Turbo Pascal Programming Techniques," presents a selection of advanced programming topics.

Chapter 13, "Graphics," examines a selection of procedures and functions from Turbo Pascal's standard GRAPH unit, and presents a sample programming exercise that demonstrates these routines in action.

Chapter 14, "Date-Arithmetic Procedures," develops a complete library of date-handling routines that you can use in business applications that work with chronological information. These routines include a date-input function, scalar-date conversion functions, a date-display function, and a day-of-the-week function. To demonstrate the use of these routines, the chapter presents the sample program called *LateCli*, designed to generate late-payment notices for overdue client accounts.

Chapter 15, "Recursion," discusses yet another important feature in the Turbo Pascal language—the ability of a structured program module to make calls to itself in the process of completing a task. As an illustration of this technique, the chapter presents a recursive sort routine called *QuickSort*.

Chapter 16, "Object-Oriented Programming," gives an in-depth explanation of OOP concepts and their use in Turbo Pascal version 5.5, and develops an object-oriented client billing program based on the *CliList* program earlier in the book.

This book ends with two appendices. Appendix A is a brief summary of the default Turbo Pascal editor commands. Appendix B describes the usage of each of the Turbo Pascal reserved words.

In summary, this book is designed as a hands-on tutorial to the Turbo Pascal language and environment. You will profit most from this book by concentrating on the program examples presented in each chapter. To study the techniques of Turbo Pascal programming, you should create your own working copies of these examples, run each program yourself, and, where appropriate, incorporate the routines into your own programming projects.

Version 5.5: Object-Oriented Programming

Version 5.5 of Turbo Pascal is more than just an improved Pascal compiler: it introduces a revolutionary new way to think about programming. Although it is totally compatible with Turbo Pascal 5.0, the new version provides support for "object-oriented" programming—a powerful way to write better structured and more easily modified programs in less time.

With this new version, Turbo Pascal continues its evolution from a simple structured language into a powerful development environment that extends the Pascal standard. Now, you can create new program objects that extend the capabilities of already existing Pascal programs—without any need to modify the original source code. You can create family trees of objects that inherit properties but don't repeat code, as well as objects that "know" how to respond to the same command in different ways.

Best of all—unlike previous object-oriented languages—Turbo Pascal lets you do as little or as much object-oriented programming as you like. You can ignore the object features completely and write your programs in straight Pascal, or you can use OOP concepts every chance you get.

Until now, object-oriented programming has not been generally available on PCs. It was almost exclusively the province of artificial intelligence researchers and relatively little-known languages such as C++, Smalltalk, and Apple's Object Pascal. Because of this, it has had an air of mystery that is completely undeserved. But far from being an oddball approach that's only good for exotic applications, object-oriented programming is a natural extension of structured programming techniques that can benefit almost everyone.

Object-oriented programming isn't all there is to Turbo Pascal 5.5. Both Turbo Pascal's integrated debugger and its smart linker have been enhanced to support objects. For large programs, the overlay manager has been improved as well.

Just like Turbo Pascal 5.5, this new edition of *Mastering Turbo Pascal* is totally compatible with earlier versions of Turbo Pascal. All the information about Turbo Pascal 5.0 has been carried forward from the previous edition of the book, and new sections about version 5.5 are clearly marked.

No matter what version of Turbo Pascal you have, *Mastering Turbo Pascal* will help you do just that: become a "master" of today's most popular PC programming language.

Installing Turbo Pascal

Turbo Pascal version 5 is stored on three disks that you receive with the original software package. Installing the compiler for use on your computer is a matter of gathering together copies of the necessary files, either onto a floppy disk or into a designated subdirectory on your hard disk. You should use the INSTALL program—included on the main Compiler disk—for copying the various parts of the system and storing them appropriately on your disk. Some of the program files are "packed" into archive files on disk; the INSTALL program automatically unpacks them and makes copies for you.

The original disks contain many different program files, utilities, and sample Pascal source code files. To perform all of the programs and exercises presented in this book, you need access to the following files:

TURBO.EXE   This is the main file for the Turbo Pascal development environment. When you enter the TURBO command from the DOS prompt, this is the program file that is executed. (Chapter 1 introduces you to the development environment.)

TURBO.HLP   This file contains Turbo Pascal's context-sensitive Help facility. (You'll learn about this facility in Chapter 1.)

TURBO.TPL   This is the Turbo Pascal library file. It contains most of the standard units included with the compiler. (These units are described in Chapter 3.)

GRAPH.TPU   This is the GRAPH unit, a standard unit that is not incorporated into TURBO.TPL. (Chapter 13 discusses the procedures and functions included in this unit. In addition to GRAPH.TPU, you will need at least one .BGI file and a collection of .CHR files to perform the sample program in Chapter 13.)

TINST.EXE   This program is the Turbo Pascal installation utility. You can use it to customize the development environment and the editor. (This program is described in Chapter 2.)

PART

The Turbo Pascal Environment

I

C H A P T E R

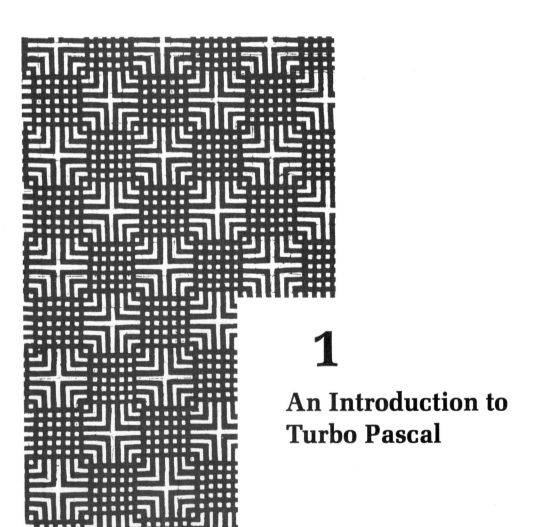

1

An Introduction to Turbo Pascal

Turbo Pascal, version 5.0, is both a professional programming language and an ideal environment for developing Pascal programs. The Turbo Pascal package includes several interrelated programming tools:

- A fast, versatile, and powerful version of the Pascal language.

- A library of *units* that provide many procedures and functions that you can use in programs.

- A built-in, full-screen editor in which you can enter and edit the source code of a program.

- A compiler that produces fast machine-language programs from your Pascal code.

- A debugger that allows you to step through a program performance line-by-line, examining changes that occur in the values of variables and expressions during the performance.

- A menu-driven development environment that integrates all these elements and streamlines the process of creating, testing, and perfecting Pascal programs.

In Part I of this book you will read in detail about the development environment, and in Parts II and III you'll master the features of the language itself. But before you begin a systematic study of these programming tools, this first chapter gives you the opportunity to explore the Turbo Pascal package informally, finding out how it works and what programming tasks you can accomplish with it.

This chapter also guides you through a first hands-on programming exercise with Turbo Pascal. While working through this exercise, you'll examine the main steps in the process of developing a Turbo Pascal program. These steps include:

- Using the built-in editor to enter the lines of the program and to save them in a text file on disk.

- Compiling the program in the computer's memory, and then editing the program, if necessary, to correct any syntax errors discovered during the initial compilation.

- Running the program and evaluating its performance.

- Using the built-in debugger, if necessary, to investigate problems in the program's behavior. (The Turbo Pascal debugger is a set of tools that help you locate and correct logical errors in your program's design.)

- Creating a stand-alone compiled program file that can be performed directly from DOS.

You'll learn when and why to perform each of these steps, and you'll find out how to use menu commands and options to accomplish each part of the process.

In short, the goals of this chapter are to present an informal survey of the overall design and capabilities of Turbo Pascal; to give you some initial hands-on experience with the system; and, finally, to prepare you for a more systematic study of the development environment and the language in chapters to come.

The first section of this chapter presents an overview of the elements included in the Turbo Pascal package. You'll probably want to start up Turbo Pascal on your computer right away so you can experiment with keyboard operations as you read the following sections. To start up the development environment, simply select the disk or directory where you have installed the various Turbo Pascal files and type **TURBO** at the DOS prompt. (If you have not yet installed Turbo Pascal on your computer, see the introduction.)

The Elements of Turbo Pascal

When you begin working with Turbo Pascal 5.0, your screen appears as shown in Figure 1.1. The top of the screen displays the following main menu line:

File Edit Run Compile Options Debug Break/watch

Most of these words represent vertical menus that drop down on the screen. The F10 function key is a toggle that moves you between the main menu and the windows below the menu. When the main menu is active, you use the right- or left-arrow keys (→ or ←) to select a menu, and the Enter key or the down-arrow key (↓) to display a menu on the screen. You'll learn much more about the menus in the course of this chapter.

The area below the menu line is initially organized into two windows, called Edit and Watch. The *Edit* window is where you develop the text of your program listing, and the *Watch* window is designed to display specific information about your program while you are using the built-in debugger.

You can activate either window at any point during your work, using special keyboard commands. For example, to activate the Edit window while one of the menus is displayed on the screen, you press

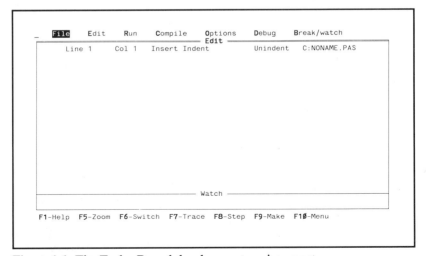

Figure 1.1: The Turbo Pascal development environment

Alt-E

This notation means, "Hold down the Alt key while you type the E key." The Edit window allows you to examine and modify the source code of your current program. When the Edit window is active, a double-line border appears at the top of the window, and a flashing cursor appears at the current position inside the window. You can begin entering the source code of a new program, or you can edit the program currently in the Edit window.

Whenever the Edit window is active you can switch to the Watch window by pressing the F6 function key. Later in this chapter, you'll learn how to use the Watch window in debugging activities.

A third window is also available in the Turbo Pascal development environment. This is the Output window, which displays the on-screen results of a program performance. While the Watch window is active you can switch to the Output window by pressing Alt-F6; the result is shown in Figure 1.2. As you can see, the environment screen is now divided into the Edit window and the Output window. (Press Alt-F6 to switch back to the Watch window, and then F6 to activate the Edit window again.)

Alternatively, you can press Alt-F5 to switch to a full-screen version of the Output window, devoting the entire screen space to the output from a program. Note that the Output window initially contains the

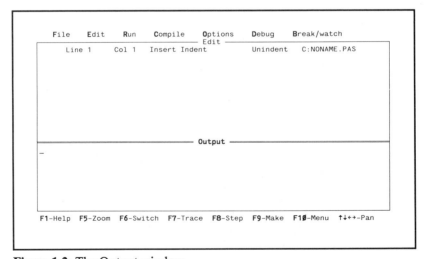

Figure 1.2: The Output window

DOS screen, showing the commands you performed in DOS just before starting the current session with Turbo Pascal. In contrast, after a program performance, the Output window shows the information that the program displays on the screen. You can press any key to return to the Turbo Pascal development environment from the full-screen Output window.

At the bottom of the environment screen, Turbo Pascal summarizes the operations that you can perform with some of the function keys (F1 to F10) on your keyboard:

F1-Help F5-Zoom F6-Switch F7-Trace F8-Step F9-Make F10-Menu

The Turbo Pascal documentation calls these the *hot keys*; some of them are shortcuts for operations that can also be performed through menu commands. Other hot keys are designed to help you work with the Edit, Watch, and Output windows. For example, you have already seen that the F6 key is a toggle that activates either Edit or Watch. In addition, you can press the F5 key to perform the *Zoom* operation, which expands the currently selected window to fill the entire screen space. Press F5 again if you want to restore the two windows to their original sizes. Another function key already mentioned, F10, toggles control between the top menu line and a selected window.

Table 1.1 summarizes the basic uses of the function keys in Turbo Pascal. You'll learn more about these and other keyboard operations as you continue in this chapter. You'll also discover that the bottom line shows a different set of hot keys depending on the context of your current activity. For now, let's look further at the purposes of the windows and the menu.

The Edit Window

The Edit window is where you initially create a program file, or revise a file that you have created previously and stored on disk. This window provides a full-screen editor. While you are in the editor, you can use the direction keys on your keyboard's number pad to move up and down to any line of the program you are currently working on, or to scroll the screen display forward or backward to any portion of the file.

Table 1.1: The Function Keys in Turbo Pascal

F1	Displays context-sensitive help messages on the screen.
F2	Saves the current program file to disk.
F3	Invokes the Load command to read a program file into the editor from disk.
F4	Performs the current program up to the line at which the cursor is positioned in the Edit window (a debugging operation).
F5	Zooms the active window.
F6	Switches between the Edit, Watch, or Output window (depending on which window is currently active and which windows are displayed on the screen).
F7	Runs the program one line at a time using the Trace mode. (Traces through each line of the program, including lines that are contained inside of the program's procedures and functions; this is a debugging operation.)
F8	Runs the program one line at a time, but does not trace through the lines of procedures and functions (a debugging operation).
F9	Performs the Make operation, one of the ways to compile the current program.
F10	Toggles between the menu line at the top of the screen and a selected window.

To help you develop a program file, the Turbo Pascal editor has many of the essential features of a complete word processing program. In addition to basic editing functions like inserting and deleting, you can also perform more elaborate operations like search-and-replace, block moves, and block copies. In fact, the editor uses keyboard commands that are similar to the WordStar word processing program. If you are already familiar with WordStar, you will feel perfectly at home in the Turbo Pascal editor. We'll take a brief look at the editor commands later in this chapter and then continue the discussion in Chapter 2.

Once you create a program file in the editor, you are ready to try compiling the program. The compilation process translates the commands and structures of your program file into an efficient machine code that the computer can perform. In this context, the original program that you type into the Edit window is called the *source code*, and the result of the compilation is known as the *object code* or the *run code*.

Compilation is a distinct step during the development of a program, a step that must be completed successfully before you can run the program. Turbo Pascal is a very fast and efficient compiler, so the compilation step seldom takes very long. The resulting compiled object code is fast, compact, and efficient.

The Output Window

A successfully compiled program is ready to be performed. The Output window is where Turbo Pascal displays any output text and input prompts that your program produces. If your program expects to read input from the keyboard at some point during a performance, the output screen is displayed until the input operation is complete.

On the other hand, if your program simply displays a series of text lines on the screen, Turbo Pascal 5.0 does not keep the output displayed on the screen when the performance is complete. Instead, you are returned immediately to the menu-driven development environment at the end of the performance. If you want to look back at the output that a program has produced, you must press Alt-F5. This keyboard combination displays the full-screen Output window. Press any key to return to the development environment.

Alternatively, you can perform the following steps to activate and zoom the Output window:

1. Press F6 to activate the Watch window.

2. Press Alt-F6 to switch to the Output window. (The Watch window disappears from the screen.)

3. Press F5 to zoom the Output window.

In this case, the Output window expands over most of the screen, but the menu line and the bottom line of keyboard instructions remain. To return to the original screen organization—with both the Watch window and the Edit window—perform these same keyboard operations in reverse (F5, Alt-F6, F6).

The Turbo Pascal language has several procedures that potentially control the appearance of text on the output screen. For example, among the most commonly used output commands are WRITELN and WRITE, both of which display items of information on the screen; GOTOXY, which positions the cursor at a particular screen location; and CLRSCR, which clears the screen of its current information. The effects of these and other output commands appear in the Output window.

The Watch Window

The Watch window is designed to help you investigate changing data values during your program's performance. Specifically, you can use this window to display the values of specific variables and expressions used in your program. You may want to do so when a program is producing some unexpected and undesired result. The Watch window is thus an essential part of Turbo Pascal's *debugging* facilities—the tools you use to locate and correct problems in the logical design of a program.

In general, you use commands in the Break/watch menu to specify exactly what you want to see in the Watch window. Then you perform your program in one of the line-by-line debugging modes. As each line of your program is performed, Turbo Pascal shows you the current value of any variable or expression you have placed in the Watch window.

You'll have an opportunity to experiment with the Watch window later in this chapter. For now, let's proceed to a discussion of the Turbo Pascal menu commands.

The Main Menu

As you have seen, the Turbo Pascal Main menu consists of the seven commands that appear at the top of the screen:

File   Edit   Run   Compile   Options   Debug   Break/watch

From the Edit, Watch, or Output window, you activate the Main menu by pressing F10. When you do so, the currently selected menu will appear in a reverse-video display or a distinct color, both called a *highlight*. You can use either of the following keyboard techniques to display one of the vertical menus:

- Use the right- or left-arrow (→ or ←) keys to move the highlight to the menu you wish to work with, and press the Enter key to display the selected menu.

- With the menu line activated (F10), simply press the letter that represents a given menu: **F**, **R**, **C**, **O**, **D**, or **B**.

You'll learn additional keyboard techniques later in this chapter.

One of the seven menu commands—Edit—results in immediate action: it moves the cursor into the Edit window, where you can either begin entering a Turbo Pascal program or edit the program that is currently stored in the memory.

In contrast, the other commands display further menu options for you to choose from. When you select one of these commands, a menu of commands appears on the screen in a vertical list, immediately below the Main menu command. For example, here is the File command's menu:

```
File
Load          F3
Pick          Alt-F3
New
Save          F2
Write to
Directory
Change dir
OS shell
Quit          Alt-X
```

This kind of vertical menu is sometimes called a *drop-down* menu, because it appears as though a list of options has dropped down from somewhere inside the top of the display screen. Turbo Pascal supplies two alternative keyboard techniques for selecting commands from such a menu:

- Use the ↑ or ↓ key to position the highlight over a target command, and press the Enter key to perform the command.

- Press the first letter of the command.

For example, to select the Load option from the File menu, you can use the direction keys to highlight the first option (if it is not already highlighted) and then press Enter. Alternatively, you can just press the L key.

From the Main menu level, an economical way to perform any command that is located inside a menu is simply to press two keys in succession: first the letter key that represents the appropriate Main menu selection, then the letter key that represents the specific command in the menu. For instance, to perform the Quit command in the File menu you can simply press F and then Q. This particular command drops you out of Turbo Pascal and returns you to DOS. Alternatively, you can use a keyboard shortcut if one is available for the command you want to perform. For example, pressing Alt-X is the shortcut for the Quit command. As you can see, Turbo Pascal lists shortcut keys in the menus themselves.

Here are brief summaries of the Turbo Pascal menus (all of which we'll examine in greater detail in Chapter 2):

- The File menu gives you a variety of commands that help you work with disk files. For example, you can save your current program on disk as a program file using the Save command; or you can use either the Pick command or the Load command to load an existing program file from disk into the Edit window. (The File commands always save and read programs as ASCII text files.) In addition, you can examine the current directory or change the directory. Finally, the File command gives you two ways to exit from Turbo Pascal—a temporary exit that allows you to perform DOS commands and then return to your Pascal programming project (*OS shell*), and a permanent exit (Quit).

- The Run menu offers you several ways to run a program. The first command in the menu, Run, initiates a performance, normally proceeding from the beginning to the end of the program. Other commands in this menu act as debugging tools, allowing you to run a portion of the program (the *Go to cursor* command), or to trace through the program one line at a time (the *Trace into* and *Step over* commands). The Run menu also has a *Program reset* command, which terminates a line-by-line debugging session. Finally, the menu includes a command named *User screen*; this command displays the full-screen Output window. (As you recall, the shortcut for this operation is Alt-F5.)

- The Compile menu provides a number of options for compiling the program that is currently in the editor. The Compile, Make, and Build commands all perform different compilation sequences, depending on the requirements of the current programming project. (You'll learn about the distinctions between these commands in Chapter 2.) In addition, the Destination option gives you the choice between storing the compiled code in memory or creating an .EXE file on disk for the compiled program. A program compiled to memory can be performed only as long as you remain in the Turbo Pascal environment. An .EXE file, on the other hand, is a stand-alone executable program that you can perform directly from DOS. The nearly automatic creation of .EXE files is one of the important advantages of the Turbo Pascal package.

- The Options menu supplies a set of commands that control the behavior of the compiler and certain characteristics of the development environment. For example, you can use commands in this menu to specify directory locations for the various types of files that Turbo Pascal creates and works with. The Options menu also lets you create and read special setup files, recording your own preferred settings for the compiler, the editor, and the development environment.

- The Debug menu controls some of Turbo Pascal's debugging tools. In particular, the menu includes switches for turning debugging on and off. (Normally you leave debugging on while you're working in the development environment. However, before you produce the final compiled version of a program, you may want to turn debugging off in order to conserve memory space.) Other commands in the Debug menu allow you to evaluate expressions during a debugging session (Evaluate); examine the order of procedure and function calls in effect during a particular point in a debugging session (*Call stack*); and to locate a named procedure or function that is used in the program (*Find function*). Finally, a command called *Display swapping* gives you control over the display of the Output screen during a debugging session.

- The Break/watch menu supplies two kinds of debugging tools. First, the *Add watch* command allows you to insert *watch expressions*—sometimes called simply *watches*—into the Watch window during a debugging session. A watch is usually a variable or expression that is used in the program you are developing. During the program performance Turbo Pascal displays the current value of each watch expression inside the Watch window, showing you exactly how each part of the program affects the watches. (You can use other commands in the Break/watch menu to remove or edit watch expressions.) In addition, the Break/watch menu lets you establish *breakpoints* in your program. A breakpoint is a line at which you want the program performance to stop so that you can investigate the program's behavior at that point. You'll learn more about breakpoints and watch expressions later in this chapter.

Some of the Turbo Pascal menus result in further submenus of their own. In fact, you may sometimes find yourself working with a command or option that is located several levels deep in the submenus. Next we'll discuss the techniques for backing out of these menu levels, and for requesting helpful information about the commands that they offer.

Techniques for Using Menus

When a menu command supplies a further submenu of its own, a new framed list of options pops up on the screen, superimposed directly over other information. We sometimes call such a list of options a *pop-up menu*.

For example, Figure 1.3 shows the pop-up menu resulting from the Compiler command of the Options menu. As you can see, this menu

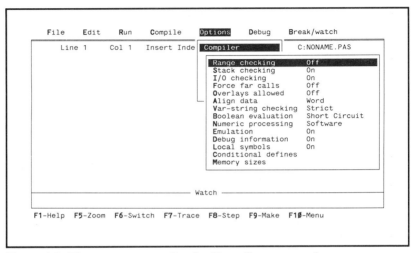

```
   File    Edit    Run    Compile   Options   Debug   Break/watch
  ┌─────────────────────────────────┬─────────────────────────────┐
  │      Line 1     Col 1    Insert Inde│Compiler          C:NONAME.PAS
  │                                  ├─────────────────────────────┤
  │                                  │ Range checking      Off      │
  │                                  │ Stack checking      On       │
  │                                  │ I/O checking        On       │
  │                                  │ Force far calls     Off      │
  │                                  │ Overlays allowed    Off      │
  │                                  │ Align data          Word     │
  └─                                 │ Var-string checking Strict   │
                                     │ Boolean evaluation  Short Circuit
                                     │ Numeric processing  Software │
                                     │ Emulation           On       │
                                     │ Debug information   On       │
                                     │ Local symbols       On       │
                                     │ Conditional defines          │
                                     │ Memory sizes                 │
                                     └─────────────────────────────┘

  ───────────────────────────── Watch ─────────────────────────────

  F1-Help  F5-Zoom  F6-Switch  F7-Trace  F8-Step  F9-Make  F1Ø-Menu
```

Figure 1.3: The pop-up menu for the Compiler command

contains over a dozen options, controlling various aspects of the compiler's behavior. We'll examine these options in Chapter 2. As usual, you select one of these options either by moving the highlight and pressing the Enter key, or by pressing the first letter of the option you want.

Sometimes a pop-up menu option results in yet another menu. You can always back out of any menu simply by pressing the Escape key (labeled Esc on your keyboard). If you are viewing a list of options that is several layers deep in the hierarchy of submenus, press the Escape key once for each menu that you wish to back out of. Pressing Escape often enough will always take you back eventually to the top line of the Main menu. Finally, from the top-line menu, you can press the Escape key yet again to move down into the currently selected window.

There are also several ways to activate the Main menu line when you have been working in the editor. As you have seen, the simplest way is to press the F10 function key. For example, if the cursor is inside the Edit window, and you want to try compiling the program you have been creating or revising, you can press F10 to return control to the Main menu level. Then press C to display the Compile menu.

If your fingers insist on using WordStar command sequences, you can also type Ctrl-K-D or Ctrl-K-Q to move to the Main menu from the editor. Alternatively, you can move directly from the editor to a specified drop-down menu by holding down the Alt key and pressing the first letter of the desired command. The following list shows the keyboard combinations that you can type to display menus if you are currently working in the editor:

Keys	Option
Alt-F	The File menu
Alt-E	The Edit command
Alt-R	The Run menu
Alt-C	The Compile menu
Alt-O	The Options menu
Alt-D	The Debug menu
Alt-B	The Break/watch menu

Another important feature of the Turbo Pascal environment is *context-sensitive help*; we'll discuss this feature in the next section.

The Help Facility

Turbo Pascal's built-in help facility can supply a brief description of any option that appears in any menu. To access these descriptions, you simply position the highlight over the target option and press the F1 function key. Turbo Pascal automatically displays a Help box on the screen, with an explanation of the selected option. For example, Figure 1.4 shows the Help box for the Destination option of the Compile menu. To display this Help message on your own screen, follow these steps:

1. Press **Alt-C** to display the Compile menu.
2. Use the up- or down-arrow keys (↑ or ↓) to highlight the Destination option.
3. Finally, press **F1** to view the Help screen.

You can press F1 at any time during your work in the Turbo Pascal environment, and an appropriate Help message will appear on the screen. This feature often saves you the trouble of having to search for information in the printed documentation. Furthermore, some Help screens contain highlighted key words directing you to additional

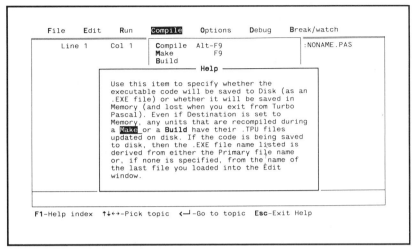

```
      File    Edit    Run    Compile    Options    Debug    Break/watch

         Line 1       Col 1      Compile  Alt-F9              :NONAME.PAS
                                 Make        F9
                                 Build
                              ─── Help ───

                     Use this item to specify whether the
                     executable code will be saved to Disk (as an
                     .EXE file) or whether it will be saved in
                     Memory (and lost when you exit from Turbo
                     Pascal). Even if Destination is set to
                     Memory, any units that are recompiled during
                     a Make or a Build have their .TPU files
                     updated on disk. If the code is being saved
                     to disk, then the .EXE file name listed is
                     derived from either the Primary file name
                     or, if none is specified, from the name of
                     the last file you loaded into the Edit
                     window.



      F1-Help index  ↑↓←→-Pick topic  ←┘-Go to topic  Esc-Exit Help
```

Figure 1.4: The Help screen for the Destination command

Help screens that you may also want to consult. If you select one of these key words (using the arrow keys) and then press Enter, a new Help screen appears on the screen. This is a good way to find information that is related to your current activity.

The Help facility also has an index, which you can view at any time by pressing the F1 key twice in succession. This multipage index lists several dozen topics that you can select and read about. Use the arrow keys to select a topic from the list, and press the Enter key to view the corresponding Help box. Note that the very first entry in the index is called "Help on Help." This entry gives you a guide to using the Help facility, and also contains key words that direct you to several other introductory topics about the features of Turbo Pascal.

Finally, you can also request Help screens for the Pascal language itself. These screens describe the syntax of a particular reserved word, procedure, or function. To display a language Help screen, follow these steps:

1. Type the Pascal reserved word or name in the editor.

2. Position the cursor inside or next to the word or name.

3. Press **Ctrl-F1**.

In response, Turbo Pascal displays a box summarizing the syntax and usage of the word you have typed. For example, Figure 1.5 shows the Help message for the WRITELN procedure.

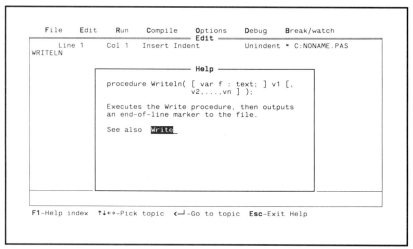

```
       File    Edit    Run    Compile    Options    Debug    Break/watch
                                         Edit
       Line 1      Col 1    Insert Indent          Unindent * C:NONAME.PAS
WRITELN

                                  Help
       procedure Writeln( [ var f : text; ] v1 [,
                          v2,...,vn ] );

       Executes the Write procedure, then outputs
       an end-of-line marker to the file.

       See also  Write




  F1-Help index  ↑↓↔-Pick topic  <⌐-Go to topic  Esc-Exit Help
```

Figure 1.5: The Help screen for the WRITELN procedure

We have discussed the highlights of the Turbo Pascal environment; we'll return to these features and examine them in greater detail in Chapter 2. Now, before beginning this chapter's programming exercise, let's briefly survey the major elements of the Turbo Pascal language. If you are relatively new to programming, some of the concepts and terminology included in the next section may be unfamiliar; Part II of this book will introduce you to each of these topics.

The Pascal Language

Pascal is known as a highly structured language. In the context of Pascal programming, the word *structure* encompasses many different characteristics, some of which are obvious and others more subtle. Briefly, Pascal encourages a particular programming style that relies on the following general features:

- *Modular* program organization, in which each important activity of a program is isolated into its own self-contained section of code.

- *Control structures* that perform decisions and repetitions in Pascal programs. (If you are a BASIC programmer, you might be accustomed to designing decisions and loops around the GOTO command. While the GOTO command is available in Turbo Pascal, it contradicts the spirit and aesthetics of structured programming; most programmers therefore avoid using it.)

- A rich collection of *data structures*, allowing you to organize information in a variety of clear and convenient ways.

- Strict requirements for defining variables and procedures. You must define all data types, variables, procedures, and functions before you use them. In the organizational scheme of a Pascal program, the main program section is located at the bottom of the program listing; by making calls to the procedures and functions located above it, this section controls the entire action of the program.

To be more specific, the following features of the Turbo Pascal language are essential for designing successful structured programs:

- Functions and procedures. These are self-contained structures into which you can organize each different section of your program. Procedures and functions are *called* from some controlling point in your program; they can receive data values as *parameters* passed from the controlling module, and can also pass information back to the control point.

- Global and local variables. You can declare and use local variables in any procedure or function. Data values stored in local variables remain private to the routines that use them. You can also declare global variables, which are available anywhere in a program.

- Structured IF decisions and CASE structures. These allow you to design complex decision-making procedures without the use of GOTO commands.

- Structured loops. These control the repetitive processes in a Pascal program. Turbo Pascal supplies a variety of loop structures, in which you can specify the number of repetitions that should be performed (FOR loops), the condition over which the looping should continue (WHILE loops), or the point at which the looping should stop (REPEAT/UNTIL loops).

- User-defined data types and structures. These include arrays, records, sets, subranges, enumerated types, and typed files. (Turbo Pascal also supports the pointer variable, an atypical data structure that we'll discuss in Chapter 8.)

We'll return frequently to the topic of structured programming throughout this book. A few other important language features are available in Turbo Pascal:

- Support for separately compiled *units*, in which you can build your own libraries of general-purpose procedures and functions.

- A collection of *standard units* that are included in the Turbo Pascal package. These units provide a built-in library of functions and procedures.

- Support for the 8087 numeric coprocessor chip. If you have installed this chip in your computer, Turbo Pascal can use it to work with extended numeric data types.

- Recursion, the process by which a function or procedure calls itself to streamline the performance of special kinds of repetitive tasks.

- Version 5.5 adds support for objects, which are user-defined data types that contain their own procedures, functions, and data. Objects can be derived from other objects and inherit their properties, as well as being able to respond in unique ways to the same program commands.

This is a preview of the topics we'll be discussing in Parts II and III of this book.

Now let's turn to this chapter's introductory programming project. The program we'll work with, called *Today*, is a simple tool designed for exchanging messages between the users of a given computer system. We'll begin in the next section by looking at a sample of the program's output.

An Introductory Programming Exercise: The *Today* Program

To understand the purpose of the *Today* program, imagine yourself in the following situation: For some weeks you have been working on a series of business application programs designed to run on a friend's personal computer. You typically go to your friend's office each evening to work on this project, and your friend runs and tests your programs the next morning. When you finish your work each evening, you write a note to leave for your friend, describing the work you have done and the programs that need further testing. The *Today* program gives you a convenient way to present this information to your friend directly on the computer screen.

Let's say you have compiled the *Today* program as an executable program file, stored on disk under the name TODAY.EXE. To perform the program—and read your note—your friend only needs to enter the word TODAY as a command at the DOS prompt:

```
C>TODAY
```

The program then performs the following tasks:

1. It displays today's date and the current time on the screen.

2. The program opens a text file named MESSAGE.TXT and displays its contents, line by line, on the screen.

3. If MESSAGE.TXT contains more than one screenful of information, *Today* displays the text one screen at a time.

To prepare a particular message for your friend, you simply create the text file MESSAGE.TXT, and enter as many lines of information into the file as you wish. (You can use any text editor or word processor to create this file. In fact, you can even use Turbo Pascal's own editor.) For example, you might use MESSAGE.TXT to store a note such as the one shown in Figure 1.6. When your friend runs the *Today* program the next morning, the program produces the output shown in Figure 1.7.

Notice that the program displays the date and the time in clearly readable formats, and then displays a line of dots both before and after the message. When you examine the program listing in the next section of this chapter, you'll find several procedures and functions that contribute to this output format.

Before going further with this exercise, you should take a moment now to create a file on disk called MESSAGE.TXT. Employ your usual word processor or text editor to create the file. You can simply copy the message from Figure 1.6, or you can write a message of your own. This file will allow you to test the performance of the *Today* program once you have entered the listing into the Turbo Pascal editor.

Keep in mind that the primary goal of this first chapter is to help you become familiar with the Turbo Pascal development environment, not the Pascal language itself. Nonetheless, you'll have the opportunity to look briefly at the listing of the *Today* program in the upcoming sections.

```
Hello R.B.,

   I have revised the following programs:

      HOURS.PAS
      CLIADDR.PAS
      CLIMENU.PAS
      CLIPROF.PAS

   Most of the revisions are designed to improve the screen
displays and the keyboard input processes. Please let me know
if you come across any problems.
   You'll find .EXE versions of all these programs on this disk.
   Hope to hear from you this afternoon.

                         M.J.
```

Figure 1.6: A sample note stored as MESSAGE.TXT

```
Today is Mon., Feb. 29, 1988.   The time is  8:53 am.

.......................................................

Hello R.B.,

   I have revised the following programs:

       HOURS.PAS
       CLIADDR.PAS
       CLIMENU.PAS
       CLIPROF.PAS

Most of the revisions are designed to improve the screen
displays and the keyboard input processes. Please let me
know if you come across any problems.
     You'll find .EXE versions of all these programs on
this disk.
     Hope to hear from you this afternoon.

                        M.J.
.......................................................
```

Figure 1.7: Output from the *Today* program

The Listing of the *Today* Program

The listing of the *Today* program appears in Figure 1.8. *Today* may at first seem rather long for a first program exercise, but you'll find that a large portion of the listing consists of comments that document the program's activities.

There are several important characteristics you should notice about the *Today* program. First, consider the structure of the program. The listing is divided into several small parts. The main program section (located at the bottom of the listing) is preceded by five self-contained routines: three procedures and two functions. You'll study the structure and characteristics of Turbo Pascal procedures and functions in Chapter 4. For now, let's take a quick look at the routines in this program and see what they do.

A *function* begins with a FUNCTION heading that supplies the name of the routine; the primary purpose of a function is to supply a data value to the program that calls it. The functions in this program are named *DateString* and *TimeString*. The first of these returns a string of characters representing the current date in the format *Day., Mo. dd, yyyy*, as in this example:

Wed., Aug. 3, 1988

```
PROGRAM Today;

  { The Today program displays today's date on the screen,
    along with the current time. The program then displays
    the contents of the text file MESSAGE.TXT. }

  USES DOS;    { DOS supplies GETDATE and GETTIME. }


  FUNCTION DateString: STRING;

    { The DateString function converts the numeric
      values supplied by the GETDATE procedure into a
      date string, in the format 'Day., Mo. dd, yyyy'. }

    CONST

      { Set up arrays for the three-character
        day and month strings. }

      days: ARRAY[0..6] OF STRING[3] =
        ('Sun','Mon','Tue','Wed','Thu','Fri','Sat');
      months: ARRAY[1..12] OF STRING[3] =
        ('Jan','Feb','Mar','Apr','May','Jun',
         'Jul','Aug','Sep','Oct','Nov','Dec');

    VAR
      year, month, day, weekday: WORD;
      yearStr, monthStr, dayStr, weekdayStr: STRING;

    BEGIN    { DateString }

      GETDATE(year, month, day, weekday);

      { Convert numeric date values to strings. }

      STR (year, yearStr);
      STR (day, dayStr);
      IF LENGTH(dayStr) = 1 THEN
        dayStr := ' ' + dayStr;

      { Get the appropriate day and month strings. }

      weekdayStr := days[weekday] + '., ';
      monthStr := months[month] + '. ';

      { Concatenate to produce final result. }

      DateString := weekdayStr + monthStr +
                    dayStr + ', ' + yearStr

    END;    { DateString }


  FUNCTION TimeString: STRING;

    { The TimeString function converts the numeric
      values supplied by the GETTIME procedure into a
      time string in the format 'hh:mm am/pm'. }

    VAR
      hour, minute, second, hundredth: WORD;
      ampm: STRING[2];
      hourStr, minuteStr: STRING;
```

Figure 1.8: The listing of the *Today* program

```
      BEGIN    { TimeString }

        GETTIME (hour, minute, second, hundredth);

        { Convert 24-hour time into am/pm format. }

        IF hour > 11 THEN
          BEGIN
            ampm := 'pm';
            IF hour > 12 THEN DEC (hour, 12)
          END
        ELSE
          BEGIN
            ampm := 'am';
            IF hour = 0 THEN hour := 12
          END;

        { Convert numeric time elements into strings. }

        STR (hour, hourStr);
        STR (minute, minuteStr);
        IF LENGTH(hourStr) = 1 THEN
          hourStr := ' ' + hourStr;
        IF LENGTH(minuteStr) = 1 THEN
          minuteStr := '0' + minuteStr;

        { Concatenate to produce final result. }

        TimeString := hourStr + ':' + minuteStr + ' ' + ampm

      END;     { TimeString }


  PROCEDURE TodaysMessage;

    { The TodaysMessage procedure opens the text file
      named MESSAGE.TXT, and displays the file's contents,
      line by line, on the screen. }

    CONST
      messageFileName = 'MESSAGE.TXT';
      screenStop      = 18;
      dots            = 60;

    VAR
      messageFile: TEXT;
      messageLine: STRING;
      screenLines: BYTE;


    PROCEDURE LineOfChars (DispChar: CHAR; lineLength: BYTE);

      { The LineOfChars procedure displays a line of DispChar
        characters on the screen. The argument passed to
        lineLength is the number of characters in the line. }

      VAR
        i: INTEGER;

      BEGIN    { LineOfChars }

        FOR i := 1 TO lineLength DO
          WRITE (DispChar);
        WRITELN

      END;     { LineOfChars }
```

Figure 1.8: The listing of the *Today* program (continued)

```
      PROCEDURE WaitForEnter;

        { The WaitForEnter procedure displays a prompt
          on the screen, and waits for the user to press
          the Enter key. }

        BEGIN
          WRITELN;
          WRITE ('Press <Enter> to continue. ');
          READLN;
          WRITELN
        END;


      BEGIN    { TodaysMessage }

        LineOfChars ('.', dots);
        WRITELN;

        { Identify the file's name on disk, and open the file. }

        ASSIGN (messageFile, messageFileName);
        RESET (messageFile);

        { Loop through the file, line by line, until the
          end of the file is encountered. }

        screenLines := 0;
        WHILE NOT EOF(messageFile) DO
          BEGIN

            { Read a line, then display it on the screen. }

            READLN (messageFile, messageLine);
            WRITELN (messageLine);
            INC (screenLines);
            IF screenLines = screenStop THEN
              BEGIN
                screenLines := 0;
                WaitForEnter
              END
          END;

        CLOSE (messageFile);
        LineOfChars ('.', dots)

      END;    { TodaysMessage }

      BEGIN    { Today }

        WRITELN;
        WRITE ('Today is ', DateString, '.   ');
        WRITELN ('The time is ', TimeString, '.');

        WRITELN;
        TodaysMessage

      END.    { Today }
```

Figure 1.8: The listing of the *Today* program (continued)

Likewise, the *TimeString* function returns a string of characters representing the current time in the format *hh:mm am/pm*, as in this example:

8:53 am

A *procedure* in Pascal begins with a PROCEDURE heading that supplies the name of the routine. The procedures in the *Today* program are named *TodaysMessage*, *LineOfChars* and *WaitForEnter*. The *TodaysMessage* procedure is responsible for opening a text file, MESSAGE.TXT, and displaying its contents on the screen; *LineOfChars* displays a line of characters on the screen; and *WaitForEnter* creates a user-controlled pause between each screenful of information.

These latter two procedures are actually defined *locally* as parts of *TodaysMessage*. As we'll see in Chapter 4, a local procedure is only available for use within the performance of the procedure that contains it.

Each of the functions and procedures in the *Today* program has its own carefully defined task to perform; when the task is complete, control of the program's activities returns to the main program section in an orderly fashion. Note that the program contains no GOTO statements cluttering up the logical flow of control.

The main program section, found at the end of any program listing, controls the program's action by making calls to the procedures and functions located above it. In *Today*, the main program contains a series of WRITE and WRITELN statements, which produce the beginning of the program's screen output. Inside these statements you will find calls to the *DateString* and *TimeString* functions:

```
WRITE ('Today is ', DateString, '.     ');
WRITELN ('The time is   ', TimeString, '.');
```

Finally, the main program ends with a call to the *TodaysMessage* procedure:

```
TodaysMessage
```

We'll discuss the format of function calls and procedure calls in Chapter 4.

If this is your first look at a Pascal program, you should examine the program's punctuation—in particular, the notation for separating different statements and blocks of code. In general, each statement of a Pascal program ends with a semicolon character (;) to separate it from the next statement in the program. A *block* of statements is enclosed between the words BEGIN and END. For example, all of the performable statements in a procedure or function appear inside one BEGIN/END block. Additional blocks are often *nested* inside the main block of a routine: that is, they are contained completely within the code of the main block. We'll see examples of nesting when we look in greater detail at procedures and functions in the next few chapters.

Inside a block, each statement ends with a semicolon; however, the semicolon is optional for the last statement in a block—that is, the statement located just before the END marker. We can represent this notation as follows:

```
BEGIN
    statement;
    statement;
    statement
END;
statement;
```

Notice that the block may end with a semicolon after the word END, to separate it from the next statement or the next block of statements. The main program section of a program also consists of a BEGIN/END block, but in this case the final END is followed by a period rather than a semicolon:

```
BEGIN
    statement;
    statement;
    statement
END.
```

We'll discuss the various uses of BEGIN/END blocks as we examine the Pascal language in Part II of this book.

Finally, you should notice that the listing of the *Today* program contains many *comments*: notes explaining the purpose of certain program passages. A comment line in Turbo Pascal is enclosed in curly brackets:

```
{ A Turbo Pascal program comment. }
```

Alternatively, you can use the following format for comments:

```
(* A Turbo Pascal program comment. *)
```

We will use curly brackets for comments in this book.

You can place comments wherever they seem useful in a Pascal program. A comment can be more than one line long, as long as it begins and ends with the required brackets, as in this example:

```
{ The WaitForEnter procedure displays a prompt
on the screen and waits for the user to press
the Enter key. }
```

Sometimes it is also useful to place a comment at the end of a program line. In particular, brief comments can be helpful to identify the beginning and end of long or important blocks of statements. For example, to identify the main program sections of programs in this book, we'll always supply the program name itself as a comment; here is the main program section of the *Today* program:

```
BEGIN   { Today }

    WRITELN;
    WRITE ('Today is    ', DateString, '.      ');
    WRITELN ('The time is   ', TimeString, '.');

    WRITELN;
    TodaysMessage

END.    { Today }
```

You do not need to skimp on commenting Turbo Pascal programs; comment lines are ignored during the compilation process and therefore have no effect on either the size or the performance of the resulting object code.

Finally, you should notice how the *Today* program is presented on the printed page. Four particular techniques—all easy to achieve within the context of the Turbo Pascal editor—help make the program listing easy to read:

- Indentation sets off lines contained within blocks of code that define procedures, functions, loops, and decisions.

- A generous number of blank lines are used to separate distinct sections of code.

- Pascal's *reserved words*, and the standard procedures and functions included in the language, are all typed in uppercase letters. (Reserved words are the core of the Pascal language; you'll find a quick reference guide to all reserved words in Appendix B.) While alphabetic case is not significant to the compiler, using uppercase letters makes reserved words easier to spot within a program listing.

- Long statements are broken up into several lines of code.

This final technique requires some explanation. Sometimes long instruction lines are unavoidable in Pascal programs. Unfortunately, if a line contains more characters than the maximum line length of your printer, a "wraparound" effect will occur. This means that the long instruction will be printed on two or more lines. As a result, however, the line might be broken at arbitrary and undesirable locations, making the instruction difficult for people to read.

You can avoid this problem by breaking up a long statement at points that make sense to you. A semicolon ends a statement, regardless of the number of lines the statement takes up in the program listing. For example, consider these two statements from the *TimeString* function:

```
IF LENGTH(hourStr) = 1 THEN
   hourStr : = '  ' + hourStr;
IF LENGTH(minuteStr) = 1 THEN
   minuteStr : = '0' + minuteStr;
```

Here, the Pascal compiler reads the semicolon character—*not* the carriage return—as the end of each of statement. These statements are more readable for having been broken into two lines each.

Now that you have looked briefly at the program listing of the *Today* program, you can begin entering it into the Turbo Pascal editor. In the next section of this chapter you'll learn a few essential editor operations—just enough to get started with this first program example.

Working with the Turbo Pascal Editor

If you haven't started up Turbo Pascal on your computer yet, do so now. (Type **TURBO** from the DOS prompt.) The first screen includes a copyright notice; press any key to activate the Turbo Pascal development environment. At this point your screen should look like Figure 1.1.

The first task ahead of you is to enter the entire *Today* program listing into the Turbo Pascal editor. You'll begin this task by moving the cursor into the Edit window, and, for convenience, performing the Zoom operation so that the entire screen is devoted to the editor. From the Main menu, press F10 to activate the Edit window, and then press F5 to zoom the window.

Once the cursor (a single flashing underscore character) appears in the editor, you are ready to begin typing the program listing. The top line of the Edit window always displays several important items of information. Initially the line looks like this:

```
Line 1   Col 1   Insert   Indent      Unindent  C:NONAME.PAS
```

The last item of information in this message line is the name of the file you are currently working on. When you first start out, the editor always supplies the default name NONAME.PAS for your file. (In addition, Turbo Pascal places an asterisk just before the file name if you have made any unsaved changes in the current program. This serves as a reminder that you haven't yet saved your revised file to disk.)

The Insert, Indent, and Unindent messages at the top of the Edit window indicate the current status of three toggles available in the editor. We'll discuss these options shortly.

The Line and Col messages show you your current line and column position in the editor; at least one of these position numbers changes every time you press a key or move the cursor. Begin now by typing the first line of the *Today* program, and notice how the Col position increases for each new character that you type:

```
PROGRAM Today;
```

Don't forget the semicolon at the end of this first line. When you press the Enter key at the end of the line, the Line position increases to 2 and the Col position becomes 1 again, showing you that you are now at the first column position of the second line.

Now that you have actually begun entering the program you should learn next how to save your work in a disk file. An operation that we call *save-and-continue* allows you to save the current contents of the Edit window and then continue editing. To avoid losing any of your work, you should perform this operation often.

The Save-and-Continue Operation

When you first save your file, you'll usually want to supply a more descriptive name than the default NONAME.PAS. There are several ways to save the file you are currently working on in the editor. The easiest way to save your work and then continue in the editor is to press the F2 function key. In response, Turbo Pascal displays an input box in the upper-left corner of the screen, prompting you for the name under which you wish to save the file:

```
Rename NONAME
C:\NONAME.PAS
```

You can enter any legal file name; the entire current contents of the Edit window will be saved on disk under the name that you specify. If you omit the extension, Turbo Pascal adds the default extension .PAS for the Pascal program file. (If you were simply to press the Enter key, your file would receive the default name NONAME.PAS; normally, however, you should enter a name of your own devising.)

Try it now, even though you have only entered one line of the program listing so far. Press F2, and enter the name **TODAY** as the new name for your file. (You can also specify a disk drive and/or a path name if you want to save the program to a drive other than the default; for example, you could type **C:\TP\PROGS\TODAY**.) Turbo

Pascal saves your program file on disk and then returns you to your work in the Edit window at the same position where you left off.

The top line of the Edit window now shows you the name you have given to your program file:

C:TODAY.PAS

Notice the default .PAS extension name.

After you have saved your file once, Turbo Pascal makes it very easy for you to perform the save-and-continue operation at any subsequent point in the development of your program. Just press the F2 function key again, and the current contents of the Edit window will be saved again as the new version of TODAY.PAS.

Furthermore, Turbo Pascal by default automatically copies the *previous* version of TODAY.PAS into a backup file, called TODAY.BAK. This means that you always have two versions of your file on disk—the versions that appeared in the Edit window at the time of each of your last *two* save operations. (If you do not want Turbo Pascal to maintain automatic backup files of your programs, you can turn this feature off using the *Backup files* option, located in the Environment submenu of the Options menu. We'll look at this command in Chapter 2.)

In short, remember to press F2 at reasonably frequent intervals during your work in the editor. This will help you to prevent the accidental loss of your work in a power failure or some other unexpected event.

With this cautionary note in mind, let's continue exploring the features of the editor.

Essential Editing Commands

Continue typing the lines of the *Today* program into the editor. For the moment, don't worry too much about typing errors; just concentrate on entering the listing. While you are typing, notice that you can use the Backspace key to "erase" the character just to the left of the cursor, and the arrow keys (located on the number pad of your keyboard) to move the cursor to a new position in the Edit window: up, down, right, or left. Press the Enter key at the end of each line. Save your work at least once or twice while you are typing the program.

Unless you are a perfect touch typist, you will probably find you have made some errors in the listing. To correct these errors, you'll want to learn how to accomplish a few essential tasks in the editor; these are the same operations that you must master first whenever you are faced with learning a new editing or word-processing environment:

- Moving the cursor around your file

- Deleting errors

- Inserting information

As we have seen, the Turbo Pascal editor borrows its command format from the WordStar word processing program. This means that most of the editing operations involve *control* commands: pressing the Ctrl key along with a combination of one or more additional keys. If you already know WordStar, you can skip the rest of this section; just correct the program listing on your own, and get ready to attempt a compilation.

If you do not know WordStar, the following notes will serve as an introduction to the basic editing operations. Appendix A, at the end of this book, provides a summary of all the editing commands, and Chapter 2 explains a few of the more advanced operations. To complete the *Today* exercise, however, you should just concentrate on learning a few of the most important operations.

Moving the Cursor

As you have seen, the arrow keys on the number pad provide the easiest method of moving the cursor. The up- and down-arrow (↑ and ↓) keys move the cursor up or down by one line at a time; the right- and left-arrow (→ and ←) keys move the cursor to the right or left by one column at a time. (If pressing these keys yields a number rather than a cursor move, you must turn the number pad off by pressing the NumLock key.)

If you prefer, the editor also provides alternative Ctrl-key commands for moving the cursor:

- Ctrl-E moves the cursor up one line.

- Ctrl-X moves the cursor down one line.

- Ctrl-D moves the cursor to the right one column.

- Ctrl-S moves the cursor to the left one column.

To move the cursor one word to the right or left, use these keyboard combinations:

- Ctrl-F moves one word to the right.
- Ctrl-A moves one word to the left.

In both cases, the cursor moves to the first letter of the word to the immediate right or left.

For page-long moves, you can use the convenient PgUp and PgDn keys, also located on the number pad; these keys scroll the file in the editor up or down by an entire screenful of information. Ctrl-R and Ctrl-C are the alternatives to PgUp and PgDn, respectively.

Finally, to move the cursor to the very top or the very bottom of your file, you can use the following commands:

- Ctrl-Q-R (or Ctrl-PgUp) moves the cursor to the top of the file.
- Ctrl-Q-C (or Ctrl-PgDn) moves the cursor to the bottom of the file.

The notation "Ctrl-Q-R" means "Hold down the Ctrl key and strike the Q key concurrently; then release both keys and type the R key." When you type Ctrl-Q, the editor displays the characters ^Q at the upper-left corner of the Edit window, and waits for you to press the next character. If you change your mind about the move, just press the Escape key.

Deleting Information

The Backspace key (located just above the Enter key) deletes the single character that is just to the left of the cursor position. In contrast, the Del key (located below the number pad) deletes the single character at the cursor position. If you move the cursor inside a line of code and press one of these two keys, the characters located to the right of the cursor position will all move to the left to fill in the space left by the deleted character.

For some users, the default operations performed by the Backspace and Del keys may seem inconvenient. For example, you might prefer to use the Del key to delete the character to the left of the cursor. Happily, the Turbo Pascal package includes a simple utility program, called TINST, that you can use to modify these and other editing operations. We'll explore this program in Chapter 2.

You can delete an entire word by positioning the cursor at the beginning of the word and pressing Ctrl-T. The Ctrl-Y command deletes an entire line of text; as a side effect, the lines below the deleted line will all move up by one row.

The editor has a simple Undo command, which you can use in some restricted cases. Let's say you move the cursor to an existing line of text and edit the line (by deleting or inserting some information), and then change your mind about the editing you've done. Before moving the cursor to another line, you can press Ctrl-Q-L to restore the current line to its original contents. However, once you move the cursor to another line, the Undo command is no longer available for the line that you just edited. Unfortunately, Undo does not bring back lines that you have deleted entirely with Ctrl-Y.

Inserting or Typing over Information

The editor has two typing modes: insert and typeover. In the *insert* mode, you can move the cursor to a position within an existing line and insert new information inside the line. Text located at the right of the cursor automatically moves further to the right to make room for the insertion. In the *typeover* mode, any new text that you enter inside an existing line will take the place of the line's previous contents.

You can toggle between the insert and typeover modes by using either one of the following keyboard commands:

- Press the key labeled Ins (located to the left of the Del key).
- Press Ctrl-V.

The Insert message, displayed at the top of the Edit window, indicates which mode you are in at any given time. If you see Insert, you'll know you are in the insert mode. If the message is missing, you are in the typeover mode.

In the insert mode, you can insert blank lines at any location in your program listing by simply pressing the Enter key. In the typeover mode, the Enter key simply moves the cursor down to the next existing line. In either mode you can use Ctrl-N to insert a blank line.

Indents and Tabs

As we've already discussed briefly, indenting within program structures is a way of making listings more readable. In this book we'll indent program lines within procedures, multiline functions, loops, and decision structures. We'll use conservative two-space indents, which are easy to enter from the keyboard (just press the space bar twice at the beginning of a new line), yet wide enough to produce the desired visual effect in the printed listing.

The Turbo Pascal editor has a convenient feature that helps you maintain correct indenting within program structures. Once you establish an indent for one line, the editor automatically starts the next line at the same column position when you press the Enter key. For example, consider the following block of code from the *Wait-ForEnter* procedure:

```
BEGIN
  WRITELN;
```

To indent the first line inside the block, you press the space bar until you have arrived two spaces in from the BEGIN line. However, when you complete this line and press Enter, the cursor automatically stops on the next line at the indent position that you have established for the block:

```
BEGIN
  WRITELN;

  _
```

As long as you are entering lines inside the block, you do not need to worry about indenting after the first line; just press Enter and start typing:

```
BEGIN
  WRITELN;
  WRITE ('Press <Enter> to continue. ');

  _
```

You'll want to align the block's END marker with the initial BEGIN marker. To do this you can simply press the Backspace key once to move back from the automatic indent:

```
BEGIN
  WRITELN;
  WRITE ('Press <Enter> to continue. ');
  READLN;
  WRITELN
END;
```

This illustrates the editor's *unindent* feature: pressing the Backspace key moves the cursor back to the previous indent level.

If you don't like automatic indent and unindent features, you can toggle them off:

- Press Ctrl-O-I to turn off the indent feature. When you do so, the word *Indent* disappears from the message line at the top of the Edit window. To toggle the feature back on again, press Ctrl-O-I a second time, and the Indent message reappears.

- Press Ctrl-O-U to turn off the unindent feature. The word *Unindent* disappears from the top of the Edit window. Subsequently the Backspace key moves the cursor backward by one space at a time. To toggle unindent back on, press Ctrl-O-U again.

The editor has another toggle available; this one affects the behavior of the Tab key. Press Ctrl-O-T to toggle this option on; the words *Tab Fill* appear on the top line of the Edit window, just before *Unindent*. The Tab key subsequently produces eight-space tabs in the Turbo Pascal editor. (You can change the number of spaces in a tab stop by displaying the Options menu, selecting the Environment command, and then selecting the *Tab size* command. Enter an integer representing the number of spaces you want to include between tab stops.)

You can toggle the Tab Fill option off by pressing Ctrl-O-T again. Note that this option is off by default in the Turbo Pascal editor. When the Tab Fill option is off, the Tab key produces a rather unusual effect. Each time you press Tab, the cursor moves forward to the starting position of the next word in the line immediately above the current line.

You should decide on an indenting scheme that appeals to your own sense of programming aesthetics, and then set the editor's Indent, Unindent, and Tab toggles accordingly.

The Turbo Pascal editor has many other features and commands that we haven't examined here, but these few are enough to get you started. Finish entering the *Today* listing now, and then go back and proofread your work. Try to catch any typing errors that you may have made, and use the various editing features to correct them. You can be sure that the compiler will find any typographical errors that you don't catch yourself, but it's always a good idea to try for a perfect program listing before you attempt to compile.

Compilation is the next step in the development of the program. In the upcoming sections, you'll examine two distinct ways to compile and run the *Today* program.

Compiling a Program

The Turbo Pascal compiler can store the object code for your program in the computer's memory, or in a file on disk. Normally, you'll want to compile directly to memory while you are developing a program; then you can run and debug the program within the Turbo Pascal environment. All of Turbo Pascal's development tools—including the editor, the filing system, the compiler, and the debugger—remain available to you while you are testing, correcting, and fine-tuning the performance of your program.

When your program is behaving just the way you want it to, and you are convinced that you have tested its performance adequately, you'll probably want to create a stand-alone program file containing the executable code. To do this, you go back to the Compile menu to change the Destination option, then compile the program one final time. The result is an executable program file that runs directly from DOS, independent of the Turbo Pascal development environment. We'll try both kinds of compilations with the *Today* program.

Compiling to Memory

Once you have examined and corrected your program listing within the editor, press the Alt-C keyboard combination and then C again to start the compiler directly from the editor. (Alternatively, press the Alt-F9 keyboard combination, the shortcut for the Compile command.) No matter how carefully you have checked your listing, the

first compilation is seldom successful. Almost always the compiler
will find some problem in the program: a misspelled command word,
a syntax error, a mistake in punctuation, a missing argument, or anything else that would prevent the program from running correctly.
These are called *compile-time errors*.

Perhaps the two most common errors in Pascal programs are missing semicolons and unmatched BEGIN and END markers for nested
blocks of code. Until all such errors have been cleaned out of your
program, Turbo Pascal cannot begin a performance of the program.
In the next section we'll examine what happens when the compiler
finds an error.

Correcting Compile-Time Errors

Compile-time errors are usually rather easy to correct. When such
an error occurs, the compilation process stops, and Turbo Pascal displays a message on the screen indicating the nature of the problem.
Conveniently, you are returned to the editor, with the cursor positioned at the program location where the error occurred. You simply
correct your mistake and try compiling again.

Let's look at an example of a compile-time error. (You may well find
other examples of your own when you compile the *Today* program; if
you don't, you can simulate this one by intentionally introducing the
error into your program listing.) Imagine that you forgot to type a
semicolon at the end of a WRITELN statement in the main program
section, at the bottom of the listing:

```
WRITELN
TodaysMessage
END. { Today }
```

Assuming this is the first error in your program, the compiler locates the
mistake and stops the compilation. You will be returned to the editor,
where the cursor will be positioned just below the *T* of *TodaysMessage*.
At the top of the Edit window, you will see the following error message:

```
Error 85: ";" expected.
```

All the error messages produced by the Turbo Pascal compiler are
numbered; as you can see, the error code for a missing semicolon is
85. (You'll find a list of Turbo Pascal's error messages in the Turbo
Pascal documentation.)

Sometimes error messages seem quite clear, and other times you may find yourself still wondering exactly what the problem is. Often the position of the cursor is as clear a hint as the error message. On the other hand, there may be some special occasions when the cursor position is not the true location of the error at all.

In any event, your task is to determine exactly what the error is that stopped the compiler, and to correct the error in the editor. In this case, you'll simply add the missing character to the end of the WRITELN statement. Once this is done, you can try another compilation. If your listing contains additional errors, this process must continue until you have corrected them all. The compiler finds one error at a time; you fix it and try again.

When the compilation of the *Today* program is finally successful, you will see no error message at the end of the process. During a compilation, Turbo Pascal displays a special message box on the screen that gives you information about the destination of the compilation and the number of lines that have been compiled. After a successful compilation, this box prompts you to press any key to return to the editor.

A Trial Run of the *Today* Program

Before you try running the program, perform the following two tasks:

1. Press **F2** to save the final version of the program on disk.

2. Display the File menu and select the *Change dir* command. Enter the drive and directory location of the MESSAGE.TXT file that you created earlier in this chapter. (This step, which insures that the *Today* program will be able to find your text file, is necessary only if the file is located somewhere other than the current directory where you saved the program file.)

Now you are ready to run the program. Press **Alt-R** to display the Run menu, then press **R** to perform the Run command. When the performance is complete, you are returned automatically to the development environment. To view the program's output, press **Alt-F5** for the full-screen Output window.

As you saw earlier in this chapter, the *Today* program displays the current date and time on the screen, followed by the contents of the MESSAGE.TXT file. Assuming the file is short, the Today program does not elicit input from the keyboard, but simply displays a series of messages on the screen. For this reason, the Output window flashes only briefly onto the screen, and you must use Alt-F5 to see any of the output.

However, if your message file is longer than one screen, *Today* supplies the text one screen at a time, displaying the following prompt at the bottom of each screen:

Press <Enter> to continue.

After you have read the current screen, you simply press the Enter key to receive the next screen of information. When the program performance is finished, you are returned to the development environment. Then you can still review the last screen of the output by pressing Alt-F5.

Significantly, compile-time errors are not the only kinds of problems you may experience during the development of a program. Other errors may actually interrupt the program's performance; these are called *run-time errors*. We'll look at an example of such an error in the next section.

Run-Time Errors

Run-time errors are problems that the compiler cannot catch in advance, but that cause the computer to terminate a program performance before the program is actually finished. Unexpected input values, invalid calculations, flawed program logic, disk access problems, inappropriate screen output commands—all of these can cause run-time errors.

For example, the current version of the *Today* program generates a run-time error if the program cannot locate the file MESSAGE.TXT on disk. This error occurs either if you have not created the file or if the file is located somewhere other than the current disk and directory.

Let's deliberately create a situation that results in a run-time error, so we can see how Turbo Pascal reacts. Begin by performing these steps:

1. Display the File menu and select the *OS shell* command. This command performs a temporary exit into DOS from the Turbo Pascal environment.

2. From the DOS prompt, use the RENAME command to assign a new name to your MESSAGE.TXT file, as in this example:

```
C>RENAME MESSAGE.TXT TEMP.TXT
```

As a result of this particular command, your message file is now stored under the name TEMP.TXT.

3. To return to Turbo Pascal, simply enter the EXIT command from the DOS prompt:

```
C>EXIT
```

The *Today* program should still be in the editor when you return to Turbo Pascal. The only difference is that the program will no longer be able to find a file named MESSAGE.TXT. Run the program again, and look at the result in the Output window. The program still displays the date and time on the screen, but an error occurs when the program tries to open the message file. Press Alt-F5, and you will see something like the following output:

```
Today is Wed., Aug. 3, 1988.  The time is  8:23 am.
..........................................................
Runtime error 002 at 1DDD:03C5.
```

As you can see, Turbo Pascal supplies an error message. This message supplies the error number (002 in this case, representing the "File not found" error), and an address at which the error occurred in the program (here displayed as 1DDD:03C5, although this address may vary depending on how you have entered the source code of your program).

Conveniently, the Turbo Pascal environment is ready to interpret this message for you in a very practical way. Inside the editor, Turbo Pascal automatically scrolls down to the problem point in the program and places the cursor at the line where the performance terminated:

```
RESET (messageFile);
```

The purpose of this statement is to open the message file so that the program can read the information stored in the file. The RESET procedure causes a run-time error whenever the target file cannot be found.

In addition to pointing you to the error, Turbo Pascal conveniently displays a run-time error message at the top of the Edit window. Here is the message you'll see for this particular error:

Error 2: File not found

This error message indicates that Turbo Pascal is unable to locate the file MESSAGE.TXT.

Correcting run-time errors can sometimes prove more difficult than correcting compile-time errors. Run-time errors will sometimes make you rethink the actual design of your program—anticipating certain problems that might occur in a program, and setting up alternative courses of action that can be taken in the event these problems do come up. This requires that you test your program's performance thoroughly in advance and try to imagine all the things that could possibly go wrong during the performance. Then, you must establish techniques to handle the potential problems. We'll see how this can be done in Chapter 3. For the moment, let's leave *Today* the way it is, despite the potential run-time error we've found.

Before you continue working with this program, be sure to change the name of your message file back to MESSAGE.TXT. Use the *OS shell* command again to exit temporarily to DOS, and enter this command:

C>RENAME TEMP.TXT MESSAGE.TXT

Then enter the word **EXIT** from the DOS prompt to return to Turbo Pascal.

Even if your program compiles successfully and contains no problems that can potentially interrupt a performance, there is yet a third kind of error that you may have to worry about: the program may simply produce incorrect, unexpected, or undesirable output results. These results may come from flaws in the way you have planned and structured your program.

For example, if a program performs a detailed numeric calculation, there may be an error in the steps of the calculation itself. This error may not prevent a performance from proceeding to the end of the program; but an incorrect calculation is of no use to you at all. Likewise, a program that builds text messages on the screen may make mistakes in the way it puts information together, resulting in misleading or incorrect output. These kinds of errors, which produce unsuitable results, even though the program compiles and performs "successfully" from beginning to end, can be the most difficult ones of all to locate and fix.

Fortunately, Turbo Pascal 5.0 has a group of tools that will help you find the sources of incorrect output, and produce programs that perform exactly as you want them to. These tools are accessed via the Run, Debug, and Break/watch menus. Together these tools are called the *debugger*. You'll take your first look at the debugger in the upcoming exercise.

Using the Built-in Debugger

Turbo Pascal's built-in debugger is designed to let you control and investigate the performance of a program, line by line. In particular, you can

- Establish breakpoints at which you want the normal performance to be interrupted.

- Trace through all or part of the program one line at a time.

- Watch changes that occur in the values of key variables or expressions in your program while the program is running.

During a *debugging session*, you use these features to examine the progress of a program's performance.

To see exactly how these features work, let's introduce an error into the *Today* program; then we'll go back and investigate the program as though the location of the error were actually unknown. Normally, of course, you will use the debugger when you really do not know what is going wrong with your program. Nonetheless, this exercise will give you a good idea of the sorts of investigations you can perform with the debugger.

An Exercise with the Debugger

We'll create an error in the section of the program that builds the text representation of today's date. This section, located near the top of the program, is the *DateString* function. Here is the function's *heading*:

```
FUNCTION DateString: STRING;
```

Let's take a brief look at this function's activities. It begins by calling on a built-in Turbo Pascal procedure named GETDATE; this procedure reads the current date from the computer's internal calendar, and supplies four numeric values representing the parts of the date:

```
GETDATE(year, month, day, weekday);
```

The job of *DateString* is to convert these four numbers into a readable string of text. For example, suppose GETDATE supplies values of 1988, 8, 3, and 3, respectively; the *DateString* function builds the text string *Wed., Aug. 3, 1988* from these numeric values. (Note that the *weekday* value of 3 represents Wednesday, counting forward from Sunday, which is represented by 0.)

As you can see, one of the tasks that *DateString* must perform is to convert the numeric *weekday* value into a text abbreviation for the day of the week. The GETDATE function supplies a value of 0 to 6, representing the days from Sunday to Saturday. *DateString* sets up a list of weekday abbreviations in an *array* called *days*. (You'll learn about arrays, and other Turbo Pascal data structures, in Part II of this book.) Here are the lines that creates this list:

```
CONST
   days: ARRAY[0..6] OF STRING[3] =
   ('Sun','Mon','Tue','Wed','Thu','Fri','Sat');
```

Without worrying too much about programming details at this point, you can see that the order of the list—'Sun' to 'Sat'— corresponds correctly to the numeric codes—0 to 6—supplied by the GETDATE procedure. The program uses the numeric value of *weekday* to select the correct abbreviation from this list; the text abbreviation is then stored in the variable *weekdayStr*. Here is where we'll fabricate an error in the program. We'll make a small change in the order of this list; as a result, the program will report the weekday incorrectly. By establishing *weekday* and *weekdayStr* as watch variables, we'll be able to observe this error in progress.

Make sure you have saved the correct version of the *Today* program to disk. Then go into the editor, and make the following change in the list of weekdays:

```
days: ARRAY[0..6] OF STRING[3] =
   ('Mon','Tue','Wed','Thu','Fri','Sat','Sun');
```

The list now goes from 'Mon' to 'Sun' rather than 'Sun' to 'Sat'. As a result, the weekday in the program's date output will be off by one day; for example:

Today is Thu., Aug. 3, 1988.

Imagine now that you have just run the program for the first time, and you have noticed this mistake in the output. You can reasonably guess that the problem is located inside the *DateString* function. You decide to use Turbo Pascal's built-in debugging facilities to find out what is going wrong. Here are the steps you take:

1. Inside the editor, move the cursor to the first executable line in the *DateString* function:

   GETDATE(year, month, day, weekday);

2. Press **Alt-B** to display the Break/watch menu, and then press **T** to perform the *Toggle breakpoint* command. (Alternatively, you can use the keyboard shortcut, Ctrl-F8.) In response, Turbo Pascal highlights the line where the cursor is located in the editor. This line is now a breakpoint: a point where the program performance will be interrupted.

3. Press **Alt-B** again, and then press **A** to perform the *Add watch* command. An input box appears on the screen, as you can see in Figure 1.9. Into this box, enter the following variable name:

   weekday

   Press the Enter key, and this name appears inside the Watch window in the following way:

   weekday: Unknown identifier

4. Add a second watch expression to the Watch window, but this time use a somewhat more efficient technique: in the editor, position the cursor just below the first *w* in this program line:

   weekdayStr : = days[weekday] + '., ';

Then press **Ctrl-F7**, the keyboard shortcut for the *Add watch* command. Taking its cue from the position of the cursor, Turbo Pascal automatically inserts the variable name *weekdayStr* into the input box that appears on the screen. You can now just press Enter to accept this name as the new watch expression. The Watch window now contains two expressions, as shown in Figure 1.10.

5. Press **Alt-R** and then **R** to run the program. The performance stops at the breakpoint you have established—the first executable line in the *DateString* function.

6. Now press the **F7** key repeatedly to perform the *DateString* function one line at a time. (F7 is the shortcut for the *Trace into* command in the Run menu.) As you do so, keep an eye on the Watch window. Whenever the performance of a given program line changes the value of one of the two watch variables, the Watch window displays the new value. By the time you perform the final line in the program, the Watch window will contain the current values of the variables *weekdayStr* and *weekday*; for example:

weekdayStr: 'Thu.,'
weekday: 3

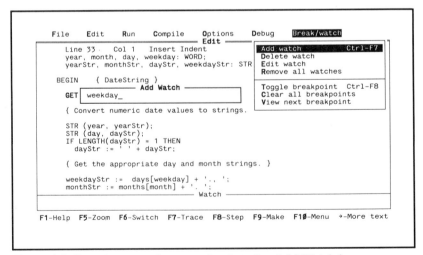

Figure 1.9: Entering a watch expression into the Add Watch box

```
   File    Edit    Run    Compile    Options    Debug    Break/watch
                                 ═══ Edit ═══
   ┌────────────────────────────────────────────────────────────────┐
   │  Line 44    Col 7    Insert Indent          Unindent   C:TODAY.PAS│
   │  yearStr, monthStr, dayStr, weekdayStr: STRING;                  │
   │                                                                  │
   │  BEGIN     ( DateString )                                        │
   │                                                                  │
   │    GETDATE(year, month, day, weekday);                          │
   │                                                                  │
   │    ( Convert numeric date values to strings. )                  │
   │                                                                  │
   │    STR (year, yearStr);                                          │
   │    STR (day, dayStr);                                            │
   │    IF LENGTH(dayStr) = 1 THEN                                    │
   │      dayStr := ' ' + dayStr;                                     │
   │                                                                  │
   │    ( Get the appropriate day and month strings. )               │
   │                                                                  │
   │    weekdayStr := days[weekday] + '., ';                         │
   │    monthStr := months[month] + '. ';                            │
   │                             ─── Watch ───                        │
   │•weekdayStr: Unknown identifier                                   │
   │ weekday: Unknown identifier                                      │
   └────────────────────────────────────────────────────────────────┘
   F1-Help  F5-Zoom  F6-Switch  F7-Trace  F8-Step  F9-Make  F10-Menu
```

Figure 1.10: Using the Watch window

If you had not already known where the error is located in your program, this information in the Watch window would give you a good idea. Clearly the *DateString* function has established a correspondence between the numeric *weekday* codes and the incorrectly ordered days of the week. Thanks to the debugger, you have been able to investigate the action of this function in detail. Your next step would be to make specific changes in the function and then run the program again.

When you complete a debugging session, you have to notify Turbo Pascal that you want to return to normal operations inside the development environment. You do this by performing the *Program reset* command in the Run menu. In addition, you'll want to deactivate any breakpoints you have established, and remove the watch expressions from the watch window. None of these steps occur automatically—even if you load a new program into the editor—so you have to take care to perform them explicitly yourself.

So, to prepare for the final exercise in this chapter, perform these steps:

1. Press **Alt-R** to display the Run menu, and then press **P** to perform the *Program reset* command. (Alternatively, press Ctrl-F2, the keyboard shortcut for Program reset.)

2. Press **Alt-B** to display the Break/watch menu, and then press **R** to perform the *Remove all watches* command. This action clears the Watch window.

3. Press **Alt-B** again, and then press **C** to perform the *Clear all breakpoints* command.

4. Press **Alt-F** to display the File menu and press **N** to perform the New command. Turbo Pascal recognizes that you have made changes in the *Today* program, and asks you if you want to save the changes:

   \TODAY.PAS not saved. Save? (Y/N)

   Press the **N** key to abandon the changes you have made.

5. Display the File menu again, and perform the Load command to load the original version of the *Today* program back into the editor.

6. Display the Compile menu and press **C** to recompile the program. Then run the program to make sure that the original version is working properly.

Once you have developed and tested a program within the Turbo Pascal environment, you are ready to create a stand-alone executable program file. The next section outlines this procedure, the final step of this introductory exercise.

Generating an Executable Program File

Clearly it is a great advantage to be able to run a finished program directly from DOS, without having to go back to the Turbo Pascal environment for each performance. In order to achieve this, you simply instruct the Turbo Pascal compiler to store the object code from your program in an .EXE program file rather than in memory.

Turbo Pascal makes this process much easier than it is in some other compilers. Along with the object code of your program, an .EXE file must contain the necessary Pascal-language routines; your program depends on the presence of these routines for a successful performance. To incorporate these resources into a single file along with your object code, some compiler packages require you to perform an extra step called *linking*. In contrast, Turbo Pascal performs the linking step automatically.

To create a stand-alone program file, you begin by changing the Destination option in the Compile menu. Display the Compile menu and examine the Destination command. Its default status is as follows:

Destination   Memory

This means that Turbo Pascal is currently set to store compiled program code in the computer's memory. To change this option, select the Destination command by pressing the **D** key. When you do so, the option changes to the following status:

Destination   Disk

Now press the **C** key to perform the Compile command. The compilation process may take a few seconds longer than it did when the object code was stored to memory. During this step Turbo Pascal is creating an .EXE file and linking together the necessary Pascal-language resources.

When the compilation is complete, the compile message box prompts you to press any key to return to the editor. To test the stand-alone program, you can now exit from Turbo Pascal and return to DOS. Display the File menu and select the Quit command (or press Alt-X).

At the DOS prompt, begin by entering the **DIR** command to examine a directory of your disk. You should find a file named TODAY-.EXE. This is the executable version of the *Today* program. To run the program, simply enter the program's name from DOS:

C>TODAY

The program is loaded into memory and the performance begins. As you can see, this is the same program that you worked with earlier in the Turbo Pascal Output window. The same messages appear on the screen. But now, when the performance is complete, you are returned once again to the DOS prompt.

Summary

The Turbo Pascal environment includes all the tools and resources you need to develop, compile, debug, and test your own Pascal programs. You access these tools through an easy-to-learn system of menu commands, and you can view the results of your work in the Output window.

The Turbo Pascal language is an extension of Standard Pascal. Version 5.0 of Turbo Pascal contains several significant improvements over previous versions. Perhaps most significantly, version 5.0 allows you to develop a program from separately compiled *units*. We'll discuss the use of units in Chapter 3.

In this chapter we have gone through the process of developing, correcting, and compiling a program, and finally creating a stand-alone executable program file. Here is a quick review of the steps you will typically follow to create such a program:

1. Enter the program listing into the Turbo Pascal editor.

2. Check the listing, and use the editor commands to correct any errors you find.

3. Try compiling the program.

4. If the compiler finds an error, you will be returned to the editor at the probable location of the problem. Correct the error, and repeat the compilation process until no more errors are found.

5. Run the program, and examine its output in the Output window.

6. Test the program thoroughly for potential run-time errors caused by events such as file access and user input.

7. If the program does not produce the output that you want, or if there is some other difficult problem in the program's behavior, use Turbo Pascal's built-in debugging resources—including watch expressions and breakpoints—to investigate the program's performance.

8. When you are satisfied with the program's performance, change the compiler Destination option to Disk, and compile

the program one final time. You can perform the resulting .EXE program file directly from DOS.

In Chapter 2 we'll examine the Turbo Pascal menu system and editor more closely, looking at the many features that we did not cover in this chapter.

C H A P T E R

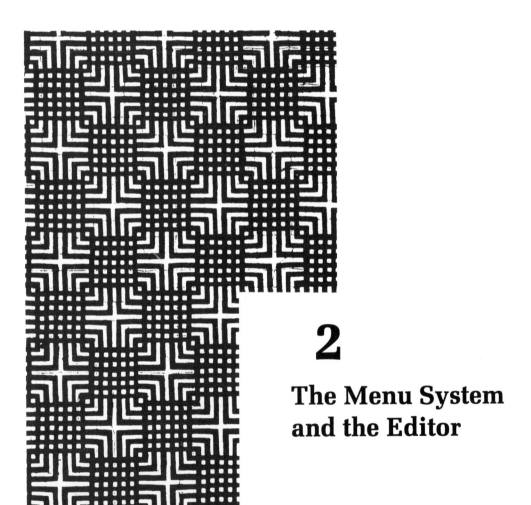

2

The Menu System
and the Editor

As you learned in Chapter 1, the features of the Turbo Pascal environment are controlled via an elaborate, multi-layered menu system. The system consists of a Main menu, and sets of corresponding dropdown and pop-up menus. The Main menu appears at the top of the screen as follows:

File   Edit   Run   Compile   Options   Debug   Break/Watch

Except for the Edit command, each selection in the Main menu displays a vertical menu on the screen, listing additional options for you to work with. Many of these options in turn result in pop-up menus, which further extend your choices for controlling the system. The options and commands available in these menus are the main subject of this chapter. You'll learn how these options affect the various resources of the system: the compiler, editor, debugger, windows, display screen, and other resources you use in the course of developing a Pascal program.

After examining the menu system, you'll take another look at the Turbo Pascal editor. Chapter 1 presented a number of the basic editing functions, such as inserting, deleting, and moving the cursor. In this chapter you'll work with several of the more advanced features. As an exercise with the editor, you'll create an *include file*: an external file of source code that the compiler incorporates into a primary program at compile time.

Finally, you'll learn how to use the TINST program to customize keyboard operations for the editor. In short, this chapter is designed to complete your introduction to the Turbo Pascal environment. Many of the features you'll read about in this chapter are tools that you'll use every time you work on a programming project. Others are more specialized and advanced tools that you'll use only occasionally when the need arises. For this reason, you might find yourself referring back to this chapter later to review features that you seldom use. A good strategy is to go through the entire chapter once now and then to look back at specific sections later as needed.

At several points during your work in this chapter you'll want to have a sample program file on hand in order to experiment with particular commands and options. The source code file for the *Today* program will fill this need nicely. Make sure that you have the program available on disk, in the file named TODAY.PAS. One of your first tasks will be to load the program back into the editor.

The File Menu

You can use commands in the File menu to save a new program file onto disk, to load an existing file from disk, to work with a disk directory, or to exit from the Turbo Pascal environment. The File menu contains the following list of nine options:

Load	F3
Pick	Alt-F3
New	
Save	F2
Write to	
Directory	
Change dir	
OS shell	
Quit	Alt-X

Most of these commands are easy to use. We'll examine them in the order in which they appear in the menu.

The Load Command

Load, the first command in the File menu, reads an existing program file from disk and loads the file into the Turbo Pascal editor. Once a file is in the editor, you can modify it, compile it, and run it.

When you select the Load command, an input box titled *Load File Name* pops immediately onto the screen, prompting you to specify the name of the file that you want to load into the editor. Assuming you remember the exact name of the file you want to load, you can enter that name directly and press the Enter key to confirm. If your file is stored somewhere other than the default drive and path, you can enter a complete path name to indicate the exact location of the file. When you do not include an extension, Turbo Pascal automatically appends the default .PAS extension to your file name before seaching for the file on disk.

Try loading the *Today* program into the editor. Enter the name of the file as follows:

Load File Name
TODAY

If the file is located in another directory or on another disk, enter a complete path, such as **C:\TP\PROGS\TODAY**. In either case, Turbo Pascal assumes that your program file has an extension of .PAS; thus the file TODAY.PAS is loaded into memory. As soon as Turbo Pascal reads the file, you will see the program appear in the Edit window.

If Turbo Pascal cannot find the file that you have identified by name, the name you supply nonetheless becomes the new file name in the Edit window. No error message appears. In this case, the Edit window remains empty; the newly named file does not actually exist on disk until you save it.

There is an interesting alternative to entering a specific file name into the Load input box. You can enter a name that contains one or more of the two DOS *wild-card* characters, the asterisk (*) and the question-mark (?). The asterisk represents any number of characters in the file name; each question mark represents a single character.

A name that contains wild-card characters is sometimes called a *mask*. For example, when the Load input box first appears on the screen, you see the following mask:

*.PAS

If you press the Enter key to accept this mask, Turbo Pascal shows you a list of all the Pascal program files (with extensions of .PAS) contained in the current directory. As another example, imagine that you have developed several versions of the *Today* program, named *Today1*, *Today2*, *Today3*, and so on. To request a directory listing of all these files, you could enter the following mask:

TODAY?.*

Figure 2.1 shows a directory listing that appears on the screen as the result of a mask. Notice that the directory includes files with both .PAS and .BAK extensions; this is the result of the asterisk character in the second part of the directory mask.

To select a file from this list and load the file into the Edit window, you can use the arrow keys to move the highlight to the target file. (Conveniently, in a list that contains more file names than this example you can simply press the first letter of the file name you want; the highlight automatically jumps to the first file name in the directory that starts with that letter. You'll notice that the files appear in alphabetical order in the list.) Press the Enter key to complete the load operation.

As always, if you change your mind about performing an operation before you actually complete it, press the Escape key to back out of a menu, an input box, or a directory box.

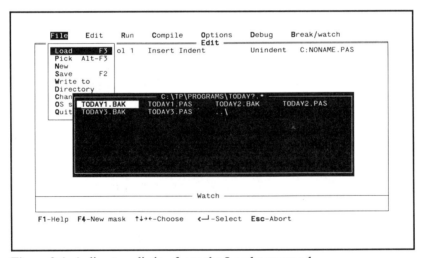

Figure 2.1: A directory listing from the Load command

The Pick Command

The Pick command gives you an easy way to reload a program file that you have already worked with at least once during the current session with the Turbo Pascal environment. The command presents a list of up to eight files that you have loaded from disk during this session and allows you to pick out the one that you wish to reload.

To perform the Pick command, display the File menu and press the **P** key. Alternatively, you can use the shortcut sequence Alt-F3 to invoke Pick. Use the ↑ and ↓ keys to select a file from the Pick list, and then press Enter to load the file.

When you first invoke the Pick command, the initial file selection is the file that you worked with most recently before your current file. To reload this file, you simply press the Enter key in response to the Pick list. This feature makes it very easy to switch between two different source files (for example, a primary file and an include file) that you are developing for a given programming project. From the editor, you can also simply press Alt-F6 as a keyboard shortcut for performing this file switch.

The last option in the Pick list is always displayed as follows:

—load file—

If the Pick file list does not contain the file that you are looking for, you can select this final option. The effect is the same as selecting the File menu's Load command.

Normally the current Pick list is lost when you exit from the Turbo Pascal environment. However, you can save the current list in a *Pick file* and then reload the list in a subsequent session with Turbo Pascal. Use the *Pick file name* command, located in the Directories submenu under the Options menu, to save the current Pick list. (You'll learn more about this command later in this chapter.)

The New Command

The New command erases the current program file from the Edit window and restores the default file name of NONAME.PAS. If you have done some work in the Edit window without saving your work in a disk file, Turbo Pascal asks you to verify this operation. For example, if you are working with the *Today* program in the Edit window and have made some changes, you will see a confirmation message such as

C:\TODAY.PAS not saved. Save? (Y/N)

If you press Y, the file is saved on disk before it is erased from the Edit window. Otherwise, if you press N, no save operation occurs, and the work you have just done in the Edit window is lost. (In this example, the original version of *Today* would remain on disk, however.)

In certain circumstances, it can be important *not* to save a program file. For example, let's say you have loaded a program into the Edit window, and then made a series of inadvertent and undesirable changes in the file. To return to the correct version of the file, you'll want to abandon the version that is currently in the Edit window and reload the original from disk.

To accomplish this you can perform the New command first, to clear the Edit window, then the Load or Pick command to load in the original version of the file. Alternatively, you can go directly to the Load or Pick command and select the file name. Again, Turbo Pascal asks you whether you want to save the revised contents of the editor. In this case, you want to abandon the incorrect Edit window version of the program before loading in the correct disk version, so you must press the N key in response to the prompt.

The Save Command

The Save command saves the program currently stored in the editor. As you learned in Chapter 1, F2 is the keyboard shortcut for this command. If you are saving your file for the first time, and the file still has the default name NONAME.PAS, Turbo Pascal gives you an opportunity to supply a more descriptive name of your own. An input box appears on the screen with the following title and file name:

Rename NONAME
C:\NONAME.PAS

As soon as you begin typing a new name, the current name in the input box disappears. If you want to save your file to some location other than the current default disk and path, you can supply a complete path name. Press Enter to confirm the new name, and Turbo Pascal saves your program file on disk. If you supply no extension, the file receives the default .PAS extension.

If you have already saved the current program file on disk at least once before, Turbo Pascal automatically renames the existing disk version, assigning it a .BAK extension name. This means that you always have both the current version and the previous version of your program on disk. (However, you'll find a command in the Options menu that allows you to turn off the automatic backup procedure if you want to. We'll discuss this option later in the chapter.)

The *Write To* Command

The *Write to* command gives you the opportunity to change the name of the program file currently stored in the editor. When you pull down the File menu and select *Write to*, an input box entitled *New Name* pops onto the screen asking you for the new name of the file. When you type a name and press the Enter key, Turbo Pascal saves a copy of the current program on disk under the file name you have supplied. The new file name also appears at the top of the Edit window. Any previous version or versions of the program that are already stored on disk remain where they are, undisturbed by the *Write to* command.

The *Write to* command is useful when you want to keep a permanent disk copy of an original program before you create a new version of the same program. For example, let's say you make some changes in the *Today* program, and you decide to save the new version under the file name NEWTODAY.PAS. You can use the *Write to* command to create a file for the new version without losing the original version.

The Directory Command

The Directory command simply displays a directory box on the screen, showing you a list of file names. When you select this command, an input box pops up, prompting you to enter a mask. The default mask is *.*, which means that all files from the current directory will be displayed.

When a directory contains one or more subdirectories, you can open a selected subdirectory and view its contents. Simply move the directory highlight to the target subdirectory and press Enter. A new directory box appears on the screen, showing the files stored in the subdirectory. This feature applies to all menu commands that display directory boxes on the screen.

By the way, the Directory command also lets you load a selected program file (or other text file) into the editor if you so choose. In this way, the Directory command behaves identically to the Load command.

The *Change Dir* Command

You can use the *Change dir* command to change the current default disk drive and/or directory path. An input box appears on the screen for entering the new directory. After you change the directory, any subsequent save or load operations use the new directory by default.

The *OS Shell* Command

The *OS shell* command provides a temporary exit from Turbo Pascal. You can use this command whenever you need to perform one or more DOS commands in the middle of a session with Turbo Pascal; *OS shell* drops you into DOS, where you can perform any necessary operating system activities. Then, to return to Turbo Pascal, you enter the word EXIT from the DOS prompt. You'll find that your current work in the editor is undisturbed. Furthermore, any option settings that you established before the exit remain in effect.

When you return to Turbo Pascal from a temporary exit, the contents of the DOS screen remain in the Output window, recording some or all of the operating system activities you just completed. (Press Alt-F5 to see the Output window.)

You might want to exit temporarily from Turbo Pascal whenever you need to perform a file or disk operation that is not available in the File menu. For example, the following DOS commands have no equivalent in Turbo Pascal:

- ERASE, for removing one or more files from a disk
- COPY, for copying more than one program file from one directory to another

- FORMAT, for formatting a new disk
- RENAME, for renaming a file on disk

Furthermore, you can exit from Turbo Pascal in order to work temporarily in another software program. For example, you might prefer to develop long program listings in your regular word processing environment, rather than in the Turbo Pascal editor. In this situation, the *OS shell* command provides a means of moving back and forth between Turbo Pascal and the outside word processing program. (Of course, your computer system must have adequate memory to handle both software packages at once.)

The Quit Command

The Quit command exits from Turbo Pascal and returns you to DOS. (The keyboard shortcut for the Quit command is Alt-X.) Unlike the *OS shell* command, Quit is a permanent exit; it does not retain your current Turbo Pascal activities. To return to Turbo Pascal after Quit, you must rerun the program by entering TURBO at the DOS prompt.

If the editor contains an unsaved program file at the time you select the Quit command, Turbo Pascal asks you if you want to save the file before quitting. You respond by pressing Y or N. Turbo Pascal can save only your source code as you exit from the development environment. If you have compiled the program to memory, this compilation is lost when you exit from Turbo Pascal. To save an executable version of the program to disk, you must first change the Destination option in the Compile menu, as you saw in Chapter 1.

The Run Menu

The Run menu offers several different ways to initiate a program performance. Here are the six commands in the menu, along with their keyboard shortcuts:

Run	Ctrl-F9
Program reset	Ctrl-F2

Go to cursor	F4
Trace into	F7
Step over	F8
User screen	Alt-F5

Using the Run command, this menu's first entry, you can start a normal run of your program. In contrast, other commands in the Run menu represent some of Turbo Pascal's debugging facilities. Significantly enough, this is the only menu in which every one of the commands has a keyboard shortcut, giving you easy access to all of these important commands.

The Run Command

The Run command initiates a performance of the current program. If you have not already compiled the program, or if you have changed the program in the editor since the last compilation, Run compiles the code (performing the equivalent of the Make command in the Compile menu). At the end of a performance, Turbo Pascal does not hold the Output screen on display. If you want to review the screen output from the program, you can press Alt-F5 (the shortcut for the *User screen* command in the Run menu) to display the output in a full-screen mode.

During a debugging session, the Run command resumes the program performance from the point at which the program was interrupted. You'll learn more about this feature as you continue in this chapter.

The *Program Reset* Command

The *Program reset* command deactivates some aspects of a current debugging session.

In Chapter 1 you worked through a first debugging exercise—establishing a breakpoint, inserting some watch expressions in the Watch window, and then stepping through the program performance one line at a time. In the course of this chapter you'll review the various debugging facilities in more detail. Specifically, you'll learn about commands in the Run, Debug, and Break/watch menus that allow you to

- Establish breakpoints at lines where you want the performance to be interrupted (the *Toggle breakpoint* command in the Break/watch menu).

- Perform the program up to the current cursor position in the editor, using the *Go to cursor* command.

- Perform the program one line at a time using either the *Trace into* or the *Step over* command.

- Examine the value of a particular expression in reference to the current program (the Evaluate command in the Debug menu).

- Examine specific watch expressions in the Watch window during a debugging session (the *Add watch* commmand in the Break/watch menu).

- Interrupt the program from the keyboard by pressing Ctrl-Break.

After you interrupt a program performance for debugging, the Run command normally resumes the program performance at the point at which it was interrupted. However, if you want to terminate the debugging session and start a normal performance from the beginning of the program, you may have to go through some or all of the following steps:

1. Perform the *Program reset* command (Ctrl-F2) so that you can rerun the program from the beginning.

2. Perform the *Clear all breakpoints* command to deactivate any breakpoints you have established.

3. Perform the *Remove all watches* command to clear the Watch window.

4. Perform the Run command to rerun your program.

The *Program reset* command releases some of the extra memory that Turbo Pascal requires for use during a debugging session. However, notice that *Program reset* does not clear breakpoints or watches;

you have to take both of these actions yourself when it is appropriate to do so. Furthermore, *Program reset* does not reinitialize variables used in your program.

The *Go To Cursor* Command

The *Go to cursor* command initiates a program performance and then stops the performance at the line where you have positioned the cursor in the editor. (The cursor line is not included in the partial performance.) This convenient command allows you to start a debugging session, running your program up to a point where you expect to find a particular problem.

If you are running your program for the first time (or immediately after performing the *Program reset* command), *Go to cursor* starts the performance at the beginning of the program. On the other hand, if you are already in a debugging session, *Go to cursor* starts immediately after the last line that was executed, and continues to the point where you have placed the cursor.

Like the Run command, the action of *Go to cursor* is affected by any breakpoints you have established for your debugging session. In other words, if you place a breakpoint before the current cursor position, the breakpoint determines where the performance will stop.

The *Trace Into* Command

During a debugging session, *Trace into* performs the next executable line in your program. If you want to run through the program one line at a time, you invoke the *Trace into* command repeatedly. (Recall that the shortcut for this command is F7.) If a debugging session is not currently active, *Trace into* initiates a session and performs the first executable line in the controlling section of your program. On the other hand, if you have already started a debugging session, *Trace into* performs the line located after the previously executed line.

When *Trace into* encounters a procedure call or a function call, control is transferred to the location of the corresponding procedure or function. (If the procedure or function is located in an external file—a unit or an include file—Turbo Pascal temporarily loads the file into memory for the purposes of the debugging session.) Pressing F7 subsequently steps line by line through the routine that has been called.

The *Step Over* Command

Like *Trace into*, the *Step over* command performs the next executable line in your program, giving you another tool for stepping through a performance line by line. However, when *Step over* encounters a procedure call or function call, the entire procedure or function is performed at once. *Step over* does not transfer control to the called routine for a line-by-line performance.

The shortcut for *Step over* is F8.

The *User Screen* Command

The *User screen* command displays the Output window on the full screen, temporarily removing the Turbo Pascal menu and window environment from view. The equivalent keyboard command is Alt-F5. The Output window shows you the screen output from a previous program performance, or the commands you performed in DOS before starting up Turbo Pascal.

Press any key from the keyboard to return to the development environment from the full-screen Output window.

The Compile Menu

The Compile menu gives you a number of options for compiling your current program, including three different commands that actually initiate compilation. This menu contains the following list of commands:

Compile	Alt-F9
Make	F9
Build	
Destination	
Find error	
Primary file	
Get info	

You have already seen the Compile command in action in Chapter 1. The Make and Build commands are alternative techniques for compiling a program that consists of multiple files. Since the action resulting from Make or Build commands depends on the current status of the *Primary file* command, we'll examine the Compile menu commands slightly out of order.

The Compile Command

The Compile command initiates the compilation process, always working on the file that is currently in the editor. As you have seen, Turbo Pascal displays a compile box on the screen during compilation, giving you information about the number of lines compiled and the destination of the object code. If the compilation is successful (that is, if there are no compile-time errors in your program), this box remains on the screen for you to examine when the process is over. On the other hand, if the compiler finds an error in your program, Turbo Pascal activates the editor and scrolls down to the program line at which the error occurred. You'll find an error message at the top of the screen.

The Alt-F9 keyboard combination is a shortcut for performing the Compile operation.

The other two compile commands, Make and Build, behave the same as Compile if your program consists of only one program file. But Make and Build have special uses when you are building a program that consists of more than one file. Before discussing these two commands, let's look at the *Primary file* command. (You'll learn much more about programs that consist of multiple files later in this chapter and in Chapter 3.)

The *Primary File* Command

Turbo Pascal gives you two ways to build programs from multiple Pascal program files. The simpler technique allows you to store procedures, functions, or other sections of source code as individual include files, stored on disk. To incorporate an include file into a program, you insert a *compiler directive* in the source code of the primary program file. A compiler directive gives a special instruction to the compiler; for example, the *include* compiler directive instructs the compiler to read an include file into the program at compile time. We'll examine this technique later in this chapter.

The second technique, using separately compiled *units*, is more complex, but also more powerful. A unit is a collection of procedures and functions stored independently on disk as compiled code. The USES statement, at the top of a program, identifies units that the program requires. Building programs with units is the subject of Chapter 3.

Using either technique, you may sometimes find yourself developing a program that consists of a main file, along with one or more secondary include files or unit files. Since only one source code file resides in the editor at a time, this kind of development process obviously requires careful attention to file management.

The *Primary file* command is a tool that can simplify your work with multiple program files. You can use this command to tell Turbo Pascal the name of the main program file in a multiple-file project. Once you have done so, both the Make and Build commands direct the compiler to work on the designated primary file, regardless of which file is currently stored in the editor.

For example, let's say you are developing a program that uses an include file. Imagine that the include file consists of a general-purpose routine that you have saved independently on disk so that you can use it in other programming projects. Currently the include file is in the editor, and you are fine-tuning its performance. The main program file is stored on disk, but you would like to be able to run the program and test the results of your changes to the include file. (Assume that the main program file contains the appropriate compiler directive for reading the include file at compile time.)

To run the program, pull down the Compile menu and select the *Primary file* command. Turbo Pascal displays an input box entitled *Primary File* on the screen. You can enter a file name into this box directly from the keyboard. (Alternatively, you can simply press the Enter key in response to the default ∗.PAS file mask; Turbo Pascal presents a directory box, from which you can select a primary file to enter into the box.) When you complete your entry or selection, the Primary file line in the Compile menu shows the name of your primary file, as in this example:

Primary file: MAINPROG.PAS

If you subsequently use either the Make command or the Build command to compile the program, Turbo Pascal reads your designated primary file into memory and compiles it. The include file remains in the editor, where you can continue making changes after each compilation and performance.

After you have finished working on this particular project, and before you try to compile some other program, you must remember to remove the old file name from the Primary file line. To do so, select the *Primary file* command, and press Ctrl-Y to erase the current contents of the input box.

The next two sections discuss the Make and Build commands in detail.

The Make Command

The Make command compiles the primary file, if you have designated one. If not, Make compiles the file that is currently in the editor. In addition, Make causes the compiler to examine any unit files that are part of the current programming project (that is, any files that are designated in the USES statement in the primary file). If you have revised the source file of a given unit since the last compilation, the Make operation recompiles that unit. (To determine whether or not to recompile a unit source file, Make examines the date and time stamps on both the source file and the object file.)

The F9 function key is the shortcut for performing the Make operation.

The Build Command

Like Make, the Build command compiles the primary file, or the file currently in the editor if you have not designated a primary file. Build also recompiles the available source code for unit files that are part of the current programming project, whether you have revised them or not since the last compilation. Use Build if you want to force a recompilation of every part of your program.

The Destination Command

You use the Destination command to specify where you want Turbo Pascal to store the object code produced by the compiler. This command determines the results of the Compile, Make, and Build commands. As you saw in Chapter 1, the command has two settings; the default setting stores the object code only in memory:

Destination   Memory

This is the setting you will normally want to use while you are developing a program inside the Turbo Pascal environment.

The alternative setting creates an .EXE file on disk for the object code:

Destination   Disk

The result is a stand-alone program that can be executed directly from DOS. Turbo Pascal automatically links the necessary Pascal-language resources with the object code of your own program to produce an .EXE file.

The *Find Error* Command

You have seen how Turbo Pascal behaves in the event of a run-time error when you are running a program inside the development environment; conveniently, the editor scrolls directly down to the program location at which the error occurred. But what happens if a run-time error terminates a compiled Turbo Pascal .EXE program that you are running directly from DOS? First, you will be returned to the DOS prompt, of course. You will also receive a rather cryptic message line explaining the error that has occurred, such as

Runtime error 002 at 0000:03C5.

This message line contains two important pieces of information: the error number and the address of the error in the program. You can use the error number to find out what kind of event caused the termination of your program, by checking the list of run-time errors, organized in numeric order, contained in the Turbo Pascal documentation.

To translate the error address into an actual location in the program listing, you must perform these steps:

1. Write down the address that you see on the message line.

2. Return to Turbo Pascal.

3. Reload your source code into the editor.

4. Pull down the Compile menu, and select the *Find error* command.

5. Enter the address into the resulting input box.

After you complete this procedure, Turbo Pascal quickly determines the location in your source code where the performance failure occurred. In the editor the cursor appears at the target line in the program.

To try this feature out, return to DOS for another performance of the program TODAY.EXE. (You created this executable program file at the end of Chapter 1.) Recall that the program reads a text file named MESSAGE.TXT. Before you run the program this time, rename the message file so that Today will not be able to find it:

```
C>RENAME MESSAGE.TXT TEMP.TXT
```

As you saw in Chapter 1, the *Today* program terminates with a run-time error if the program cannot locate the MESSAGE.TXT file. Run the program by entering

```
C>TODAY
```

When the program terminates, make note of the error address and follow the steps outlined above. Turbo Pascal should direct you to the following line as the source of the run-time error:

```
RESET (messageFile);
```

The *Find error* command proves especially useful in programs that are much longer than *Today*. If you take care to test your programs carefully inside the Turbo Pascal environment, you may not have to use this command very often. You will have already prepared for potential run-time errors by the time you have created an .EXE file. However, from time to time an unexpected error pops up, and you'll have to search it out. In this situation, the *Find error* command can save you a lot of time.

The *Get Info* Command

The *Get info* command presents a pop-up window on the screen, containing a variety of information about your current programming project. The window tells you about the source file (name, size, and primary file, if any) and about the last compilation (number of lines compiled, destination of the code, and any compile-time or run-time errors that resulted from the compilation or the subsequent performance). Figure 2.2 shows an example of the *Get info* window describing a compilation of the *Today* program.

The Options Menu

The Options menu contains seven commands that control various characteristics of the compiler and the development environment. Here is the menu list:

Compiler
Linker
Environment
Directories
Parameters
Save options
Retrieve options

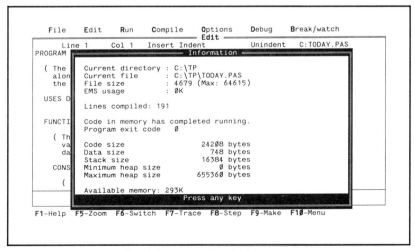

Figure 2.2: An example of the *Get info* window

The first four commands, Compiler, Linker, Environment, and Directories, result in pop-up submenus that supply a large set of options. Many of these options are required only for special situations, but you should be aware that they exist in case you ever need them.

The Compiler Options

The pop-up menu for the Compiler options appears in Figure 2.3. The options in this menu represent a range of compiler characteristics, each of which you can control in two ways: by changing a setting in this menu or by including a particular compiler directive directly in your program's source code. Before we turn to the Compiler menu options, let's briefly discuss the use of compiler directives.

Compiler Directives

A *compiler directive* is an abbreviated command that instructs the compiler to assume a certain condition or to perform a particular action during the compilation of a program. The name of each compiler directive begins with a dollar sign character ($) and must be enclosed in comment delimiters inside a program listing.

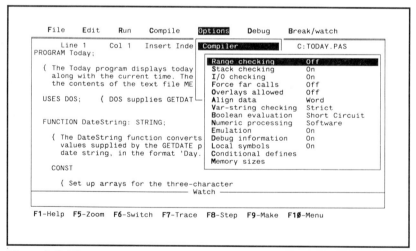

Figure 2.3: The pop-up menu for the Compiler options

For example, the $R directive corresponds to the *Range checking* command, the first option in the Options/Compiler menu. (We'll look at this command shortly.) The $R directive has two formats. The following format turns range checking on:

```
{$R + }
```

Using this is equivalent to selecting the *Range checking* command and turning its status On:

```
Range checking      On
```

The following format of the $R directive turns range checking Off:

```
{$R – }
```

This is the same as setting the Range checking command to off.

Like $R, a number of compiler directives are switches that turn certain conditions on or off. Each of these switches has a default status of on or off; you change the status by selecting the appropriate option in the Compiler menu or by including a compiler directive in your source code.

Another category of compiler directive requires that you supply one or more items of information—*parameters*—to complete the command. For example, the $M directive controls the size of two special memory areas called the *stack* and the *heap*. To use this directive you supply three numbers, representing the stack size and the minimum and maximum size of the heap; for example:

```
{$M 32768, 0, 0}
```

Including this directive in your program listing is equivalent to selecting the *Memory sizes* command in the Compiler submenu and entering these three numeric settings into the corresponding input boxes.

Finally, a third category of compiler directives controls Turbo Pascal's capacity for *conditional compilation*. Using this feature, you can designate blocks of code that the compiler will either translate or ignore, depending on specified conditions. We'll discuss this topic later in this chapter.

Now let's examine the various options of the Compiler submenu; as we go through these options we'll also note the compiler directives that produce the same results.

The *Range Checking* Option

When you compile a program with the *Range checking* option toggled to on, the resulting code checks to make sure that the following data values are within appropriate ranges:

- Subscripts for accessing array elements
- Subscripts into string variables
- *Scalar* data values, such as integers, characters, and enumerated type values

Once the *Range checking* option is activated, if any subscript or value is out of range, the program terminates with a run-time error. (We'll discuss scalar data types in Chapter 4 and arrays in Chapter 6.)

This command is toggled off by default. You might want to switch it on during program development, when the range checking feature is particularly useful. However, this option results in less economical code, so be sure to switch it back off again after you have tested your program and before you begin the final compilation.

As you have seen, the compiler directive equivalent to the Range checking option has the following two formats:

{$R + }   Switches range checking on.

{$R − }   Switches range checking off.

The *Stack Checking* Option

The *stack* is the memory segment in which Turbo Pascal keeps track of local variables in a program's procedures and functions. When one routine calls another during the performance of a program, the new routine's local variables are allocated to the stack. When the routine later relinquishes control, the local variables are released from the stack.

When you compile a program with the *Stack checking* option activated, the compiler includes code in your program to check the status of the stack every time a procedure or function is called. If there is not enough stack space for the local variables of a given routine, a run-time error occurs.

The *Stack checking* option is on by default; you should generally leave it activated for all compilations. The $S compiler directive corresponds to the *Stack checking* option:

{$S + }   Switches stack checking on.

{$S − }   Switches stack checking off.

By default, Turbo Pascal allocates 16K of memory for the stack. You can use the Compiler submenu's *Memory sizes* option to change the amount of stack space for a given program.

The *I/O Checking* Option

The *I/O checking* option determines whether the compiler will generate code to check for input and output errors. This option is *on* by default; a program compiled under this setting results in a run-time error when an input or output error occurs. A few common input and output errors are

- Entering an inappropriate type of input data from the keyboard during a program performance.

- Attempting to read from or write to a file that is not open.

- Attempting to open and read (RESET) a file that does not exist on disk.

Input and output errors, like all run-time errors, normally stop a program, creating an undesirable interruption in the performance. You saw an example in Chapter 1, when the *Today* program could not locate the MESSAGE.TXT file. Since input and output errors are so common, Turbo Pascal supplies some special tools for handling these events. Specifically, when the *I/O checking* option is off, a program can check the Turbo Pascal function named IORESULT after each input or output operation. For a successful input or output operation, IORESULT returns a value of 0. For an I/O error, IORESULT returns an integer code value, representing the particular error that has occurred. The program can use this value to determine what to do next.

The $I compiler directive is equivalent to the I/O checking switch:

{$I + }   Switches I/O checking on.

{$I – }   Switches I/O checking off.

This directive is a useful tool in programs that contain the potential for input and output errors. You can use the directive to switch I/O checking off temporarily for individual input or output operations. For example, the following code presents a solution for preventing the I/O run-time error in the *Today* program:

```
{$I – }
  RESET (messageFile);
{$I + }

IF IORESULT = 0 THEN
  BEGIN
    { Read the file. }
  END
ELSE
  WRITELN ('Can''t find ', messageFileName);
```

In this passage, the $I directive turns I/O checking off just before the RESET command is performed, and on again after RESET. Then the program checks the value of IORESULT. If the value is 0, the file has been opened successfully and the program can read it. However if IORESULT returns any value other than 0, an I/O error has occurred. In this case, the program displays the date, the time, and then an error message that tells the user what has happened:

Can't find MESSAGE.TXT

You'll learn more about input and output errors, and the role of the $I directive, in Chapters 3 and 4. Note that Turbo Pascal also has an *include file* compiler directive that is also named $I. Even though these two directives have the same name, they perform very different operations, as you'll see later in this chapter.

The *Force Far Calls* Option

Force far calls is an advanced option for special-purpose programming projects. A *far call* is a complete calling address for a particular procedure or function that may reside in a different 64K memory segment than the primary program segment. (A far call contains both the segment address and the offset address within the designated segment.)

A *near call* is an address that is inside the same memory segment as the main program. (A near call contains only the offset address within the current segment.) Normally the *Force far calls* option is off; under this status, the compiler generates near calls for all procedures and functions except those provided to the main program by a unit. When the *Force far calls* option is on, the compiler generates far calls for all procedures and functions. (Far calls must be enabled in a programming project that uses *overlays*; this subject is introduced briefly in the next section.)

The $F compiler directive allows you to turn the *Force far calls* option on or off for particular procedures and functions in your program:

{$F + }   Generates far calls for subsequent routines.

{$F − }   Generates near calls for subsequent routines.

The *Overlays Allowed* Option

Overlays are sections of code that may reside alternately in the same part of memory during a program performance, allowing you to run a program that is larger than the memory actually available in your computer. The basic idea is that an overlay is loaded into memory at the point when its routines are required during the performance, and then remains in memory until it is replaced by a different overlay.

Turbo Pascal supports the use of overlays in programming projects that use units. The *Overlays allowed* option determines whether or not the compiler will generate the code necessary for a unit overlay. You must switch this option to its On setting (or use the {O + } compiler directive) for compiling a unit that you plan to use as an overlay. In programming projects that do not use overlaid units, you can retain the default Off setting.

The $O compiler directive allows you to turn the overlays option on or off for particular units:

{$O + }   Generates overlay code.

{$O – }   Does not generate overlay code.

(You'll learn a little more about overlays in Chapter 3. For complete coverage of this advanced topic, consult the Turbo Pascal documentation.)

The *Align Data* Option

Align data is an advanced option for improving the efficiency of data access on computers that are controlled by 8086, 80286, or 80386 microprocessors. You can choose either of two settings for this option: *Word* or *Byte*. Under *Word*, the default setting, Turbo Pascal stores each simple variable and typed constant at an even-numbered address in memory. A blank byte of memory is used, if necessary, to pad between two consecutive items so that each item can start at an even address. The 80x86 family of microprocessors can access data faster at even addresses than at odd addresses, so the *Word* setting improves performance on these machines. (The *Word* setting has no effect on storage of complex data structures, including records and arrays; nor does it affect items that are only one byte in length.)

Under the *Byte* setting, variables and typed constants are stored consecutively without padding, at even or odd addresses. You can switch to this setting if you are running Turbo Pascal on an 8088 microprocessor; on this machine the *Word* setting has no effect on access speed.

The $A compiler directive switches between the *Word* and *Byte* alignment settings in a program:

{$A + }   Switches to word alignment.

{$A – }   Switches to byte alignment.

The *Var-String Checking* Option

The *Var-string checking* option determines how strictly the compiler will check string-type values sent to procedures and functions. The default status of this option appears as follows:

Var-string checking   Strict

When you select this option to toggle its status, the menu line appears as follows:

Var-string checking   Relaxed   .

Under the Strict status, a string variable that is passed *by reference* must have the same defined type as the formal VAR parameter defined in the PROCEDURE or FUNCTION heading of the called routine. (If the types are not the same, a compile-time error occurs.)

Under the Relaxed status, the length of the string argument passed to a procedure or function does not have to match the defined length of the formal parameter. (We'll discuss procedures, functions, arguments, and parameters—and the special vocabulary for describing these elements—in Chapter 4.)

The $V compiler directive is equivalent to the *Var-string checking* option:

{$V + }   Switches to strict string-variable checking.

{$V − }   Switches to relaxed string-variable checking.

The *Boolean Evaluation* Option

The *Boolean evaluation* option determines how the Turbo Pascal evaluates compound logical expressions (using the logical operators AND and OR). This option has two settings—the default

Boolean evaluation   Short Circuit

and the toggled

Boolean evaluation   Complete

Under the default Short Circuit status, Turbo Pascal evaluates as few components of the compound logical expression as possible, as in these examples:

- Given the expression *a AND b*, if *a* is FALSE, Turbo Pascal does not evaluate *b*.

- Given the expression *a OR b*, if *a* is TRUE, Turbo Pascal does not evaluate *b*.

In contrast, the Complete status forces Turbo Pascal to evaluate all components of a compound logical expression, regardless of the value of initial components. (We'll discuss logical expressions and operators, and the two evaluation modes, in Chapter 5.)

The $B compiler directive is equivalent to the *Boolean evaluation* option:

{$B + }   Forces *complete* evaluation of logical expressions.

{$B − }   Allows *short-circuited* evaluation.

The *Numeric Processing* Option

The Turbo Pascal compiler can generate code that takes advantage of the 8087 or the 80287 math coprocessor chips. The presence of this chip in your computer system therefore results in programs that may perform faster and more efficiently than in a system that lacks the chip. In addition, your programs can use an extended set of *floating-point* data types named SINGLE, DOUBLE, EXTENDED, and COMP. (The standard floating-point data type is named REAL; you'll learn about all these types in Chapter 4.)

Turbo Pascal can also *emulate* the operations of the 8087/80287 coprocessor in a system that does not include the chip. Under this emulation, the extended numeric data types are available even when the coprocessor chip is not present; however, performance will be slower.

The *Numeric processing* option determines whether or not a program can use the extended 8087 data types. The option's default status appears as follows:

Numeric processing   Software

Under this status, the only floating-point data type available is REAL. The extended types cannot be used.

When you toggle the *Numeric processing* option, the status changes as follows:

Numeric processing   8087/80287

Under this status, the compiler generates code for the extended floating-point data types. Depending on the status of the Emulation option ($E, discussed in the next section), the presence of the 8087 chip will be required, or its operations will be emulated if necessary.

The $N compiler directive is equivalent to the *Numeric processing* option:

{$N + }   Switches to the *8087/80287* setting.

{$N − }   Switches to the *Software* setting.

The Emulation Option

The Emulation option has meaning only when the *Numeric processing* option is switched to its 8087/80287 setting. Under this setting, you can activate or deactivate emulation of the 8087 operations.

The default Emulation setting is On. In this case, Turbo Pascal checks to see if your system has an 8087 chip or not. If the chip is available, it is used for performing all floating-point operations. If the chip is not present, Turbo Pascal emulates its operations, resulting in slower performance.

If Emulation is set to Off and *Numeric processing* is switched to the 8087/80287 setting, the resulting compiled program will require the presence of a math coprocessor chip. The program will not run on a system that does not include the chip.

Under the default *Software* setting of the *Numeric processing* option, Turbo Pascal ignores the setting of the Emulation option.

The $E compiler directive is equivalent to the Emulation option:

{$E + }   Generates emulation code (numeric processor chip is optional).

{$E − }   Does not generate emulation code (numeric processor chip is required).

This directive has no effect if the {N − } directive is used, switching numeric processing to the software mode.

The *Debug Information* Option

When the *Debug information* option is On—the default setting—the compiler generates the information required for successful use of the built-in debugger. (The *Integrated debugging* option in the Debug menu must also be On for debugging sessions.) In addition, the debug information allows Turbo Pascal to locate the source of run-time errors.

You have seen what normally happens in the development environment when a run-time error occurs: Turbo Pascal scrolls to the problem line in the editor, and the compiler supplies an appropriate error message. If you switch *Debug information* off, a run-time error still results in an appropriate error message, but Turbo Pascal does not scroll to the line that caused the error.

Furthermore, when this option is off you cannot trace through a program in either of the line-by-line debugging modes (*Trace into* or *Step over*), and you cannot use breakpoints to interrupt the program performance at specific lines.

The $D compiler directive is the equivalent to this option:

{$D + }   Switches debug information on.

{$D – }   Switches debug information off.

The *Local Symbols* Command

The *Local symbols* option determines whether the compiler will generate information about variables and constants that are local to a program's procedures and functions. When this option is On—the default setting—the compiler allows you to set up watch expressions to examine the values of these data structures during a debugging session. When the option is switched Off, Turbo Pascal cannot display the values of local variables and constants in the Watch window.

The $L compiler directive is the equivalent to the *Local symbols* option:

{$L + }   Generates information about local variables and constants.

{$L – }   Does not generate information about local variables and constants.

If the *Debug information* option is Off, Turbo Pascal ignores the setting of *Local symbols*.

The *Conditional Defines* Option

Turbo Pascal supports *conditional compilation*, by which you can direct the compiler to include or ignore certain marked sections of your source code. You control this feature via a special set of compiler directives; specifically, these directives provide a variety of IF/ELSE/ENDIF-style structures that you use to mark sections of code that are subject to conditional compilation. Table 2.1 gives a brief summary of the available directives.

Table 2.1: Compiler Directives for Conditional Compilation

{$IFDEF *symbol*}	Directs Turbo Pascal to compile the subsequent block of code only if *symbol* has been defined. (The end of the block is marked by an {$ELSE} or {$ENDIF} directive.)
{$IFNDEF *symbol*}	Directs Turbo Pascal to compile the subsequent block of code only if *symbol* has not been defined.
{$IFOPT *option*}	Directs Turbo Pascal to compile the subsequent block of code only if *option* is set as specified. (The *option* argument is a setting for any of Turbo Pascal's switch-type compiler directives; for example N + .)
{$ELSE}	Marks the beginning of the block of code that will be compiled if the corresponding $IFDEF, $IFNDEF, or $IFOPT directive has resulted in a false condition.
{$ENDIF}	Marks the end of a block of conditionally compiled code.
{$DEFINE *symbol*}	Defines a named *symbol* for use in subsequent $IFDEF or $IFNDEF directives.
{$UNDEF *symbol*}	Releases the definition of a named *symbol* for subsequent $IFDEF or $IFNDEF directives.

You can use the *Conditional defines* option to define special named symbols for use in the $IFDEF or $IFNDEF directives. The result of these two conditional directives depends on the existence of a particular named symbol.

For example, consider the following short demonstration:

```
PROGRAM Test;
  USES PRINTER;

  BEGIN
    {$IFDEF printerOn}
      WRITELN (LST, 'Output to the printer.')
    {$ELSE}
      WRITELN ('Output to the display screen.')
    {$ENDIF}
  END.
```

The portion of this program that will actually be compiled depends on whether or not you have defined the symbol *printerOn*. To test the program, begin by selecting the *Conditional defines* command and entering the name **printerOn** into the input box that Turbo Pascal supplies. When you compile and run the program, a line of text will be sent to your printer; the following program line has been compiled and performed:

```
WRITELN (LST, 'Output to the printer.')
```

Now, to complete the exercise, select the *Conditional defines* command again, and press **Ctrl-Y** to erase the contents of the input box. Compile and run the test program again, and a line of text will appear on the screen. The following line has been compiled:

```
WRITELN ('Output to the display screen.')
```

The $DEFINE compiler directive is equivalent to the *Conditional define* command. For example, the following directive defines the *printerOn* symbol:

```
{$DEFINE printerOn}
```

Version 5.0 of Turbo Pascal automatically defines four named symbols for use in conditional compilation directives, as follows:

- *ver50* indicates that the current version is 5.0.

- *msdos* identifies the operating system under which this version runs.

- *cpu86* specifies the CPU family for which this version was designed.

- *cpu87* indicates (if defined) that an 8087 chip is present in the current system. The *cpu87* symbol is defined only if Turbo Pascal detects the 8087 chip at the beginning of a compilation.

Consult the Turbo Pascal documentation for additional information about conditional compilation.

The *Memory Sizes* Option

The *Memory sizes* option controls the size of the *stack* and the *heap*, two blocks of memory that are allocated for special purposes during the performance of a program. In many programs you will not have to worry about these memory allocations; you can just accept the default sizes. But in certain programs you may have to use the *Memory sizes* command to specify the required amount of memory for these purposes.

When you select the *Memory sizes* command, a pop-up window appears on the screen with the following three memory options and defaults:

Stack size			16384
Low	heap	limit	0
High	heap	limit	655360

You can select any one of these three options and enter a new numeric value for the corresponding memory size: the size of the stack, the minimum size of the heap, and the maximum size of the heap. As we saw earlier in this chapter, the $M compiler directive is equivalent to the *Memory sizes* command.

The second main entry in the Options menu is Linker. Select this entry, and a submenu appears on the screen offering you two options that control the linking process. We'll discuss these two options in the next section.

The Linker Options

When you compile a program, Turbo Pascal automatically *links* together all the procedures and functions that your program requires. The linking process combines object code from your primary program with code contained in the units that your program uses. The Linker submenu gives you two options related to this process.

The *Map File* Option

When the *Map file* option is in one of its active settings, and the Compile/Destination option is in its *Disk* setting, Turbo Pascal generates a special text file on disk that contains information about the compiled program. This file, which is created along with the compiled EXE file, has the same base name as the program file itself, with an extension name of .MAP. A map file is an advanced debugging tool.

When you select the *Map file* option, a menu of four settings appears on the screen:

    Off
    Segments
    Publics
    Detailed

Under the default setting, Off, no map file is created. The other three settings create map files containing varying levels of detailed information about the program. (The settings of the *Debug information* and *Local symbols* options in the Compiler submenu also affect the amount of information stored in a map file.) By the way, a map file is in ASCII text form, so you can display it on the screen or send it to your printer if you want to inspect its contents.

The *Link Buffer* Option

By default, Turbo Pascal loads all required routines directly into the computer's memory to carry out the process of linking together the parts of a program. However, if you are developing a very long program, you may need to direct Turbo Pascal to make use of disk memory during the linking.

The *Link buffer* command controls this option. The default setting is

Link buffer   Memory

To toggle this setting, you select the *Link buffer* command in the Linker submenu; the new setting appears as follows:

Link buffer   Disk

The third entry in the Options menu is Environment. This command presents a pop-up menu with a variety of useful options that control the behavior of the Turbo Pascal development environment. We'll examine these options in the next section.

The Environment Options

The Environment command presents a pop-up menu containing a combination of on/off switches and input options. Here are the options with their default settings:

Config auto save   Off
Edit auto save   Off
Backup files   On
Tab size   8
Zoom windows   Off
Screen size

The Environment options are mostly self-explanatory and easy to use.

The *Config Auto Save* Option

You use the *Config auto save* option to specify whether or not you want Turbo Pascal to save your new compiler and environment settings when you exit from the development environment. This command is Off by default; if you toggle it On, any settings that you change during the current session will be saved to your configuration file. (We'll discuss this file later in this chapter.)

The *Edit Auto Save* Option

The *Edit auto save* command determines whether Turbo Pascal will automatically save any revised source code file before you begin a performance of the program. Switching this option On is a safeguard against losing your program file in the event of a serious run-time error that interrupts the entire system. (In addition, your source code will be saved before you perform a temporary exit via the *OS shell* command.) The option is Off by default.

The *Backup Files* Option

The *Backup files* option determines whether Turbo Pascal will maintain a backup file when you save the current program file to disk. (A *backup file*, with extension name .BAK, stores the previously saved version of the program.) The default setting of this option is On. If you do not want backup files to be saved, switch the option to its Off setting.

The *Tab Size* Option

You use the *Tab size* command to change the default 8-space tab setting. When you select this command, an input box appears into which you can enter an integer from 2 to 16 for the new tab setting. (To activate the Tab Fill mode in the editor, press Ctrl-O-T, as discussed in Chapter 1.)

The *Zoom Windows* Option

The *Zoom windows* toggle determines whether the Zoom operation will occur automatically when you activate the Edit, Watch, or Output window. This option is Off by default; under this setting, two windows appear together on a split screen. Toggle the option On if you want the active window to take up the entire screen space.

The *Screen Size* Option

The *Screen size* command allows you to make use of the maximum number of screen lines available with your particular display hardware. When you select this command, a box appears with the following options:

```
25 line standard display
43/50 line display
```

Select the option that corresponds to your hardware.

The fourth entry in the Options menu allows you to specify various directories for storing Turbo Pascal files.

The Directories Options

As you work with Turbo Pascal over time, you will probably develop a rather large collection of files related to different applications and system functions. Establishing subdirectories to store different types of files can prove to be an advantage, particularly if you are working on a hard disk.

Using the Directories command, you can designate default paths for several different types of files.

```
Turbo            directory:
EXE & TPU        directory:
Include          directories:
Unit             directories:
Object           directories:
Pick file name:
```

For each of these options you can enter a different path, which becomes the default directory for the selected type of files. Subsequently, Turbo Pascal uses this default directory when you load or save a file of a specified type.

For the Include, Unit, and Object file directories, you can enter multiple path names, separated by semicolons. If you do so, Turbo Pascal first searches the current directory, and then all specified directory paths for the corresponding file type.

Here are brief descriptions of these directories:

- The Turbo directory is set aside for the system files, including configuration files and the Help file.

- The .EXE and .TPU directory is where Turbo Pascal saves compiled programs and compiled units to disk.

- The Include directories are where Turbo Pascal looks for a source code file referenced in an $I compiler directive. You'll learn more about the $I compiler directive later in this chapter.

- The Unit directories are where Turbo Pascal looks for .TPU files for a program that uses units.

- The Object directories are where Turbo Pascal looks for .OBJ files for a program that uses external assembly-language routines. (You use the {$L *fileName*} directive to incorporate an external assembly-language routine into the current program.)

- The *Pick file name* option allows you to save the current pick list to disk when you exit from the development environment. When you select this option, Turbo Pascal displays an input box on the screen into which you can enter a file name for the pick file. The default name is TURBO.PCK:

  ```
  Pick File Name
  TURBO.PCK
  ```

  The next time you start a session in the development environment, your previous pick list will be reloaded automatically if TURBO.PCK exists. (If you save your pick list under some other file name, you'll have to use the TINST program to establish the name as the pick file that Turbo Pascal will load. We'll discuss the TINST program later in this chapter.)

The Parameters Command

The next command in the Options menu is Parameters. The Parameters command helps you develop and test programs that contain the

PARAMSTR function, an important element of the Turbo Pascal language. Using this function, you can create a stand-alone .EXE program that accepts parameters from the keyboard when you perform the program directly from the DOS prompt. (In this context, a *parameter* is simply a data item that you send to the program.) The PARAMSTR function supplies your parameters to the program. Reading the information returned by PARAMSTR, the program can thus tailor its own performance according to the parameters you supply at run time.

While you are developing such a program, the Parameters command allows you to test the effect of the PARAMSTR function within the Turbo Pascal environment. Specifically, you can supply a sample parameter line before you use the Run command to begin a performance.

When you select the Parameters command, an input box pops up on the screen with the title

Command Line Parameters

Into this box you should enter whatever parameter line you wish to test when you subsequently run the current program.

We'll discuss program parameters and the PARAMSTR function more thoroughly in Chapter 10.

The Configuration File Commands

Configuration files represent yet another convenient feature built into the Turbo Pascal environment. A configuration file is designed to save all the options and settings that you have established in the Options menu. You can create and save as many different configuration files as you want, using the *Save options* command. Each file receives the default extension name .TP.

When you want to activate one of the configuration files you have created, you can load it into the system using the *Load options* command. As a result, the Turbo Pascal environment takes on all the settings stored in the file.

The default configuration file, which Turbo Pascal automatically activates at the beginning of each session, is called TURBO.TP.

The *Save Options* Command

The *Save options* command results in an input box, asking you for the name you wish to give to the new configuration file you will be creating:

```
Config File
TURBO.TP
```

If you accept the suggested name, you will modify the default configuration file, TURBO.TP. Enter a new name if you want instead to create a completely new configuration file. In either case, all the current settings of the Options menu will be saved in the file.

The *Retrieve Options* Option

When you select the *Retrieve options* command, an input box pops onto the screen, asking you for the name of the configuration file that you want to activate:

```
Config File
*.TP
```

As you can see, the box initially contains a directory mask; if you press the Enter key, a directory box appears on the screen showing you all the available configuration files. To select one of them, use the arrow keys to move the highlight and press the Enter key.

Alternatively, you can simply type the name of the configuration file you want to load. When you do so, the *.TB mask disappears.

Two more menus remain for us to investigate—Debug and Break/watch—both of which contain debugging options.

The Debug Menu

The Debug menu offers a collection of miscellaneous commands related to the built-in debugger. Here is the list of the commands you see when you select this menu:

Evaluate   Ctrl-F4
Call stack   Ctrl-F3
Find function
Integrated debugging
Standalone debugging
Display swapping
Refresh display

Some of these commands are switches that control the compiler's behavior, and others perform useful operations during a debugging session. Two of them are available for use only under specific circumstances: the *Call stack* command can be used only during a debugging session, and the *Find function* command is available only after you have compiled the current program. Let's look briefly at each command in this menu.

The Evaluate Command

During a debugging session, the Evaluate command gives you the opportunity to investigate the value of a variable or expression in your program. This feature is a convenient alternative to setting up a watch expression. Sometimes you may simply want a quick way to look once at a particular variable, without bothering to enter the variable into the Watch window. In this case, the Evaluate command is the best tool to use.

But the command does even more. You can also use it to *change* the value stored in a variable, and to see how this change affects the subsequent program performance. This useful feature gives you the opportunity to test a variety of data values for a particular variable, and to see how these values change your program's behavior.

When you select the Evaluate command, Turbo Pascal displays a window on the screen that contains three horizontal boxes arranged one above another. The boxes are labeled *Evaluate*, *Result*, and *New value*, respectively. You enter the variable or expression that you want to investigate into the Evaluate box. The current value of the variable or the result of the expression immediately appears in the Result box.

Once you enter a variable name (not a more complex expression) into the Evaluate box, you can select the New value box and enter an experimental value for the variable. When you subsequently continue the program performance, you'll be able to see how this new value affects the program's behavior.

Let's work through a brief exercise with the Evaluate command. Load the *Today* program into the editor if it is not there already, and follow these steps to see how the Evaluate command works:

1. Inside the editor, find the *DateString* procedure and position the cursor at the beginning of the final statement in the procedure:

   DateString : = weekdayStr + monthStr +

2. Press **Alt-R** to display the Run menu and then press **G** to select the *Go to cursor* command (or simply press **F4**). As you'll recall, this action initiates a performance of the program, and interrupts the performance at the current cursor position.

3. Position the cursor just below the *w* of the variable *weekday-Str* in the current statement line.

4. Display the Debug menu and select the Evaluate command (or press **Ctrl-F4**). The Evaluate window appears on the screen, and—thanks to the position of the cursor—the variable name *weekdayStr* is automatically entered into the Evaluate box, as shown in Figure 2.4.

5. Press the Enter key, and the current value of *weekdayStr* appears in the Result box. The value should be a three-letter abbreviation for a day of the week, such as *Thu.,* .

6. Press the ↓ key twice to select the *New value* box. To experiment with this feature, type the full name for the day of the week into the *New value* box. Since this is a string value, you should enclose it in single quotation marks—for example, **'Thursday, '**.

7. Press the Enter key to complete the new value entry. The new value appears inside the Result box.

8. Press **Alt-R** to display the Run menu and then press R to perform the Run command (or simply press Ctrl-F9). In the subsequent performance of the *Today* program, you'll see the

```
     File    Edit    Run    Compile    Options    Debug    Break/watch
                                    Edit
     Line 49    Col 21    Insert Indent          Unindent    C:TODAY.PAS
     { Convert numeric
                                          Evaluate
     STR (year, yearSt    weekdayStr
     STR (day, dayStr)
     IF LENGTH(dayStr)                         Result
        dayStr := ' ' +

     { Get the appropr                      New value

     weekdayStr :=  da
     monthStr := month

     { Concatenate to produce final result. }

     DateString := weekdayStr + monthStr +
                       dayStr + ', ' + yearStr

     END;    { DateString }
                                          Watch

 F1-Help  F8-Step  F7-Trace  F1Ø-Menu  TAB-Cycle  ←┘-Evaluate  →-More text
```

Figure 2.4: The Evaluate window

changed value of the *weekdayStr* variable in the program's output, as in this example:

Today is Thursday, Aug. 11, 1988.

The ability to change the value of a variable midway through a program performance can be extremely valuable, especially when you are first developing a program and you want to test the results of different values.

By the way, you can also use the Evaluate window as a kind of on-screen calculator, outside of any debugging session. Enter any arithmetic expression into the Evaluate box and you'll immediately see the result in the Result box.

The *Call Stack* Command

At any point during a debugging session, the *Call stack* command shows you the list of procedure and function calls that are currently controlling the program's action. In a complex program, this list gives you a clear picture of your program's flow of control.

Use the *Today* program once again to perform a short experiment with the *Call stack* command:

1. Inside the editor, scroll down to the short local procedure named *LineOfChars*, and position the cursor at the beginning of the routine's last statement:

   WRITELN

   (This procedure produces the lines of periods above and below the text message in the *Today* program's output.)

2. Press the **F4** function key to perform the program up to the current cursor position.

3. Press **Alt-D** to display the Debug menu and then press **C** to perform the *Call stack* command (or simply press **Ctrl-F3**). A window named *Call Stack* appears at the upper-right corner of the screen, containing the following list of procedure calls:

   LINEOFCHARS('.',60)
   TODAYSMESSAGE
   TODAY

   From this list, you can see the current hierarchy of control in the program: the *Today* program has called the *TodaysMessage* procedure, which in turn has called the *LineOfChars* procedure. You can also see the argument values that were sent to *LineOfChars*.

4. Press the ↓ key twice to highlight the word TODAY in the *Call Stack* list. Press the Enter key, and the editor immediately scrolls down to the point in the main program where the *TodaysMessage* procedure was called.

As you can see, this useful tool not only gives you an accurate list of current procedure calls, but it also allows you to locate the position of a particular call in the source code.

The *Find Function* Command

After you have compiled the current program, the *Find function* command is a convenient tool for locating any function or procedure in the source code. When you select this command, an input box appears on the screen, labeled *Enter subprogram symbol*. Into this box you enter the name of the procedure or function that you wish to locate. The editor immediately scrolls to the beginning of the target routine.

As an example, try this short exercise:

1. Press **Alt-D** to display the Debug menu, and then press **F** to perform *Find function*.

2. Into the resulting input box enter the name *DateString*.

3. Press the Enter key, and watch what happens in the Edit window. The editor scrolls down to the requested function, and the cursor is positioned at the beginning of this line:

```
BEGIN      { DateString }
```

Conveniently, you can even use *Find function* to examine a procedure or function that is stored in an external file (an include file or a unit). The appropriate file is loaded into the editor, and Turbo Pascal scrolls down to the requested routine.

The *Integrated Debugging* Command

Integrated debugging is a switch that has settings of On and Off. Under the default On setting, the features of the built-in debugger are available for use; in particular, you can use breakpoints and you can trace through a program performance line by line. (The *Debug information* option in the Compiler submenu must also be set to On for these features to work.)

Switching this option to Off disables debugging features. You may want to turn debugging off in order to conserve memory space when you are compiling a program to disk.

The *Standalone Debugging* Command

Standalone debugging is also a switch with On and Off settings. The default setting is Off. You'll turn this switch on if you plan to use Borland's external debugging product called *Turbo Debugger* to investigate the performance of a compiled .EXE program file that you create in Turbo Pascal. (Turbo Debugger is a separate software package, not included with Turbo Pascal.)

The *Standalone debugging* command only has meaning when you are compiling a program to disk. If you switch the command on, Turbo Pascal includes all the necessary debugging information directly in the .EXE file. The stand-alone Turbo Debugger program uses this information to help you investigate your program.

You will be able to solve the vast majority of debugging problems inside the Turbo Pascal environment, using the built-in debugger. Generally an external debugging tool such as the Turbo Debugger program is not necessary, unless you are designing very large and very complex programs.

The *Display Swapping* Command

The *Display swapping* command controls the way Turbo Pascal handles the output screen during a debugging session. When you select this command, a short menu pops up on the screen, offering three option settings:

None
Smart
Always

Under the default setting, *Smart*, Turbo Pascal switches to the output screen whenever necessary to perform an output operation, and then switches immediately back to the development environment. For most debugging sessions, you'll retain this default setting.

Under the *Always* setting, the system switches briefly to the output screen after the performance of each program line. In contrast, under the None setting the program's screen output is superimposed directly over the development environment screen.

The *None* option is best reserved for programs that do not produce screen output; otherwise, it can destroy the appearance of the development environment. Fortunately, the Debug menu offers a final command that cleans up the screen in the event that a program's output has been superimposed over the Menu system or the Edit window. This command is *Refresh display*.

The *Refresh Display* Command

The *Refresh display* command renews the screen of the development environment in the event that a program's output has been superimposed over the screen. To perform this command, press Alt-D and then R, no matter how bad the screen looks. (In some cases a program's output operations might erase even the menu line itself from the screen, so you should keep in mind that the *Refresh display* command is located in the Debug menu.) After a performance of this command, the development environment returns to its normal appearance.

Finally, let's turn once again to the Break/watch menu.

The Break/Watch Menu

You'll recall that the commands of the Break/watch menu control two of Turbo Pascal's most important debugging features: breakpoints and watch expressions. Here is the list of menu items:

Add watch	Ctrl-F7
Delete watch	
Edit watch	
Remove all watches	
Toggle breakpoint	Ctrl-F8
Clear all breakpoints	
View next breakpoint	

You experimented with most of these commands in Chapter 1. The following sections review the purpose of each command briefly; refer to Chapter 1 for examples and screens displays.

The *Add Watch* Command

You use *Add watch* to insert a new variable name or expression into the Watch window. When you select this command, an input box appears on the screen into which you can enter the new watch expression. (You can also position the cursor in front of a target variable in the Edit window before invoking the *Add watch* command. Turbo Pascal automatically inserts the variable name into the *Add Watch* input box.)

Next to each watch expression, Turbo Pascal displays the current value of the expression. This value may change many times during a program performance. If you step through your program in one of the line-by-line tracing modes, you can see exactly when the changes occur.

The Watch window expands in size to display each new entry, up to the first eight watch expressions. After that, you have to scroll the Watch window to examine expressions that are out of view. Press F6 to switch to the Watch window from the Edit window, and use the ↑ and ↓ keys to scroll through the window.

When the Watch window is active, you can simply press the Ins key to display the Add Watch input box and then add a new watch expression.

The *Delete Watch* Command

The *Delete watch* command removes the current watch expression from the Watch window. Normally the current expression is the one that you have most recently entered into the window; it is marked by a bullet (•), located just before the expression itself in the window.

You can change the current expression by activating the Watch window and using the arrow keys to highlight a new expression. When the Watch window is active, the current expression is the one that is highlighted. Inside the Watch window, you can delete the current expression simply by pressing the Del key.

The *Edit Watch* Command

The *Edit watch* command displays the current watch expression in an edit box labeled *Edit Watch*. Inside this box you can modify the expression in any way. Press Enter to complete the edit operation, or Esc to abandon the edit and retain the original watch expression.

From within the active Watch window, you can bring up the Edit Watch box by highlighting the target watch expression and pressing the Enter key. The highlighted expression will appear in the Edit box.

The *Remove All Watches* Command

The *Remove all watches* command clears the Watch window of all current existing expressions. The window returns to its original size.

The *Toggle Breakpoint* Command

The *Toggle breakpoint* command establishes a line of source code as a breakpoint, at which the program performance will be interrupted during a debugging session. To use this command, you first position the cursor in the editor at the line that you want to establish as a breakpoint. Then press Alt-D to display the Debug menu and T to perform the *Toggle breakpoint* command (or simply press Ctrl-F8). Turbo Pascal highlights breakpoint lines in the editor.

You can also use *Toggle breakpoint* to deactivate a breakpoint. Position the cursor at a highlighted line in the editor, and press Ctrl-F8. The highlight disappears, and the line is no longer a breakpoint.

The *Clear All Breakpoints* Command

The *Clear all breakpoints* command deactivates all breakpoints in the current program project.

The *View Next Breakpoint* Command

The *View next breakpoint* command scrolls the editor to the next breakpoint in the program's source code listing. If the next breakpoint is located inside an external file (an include file or a unit), Turbo Pascal loads the file into the editor so you can see the breakpoint. After you scroll to the last breakpoint in the program, the next performance of the *View next breakpoint* command scrolls back up to the first breakpoint.

This concludes our survey of the Turbo Pascal menu system. The remaining sections of this chapter introduce you to a few advanced operations in the editor.

A Second Look at the Editor

The Turbo Pascal editor is rich in features designed to help you create and revise the text of your programs. You will undoubtedly use some of these features all the time; others you may seldom use. In addition to the basic editing operations we discussed in Chapter 1, there are two categories of features that you should learn about right away, because they can prove very useful in the process of editing a program: block operations and find and replace operations. We'll examine each of these features in turn. For a summary of all the available editing operations, see Appendix A.

Block Operations in the Editor

A *block* is any contiguous portion of your program listing that you temporarily highlight in order to perform one of several available block operations. A block can be any size, but typically consists of several lines of text within your program. Marking a block of text is easy—here are the steps:

1. Move the cursor to the first character at the top of the block, and press Ctrl-K-B (hold down the Ctrl key while you strike the K key; then release both keys and press the B key). You'll notice that when you just mark the beginning of a block, no visual change occurs in the Edit window. Only when you subsequently mark the end of the text does the entire block appear in highlight.

2. Move the cursor just past the last character at the end of the block, and press Ctrl-K-K.

When you have performed these two steps, the editor highlights the entire block of text. (On a monochrome screen, the block appears as dark text against a light background, rather than the normal light against dark. On a color screen, the block appears against a distinct colored background.) You can mark only one block at a time inside the editor. If you mark a new block, the old block definition disappears.

Once you have marked a block of text, you can use a number of Ctrl-K key commands to perform any of the following operations:

Keystrokes	Operation
Ctrl-K-P	Sends the block to your printer
Ctrl-K-V	Moves the block to a new location
Ctrl-K-C	Copies the block to a new location
Ctrl-K-W	Writes the block to a disk file
Ctrl-K-H	Deactivates block markers
Ctrl-K-Y	Deletes the block

Let's use the *Today* program file to experiment with the block operations. Before starting, however, you should store the file under a new name so that the original version will be retained in the file TODAY.PAS. Use the *Write to* command from the File menu to store a copy of the program under the name NEWTODAY.PAS. (Notice that the file in the editor is now NEWTODAY.PAS rather than TODAY.PAS.) Inside the Edit window, change the name of the program as follows:

PROGRAM NewToday;

In the next section of this chapter you'll use block commands to make some special revisions to this new version of the program. Specifically, you'll perform an experiment with Turbo Pascal's *include* compiler directive.

Using Include Files in Turbo Pascal

The $I compiler directive tells the compiler to read an additional source code file into the current program during the compilation process. We refer to source code files that are read into a program in this way as *include files.* The compiler translates the source code and incorporates it into the program's object code. If you subsequently compile your program to a disk file, Turbo Pascal creates a single .EXE file for the program. In the performance of this program, you will see no indication that the source code was broken up into multiple files.

The $I directive appears in the following form:

```
{$I fileName}
```

The file name may include drive and path designations, although this information is not necessary if you have used the *Include directories* option in the Directories submenu to establish one or more subdirectories for include files. If you do not include an extension name, Turbo Pascal assumes the default .PAS extension.

An include file is a simple tool for incorporating general-purpose procedures and functions into a larger programming project. You can store the source code for such routines in individual disk files and use the $I directive to read one or more include files into the main program listing at compile time. (In Chapter 3 we'll discuss the *unit*, a more sophisticated tool you can use to develop a program from multiple files. A unit is a set of *precompiled* procedures and functions, whereas an include file simply stores the source code for such routines.)

The *DateString* and *TimeString* functions from the *Today* program are two routines that you'll be using in other programming projects later in this book. In the following exercise, you'll create an include file to store these two functions, and you'll insert an $I directive into the *NewToday* program to read this include file at compile time.

This exercise will also give you a chance to experiment with the editor's block commands. Begin by moving the cursor to the first line of the *DateString* function:

```
FUNCTION DateString: STRING;
```

Specifically, the cursor should be located just under the *F* of FUNC-TION. Press **Ctrl-K-B** to mark the top of the block. Then move the cursor to the end of the *TimeString* function:

```
END;     { TimeString }
```

Place the cursor just after the comment, and press **Ctrl-K-K** to mark the bottom of the block. In response, the editor displays the two procedures as a block of reverse-video text, as shown in Figure 2.5.

Now perform the following operations on the block:

1. Print the procedures to paper, so that you will have a hard copy of the include file you are about to create. Make sure your printer is on, and press **Ctrl-K-P**.

2. Create a disk file containing the procedure. Press **Ctrl-K-W**, and enter the file name **CHRONINC.PAS** (for chronological include file) into the input box that appears on the screen.

3. Delete the block from the *NewToday* listing by pressing **Ctrl-K-Y**. The entire block of text disappears completely from the file.

Now enter the following $I directive into the *NewToday* program, in the place of the two deleted procedures:

```
{$I ChronInc}
```

Here is how the top of the program now appears:

```
PROGRAM NewToday;
    { The NewToday program displays today's date on the
      screen, along with the current time. The program then
      displays the contents of the text file MESSAGE.TXT. }
    USES DOS;      { DOS supplies GETDATE and GETTIME. }
    {$I ChronInc}
```

The rest of the program listing remains unchanged. Press F2 to save the revised version of *NewToday* to disk. You can try running the program now; the performance should be the same as before.

By the way, you can now use an $I directive to incorporate the *ChronInc* include file into any new program you develop. However, there is one additional requirement for using the *DateString* and *TimeString* functions successfully; you must place the following USES statement at the top of your program, after the PROGRAM statement:

```
USES DOS;
```

```
      File    Edit    Run    Compile    Options    Debug    Break/watch
                                 Edit
       Line 1      Col 1    Insert Indent              Unindent    C:TODAY.PAS
   PROGRAM Today;

     { The Today program displays today's date on the screen,
       along with the current time. The program then displays
       the contents of the text file MESSAGE.TXT. }

     USES DOS;     { DOS supplies GETDATE and GETTIME. }


     FUNCTION DateString: STRING;

       { The DateString function converts the numeric
         values supplied by the GETDATE procedure into a
         date string, in the format 'Day., Mo. dd, yyyy'. }

       CONST

         { Set up arrays for the three-character
                                 Watch

    F1-Help  F5-Zoom  F6-Switch  F7-Trace  F8-Step  F9-Make  F1Ø-Menu
```

Figure 2.5: A marked block of text in the editor

DOS is one of Turbo Pascal's *standard units*; it happens to supply two Pascal procedures required by the *DateString* and *TimeString* functions. You'll learn more about standard units and the USES statement in Chapter 3.

Find and Replace Operations

You can use the editor's Find command to locate any string of text in your current program listing, up to 30 characters long. In addition, the Find-and-replace command replaces an existing string of text with a new string that you supply. You can perform a single replacement, or you can replace the target text *globally*—that is, wherever it occurs throughout your listing.

Here are the keyboard combinations for these commands:

Keystrokes	Operation
Ctrl-Q-F	Finds string of text
Ctrl-Q-A	Finds string of text and replaces it with a supplied string
Ctrl-L	Repeats the previous Find or Find-and-replace operation

Once you have established a Find or Find-and-replace pattern, you can instruct the editor to repeat the performance by pressing Ctrl-L. Let's see exactly how these commands work.

The Find Command

When you perform the Find command, a prompt appears at the top of the Edit window asking you for the target string of text that you wish to locate:

Find:

After you have entered this text value, a second prompt appears, asking you to specify options for the Find operation:

Options:

In response to this prompt, you can enter a string consisting of any combination of five code letters: B, G, U, L, and/or W. These letters stand for the following Find options:

- B makes Find search backward, starting from the cursor position. (The default rule is to search forward from the cursor position.)

- G makes Find start searching for the target string from the beginning of the file and stop at the final occurrence in the file. (The default rule is to search from the cursor position and to stop at the next occurrence.) The B and G options together result in a search that starts from the end of the file, and stops at the first occurrence in the file.

- L lets Find search locally within a marked block of text.

- U forces Find to ignore alphabetic case differences between the target string and the matching string inside the file. (The default rule is to require an exact match, including case.)

- W finds whole words only that match the target string. (The default rule is to find any matching string, even if it embedded within a larger word.)

If you omit the letter for a given option, the Find operation will instead follow the default rule. For example, WU starts searching forward from the cursor position, and searches for whole words only without regard to case. BW searches backward from the current position for whole words that match the case specified in the target string. In response to the Options prompt, you can supply the option letters in any order, uppercase or lowercase. If you simply press the Enter key, without entering any option letters, the Find operation will follow all the default rules.

You can also include one numeric option in response to the Options prompt. This instructs Turbo Pascal to stop the search at a specified number of occurrences inside the file. For example, if you enter G3, the operation will find the third occurrence of the target string, starting from the top of the file.

For a quick exercise with the Find command, try finding all the occurrences of the BEGIN marker inside the *NewToday* program listing. Activate the editor and press **Ctrl-PgUp** to move the cursor to the beginning of the file, if necessary. Start the Find operation by pressing **Ctrl-Q-F**. Enter the word **BEGIN** as the target Find string. Then enter **W** as the option code for the search. In response, the editor finds the first BEGIN marker in the file. Now you can press Ctrl-L repeatedly to find additional occurrences. Count the number of BEGIN markers that you find. When the operation has located the last occurrence, you will see the following error message appear on the screen:

```
Search string not found.  Press <Esc>
```

Press the Escape key to exit from the Find operation.

Now find all of the END markers, beginning your search at the bottom of the file. Press Ctrl-PgDn to move the cursor to the end of the file. Then press **Ctrl-Q-F**, and enter the word **END** as the target string. Enter **WB** as the option code. The first END marker is the one that ends the program. Now press **Ctrl-L** repeatedly, and count the END markers that you find. You should, of course, find the same number of END markers as you found BEGIN markers.

The Find-and-Replace Command

The Find-and-replace command also begins by prompting you for a target string of text to find. But then this command asks you to supply the replacement text:

Replace with:

Then Find-and-replace prompts you to enter option codes for the operation. The same options are available as for the Find command, plus one additional option: N, replace without confirmation. By default, the Find-and-replace operation asks you to confirm each replacement. When the cursor is positioned at a given occurrence of the target string, you will see the following confirmation question appear in the Edit box:

Replace (Y/N):

In response to this prompt, you press Y if you want the replacement to be carried out, or N if you do not.

In contrast, if you specify the N option at the time you initiate the Find-and-replace operation, this confirmation prompt does not appear. Instead, each replacement takes place automatically.

The global option (G) causes the Find-and-replace operation to replace all occurrences throughout the file. To experiment with this operation in our sample program file, let's change all the comment delimiters to the alternative format, (*...*). You'll recall that Turbo Pascal allows both of the following comment formats:

{ This is a comment. }
(* This is a comment. *)

This exercise requires two global changes: first for the left delimiters, then for the right delimiters. Press **Ctrl-Q-A** to start the first of these operations, then answer the three prompts as follows:

Find: {
Replace with: **(***
Options: **NG**

When the operation is complete, you will find that all occurrences of the left curly bracket throughout the text have been replaced with the (* sequence. Now perform a second global operation to change the right curly bracket } to *). All the comments in the program should now be delimited in the alternative format. Try running the program again to confirm that the global operations have worked properly. There should be no change in the program performance.

The final subject of this chapter is a special utility program that you can use to customize the editor. The program is called TINST.

Customizing the Editor

The TINST program is included on the Turbo Pascal program disk; its full name is TINST.EXE. You run the program directly from DOS, as follows:

```
A>TINST
```

The program's potential purpose is to make a number of carefully controlled changes in the Turbo Pascal system. When you first run the program, you'll see the following menu appear on the screen:

Installation Menu
Compile
Options
Debug
Editor commands
Mode for display
Set colors
Resize windows
Quit/save

The first three options allow you to establish new default settings for various commands in the Turbo Pascal Compile, Options, and Debug menus. The third option (Editor commands) allows you to customize the editor keyboard commands.

The fourth option, *Mode for display*, lets you to set the correct mode for your display hardware, and the fifth option, *Set colors*, establishes new color combinations for the Turbo Pascal menu and environment screen. You can use the sixth option, *Resize windows*, to set new default sizes for the Edit, Watch, and Output windows.

Finally, the last option, Quit/save, exits from the TINST program and either abandons your changes or saves them in the TURBO.EXE program file, according to your final instructions.

Most of these options are self-explanatory; the TINST menu system is easy to use, because it operates in the same way as the Turbo Pascal menus. A particularly interesting option to experiment with on your own is the *Set colors* command. This command offers you some predesigned color combinations for the Turbo Pascal environment, or allows you to set all the colors individually. You can set colors for all of the menu and window elements, and for the text that appears inside the edit window.

Another important selection is the *Editor commands* option. You can use the option to make changes in the keyboard commands that control the editor. The *Editor commands* option shows you a multipage list of all the editor's keyboard commands. The first column of this list contains text descriptions of the editor operations, and the second contains the fixed keyboard commands that carry out these operations. The third column shows optional alternative keyboard commands for some editor operations.

To make a change, you select an existing keyboard notation and press Enter. An input box appears to accept your modified keyboard sequence. In response to this box, you press the exact keyboard sequence that you want to install for the command.

You can use the TINST program to make any changes you like in the editor's keyboard commands. This can be a particularly valuable tool if you are used to some other editing environment, and you are having trouble making your fingers conform to Turbo Pascal's default editing commands.

Summary

Turbo Pascal's Main menu offers a broad range of options. We have discussed all of these options in detail; however, during most sessions with Turbo Pascal you probably won't need to use more than a small group of them.

The Turbo Pascal editor is equally rich in features. In this chapter you experimented with the find and replace operations and block commands. These commands are useful for developing and revising program listings.

Chapter 3 discusses one final development topic to complete Part I of this book. You'll find out how to use separately compiled units to create libraries of routines for use in your Pascal programs.

C H A P T E R

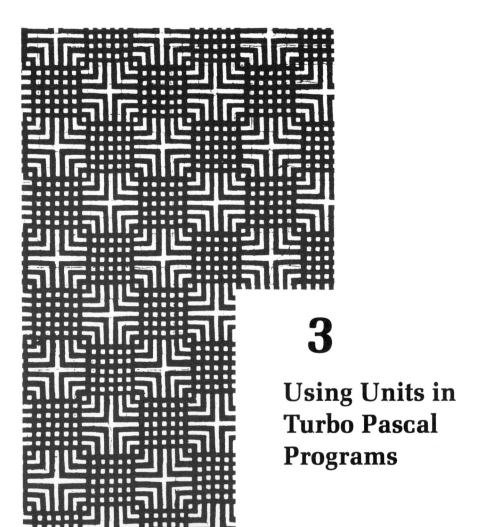

3

Using Units in
Turbo Pascal
Programs

As you develop applications in Turbo Pascal's structured programming environment, you will inevitably begin creating your own collection of general-purpose procedures and functions. To avoid having to reinvent these general tools each time you begin a new programming project, you'll need an effective way to "share" these routines with other programs. For example, suppose you develop a general-purpose input routine for one program; you'll want a convenient technique for making that routine available to any other program you write.

In Chapter 2 we briefly discussed two different techniques for building a Turbo Pascal program from multiple program files. The simpler of the two techniques is to read additional blocks of source code into a primary program as *include files*. You use the $I compiler directive to read an include file into a program file at compile time.

A second, more sophisticated technique is to build compiled *units*, containing Turbo Pascal procedures and functions that you have developed. This powerful and efficient technique allows you to create your own library of compiled routines for use in any programming project. In effect, creating a unit is a way to expand and customize Pascal, incorporating your own general-purpose routines into the working language.

In this chapter you'll learn the steps for building a unit and for using a unit's routines in a subsequent programming project. The process of creating a unit is not very different from the process of developing an entire program, although a unit requires a distinct organizational scheme.

Significantly, the Turbo Pascal package includes its own library of units; they are called the *standard units*, and they supply many of the language's "built-in" procedures and functions. For convenience, some of these standard units are gathered into a single *library* file called TURBO.TPL. (The Turbo Pascal package does not include the source code for these units, just the compiled object code.) This chapter introduces you to the eight standard units, most of which you'll use in the various programming projects presented later in this book.

To illustrate both "user-defined" units and the standard units, we'll examine a program called *Hours* in this chapter. The *Hours* program represents the beginning of a client-billing application that we'll develop and expand throughout the chapters in Part II. Along with the *Hours* program, we'll create a unit, *ChrnUnit*, containing two functions presented in Chapter 1: *DateString* and *TimeString*.

Before looking at *Hours*, let's begin our discussion of units.

Creating a Unit

In Chapter 2 you experimented with the editor's block commands and saw how to transfer a block of code to its own file on disk. You can easily use these block commands to create independent files for the source code of general-purpose routines you write. Then you can gather a collection of such routines into a single file. But before you can compile a collection of routines as a unit, you must supply some additional organizational elements. Specifically, you must write a unit heading and create two special unit sections.

The heading of a unit is always a UNIT statement, which identifies the name of the unit itself. The syntax of this statement is

UNIT *UnitName*;

Like other identifiers in Turbo Pascal, a unit name begins with a letter and may contain letters, digits, and underline characters. The name you supply may contain any number of characters, but only the first 63 are significant.

Following the UNIT heading, the unit is divided into two sections, identified by the Pascal reserved words INTERFACE and IMPLE-MENTATION. Broadly, the *INTERFACE* section contains a list of all the PROCEDURE and FUNCTION headings from the routines contained in the unit. The *IMPLEMENATION* section contains the actual source code for these routines. Here is a simple outline of a unit's structure:

```
UNIT UnitName;

    INTERFACE
      { PROCEDURE headings and
        FUNCTION headings }

    IMPLEMENTATION
      { source code for
        procedures and functions }

END. { end of unit }
```

Notice that the reserved word END, followed by a period, marks the end of the unit.

Actually, both the INTERFACE and the IMPLEMENTATION sections of a unit may also contain declarations for constants, types, and variables. You'll learn about the syntax and usage of these declarations in Chapter 4. For now, let's concentrate on the distinctions between the INTERFACE and the IMPLEMENTATION sections of the unit structure.

The INTERFACE section declares all the unit's *public* elements— that is, the constants, types, variables, procedures, and functions that will be available to the program that ultimately uses the unit. This section contains the complete heading of each public procedure and function, but not the actual code defining the action of the routines.

The IMPLEMENTATION section defines constants, types, variables, procedures, functions, and blocks of source code that are *private*—that is, defined for use only inside the unit itself. The IMPLEMENTATION section also contains the complete source code defining all procedures and functions that the INTERFACE section declares as public.

Finally, a unit can end with an optional BEGIN/END block called the *initialization section*. In this section you include any statements that you want Turbo Pascal to perform initially, whenever the unit is used in a program. For example, you might want to display some messages on the screen, make advance calls to certain procedures or functions, or initialize some variables. If the initialization section exists, it is performed when the unit is first referenced in the primary program file. A unit that does not have this section simply ends with the reserved word END.

You use the Turbo Pascal editor to develop the source code for a unit, just as you would for a primary program file. When you ultimately compile the code to disk, the compiler recognizes the structure of your program as a unit and saves the resulting object code in a file that has the extension name .TPU (for Turbo Pascal unit) rather than .EXE. In short, here are the steps for creating a unit:

1. Enter the unit's source code into the editor, starting with a UNIT heading, and including the INTERFACE and IMPLE-MENTATION sections.

2. Save the unit in a disk file. (You'll use the unit's actual name as the file name for storing the source code. The default extension for a unit's source code file name is .PAS. For example, you'll save a unit named *UnitName* under the file name UNITNAME.PAS.)

3. Try compiling the unit to memory, and correct any errors that the compiler finds. Repeat this process until the compilation is successful.

4. Press **Alt-C** to display Compile menu and then press **D** to toggle the Destination option to its Disk setting. Press **C** to compile the unit a final time. Turbo Pascal gives the object code file an extension name of .TPU. Once this .TPU file is stored on disk, your unit is available for use in any subsequent programming project.

In the following brief exercise you'll practice these steps by developing an experimental unit named *TestUnit*. This unit contains two routines: a procedure named *TestProc* and a function named *TestFun*. This particular unit is designed as an exercise, not as a useful set of routines; the *TestProc* procedure simply displays a message on the screen identifying itself, while *TestFun* returns an identifying string value. The listing for *TestUnit* is given in Figure 3.1.

Each of the routines receives a string value as an argument. The *TestFun* function also returns a string as its result. (We'll discuss arguments and return values in Chapter 4.) These characteristics are defined in the PROCEDURE and FUNCTION headings listed in the INTERFACE section of the unit:

```
PROCEDURE TestProc (inString1: STRING);
FUNCTION TestFun (inString2: STRING): STRING;
```

In contrast, the IMPLEMENTATION section requires only the following abbreviated headings for the two public routines:

```
PROCEDURE TestProc;
FUNCTION TestFun;
```

```
UNIT TestUnit;

  INTERFACE

    PROCEDURE TestProc (inString1: STRING);
    FUNCTION TestFun (inString2: STRING): STRING;

  IMPLEMENTATION

    PROCEDURE TestProc;

      BEGIN    { TestProc }
        WRITELN ('This is TestProc.');
        WRITELN ('Received the following argument:');
        WRITELN (inString1)
      END;    { TestProc }


    FUNCTION TestFun;

      VAR
        tempString: STRING;

      BEGIN    { TestFun }
        tempString := 'This is TestFun. Received ' +
                      'the following argument: ' +
                      inString2;
        TestFun := tempString
      END;    { TestFun }

  END.    { TestUnit }
```

Figure 3.1: The listing of *TestUnit*

(Actually, Turbo Pascal allows you to include complete PROCE-DURE and FUNCTION headings in the IMPLEMENTATION section; however, only the abbreviated form is necessary for public routines.) Following these headings, the IMPLEMENTATION section of *TestUnit* contains the source code defining the behavior of these two routines. Notice the strict punctuation required in the IMPLEMENTATION section. The final routine in the section must end with a semicolon, even though the next word in the listing is simply the END marker that closes the unit:

```
    END;  { TestFun }
END.    { TestUnit }
```

To work through this exercise, enter the *TestUnit* listing into the editor. Save the source code under the file name TESTUNIT.PAS. Then compile the unit and correct any typographical errors that the compiler might find. Once the unit compiles successfully, pull down the Compile menu, toggle the Destination option to its Disk setting, and compile the unit again, this time creating a disk file. If you look at your directory, you'll find that Turbo Pascal has created a file named TESTUNIT.TPU. This is your compiled unit.

Next let's look at the USES statement.

The USES Statement

Once you have developed and compiled a unit, you need a way to incorporate its routines into your current program. The USES statement is the tool for this task.

A USES statement at the top of a program lists one or more units that the program requires. The syntax of this statement is

```
USES Unit1, Unit2, Unit3, ...;
```

The names listed in the USES statement are assumed to be the base file names of the units stored on disk—for example, UNIT1.TPU, UNIT-2.TPU, and UNIT3.TPU. When the compiler encounters the USES statement, it searches on disk for each unit and prepares to incorporate the unit's public routines into the current program.

The USES statement must appear immediately after the PRO-GRAM heading in a program listing. (Significantly, a unit may also contain USES statements. USES may appear as the first statement in both the INTERFACE and IMPLEMENTATION sections.)

When you compile a multi-file program to disk, Turbo Pascal is very efficient about linking the routines of a unit into the final compiled code of a program. Only those public routines that a program actually uses become part of the final code. For example, if a unit contains ten public routines but a program actually calls on only three of the routines, Turbo Pascal links only the three required routines to the program.

To experiment with the USES statement, let's continue our exercise with the *TestUnit* unit. The following short program illustrates USES:

```
PROGRAM TestUses;

  USES TestUnit;

  BEGIN
    TestProc ('HELLO TESTPROC');
    WRITELN;
    WRITELN (TestFun ('HELLO TESTFUN'))
  END.
```

In this case, the USES statement instructs Turbo Pascal to link the two routines in *TestUnit* to the *TestUses* program. The program performs calls to *TestProc* and *TestFun*, sending a string argument to each.

Enter this short listing into the editor as a new program file. Compile the program and run it. The program's screen output consists of messages from each of the two routines in *TestUnit*:

```
This is TestProc.
Received the following argument:
HELLO TESTPROC

This is TestFun. Received the following argument:
HELLO TESTFUN
```

As these messages show, the program has successfully performed *TestProc* and *TestFun*.

We'll build a more significant unit—one that contains useful routines—a little later in this chapter. But first let's briefly discuss Turbo Pascal's *standard units*.

Using Standard Units

Version 5.0 of Turbo Pascal comes with eight predefined units, which are called the *standard* units. These units contain many of the procedures and functions that make up the Turbo Pascal language. The names of the standard units are SYSTEM, DOS, OVERLAY, CRT, PRINTER, GRAPH, TURBO3, and GRAPH3.

The first of these, the SYSTEM unit, contains essential declarations and definitions that are used in every program you write. Turbo Pascal automatically links appropriate resources from this unit whenever you compile a program. (Do not include SYSTEM in a USES statement; doing so results in a compile-time error.)

The other standard units contain routines that you may use selectively in programs that you write. To use a routine from one of these units, you must include the unit's name in the program's USES statement. (The Turbo Pascal *Reference Guide* tells you the unit location of each procedure and function available in the language.) The following paragraphs give introductory descriptions of these standard units:

- The DOS unit contains routines that help you perform functions associated with the operating system. For example, DOS contains the GETDATE and GETTIME procedures, which give you access to the system date and time. DOS also supplies the EXEC procedure, which allows you to perform a DOS program or utility from within a Turbo Pascal program.

- The OVERLAY unit supplies a small group of routines that are required for implementing overlays in Turbo Pascal programming projects. As you'll recall, an overlay is a block of code that may be loaded into memory when needed during a program performance—and may then be replaced in memory by another overlay when necessary. The use of overlays is a means of fitting large programs into limited memory space. In

Turbo Pascal, you can designate any complete unit as an overlay. The OVERLAY unit provides the resources you need for managing overlays. (None of the programming projects in this book is designed to use overlays; turn to the Turbo Pascal documentation if you want to learn more about this subject.)

- The CRT unit includes a variety of important and commonly used routines for controlling the display screen and for reading characters from the keyboard. For example, the CLRSCR procedure clears the screen, and CLREOL clears the current line from the cursor position. The WHEREX and WHEREY functions supply the current cursor position, and the GOTOXY procedure positions the cursor at a specified location. The READKEY function reads one keystroke of input from the keyboard.

- The PRINTER unit gives you a simple technique for sending output to your printer rather than to the display screen. PRINTER defines a text file named LST. When you use WRITELN or WRITE to send data to this text file, Turbo Pascal directs the output to the printer.

- The GRAPH unit is a large and sophisticated collection of graphics routines. We'll discuss some of the procedures and functions from this unit in Chapter 13.

- The TURBO3 and GRAPH3 units contain routines from version 3.0 of Turbo Pascal. In many cases the routines in these units have been replaced with newly designed procedures and functions in version 5.0; however, TURBO3 and GRAPH3 supply a high level of compatibility for programs developed in version 3.0. (If 5.0 is the only version of Turbo Pascal you plan to work with, you won't need to use these two units.)

We'll continue discussing these units and the routines they contain throughout this book.

For convenience, five of the eight standard units are packaged in a special library file named TURBO.TPL. The units in this important file are SYSTEM, DOS, OVERLAY, CRT, and PRINTER. This library file gives Pascal efficient access to the five standard units the file contains. (Since the GRAPH unit is very large, it is not included in the library file; instead it is in the file GRAPH.TPU. Likewise, TURBO3 and GRAPH3 are not included in the library, since they are used only in special circumstances.)

By the way, the Turbo Pascal package includes a useful program named TPUMOVER.EXE that you can use for managing the TURBO.TPL library file. Specifically, TPUMOVER lets you remove unused units from the library (for example, OVERLAY); it also allows you to move your own units into the library file. (See the Turbo Pascal documentation for complete instructions on using this utility.)

With this much background information on the standard units, let's now examine a unit that we'll use in many of the programs in this book. In Chapter 2 we transferred the *DateString* and *TimeString* functions into an include file named CHRONINC.PAS. Now we'll transform this file into a unit and compile the unit as CHRNUNIT.TPU.

The *ChrnUnit* Unit

Begin this exercise by making a copy of the CHRONINC.PAS include file. Call the copy CHRNUNIT.PAS, and load the file into the Turbo Pascal editor. The file already contains the source code for the two chronological functions used in the *Today* program, *DateString* and *TimeString*. To create a unit you need to add a UNIT heading, an INTERFACE section, the IMPLEMENTATION heading, and an END marker at the end of the unit. Figure 3.2 shows the complete listing of this unit; the new elements of the unit file are displayed in boldface.

Notice that this unit uses the standard DOS unit:

```
INTERFACE

   USES DOS;     { The DOS unit supplies the GETDATE
                   and GETTIME procedures. }
```

DateString and *TimeString* use the Turbo Pascal procedures GETDATE and GETTIME to read the system date and time, respectively. Since this USES statement is included in the unit itself, a primary program that uses *ChrnUnit* does not have to reference the DOS unit in a

```
UNIT ChrnUnit;

{ This unit supplies two chronological functions:

    DateString gives a string representing today's date.
    TimeString gives a string representing the current time. }


INTERFACE

  USES DOS;      { The DOS unit supplies the GETDATE
                   and GETTIME procedures. }

  FUNCTION DateString: STRING;
  FUNCTION TimeString: STRING;

IMPLEMENTATION

  FUNCTION DateString;

    { The DateString function converts the numeric
      values supplied by the GETDATE procedure into a
      date string, in the format 'Day., Mo. dd, yyyy'. }

    CONST

      { Set up arrays for the three-character
        day and month strings. }

      days: ARRAY[0..6] OF STRING[3] =
        ('Sun','Mon','Tue','Wed','Thu','Fri','Sat');
      months: ARRAY[1..12] OF STRING[3] =
        ('Jan','Feb','Mar','Apr','May','Jun',
         'Jul','Aug','Sep','Oct','Nov','Dec');

    VAR
      year, month, day, weekday: WORD;
      yearStr, monthStr, dayStr, weekdayStr: STRING;

    BEGIN    { DateString }

      GETDATE(year, month, day, weekday);

      { Convert numeric date values to strings. }

      STR (year, yearStr);
      STR (day, dayStr);
      IF LENGTH(dayStr) = 1 THEN
        dayStr := ' ' + dayStr;

      { Get the appropriate day and month strings. }

      weekdayStr :=  days[weekday] + '., ';
      monthStr := months[month] + '. ';

      { Concatenate to produce final result. }

      DateString := weekdayStr + monthStr +
                    dayStr + ', ' + yearStr

    END;    { DateString }
```

Figure 3.2: The listing of *ChrnUnit*

```
FUNCTION TimeString;

  { The TimeString function converts the numeric
    values supplied by the GETTIME procedure into a
    time string in the format 'hh:mm am/pm'. }

  VAR
    hour, minute, second, hundredth: WORD;
    ampm: STRING[2];
    hourStr, minuteStr: STRING;

  BEGIN     { TimeString }

    GETTIME (hour, minute, second, hundredth);

    { Convert 24-hour time into am/pm format. }

    IF hour > 11 THEN
      BEGIN
        ampm := 'pm';
        IF hour > 12 THEN DEC (hour, 12)
      END
    ELSE
      BEGIN
        ampm := 'am';
        IF hour = 0 THEN hour := 12
      END;

    { Convert numeric time elements into strings. }

    STR (hour, hourStr);
    STR (minute, minuteStr);
    IF LENGTH(hourStr) = 1 THEN
      hourStr := ' ' + hourStr;
    IF LENGTH(minuteStr) = 1 THEN
      minuteStr := '0' + minuteStr;

    { Concatenate to produce final result. }

    TimeString := hourStr + ':' + minuteStr + ' ' + ampm

  END;     { TimeString }

END.     { ChrnUnit }
```

Figure 3.2: The listing of *ChrnUnit* (continued)

separate USES statement in order to gain access to GETDATE and
GETTIME. (On the other hand, a primary program is allowed to use
any unit, even one that is also used within another unit. For example,
a program that requires the use of other DOS-related routines may
reference the DOS unit along with *ChrnUnit*.)

Once you have entered the new structural elements of the unit file,
compile the unit to disk to create CHRNUNIT.TPU. You'll use this
unit in this chapter's main program example, the *Hours* program.
This program, the first in a series of client-billing applications presented in this book, is introduced in the next section.

The *Hours* Program

For the purposes of internal accounting or billing, business people are often required to keep track of the number of hours they spend on particular jobs. This task applies to self-employed people as well as employees. For example, a self-employed computer programmer who has several clients might want to set up an account for each client and keep records of the number of billable hours worked each day on each account. Likewise, an attorney at a large law firm may have to keep accurate daily records of the amount of time spent on projects for different clients, even down to the detail of 15-minute telephone calls.

The *Hours* program is a tool designed to simplify the task of maintaining these work-hour records. The program is relatively simple, but can nonetheless serve a purpose in real work situations. Before we examine the program's listing, let's see how it works.

Running the Program

When you run the *Hours* program, it begins by giving you the current date and time and then asks you for two items of information: the name of the account (or project) you have been working on, and the number of billable hours you wish to record in this account. Given the account name that you supply, the program devises a file name for storing your billable hours on disk; the file's base name consists of the first eight letters of the account name you supply. The extension name is always .HRS. For example, if your account name is *Benton*, the resulting file name is BENTON.HRS.

If you have already recorded entries in a given account on some date in the past (during a previous performance of the program), *Hours* opens the account file and appends your new record at the end of the file. On the other hand, if this is your first entry for a given account, *Hours* creates a new account file on disk for you and records a first entry into the account.

After eliciting the appropriate input information from you and storing the information in the correct file on disk, the program adds up the number of hours you have accumulated in this account to date. This number is displayed on the screen for you as the program's final line of information. Here is a complete example of a dialog conducted by the program, along with the subsequent output information:

Date: Thu., Mar. 10, 1988   Time: 3:57 pm

Recording Billable Hours

Account name?   **SmithCo**
Billable hours?   **5.5**

Total hours to date for this account: 48.00

You can see the two input items (shown here in boldface) and the current total number of hours for the account.

The program can maintain as many account files as you wish, as long as you take care to supply a unique account name for each file. Inside each file, a record line consists of three data items: the date of the entry, the time of the entry, and the number of work hours you recorded for this entry. (To use this program appropriately, you should record an entry as soon as you complete a period of work for a given account.) For example, here is how one such file might appear after a series of chronological entries:

```
Thu., Mar. 10, 1988  3:49 pm 5.50
 Fri., Mar. 11, 1988  4:50 pm 4.50
Sat., Mar. 12, 1988 10:18 am 3.50
Mon., Mar. 14, 1988  5:30 pm 6.50
Tue., Mar. 15, 1988 12:19 pm 3.00
Wed., Mar. 16, 1988  4:51 pm 2.50
Thu., Mar. 17, 1988  3:09 pm 1.00
 Fri., Mar. 18, 1988  2:01 pm 3.50
Mon., Mar. 21, 1988  5:08 pm 3.50
Tue., Mar. 22, 1988  4:00 pm 1.00
Wed., Mar. 23, 1988  1:32 pm 2.00
Thu., Mar. 24, 1988  2:19 pm 3.50
 Fri., Mar. 25, 1988  3:52 pm 2.50
Mon., Mar. 28, 1988  6:44 pm 5.50
```

Each entry is stored as an individual line of text. This is called a *sequential data file*; we'll discuss the programming techniques for working with such files in Chapter 10.

The *Hours* program allows you to examine a directory list before you attempt to open an account file. Accordingly, the program anticipates several different possible input strings in response to the *Account name?* prompt. First, if you simply press the Enter key, without typing any other keys first, the program responds by displaying a list of all the .HRS account files in the current directory. In addition, *Hours* accepts any input string that contains one or both of the DOS wild-card characters: the asterisk and/or the question mark. In response, the program displays a list of directory files that match the mask string. If no files match your mask, the program instead displays a *File not found* message.

Figure 3.3 shows some additional sample output from *Hours*, illustrating the program's ability to display directory lists. The first directory in this output is the result of pressing the Enter key in response to the *Account name?* prompt. The second displays files that match a particular mask, SMI*.HRS. You can view as many directory lists as you want during a given program performance. The *Account name?* prompt reappears after each list. When you are ready to continue with the program, simply enter an actual account name.

By the way, *Hours* does not expect you to enter an extension name with your account name. If you do, the program ignores the extension, and always adds its own .HRS extension to the first eight characters of the account name you supply.

Since each account file is stored on disk, the *Hours* program in effect creates permanent chronological records of your work for individual clients or projects. *Hours* is designed only to create and maintain the files and to supply you with the current total hours in a given file at the time of an update. In later chapters you'll find additional Turbo Pascal programs that read these account files and perform other operations, such as

- Producing a billing invoice for a given account

- Printing a table summarizing the activities in several accounts at once

- Maintaining additional information about each account, such as addresses, contacts, phone numbers, and payment records

```
     Date: Fri., Mar. 11, 1988   Time:  5:29 am
    _____

             Recording Billable Hours
    _____

   Account name?

   ..................................................

    Volume in drive B has no label
    Directory of  B:\

   SMITHCO  HRS    ACMECO   HRS    ABCINC   HRS    XYZLTD   HRS
   SMITHSUB HRS    SMITHLTD HRS    SMICORP  HRS       __

           7 File(s)     83968 bytes free

   ..................................................

   Account name? SMI*.HRS

   ..................................................

    Volume in drive B has no label
    Directory of  B:\

   SMITHCO  HRS   SMITHSUB HRS    SMITHLTD HRS    SMICORP  HRS
           4 File(s)     83968 bytes free

   ..................................................

   Account name? _
```

Figure 3.3: Output from the *Hours* program

Since all of these programs will work with the same sets of data, the account files stored on disk serve as the permanent communication link among the programs.

Let's now look briefly at the program listing for *Hours*.

The Program Listing

The listing of the *Hours* program appears in Figure 3.4. The first thing you'll notice as you examine the listing is that the program uses three units:

```
USES  CRT,      { Supplies CLRSCR, CLREOL, GOTOXY,
                         WHEREY, and WHEREX }
      DOS,      { Supplies EXEC }
      ChrnUnit;{ Supplies DateString and TimeString }
```

As you have seen, CRT and DOS are two of Turbo Pascal's standard units, and *ChrnUnit* is the unit you created earlier in this chapter to supply the *DateString* and *TimeString* functions.

The optional comments incorporated into the USES statement show the particular routines that the program needs from each unit.

```
PROGRAM Hours;

  { The Hours program creates and maintains chronologically
    organized project databases, for keeping track of the
    number of work hours spent on a given project. }

  USES CRT,          { Supplies CLRSCR, CLREOL, GOTOXY,
                               WHEREY, and WHEREX }
       DOS,          { Supplies EXEC }
       ChrnUnit;     { Supplies DateString and TimeString }

  { Specify heap size, for successful use of EXEC. }
  {$M 16384, 0, 0}

  CONST
    fixedLineLength = 48;

  VAR
    accountFile:     TEXT;
    accountFileName: STRING;
    openFile:        BOOLEAN;


  PROCEDURE LineOfChars (displayChar: CHAR;
                         lineLength:  BYTE);

    { The LineOfChars procedure displays a line of
      displayChar characters on the screen. The
      argument passed to lineLength is the number
      of characters in the line. }

    VAR
      i: INTEGER;

    BEGIN     { LineOfChars }
      FOR i := 1 TO lineLength DO
        WRITE (displayChar);
      WRITELN
    END;     { LineOfChars }


  PROCEDURE AccountUpdate;

    { The AccountUpdate procedure records the date, the time,
      and a real number representing billable work hours into
      the target account file. This procedure includes the
      local routines named GetFileName and InReal. }

    VAR
      inHours: REAL;


    FUNCTION GetFileName: STRING;
```

Figure 3.4: The listing of the *Hours* program

```
{ The GetFileName function elicits a file name or a
  DIR-style mask from the user at the keyboard. }

VAR
  goodName,
  dirRequest: BOOLEAN;
  inName: STRING;
  periodPos: BYTE;


PROCEDURE Directory (mask: STRING);

  { The Directory procedure uses the EXEC command to
    display a list of selected files on the screen. }

  BEGIN     { Directory }
    LineOfChars ('.', 75);
    EXEC ('\COMMAND.COM', '/C DIR ' + mask + ' /W');
    LineOfChars ('.', 75)
  END;     { Directory }


BEGIN     { GetFileName }
  goodName := FALSE;

  WHILE NOT goodName DO
    BEGIN
      WRITELN;
      WRITE ('Account name? ');
      READLN (inName);

      { If the user simply presses <Enter>, display
        all the HRS files in the current directory. }

      IF inName = '' THEN
        Directory ('*.HRS')
      ELSE
        BEGIN

          { Search for wildcard characters in the input. }

          dirRequest :=
            (POS('*', inName) <> 0)
            OR (POS('?', inName) <> 0);
          IF dirRequest THEN
            Directory (inName)
          ELSE
            goodName := TRUE;

            { Eliminate any user-supplied extension. }

            periodPos := POS('.', inName);
            IF periodPos <> 0 THEN
                  inName := COPY(inName, 1, periodPos - 1);
          END
        END;

      { Add HRS as the extension, and return the file name. }

    GetFileName := inName + '.HRS'
  END;     { GetFileName }
```

Figure 3.4: The listing of the *Hours* program (continued)

```
FUNCTION InReal (prompt: STRING): REAL;

  { The InReal function reads a real number from the
    keyboard, and avoids the run-time error that would
    normally result from an invalid numeric entry. }

  VAR
    tempReal:    REAL;
    goodInput:   BOOLEAN;
    saveX, saveY: BYTE;

  BEGIN    { InReal }

    { Repeat the input process until the user
      enters a valid real number. }

    REPEAT

      { Record the current cursor position }

      saveX := WHEREX;
      saveY := WHEREY;

      WRITE (prompt);

      { Turn off input error checking temporarily }

      {$I-}
        READLN (tempReal);
      {$I+}

      goodInput := (IORESULT = 0);

      { If the input is not valid, clear the entry
        from the screen. }

      IF NOT goodInput THEN
        BEGIN
          GOTOXY (saveX, saveY);
          CLREOL
        END
    UNTIL goodInput;

    { When the looping ends, return tempReal as
      the result of the function. }

    InReal := tempReal
  END;    { InReal }


BEGIN    { AccountUpdate }

  { Call the GetFileName function to elicit
    a target file name. }

  accountFileName := GetFileName;
  ASSIGN (accountFile, accountFileName);
  openFile := TRUE;

  {$I-}

  { First try to open the file in the APPEND mode. }
```

Figure 3.4: The listing of the *Hours* program (continued)

```
        APPEND (accountFile);

        IF IOResult <> 0 THEN
          BEGIN

            { If the file does not exist yet, try opening it
              for output, as a new file. }

            REWRITE (accountFile);
            {$I+}

            { If the REWRITE produced an error, the file name
              cannot be used for some reason. }

            IF IOResult <> 0 THEN
              BEGIN
                WRITELN;
                WRITELN ('    *** Can''t open file.');
                openFile := FALSE
              END
          END;

      { If the file has been opened successfully, elicit
        the number of billable hours, and then store the
        current date, the current time, and the billable
        hours in the file. }

      IF openFile THEN
        BEGIN
          inHours := InReal('Billable hours? ');

          WRITE (accountFile, DateString, ' ', TimeString, ' ');
          WRITELN (accountFile, inHours:5:2);
          CLOSE (accountFile)
        END
    END;       { AccountUpdate }


FUNCTION TotalAccount: REAL;

  { The TotalAccount function opens the target account
    file again, this time for reading, and finds the
    total number of hours currently recorded in the account. }

  CONST
    chronInfoLength = 29;

  VAR
    hours,
    total:    REAL;
    chronLine: STRING[chronInfoLength];

  BEGIN
    total := 0.0;

    RESET (accountFile);

    { Read each line of the file, from the beginning. }

    WHILE NOT EOF(accountFile) DO
      BEGIN

        { Read the date and time as a single (unused) string
          value, then read the number of hours as a real
          number. }
```

Figure 3.4: The listing of the *Hours* program (continued)

```
              READLN (accountFile, chronLine, hours);
              total := total + hours
          END;

       CLOSE (accountFile);
       TotalAccount := total
    END;


BEGIN   { Hours }
   CLRSCR;
   WRITELN (' Date: ', DateString, '  Time: ', TimeString);
   LineOfChars ('_', fixedLineLength);
   WRITELN;
   WRITELN ('        Recording Billable Hours ');
   LineOfChars ('_', fixedLineLength);

   { Open an account file, and record a new entry. }

   AccountUpdate;
   LineOfChars ('_', fixedLineLength);
   WRITELN;

   { If a file has been opened successfully, open it again
     to find the total number of hours in the account. }

   IF openFile THEN
      BEGIN
         WRITE (' Total hours to date for this account: ');
         WRITELN (TotalAccount: 6: 2);
         LineOfChars ('_', fixedLineLength)
      END

END.   { Hours }
```

Figure 3.4: The listing of the *Hours* program (continued)

Without comments, the USES statement would appear simply as

USES CRT, DOS, ChrnUnit;

In this book we'll use capitalization to distinguish between standard units and user-defined units; the names of standard units appear in all uppercase letters, whereas the names of user-defined units are in mixed uppercase and lowercase.

As you enter the *Hours* listing into the Turbo Pascal editor, you'll notice that the program is organized into the following major routines:

- The *AccountUpdate* procedure conducts the program's input dialog and then records a new entry into the account you have specified. This procedure has two local routines of its own: the *GetFileName* function, to elicit an account name (and to display a directory listing if necessary); and the *InReal* function, to elicit and read a real number from the keyboard.

- The *TotalAccount* function computes the total number of work hours that are currently recorded in the account file you have specified.

There is no syntactical distinction in Turbo Pascal between calls to routines that are supplied by units and calls to routines that are part of the primary program file. The main program section of *Hours* (at the bottom of the listing) makes calls to *DateString, TimeString, AccountUpdate* and *TotalAccount*. In addition, the *LineOfChars* procedure is called to display lines of characters across the screen; you may remember this short procedure from the *Today* program. (We'll discuss the syntax of procedure calls and function calls more formally in Chapter 4.)

Once you have entered the *Hours* program, check your work carefully and then save the program to disk by pressing the **F2** function key. If you have saved *ChrnUnit* at some location other than the current directory, you have to make its location known to the system: pull down the Options menu, select the Directories option, and enter the unit's directory location. Then compile the program, and correct any errors that the compiler finds. When the compilation is finally completed successfully, try running the program. Begin by creating some experimental .HRS account files. You can also test the various input techniques for requesting a directory, as illustrated earlier in this chapter.

To complete the development process, you should create a stand-alone compiled version of the program. Display the Compile menu and select the Destination command, changing the setting to Disk. Then press **C** to compile the program. Exit from Turbo Pascal, and examine your directory. You'll see that the compiler has created a single .EXE file, called HOURS.EXE; this file combines the primary program along with the required routines from the units that the program uses. Try running the program. The performance should proceed just as it did inside the Turbo Pascal environment.

Summary

A unit is a collection of general-purpose procedures and functions, stored on disk in compiled form. Units streamline the process of developing applications by allowing you to share important routines among different programming projects. This chapter's programming exercise illustrates the design and use of units. We'll be developing several additional units throughout this book.

This chapter concludes our initial exploration of the Turbo Pascal development environment—the editor, the menu system, and the compiler. In Part II of this book we'll survey the elements of the Turbo Pascal language. We'll begin in Chapter 4 by examining the fundamentals of program organization: declarations, definitions, procedures, functions, and data types.

PART

A Turbo Pascal Language Tutorial

II

C H A P T E R

4

**Fundamentals
of Turbo Pascal
Programming**

In this chapter we'll examine the structure of Turbo Pascal programs, focussing on the individual elements of that structure—specifically, declarations (CONST, TYPE, and VAR), subprogram modules (PROCEDURE and FUNCTION), and the main program section. Along the way we'll examine the use of variables, data types, operations, and essential input and output commands.

If you have worked through the introductory programming exercises presented in Part I of this book, you may have already developed an intuitive understanding of many of these concepts. Nonetheless, this chapter will give you a more formal and practical knowledge, and will prepare you for more advanced topics to come.

To illustrate these introductory topics, the chapter presents a program example called *BillTime*. This program works with the .HRS account files produced by the *Hours* program, developed in Chapter 3. Specifically, *BillTime* reads an account file and generates an invoice-style summary of the billable hours recorded in the file. This chapter also presents two new units, named *StrUnit* and *InUnit*. The first of these contains several string-handling functions, and the second is designed for a variety of input routines. We'll be expanding both of these units in subsequent chapters.

Let's begin with an overview of the Turbo Pascal program structure.

Turbo Pascal Program Structure

In Chapter 1 we briefly discussed the significance of modular program design in Turbo Pascal. This design approach is the essence of *structured* programming: the process of organizing any program, regardless of its length, into a hierarchy of small, semi-independent routines. The structured approach leads to programs that are at once more reliable, easier to revise and maintain, and more readable and understandable than programs that are not designed in this way.

A Turbo Pascal program consists of several structural elements, including the following:

- A PROGRAM heading, supplying the name of the program itself. (This heading is officially optional in Turbo Pascal, but should be included in all but the most trivial of programs.)

- A USES statement, naming any units that will be linked to the program at compile time.

- A group of optional declaration statements, which define labels, constants, types, and variables for the program:

  - The LABEL part defines label identifiers for GOTO statements. (Since most Pascal programmers avoid the GOTO statement altogether, the LABEL declaration seldom actually appears in a program. None of the programs in this book use LABEL declarations.)

  - The CONST statement defines symbolic constants for use in the program.

  - The TYPE statement declares user-defined data types for use in the program.

  - The VAR statement declares variables used in the program.

- Procedures and functions, which contain the instructions for accomplishing individually defined tasks for the program. A procedure performs a defined action, whereas a function returns a single value as its primary result. (Despite this main design difference, procedures and functions have much in common, as we will see in the course of this chapter.)

- A main program section, which controls the action of the program by making calls to the procedures and functions that are included in the program.

In summary, here is a skeleton outline of a Turbo Pascal program:

```
PROGRAM ProgName;

    USES UnitName1, UnitName2, { ... };

    LABEL
        { label declarations for GOTO statements };

    CONST
        { constant declarations };

    TYPE
        { type declarations };

    VAR
        { variable declarations };

    { PROCEDURE and
        FUNCTION definitions };

BEGIN { Main Program }

    { Statements of the
        main program section }

END. { Main Program }
```

We'll examine the format of all these program components later in this chapter. All declaration sections are optional in a Turbo Pascal program; the only required part is the main program section itself.

Consequently, the simplest form of a program is a BEGIN/END block containing one or more performable statements:

```
BEGIN
    statement;
    statement;
    statement
END.
```

In the standard definition of Pascal, the declaration sections appear in a fixed order: LABEL, CONST, TYPE, and VAR. Turbo Pascal is more lenient on this point; as long as you have a reason for doing so, you can write multiple declaration sections, and they can appear in any appropriate order.

The words that identify the various parts of a program—for example, PROGRAM, USES, CONST, TYPE, VAR, PROCEDURE, FUNC-TION, BEGIN, and END—are called *reserved words*. All reserved words have fixed meanings in Turbo Pascal. Other reserved words serve in a variety of definitions and structures, including

- Data structures (for example, ARRAY, RECORD, SET, STRING)

- Operations (for example, AND, OR, NOT, DIV, MOD)

- Control structures (for example, IF, CASE, FOR, DO, WHILE, UNTIL)

Turbo Pascal has four dozen reserved words in all; they are listed in Table 4.1. (Appendix B supplies a quick reference guide to the reserved words.)

Other names that are part of the Turbo Pascal language are called *standard identifiers*. For example, the names of the "built-in" proce-dures and functions—defined in the eight units that come with Turbo Pascal 5.0—are all standard identifiers. (Officially, a standard identi-fier can be redefined in a Pascal program, although most program-mers treat these names like reserved words with fixed meanings.)

Tables 4.2, 4.3, and 4.4 list the procedures and functions in the SYSTEM, DOS, and CRT units, respectively. (Keep in mind that the SYSTEM unit is automatically linked to every program you write.) These lists include the built-in routines that we'll be using most

Table 4.1: Turbo Pascal Reserved Words

ABSOLUTE	FILE	MOD	SHR
AND	FOR	NIL	STRING
ARRAY	FORWARD	NOT	THEN
BEGIN	FUNCTION	OF	TO
CASE	GOTO	OR	TYPE
CONST	IF	PACKED	UNIT
DIV	IMPLEMENTATION	PROCEDURE	UNTIL
DO	IN	PROGRAM	USES
DOWNTO	INLINE	RECORD	VAR
ELSE	INTERFACE	REPEAT	WHILE
END	INTERRUPT	SET	WITH
EXTERNAL	LABEL	SHL	XOR

often in this book. (The PRINTER unit defines one standard identifier, LST, designed to help you send output to a printer, as we'll see later in this chapter. We'll examine the contents of the GRAPH unit in Chapter 13. Of the remaining three units, TURBO3 and GRAPH3 provide compatibility with Turbo Pascal 3.0, and OVERLAY provides the resources for implementing overlays; we won't be using these units in this book.)

Finally, the names you write yourself—as identifiers for constants, types, variables, procedures, functions, and units—are sometimes called *user-defined identifiers*. The next section outlines the rules for creating these identifiers.

User-Defined Identifiers

Identifiers in Turbo Pascal can be of any practical length; however, only the first 63 characters are significant to the compiler. Identifiers must begin with a letter of the alphabet, and can consist of any number of letters and digits. The underscore character (_) is also legal within variable names. The length of a variable name has no negative

Table 4.2: The Procedures and Functions of the SYSTEM Unit

ABS	EXIT	MEMAVAIL	RMDIR
ADDR	EXP	MKDIR	ROUND
APPEND	FILEPOS	MOVE	RUNERROR
ARCTAN	FILESIZE	NEW	SEEK
ASSIGN	FILLCHAR	ODD	SEEKEOF
BLOCKREAD	FLUSH	OFS	SEEKEOLN
BLOCKWRITE	FRAC	ORD	SEG
CHDIR	FREEMEM	PARAMCOUNT	SETTEXTBUFF
CHR	GETDIR	PARAMSTR	SIN
CLOSE	GETMEM	PI	SIZEOF
CONCAT	HALT	POS	SPTR
COPY	HI	PRED	SQR
COS	INC	PTR	SQRT
CSEG	INSERT	RANDOM	SSEG
DEC	INT	RANDOMIZE	STR
DELETE	IORESULT	READ	SUCC
DISPOSE	LENGTH	READLN	SWAP
DSEG	LN	RELEASE	TRUNC
EOF	LO	RENAME	TRUNCATE
EOLN	MARK	RESET	UPCASE
ERASE	MAXAVAIL	REWRITE	VAL
			WRITE
			WRITELN

impact on the performance of a Turbo Pascal program, nor on the ultimate size of the object code. This means that you are free to create long (and meaningful) variable names without risk of slowing down your program.

Table 4.3: The Procedures and Functions of the DOS unit

DISKFREE	FINDNEXT	GETINTVEC	SETDATE
DISKSIZE	FSEARCH	GETTIME	SETFATTR
DOSEXITCODE	FSPLIT	GETVERIFY	SETFTIME
DOSVERSION	GETCBREAK	INTR	SETINTVEC
ENVCOUNT	GETDATE	KEEP	SETTIME
ENVSTR	GETENV	MSDOS	SETVERIFY
EXEC	GETFATTR	PACKTIME	SWAPVECTORS
FEXPAND	GETFTIME	SETCBREAK	UNPACKTIME
FINDFIRST			

Table 4.4: The Procedures and Functions of the CRT Unit

ASSIGNCRT	GOTOXY	NORMVIDEO	TEXTCOLOR
CLREOL	HIGHVIDEO	NOSOUND	TEXTMODE
CLRSCR	INSLINE	READKEY	WHEREX
DELAY	KEYPRESSED	SOUND	WHEREY
DELLINE	LOWVIDEO	TEXTBACKGROUND	WINDOW

As you examine collections of Pascal programs written by different programmers, you'll discover a variety of approaches to devising variable names. For example, the *BillTime* program, which we'll be examining later in this chapter, requires a variable to store the dollar rate at which a given client is billed for an hour of work. Here is an assortment of names that might be chosen for this variable:

hourlyRate

hRate

hour_rate

billingDollarsPerHour

hrRt

hr

The longer identifiers are generally easier to understand than the short ones. The purpose of a variable named *hourlyRate* is much more obvious than that of one named simply *hr*. On the other hand, length may become a liability when you have to enter an identifier many times into a program listing. The longer the name, the more likely you are to make a keystroke error, resulting in an incorrect identifier and a compile-time error. Programmers who don't like to type tend to favor short names.

Probably the best approach to creating identifiers is a compromise between length and clarity. Avoid names that are too long to be convenient and names that are too short to be clear. In most cases, you can express the purpose of an identifier in a name that is no longer than eight or ten characters, and often shorter. You can also use certain tricks to improve clarity, such as capitalizing a letter to show that the name is made up of two words:

hourlyRate

(The compiler ignores alphabetic case in variable names. To the compiler, the names *hourlyRate* and *hourlyrate* represent the same variable.) Another trick is to use the underscore character to separate words inside a variable name, as in this example:

hourly_rate

The compiler does impose one important restriction on the use of variable names: A variable name may not be the same as any of the reserved words in the Turbo Pascal language. A reserved word may be *embedded* inside a variable name, but may not appear alone as a name. For example, the name *dividend* is a valid variable name. However, the names *div* and *end*, if used individually as identifiers, would cause compile-time errors, because DIV and END are both reserved words.

These points about identifiers apply to all names that you create for a Turbo Pascal program, including the names of constants, types, variables, procedures, and functions. In the following sections we'll discuss the declaration sections for all of these program structures, starting with the CONST section.

CONST Declarations

In the CONST section you define identifiers that represent fixed data values throughout the program performance. These identifiers are called *symbolic* or *named* constants—or, when the context is clear, simply *constants*. A named constant can represent any type of numeric value, character, or string, as we'll see in upcoming examples. (In addition, Turbo Pascal allows you to initialize *structured constants*, such as arrays and records, in a CONST declaration section. We'll examine these structures in Chapter 6.)

Here is the general format of the CONST declaration section:

```
CONST
   constantName1 = constantValue1;
   constantName2 = constantValue2;
   constantName3 = constantValue3;
   ...;
```

Each individual statement in this section assigns a value to a named constant. For example, the following CONST section declares a string constant and two numeric constants:

```
CONST
   titleLine     = 'Billable hours';
   screenWidth  = 80;
   ratePerHour  = 29.5;
```

Notice that a string constant is enclosed in single quotation marks in Pascal.

The use of named constants improves a program's readability; a named constant is a clear representation of a value that remains unchanged during the course of the program performance. Furthermore, a carefully planned collection of CONST declarations can prove to be very convenient when you are revising a program. Changing the values of a few selected constants can completely redefine the parameters of a subsequent performance.

TYPE Declarations

The TYPE section is used to declare user-defined data types and structures. (Don't worry if you're not familiar with all the terms in the following discussion; we'll look at types in greater detail later in this chapter.) Although Turbo Pascal offers a rich variety of standard data types, you may sometimes want to clarify or expand on these by writing special type identifiers and definitions for particular programming situations. (In addition, some standard types, such as records, sets, and enumerated types, contain elements that are always defined by the programmer.) After a TYPE declaration, you can use a subsequent VAR section to declare variables belonging to both standard types and user-defined types.

The general format of the TYPE section is as follows:

```
TYPE
    typeIdentifier1 = type1;
    typeIdentifier2 = type2;
    typeIdentifier3 = type3;
    ...;
```

For example, the following TYPE section declares a range type and a string type:

```
TYPE
    screenRange = 1..80;
    screenLine  = STRING[80];
```

You'll learn much more about user-defined types and the TYPE section in Chapters 6, 7, and 8.

VAR Declarations

Variables are identifiers that represent data values in a Pascal program. In contrast to less structured languages such as BASIC, Pascal requires that all variables be declared before use. (Failing to declare a variable results in a compile-time error.)

As we'll see a bit later, an *assignment statement* assigns a value to a variable. Subsequently your program gains access to the data value by referring to the variable by name. You can create as many variables as necessary to satisfy the data requirements of a given program, within the constraints of available memory. Simple variable types are designed to store single values at a time; when you assign a new value to the variable, the previous stored value is lost. More complex variable structures, such as *arrays* and *records*, can represent lists, tables, or other arrangements of data values under a single name. (Arrays and records are the subject of Chapter 6.)

In the VAR section you explicitly designate the type of each variable you create for a program. Here is the general format of the VAR section:

```
VAR
  variableName1: type1;
  variableName2: type2;
  variableName3: type3;
```

Alternatively, you can use the following syntax to define multiple variables of the same type:

```
VAR
  variableName1,
  variableName2,
  variableName3: type1;
```

For example, the following VAR section declares a string variable, along with three numeric variables belonging the standard type named BYTE:

```
VAR
  inString:      STRING;
  inLength,
  commaMarker,
  newPos:        BYTE;
```

You can use any user-defined types or standard data types to define variables. We'll begin examining data types in the next section.

Introduction to Standard Data Types

Pascal programs can work with data expressed as literal values (such as the string 'Billable hours' or the number 5) or as values represented symbolically by identifiers (such as constants and variables). Regardless of how a data value is expressed, you must take care to distinguish among the various data types that Turbo Pascal recognizes. Mixing data types in inappropriate ways results in compile-time errors.

Turbo Pascal has several categories of standard data types, of which the most commonly used are

- Integer numeric types
- Real number types
- Character and string types
- The Boolean type

These four categories are the easiest types to use and to understand, especially if your programming background includes experience with any version of the BASIC language.

We refer to the integer, character, and Boolean types as *scalars* or *ordinal types*, because they represent ordered sets of values. The scalar types, along with the real number types, are sometimes called *simple* types, because elements in these types are single values rather than structured collections of values. In contrast, the more complicated types such as records, arrays, and sets are called *structured types*. (We'll discuss structured types and additional scalar types in Chapters 6, 7, and 8.)

In one sense, the string type is in a category of its own in Turbo Pascal. A string is a sequence of characters, up to 255 characters long. String variables are *dynamic*, which means that length of the string stored in a variable can change during a program performance. This convenient characteristic is one of Turbo Pascal's extensions of the standard definition of Pascal.

The following sections summarize the properties of numeric, string, and Boolean data types.

General Characteristics of the Numeric Types

For economy, convenience, efficiency, and accuracy, Turbo Pascal provides a wide variety of integer and real-number types. Your job is to decide which type is appropriate for a given application. Sometimes the validity of a program's numeric results depends on the correct choice of numeric data types. In general you must think carefully about the characteristics of the data types that you decide to use.

Turbo Pascal handles each numeric data type in a distinctive format in memory. There are two important general properties to consider about each numeric data type: range and precision. *Range* is the characteristic that specifies the largest and smallest numbers that Pascal can handle in a given data-type format. *Precision* is a measure of the number of accurate digits that Pascal can guarantee for each data type. We'll discuss range and precision for each of the numeric data types, and also the memory requirements for each type.

Integer Types

Turbo Pascal offers five integer types: INTEGER, WORD, LONGINT, SHORTINT, and BYTE. These types supply varying ranges of whole-number values. The larger the range, the more memory is required for values in a given type: LONGINT values require four bytes each, INTEGER and WORD values require two bytes, and SHORTINT and BYTE values require one byte each. An integer has no decimal portion, and is always perfectly precise within its specified range. Here are the ranges of these five integer types:

- INTEGER values range from -32768 to $+32767$.

- WORD values range from 0 to 65535.

- LONGINT values range from about -2 billion to $+2$ billion (from $-2,147,483,648$ to $+2,147,483,647$, to be exact).

- SHORTINT values range from -128 to $+127$.

- BYTE values range from 0 to 255.

In addition to these, you can use an additional integer type called COMP. COMP can store values in the range of $\pm 9.8 \times 10^{18}$. (A COMP value requires 8 bytes of memory.) Operations with COMP values are performed on the 8087 chip or in the 8087/80287 emulation mode; for this reason, the Turbo Pascal documentation classifies COMP along with the real data types rather than the integer types.

Real Number Types

A real number can contain digits both before and after the decimal point, and may be subject to the constraints of limited precision. We also use the term *floating point* to describe these types, referring to the fact that Pascal stores real numbers in two distinct parts: the significant digits (sometimes called the *mantissa*), and the exponent that indicates the correct position of the decimal point.

Turbo Pascal offers a variety of real-number types. Their availability depends on the settings you have established for the *Numeric processing* and Emulation options in the Options/Compiler submenu, as discussed in Chapter 2. Here is a brief review of these settings:

- If the *Numeric processing* option remains in the default Software setting, only the REAL type is available, whether or not your system has an 8087 coprocessor chip.

- If the *Numeric processing* setting is 8087/80287, there are four additional numeric types: COMP (which we have already discussed), and three real types—SINGLE, DOUBLE, and EXTENDED—offering a variety of ranges and precisions for real-number applications. With the Emulation option in its default On status, Turbo Pascal emulates the operations of the 8087 if the chip is not present in your system. If Emulation is Off, a real-number application will not run without a numeric coprocessor chip.

Keep in mind that you can also use the $N and $E compiler directives to control the settings for these options.

Here are summaries of these five floating-point types:

- REAL values are positive or negative numbers as large as 10^{38} and as small as 10^{-38}. REAL numbers have a guaranteed precision of eleven digits and require six bytes of memory.

- SINGLE type values are in a range that is similar to REAL values, but have a guaranteed precision of only seven digits. SINGLE values require only four bytes of memory, the most economical of the real-number types.

- DOUBLE type values have a range of about 10^{-324} to 10^{+308}, and a precision of 15 digits. DOUBLE values require eight bytes of memory.

- EXTENDED type values have the greatest range (10^{-4932} to 10^{4932}) and the best precision (19 digits). EXTENDED values require ten bytes of memory.

The programs in this book use the type REAL exclusively for real-number applications. However, you may want to experiment with other real-number types, particularly if you have an 8087 coprocessor chip.

Characters and Strings

A character is a letter, digit, punctuation mark, or other element from the IBM PC character set. In the computer's memory, each character is actually stored as a one-byte integer code, from 0 to 255. This code, known as ASCII (American Standard Code for Information Interchange), defines the available character set, providing numeric equivalents for each of 256 characters.

Most of the first half of the ASCII code—numbers 0 to 127—is used in a standard way by all personal computers. It provides codes for the uppercase letters A to Z (65 through 90); the lowercase letters a to z (97 through 122); the digits 0 to 9 (48 through 57); the punctuation marks, control characters, and so on.

The second half of the ASCII code, 128 through 255, provides non-standard characters that are often implemented differently on different brands of computers. On the IBM PC and compatibles, these codes provide an assortment of useful display characters, including foreign-language letters; technical, mathematical, and scientific symbols; and a set of graphics characters that can be combined together to create frames, patterns, images, and shadings on the text screen.

The standard identifier CHAR defines character-type variables in Turbo Pascal. For example, the following VAR declaration defines a CHAR variable named *menuChoice:*

```
VAR
  menuChoice: CHAR;
```

This variable can store exactly one character at a time.

A *string* is a sequence of characters. The length of a string is equal to the number of characters it contains. In Turbo Pascal the maximum length of a string is 255 characters; the smallest possible string length is 0 characters. A string that contains no characters is called a *null* or *empty* string.

The reserved word STRING defines a string variable. For example, the following VAR statement defines a string named *clientName:*

```
VAR
  clientName: STRING;
```

The maximum length of a variable declared simply as STRING is 255 characters. However, you can specify a smaller maximum length for a string variable, using the following notation:

```
VAR
  variableName: STRING[maxLength];
```

For example, the following declaration defines a string whose maximum length is 8 characters:

```
VAR
  dataString: STRING[8];
```

Keep in mind that the actual length of the string stored in a STRING-type variable is *dynamic*—that is, the string can have any length up to the specified maximum. The built-in function LENGTH gives the current dynamic length of a string variable.

Finally, you can use the following notation to access a single character from a specified location in a string variable:

```
variableName[characterPosition]
```

For example, the expression

```
dateString[5]
```

yields the fifth character of the string currently stored in the *dateString* variable.

We'll continue exploring the characteristics of strings in subsequent chapters. In particular, Chapter 10 covers Turbo Pascal's built-in string functions and procedures.

Boolean Values

A Boolean value is either TRUE or FALSE. (Boolean values are named after the nineteenth-century English mathematician George Boole. We sometimes use the alternative term *logical values*.) Such a value often determines a program's choice between two or more alternative courses of action. Turbo Pascal supplies a set of relational and logical operations that produce expressions resulting in values of TRUE or FALSE. We'll discuss these operations in Chapter 5.

The standard identifier BOOLEAN defines a variable of this type, as in this example:

```
VAR
   goodName: BOOLEAN;
```

The constant logical values TRUE and FALSE are also standard identifiers in Turbo Pascal.

Once you have declared a variable of any type, you can use an *assignment statement* to store a value in the variable. We'll look briefly at this statement in the next section.

Assignment Statements

The syntax of an assignment statement is

variableName : = *expression;*

To perform this statement, Pascal evaluates the expression located on the right side of the equal sign and stores the resulting value in the variable named on the left. A variable name always appears alone at the left of the equal sign in this statement.

The expression located at the right side of the equal sign may be simple or complex. Consider these examples:

```
totAmt1 : = 5;

title1 : = 'Billable Hours';

totAmt2 : = (prevAmt + 18) * 5;
```

The first two examples simply assign constant values—the number 5 and the string 'Billable Hours'—to their respective variables. The third example assigns the result of an arithmetic expression to the variable *totAmt2*.

We have examined the CONST, TYPE, and VAR declaration sections, and we've discussed some of the standard data types. Now let's complete our overview of the Turbo Pascal program structure by looking at procedures and functions.

Procedures and Functions in Turbo Pascal

As we have seen, Turbo Pascal supports two kinds of structured blocks: procedures and functions. We refer to these blocks generically as *subprograms*, *subroutines*, or simply *routines*. The structure of a procedure is very similar to the structure of a function in Turbo Pascal. The primary difference is that a function is defined explicitly to return a value of a specified type.

A *call* to a procedure or a function is represented in a Pascal program simply by a reference to the name of the routine itself. However, the context of a call depends on whether the routine is a procedure or a function:

- A procedure call stands alone as a complete statement and results in a performance of the named procedure.

- A function call is always part of a larger statement. The name of the function represents the value that the function will ultimately return. In other words, a function call is always an operand in a statement, never a statement by itself.

Here is the general format of a procedure in Turbo Pascal:

```
PROCEDURE ProcName (parameterList);
```

```
CONST
  { local constant declarations };
TYPE
  { local type declarations };
VAR
  { local variable declarations };

BEGIN
  { body of the procedure }
END;
```

In this syntax representation, *ProcName* is the identifier that you create as the name of the procedure. The CONST, TYPE, and VAR declarations inside the procedure block define *local* constants, types, and variables for the routine.

The general format of a function is similar, but has two important distinctions:

```
FUNCTION FunctionName (parameterList): resultType;

CONST
  { local constant declarations };
TYPE
  { local type declarations };
VAR
  { local variable declarations };

BEGIN

  { body of the function, including
    an assignment statement that assigns
    a return value to the function name. }
END;
```

FunctionName is the identifying name of the function. Notice that the function heading defines the type of the function—that is, the type of value that the function will return—with the *resultType* identifier. Also, inside every function there should also be an assignment statement that identifies the exact value that the function will return. This statement takes the following form:

```
FunctionName : = returnValue
```

Like other identifiers in Turbo Pascal, a procedure name or function name must begin with a letter of the alphabet, and may contain letters, digits, and underline characters. In this book all procedure and function names begin with uppercase letters. We'll also sometimes use uppercase letters inside procedure names to clarify meaning, as in these examples:

PrintBill

GetFileName

InvoiceHeading

Each routine in a given program must have its own unique name.

Let's explore some of the essential characteristics of procedures and functions.

Parameter Lists

The parameter list, enclosed in parentheses in the PROCEDURE and FUNCTION headings, is optional. If present, the list designates variables for accepting the argument values sent from a call to the routine. We'll generally use the term *parameter* to refer to a variable listed in a procedure or function heading, and the term *argument* for a value that is actually passed to the procedure in a call. (The variables listed in the PROCEDURE or FUNCTION heading are also sometimes called *formal* parameters, and the values listed in a call to the routine are *actual* parameters.) A routine that contains no parameter list is defined to accept no arguments.

A parameter list specifies the number and type of argument values that must be sent to the procedure or function. Each variable name in the list is normally followed by a type identifier, and the parameters in the list are separated by semicolons. These variables are defined for use only inside the procedure itself; they are not available elsewhere in the program.

For example, consider the following hypothetical procedure, named *SampleProc:*

```
PROCEDURE SampleProc (stVar:    STRING;
                      numVar:    REAL;
                      intVar:    INTEGER);
```

```
BEGIN
   { body of the procedure }
END;
```

This particular procedure is defined to accept exactly three argument values, and to store the values in the parameters *stVar*, *numVar*, and *intVar*. The parameter list tells us that a call to the procedure must send a string value, a real value, and an integer as arguments to the routine.

Procedure Calls and Function Calls

A call statement directs Turbo Pascal to perform a procedure, and optionally sends argument values to the procedure:

ProcName (*argumentList*)

The procedure name (represented here as *ProcName*) refers to a procedure that is defined within the program or in a unit that the program uses. The procedure definition must be located above an actual call to the procedure.

The *argumentList*, if it exists, is a list of values that are to be sent to the procedure. The arguments appear within parentheses and are separated by commas. The list must contain the same number and type of values, in the same order, as those specified in the PROCEDURE heading of the procedure that is being called. For example, if you try to send a string argument value to a numeric parameter (or vice versa), the compiler will give you an error message, and the program will not run until you correct the error.

Values in the argument list of a call statement may be expressed as literal values, variables, or expressions. In the latter case, Turbo Pascal first evaluates the expression to a value, and then sends the value to the procedure as an argument. For example, consider the following call to the *SampleProc* procedure, which we defined earlier:

SampleProc ('XYZCorp', hours * 25.5, year)

Notice first of all that the type of each argument value must match the type of the corresponding parameter variable, in the correct order.

This CALL statement sends the following values to the *SampleProc* procedure:

- A constant string value ("XYZCorp") to the parameter *stVar*
- The REAL result of a numeric expression (*hours * 25.5*) to the parameter *numVar*
- The value stored in an integer variable (*year*) to the parameter *intVar*

In contrast, a function call does not stand alone as a statement, but rather appears as part of a larger statement. Usually a function is devoted to a sequence of operations leading up to a single calculated value. If the function receives arguments, these values will normally take part in the operations performed. The final line in most functions is an assignment statement that explicitly defines the value that the function will return to the calling program. For example, consider a hypothetical integer function named *SampleFun:*

```
FUNCTION SampleFun (p1,
                    p2,
                    p3: INTEGER): INTEGER;

    VAR
      returnVal: INTEGER;

    BEGIN

      { body of the function;
        uses p1, p2, and p3 to calculate
        an integer return value, returnVal }

      SampleFun : = returnVal

    END;
```

SampleFun receives three integer arguments, which are used to calculate a final value, *returnVal*. The function is defined to return an INTEGER-type value. The assignment statement at the end of the function specifies that *returnVal* is the return value:

```
SampleFun : = returnVal
```

The following statement contains a call to *SampleFun:*

```
WRITELN ('The result is ', SampleFun (1, 2, 3));
```

In this example, the call appears in a WRITELN statement. The call sends three integers to the function and results in a returned integer value. The WRITELN statement then displays this value as part of a message on the screen. A function call can also appear in other kinds of statements—for example, an assignment statement, or even in the argument list of a call to another routine:

```
i : = SampleFun (1, 2, 3);

SampleProc (stVar, numVar, SampleFun (1,2,3));
```

In the first of these statements, the result of *SampleFun* is stored in the variable *i*. In the second, the result is sent as the last of three arguments to the procedure *SampleProc*.

Global versus Local Declarations

We have seen that procedures and functions can have their own CONST, TYPE, and VAR sections. The location of a declaration statement determines the *scope* of the corresponding identifiers:

- Program-level declarations (located immediately below the PROGRAM heading) define *global* identifiers—that is, constants, types, and variables that are available for use at any point in the program.

- Procedure-level or function-level declarations define *local* identifiers—constants, types, and variables that are available only within a particular routine, and are dropped from memory when the performance of the routine is complete.

Furthermore, a procedure or function may have its own nested procedure or function definitions. A routine that is located completely inside the defining block of another routine is *nested* within that routine, and is local to the routine that contains it. For example, consider the following hypothetical procedure:

```
PROCEDURE Outer;

  VAR
    { variable declarations for Outer };

  PROCEDURE Inside1;

    { Inside1 is local to Outer }

    VAR
      { variable declarations for Inside1 };

    BEGIN
      { statements of Inside1 }
    END;

  PROCEDURE Inside2;

    { Inside2 is also local to Outer }

    VAR
      { variable declarations for Inside2 };

    FUNCTION Inside3: STRING;

      { Inside3 is local to Inside2 }

      VAR
        { variable declarations for Inside3 };

      BEGIN
        { statements of Inside3 }
      END;

    BEGIN
      { statements of Inside2 }
    END;

  BEGIN
    { statements of Outer }
  END;
```

In this example, the *Outer* procedure contains two local procedures, named *Inside1* and *Inside2*. These two procedures are available only to *Outer*. In addition, the *Inside2* procedure contains its own local function, named *Inside3*, which is available only to *Inside2*. Local procedures and functions are always located above the BEGIN/END block of the routine that contains them.

Here is a stylistic suggestion concerning the length of both procedures and functions: Keep routines short, ideally no more than one page long. If a routine starts to grow longer than a page, break it up systematically into two or more shorter local procedures. Short procedures are easier to write, debug, and maintain than long ones. In general, you will improve the style of your structured programs if you avoid excessively long procedures.

Finally, in the next section we'll discuss an important distinction between two kinds of parameters: *value parameters*, designed for one-way communication from the call to the routine; and *variable parameters*, designed for two-way communication.

Value Parameters and Variable Parameters

By default, the variables listed in the heading of a procedure or function are *value parameters*. When the routine is called, Turbo Pascal makes a copy in memory of each argument that is passed to the routine. These copies are for use only by the routine and are released from memory when the performance of the routine is complete. Operations performed on these value parameters have no effect on the original argument values.

However, you can use the reserved word VAR to designate *variable parameters* for a procedure or function, as in this example:

```
PROCEDURE ProcName (VAR varParam: REAL);
```

A variable parameter is passed *by reference* rather than by value. Given an argument that is passed by reference, Turbo Pascal does not actually make a duplicate copy of the value in the computer's memory. Instead, the procedure simply receives the memory location of the original argument value. The implication of this fact is very important: If the procedure changes the value of the argument, this new value will be "passed back" to the calling routine when the procedure's performance is complete.

Only an argument expressed as a variable can be sent to a VAR parameter from a procedure call or function call. An argument value that appears as an expression (for example, *a * 2*) or as a literal value (for example, 7.5) is always passed by value and cannot serve as a medium for sending information back to the calling program from the procedure. Figure 4.1 shows a program, called *VarTest*, that illustrates the difference between value parameters and variable parameters.

The program contains one procedure named *Test*, designed to accept three arguments into the formal parameters *x*, *y*, and *z*. All three of these parameters are defined as BYTE values, and the middle parameter, *y*, is designated as a VAR parameter.

```
PROGRAM VarTest;

VAR
  a, b, c: BYTE;

PROCEDURE Test (x:     BYTE;
               VAR y: BYTE;
               z:     BYTE);

BEGIN
  INC (x, 10);
  INC (y, 10);
  INC (z, 10);

  WRITELN ('Inside Test:');
  WRITELN ('x: ', x, ' y: ', y, ' z: ', z);
  WRITELN

END;


BEGIN     { ParameterTest }
  a := 5;
  b := 6;
  c := 7;

  WRITELN ('Before the call to Test:');
  WRITELN ('a: ', a, ' b: ', b, ' c: ', c);
  WRITELN;

  Test (a, b, c);

  WRITELN ('After the call to Test:');
  WRITELN ('a: ', a, ' b: ', b, ' c: ', c);

END.    { ParameterTest }
```

Figure 4.1: A program illustrating the differences between value and variable parameters

The main program section assigns initial values to the BYTE variables *a*, *b*, and *c*, and then passes these three values as arguments to the *Test* procedure:

```
Test (a, b, c);
```

The *Test* procedure uses Turbo Pascal's built-in INC procedure to increase the value of each of the corresponding parameters by 10:

```
INC (x, 10);
INC (y, 10);
INC (z, 10);
```

The effect of these three statements is the same as the following assignment statements:

```
x := x + 10;
y := y + 10;
z := z + 10;
```

(Note that Turbo Pascal also has a built-in DEC procedure, which decreases the value stored in a variable by a specified amount.)

When the performance of the *Test* procedure is complete, the two value parameters, *x* and *z*, are dropped from memory. In contrast, the value of the variable parameter *y* is "passed back" to the main program section, and becomes the new value of the variable *b*. The program displays a series of messages on the screen to demonstrate the effect of the procedure call. Here is the output of the program:

```
Before the call to Test:
a: 5   b: 6   c: 7

Inside Test:
x: 15   y: 16   z: 17

After the call to Test:
a: 5   b: 16   c: 7
```

As you can see, the variable *b* receives the changed value of the variable parameter *y* from the *Test* procedure.

To summarize all this information in a practical way, here is what you must remember about passing arguments to procedures:

- When you wish to use a variable as a medium for *two-way* communication between a procedure and a calling program, you use VAR to define a variable parameter.

- When you want to protect the value stored in a variable argument, preventing the called procedure from changing the value, you should pass the argument by value. To do so, omit VAR from the parameter list. Expressions and constants are always passed by value.

The *BillTime* program example, presented later in this chapter, contains further examples of value parameters and variable parameters.

This concludes our overview of the Turbo Pascal program structure—the CONST, TYPE, and VAR sections, and the procedure and function subprogram modules. Along the way, we've also examined structures for storing data in a program and techniques for sharing and passing data from one routine to another during the program performance. Before we turn to this chapter's program example, we'll briefly discuss two additional topics: the operations available for working with numeric and string values in Turbo Pascal, and some essential input and output operations.

Operations

Turbo Pascal has several categories of operations, each designed to be performed on a specific type of operand. These categories include the following:

- Numeric operations, which work on integer types and real-number types

- Concatenation, a string operation

- Relational and logical operations, resulting in Boolean values

- Set operations

- Address operations, for *pointer variables* (the subject of Chapter 8)

- Bit operations, which perform bit manipulations on integer values

In this chapter we'll discuss the first two categories in this list: numeric operations and concatenation. We'll discuss other operations in subsequent chapters.

Numeric Operations

The four familiar arithmetic operations are represented in Pascal by the following symbols:

* Multiplication

/ Division

+ Addition

− Subtraction

These are called *binary* operations, because they always require two numeric operands. In contrast, the minus sign can also be used to express a negative number; negation is a *unary* operation.

Two other operations are available for integers: *integer division* and the *modulo* operation. Integer division finds the whole quotient of two integers; any remainder from the quotient is simply dropped. The reserved word DIV represents this operation. For example, consider the following expression:

a DIV b

If the variable *a* contains a value of 42 in this example, and *b* is 8, the result of the expression will be 5.

The modulo operation is represented by the reserved word MOD. This operation finds the remainder from the division of two integers. For example, if *a* is 42 and *b* is 8, the following expression yields a value of 2:

a MOD b

We'll see examples of both integer division and MOD in programs presented later in this book.

In an expression that contains more than one operation, Turbo Pascal normally follows a prescribed order of precedence for evaluating each operation. Here is the order, from highest to lowest precedence:

1. Negation

2. Multiplication, division, integer division, and modulo

3. Addition and subtraction

Where there is more than one operation at the same level of precedence, operations at the same level are performed in order from left to right. For example, consider the following passage, in which all the operands are of type INTEGER:

```
a := 5;
b := 4;
c := 3;
d := 2;

x := a * b + c MOD d;
```

To assign a value to *x*, Pascal first evaluates the operations on the right side of the equal sign in this order: the multiplication, the MOD operation, and finally the addition. The variable *x* thus receives a value of 21.

If you want Pascal to evaluate an expression in some order other than the standard way, you can supply parentheses within the expression. Pascal performs operations inside parentheses before performing other operations. For example, consider how the addition of parentheses affects the result of our previous statement:

```
x := a * (b + c) MOD d;
```

In this case, the addition is performed first, then the multiplication, and finally the MOD operation. If the variables have the same values as before, the new result will be 1.

Parentheses may be *nested* in an expression—that is, one set of parentheses may appear completely within another set. Pascal performs the operation located within the innermost parentheses first, and then works its way out to outer parentheses. For example, in the following statement the addition is performed first, then the MOD operation, and finally the multiplication, for a result of 5:

```
x : = a * ((b + c) MOD d);
```

In a nested expression every opening parenthesis must be matched with a closing parenthesis character, or a compile-time error will occur.

String Operations

Concatenation is a string operation that combines two strings. The symbol for concatenation is the plus sign (+), as in the following assignment statement from the *TimeString* procedure:

```
TimeString : = hourStr + ':' + minuteStr + ' ' + ampm
```

This particular example combines five strings: three string variables, and two literal string values. The result becomes the return value of the *TimeString* function.

Turbo Pascal also has a built-in function named CONCAT that gives you an alternative format for performing concatenations. CONCAT takes a series of strings as its argument list, and returns the concatenation of all the strings; for example, the following statement is equivalent to the example from *TimeString:*

```
TimeString : = CONCAT (hourStr, ':', minuteStr, ' ', ampm);
```

In addition to CONCAT, Turbo Pascal has a useful library of built-in procedures and functions that perform a variety of string operations. We'll study these routines in detail in Chapter 10.

Figure 4.2 shows the listing for *StrUnit*, a group of special string functions that we'll use in the *BillTime* program. These functions give you a preview of some of the string operations that you can define yourself, using Turbo Pascal's own library of string routines as the foundation for your work. This first version of *StrUnit* contains the following four functions:

- *StringOfChars* supplies a string of a specified length, consisting of a repeated character. (Compare this function with the *LineOf-Chars* procedure, which appears in the *Hours* program.)

- *RightJustify* right justifies a string inside a specified field width.

- *DollarDisplay* returns a dollar-and-cent display string, given a long-integer argument that represents cents.

- *UpperCase* provides an uppercase version of a given string argument.

We'll see examples of output from these four functions when we turn to the *BillTime* program.

```
UNIT StrUnit;

  { This unit supplies a variety of string
    functions and procedures. }

  INTERFACE

    CONST
      maxScreenColumn = 80;

    TYPE
      screenRange = 1..maxScreenColumn;
      screenLine  = STRING[maxScreenColumn];

    FUNCTION StringOfChars (displayChar: CHAR;
                            lineLength: screenRange): screenLine;

    FUNCTION RightJustify (inString:    STRING;
                           fieldLength: BYTE):  STRING;

    FUNCTION DollarDisplay (inAmount: LONGINT;
                            width:    BYTE):    STRING;

    FUNCTION UpperCase (inString: STRING): STRING;

    { More to come ... }
```

Figure 4.2: The listing of *StrUnit*

```
    IMPLEMENTATION

FUNCTION StringOfChars;

    { The StringOfChars function builds a string of displayChar
      characters; the resulting string is lineLength characters
      long. }

    VAR
      i:     screenRange;
      temp: screenLine;

    BEGIN    { StringOfChars }

      temp := '';
      FOR i := 1 TO lineLength DO
          temp := temp + displayChar;
      StringOfChars := temp

    END;     { StringOfChars }

FUNCTION RightJustify;

    { The RightJustify function returns a string
      that is fieldLength in length. The inString value
      is right justified within the resulting string. }

    BEGIN    { RightJustify }

      WHILE LENGTH(inString) < fieldLength DO
        inString := ' ' + inString;
      RightJustify := inString

    END;     { RightJustify }

FUNCTION DollarDisplay;

    { The DollarDisplay produces a dollar-and-cent string
      from the numeric value inAmount (a long integer
      representing cents). The output string is right-
      justified in a string of width characters. }

    VAR
      inString:    STRING;
      inLength,
      commaMarker,
      newPos:      BYTE;

    BEGIN    { DollarDisplay }

      STR(inAmount, inString);

      WHILE LENGTH(inString) < 3 DO
        INSERT ('0', inString, 1);

      inLength := LENGTH(inString);
      newPos := inLength;

      commaMarker := 4;
      WHILE (newPos > 5) DO
        BEGIN
          INSERT (',', inString, inLength - commaMarker);
          INC (inLength);
          INC (commaMarker, 4);
          DEC (newPos, 3)
        END;
```

Figure 4.2: The listing of *StrUnit* (continued)

```
          INSERT ('.', inString, inLength - 1);
          INSERT ('$', inString, 1);

          DollarDisplay := RightJustify (inString, width)

      END;    { DollarDisplay }


  FUNCTION UpperCase;

      { The UpperCase function returns an uppercase
        version of the string argument it receives. }

      VAR
        i : INTEGER;
        outString : STRING;

      BEGIN
        outString := '';
        FOR i := 1 TO LENGTH(inString) DO
          BEGIN
            outString := outString + UPCASE(inString[i])
          END;

        UpperCase := outString
      END;

  END.
```

Figure 4.2: The listing of *StrUnit* (continued)

Screen Output and Keyboard Input

Like other microcomputer programming languages, Turbo Pascal has a strong facility for *interactive* programming. An interactive program elicits input information from the user at the computer, and then responds appropriately to the input by supplying information on the screen or sending data to a printer. Interactive programs create the illusion that the computer is reacting intelligently to the user's responses or requests. Pascal supplies several commands that make interactive programming simple and effective. We'll review some of them in the sections ahead.

Screen Output: The WRITE and WRITELN Statements

In its simplest form, the WRITELN statement displays a line of information on the screen. The WRITE procedure also sends data to the screen, but retains the final cursor position so that a subsequent WRITE or WRITELN command can display additional information on the same screen line.

Both WRITE and WRITELN take a list of data arguments in the form of constants, variables, or expressions, separated by commas. Consider this example:

```
VAR
  items,
  unitPrice: INTEGER;

BEGIN
  items : = 200;
  unitPrice : = 35;
  WRITE ('The price of ', items);
  WRITELN (' units is ', items * unitPrice)
END.
```

This passage displays a line of four data values on the screen: a literal string value, the value of a numeric variable, a second string value, and the result of an arithmetic expression. The resulting screen output is

```
The price of 200 units is 7000
```

Notice in this example that the WRITE and WRITELN commands display all four data values on a single line of output—the two string constants, the value stored in the variable *items*, and the result of the expression *items * unitPrice*.

The default output device for the WRITE and WRITELN statements is the display screen. When you want to send output to some other device, you must specify a file name as the first argument of the WRITE or WRITELN statement. For example, the PRINTER unit defines a file named LST, and associates this file with the DOS device named LPT1. You can therefore use LST to send data to the printer from a WRITE or WRITELN statement. To do so, you must include the following USES statement at the top of the program:

```
USES PRINTER;
```

When you subsequently specify LST as the first argument of a call to the WRITE or WRITELN procedure, the output is sent to the printer rather than the display screen:

```
USES PRINTER;

VAR
  items,
  unitPrice: INTEGER;

BEGIN
  items : = 200;
  unitPrice : = 35;
  WRITE (LST,'The price of ', items);
  WRITELN (LST, ' units is ', items * unitPrice)
END.
```

This example prints the line of information about unit pricing.

You can also use WRITE and WRITELN to send data to a disk file; we'll study data-file programming in Chapters 11 and 12.

To produce a blank line of output on the screen, include the WRITELN statement alone, without a list of data values. For example, this sequence results in two lines of output with a blank line between them:

```
WRITELN ('Statement one');
WRITELN;
WRITELN ('Statement two');
```

The WRITELN command supports special format notations for controlling the display of numeric data. You can specify the width of the output and the number of decimal places:

```
WRITELN (value: width: decimalPlaces)
```

In this notation, *width* and *decimalPlaces* are both literal integer values. In the following example, the WRITELN statement right-justifies a numeric value within an output field of ten spaces and displays two decimal places:

```
VAR
  outValue: REAL;
```

```
BEGIN
  outValue : = 18.766;
  WRITELN (outValue: 10: 2)
END.
```

The output value from this program is 18.77. Notice that the second decimal place has been rounded up. For integer output, you can omit the *decimalPlaces* specifier.

Turbo Pascal does not have any built-in equivalent to BASIC's PRINT USING command (which produces formatted dollar-and-cent output); however, you can easily write your own function that takes the place of this command. The *DollarDisplay* function from *StrUnit* (Figure 4.2) is an example of such a function. A call to this function takes two arguments: a long integer representing cents, and a BYTE value representing the width of the output field in which you want to right-justify the dollar-and-cent string. For example, consider the following example:

```
USES StrUnit;

BEGIN
  WRITELN (DollarDisplay (123456789, 15))
END.
```

The string value displayed on the screen is

```
$1,234,567.89
```

One final tip about WRITE and WRITELN: If you want to include the single-quote character (or apostrophe) as part of string output value, you must include a sequence of two single quotes in the corresponding string argument. For example, consider this WRITELN statement:

```
WRITELN ('Pascal''s input and output procedures.')
```

This results in the following display line:

```
Pascal's input and output procedures.
```

Keyboard Input: The READ and READLN Statements

In its simplest form, the built-in READLN procedure accepts an input value from the keyboard:

READLN (*variableName*)

This command pauses for the user to enter data, and then stores the user's response in the specified variable. The user's input must match the data type of the variable named in the READLN statement. When the user finishes typing the input value and presses the Enter key, the value is stored in the variable, and the task of the READLN statement is complete.

In an interactive program, a READLN statement is usually preceded by a WRITE or WRITELN statement, which places an appropriate input prompt on the screen. The message typically tells the user what kind of information the program expects as input. For example, consider the following passage from the *BillTime* program:

```
WRITE ('Account name? ');
READLN (inName);
```

This sequence places a prompt on the screen, and waits for the user to enter an account name:

Account name? _

READLN also allows you to accept more than one input value at a time. You can include a list of variables as the argument of the READLN statement:

READLN (*variableName1*, *variableName2*, *variableName3*, ...)

This form of the READLN statement is not generally useful for keyboard input; a program can usually exert more careful and graceful control over the input process if each input value is elicited and accepted by an individual READLN statement. However, the READLN statement is also used for reading data from disk files; in this case, one statement can conveniently read multiple data values. (We'll examine this topic in Chapters 11 and 12.)

The READ statement reads a data value from an input line and retains the position of the "file pointer" so that a subsequent READ or READLN statement can read additional data from the same line. Again, this statement is generally more important in file-handling programs than in programs that read data from the keyboard.

The READLN procedure poses a troublesome problem in some interactive programs. The problem arises when a program elicits a numeric value and the user inadvertently enters a sequence of characters that Turbo Pascal cannot read as a number. When this happens, the program performance terminates with a run-time error. For example, consider this passage:

```
WRITE ('Hourly rate? ');
READLN (hourlyRate)
```

Assume that *hourlyRate* is defined as a REAL variable. These lines display the following prompt on the screen and wait for the user to enter a real number:

```
Hourly rate? _
```

Unfortunately, if the user inadvertently enters a string of nonnumeric characters as the input, Turbo Pascal's normal reaction is to terminate the performance with a run-time error message. Inside the Turbo Pascal development environment, you will see the following error message:

```
ERROR 106: Invalid numeric format
```

Guarding against this kind of input error is an interesting programming task. Throughout the course of this chapter, and those that follow, we'll build a series of routines designed to accept data gracefully from the keyboard and avoid input errors. We'll store these routines together in a unit named *InUnit*. For the purposes of the *BillTime* program, our first version of *InUnit* contains only one routine, a function named *InReal*. This function elicits a real number from the keyboard, and provides the user's input as its return value. For example, here is the call to *InReal* from the *BillTime* program:

```
hourlyRate : = InReal ('Hourly rate? ');
```

Notice that *InReal* takes a string argument; this value is displayed on the screen as the input prompt.

The listing for *InReal*, and the first version of *InUnit*, appears in Figure 4.3. Glancing at the listing, you'll see that the function uses the {$I – } compiler directive to turn input error checking off just before the READLN statement, and then checks Turbo Pascal's built-in IORESULT function to find out whether the input is usable. (We first discussed $I and IORESULT in Chapter 2. We'll learn more about this function when we look at the *BillTime* program in the next section of this chapter.)

Sample Program: Generating Printed Reports from Account Files

The purpose of the *BillTime* program is to print a billing report from an .HRS account file produced by the *Hours* program. If you have used *Hours* repeatedly over a period time to record work-hour entries for a given client, you can now use the *BillTime* program to summarize the content of the client's file. The program opens an .HRS disk file, reads all of the entries recorded to date, and produces a printed report.

Before we turn to the program listing, let's look at an example of the program's output. Imagine an attorney who has been using *Hours* over a month-long period to record her work hours for a certain client named Smith Company. She has used the name SmithCo for the account file, and the *Hours* program has therefore saved her daily entries in the file named SMITHCO.HRS. Now, at the end of the month, the attorney wants to send a bill to her client.

Here are the chronological entries currently stored in this particular file:

```
Thu., Mar. 10, 1988   3:49 pm  5.50
 Fri., Mar. 11, 1988   4:50 pm  4.50
Sat., Mar. 12, 1988  10:18 am  3.50
Mon., Mar. 14, 1988   5:30 pm  6.50
Tue., Mar. 15, 1988  12:19 pm  3.00
Wed., Mar. 16, 1988   4:51 pm  2.50
```

```
Thu., Mar. 17, 1988   3:09 pm  1.00
Fri., Mar. 18, 1988   2:01 pm  3.50
Mon., Mar. 21, 1988   5:08 pm  3.50
Tue., Mar. 22, 1988   4:00 pm  1.00
Wed., Mar. 23, 1988   1:32 pm  2.00
Thu., Mar. 24, 1988   2:19 pm  3.50
Fri., Mar. 25, 1988   3:52 pm  2.50
Mon., Mar. 28, 1988   6:44 pm  5.50
```

As you'll recall, the *Hours* program saves three items of information for each entry: the date of the entry, the time of the entry, and the number of hours worked.

The *BillTime* program begins its performance by eliciting information from the user. First the program needs to know the name of the account file from which a report is to be printed. Then, in order to translate the hours worked into billable dollar-and-cent amounts, the program must know the hourly billing rate for this client. An input dialog designed to accept these values appears on the computer's screen.

Let's say the attorney is billing Smith Company at a rate of $112.50 per hour. When she performs the *BillTime* program, here are the input prompts that will appear on the screen and the answers that the attorney will provide:

Date: Thu., Mar. 31, 1988   Time: 4:11 pm

Print a Client's Invoice

Account name? **SmithCo**
Hourly rate? **112.50**

Like the *Hours* program, *BillHour* allows the user to request a directory listing of .HRS files by simply pressing the Enter key in response to the *Account name?* prompt. (Alternatively, the user can enter a file-name mask consisting of wild-card characters; see Chapter 3 for more information.) The attorney has skipped this step, since she already knows the name of the file she wants to work with.

```
UNIT InUnit;

   { This unit contains special input routines for accepting
     and validating data entries from the keyboard. }

   INTERFACE

     USES CRT;

     FUNCTION InReal (prompt:     STRING):     REAL;

     { More routines to come ... }


   IMPLEMENTATION

     FUNCTION InReal;

         { The InReal function displays an input prompt on
           the screen, eliciting a real number data entry.
           If the user's entry is not valid- -for example,
           if the entry contains nonnumeric characters- -InReal
           erases the entry from the screen and continues
           displaying the input prompt. }

       VAR
         tempReal:     REAL;
         goodInput:    BOOLEAN;
         saveX, saveY: BYTE;

       BEGIN
         REPEAT

           { Record the current cursor position. }

           saveX := WHEREX;
           saveY := WHEREY;

           WRITE (prompt);

           { Turn input error checking off before
             accepting the input value. (This avoids
             a run-time error if the value is not valid.) }

           {$I-}
             READLN (tempReal);
           {$I+}

           { Check IORESULT to see if the input is valid. }

           goodInput := (IORESULT = 0);

           { If not, erase the input value and try again. }

           IF NOT goodInput THEN
             BEGIN
               GOTOXY (saveX, saveY);
               ClrEol
             END
         UNTIL goodInput;

         InReal := tempReal

       END;     { InReal }

   END.    { InUnit }
```

Figure 4.3: The listing for *InUnit*

When the *Hourly rate?* prompt appears on the screen, the *BillTime* program expects the user to enter a real number, representing dollars and cents. No nonnumeric characters are allowed in this input value, not even a dollar sign. The *InReal* function (from *InUnit*) controls the input; if the user inadvertently enters a value that would otherwise result in an input error, *InReal* erases the unusable input from the screen, and repositions the input cursor at the end of the input prompt, thus eliciting another entry.

As soon as this input dialog is complete, the *BillTime* program immediately starts printing the billing report. The final report is shown in Figure 4.4.

The program begins by printing a title and the date of the report. Then the program presents a table of detail lines for the account entries. Each line contains the date, the hours billed, and the amount billed for a given chronological entry in the file. At the bottom of the table, the program presents the total number of hours worked during the period, and the total amount due for the current billing:

TOTAL —> 48.00 $5,400.00

Notice the readable dollar-and-cent format (including dollar sign and commas) that the program produces. The *DollarDisplay* function (from *StrUnit*) is responsible for this format.

```
                  *** Hourly Billing for: SMITHCO ***
                         Thu., Mar. 31, 1988

       Date                Hours Billed     @$112.50 / hour


   Thu., Mar. 10, 1988         5.50            $618.75
   Fri., Mar. 11, 1988         4.50            $506.25
   Sat., Mar. 12, 1988         3.50            $393.75
   Mon., Mar. 14, 1988         6.50            $731.25
   Tue., Mar. 15, 1988         3.00            $337.50
   Wed., Mar. 16, 1988         2.50            $281.25
   Thu., Mar. 17, 1988         1.00            $112.50
   Fri., Mar. 18, 1988         3.50            $393.75
   Mon., Mar. 21, 1988         3.50            $393.75
   Tue., Mar. 22, 1988         1.00            $112.50
   Wed., Mar. 23, 1988         2.00            $225.00
   Thu., Mar. 24, 1988         3.50            $393.75
   Fri., Mar. 25, 1988         2.50            $281.25
   Mon., Mar. 28, 1988         5.50            $618.75


        TOTAL   -->            48.00          $5,400.00
```

Figure 4.4: Output from the *BillTime* program

In summary, the *BillTime* program produces the entire report quickly and efficiently, and with a minimum of input from the user. The listing of the *BillTime* program appears in Figure 4.5. In the next section we'll examine the listing, concentrating on the program's overall structure.

The Listing of the *BillTime* Program

The action of *BillTime* is organized into five procedures and functions, along with the main program section. The main program, located at the bottom of the listing, displays the date, the time, and the program title on the screen, and then calls the procedure that does most of the work, *PrintBill*.

The *PrintBill* procedure in turn divides its work among three local routines. First, the *GetFileName* function elicits the name of the account file and displays directory listings if they are requested. (*GetFileName* has its own local procedure named *Directory*, which displays a directory list on the screen at the user's request.) Then the *InvoiceHeading* procedure prints the report's title and the column headings for the table section of the report. The *PrintBill* procedure itself prints each detail line of the report, and finally calls the *TotalLine* procedure to display the account total and to close the account file.

Looking through the program listing, you'll find that *BillTime* illustrates many of the topics we have discussed in this chapter. In particular, you should notice the global CONST and VAR declarations at the top of the program listing, and the local declarations inside most of the procedures and functions. Each routine declares all of the variables it requires for completing its own task. For example, the *PrintBill* procedure declares the following assortment of numeric, string, and Boolean variables:

```
VAR
  hours,
  hourlyRate,
  total,
  amountDue:  REAL;
  cents,
  totalDue:   LONGINT;
  dateLine:   STRING[dateInfoLength];
```

```
timeLine:     STRING[timeInfoLength];
clientName:  STRING;
okToPrint:    BOOLEAN;
```

```
PROGRAM BillTime;

    { This program prints invoice-style billing reports
      from the HRS data files created by the Hours program. }

    { Set the heap size, for successful use
      of the EXEC statement: }
    {$M 16384, 0, 0}

    USES CRT, DOS, PRINTER, ChrnUnit, InUnit, StrUnit;

    CONST
       lineLength     = 55;
       maxScreenColumn = 80;

    VAR
       accountFile: TEXT;
       accountFileName: STRING;


    PROCEDURE PrintBill;

        { The PrintBill procedure prints the invoice report
          from a selected account file. }

        CONST
           dateInfoLength = 20;
           timeInfoLength =  9;

        VAR
           hours,
           hourlyRate,
           total,
           amountDue: REAL;
           cents,
           totalDue:  LONGINT;
           dateLine:  STRING[dateInfoLength];
           timeLine:  STRING[timeInfoLength];
           clientName: STRING;
           okToPrint: BOOLEAN;


        FUNCTION GetFileName: STRING;

            { The GetFileName function elicits the name of
              an account file, and displays a directory listing
              if necessary. }

            VAR
               goodName,
               dirRequest: BOOLEAN;
               inName:     STRING;
               periodPos:  BYTE;


        PROCEDURE Directory (mask: STRING);

            { The Directory procedure displays a
              directory list on the screen. }
```

Figure 4.5: The listing of the *BillTime* program

```
    BEGIN    { Directory }

      WRITELN (StringOfChars ('.', 75));
      EXEC ('\COMMAND.COM', '/C DIR ' + mask + ' /W');
      WRITELN (StringOfChars ('.', 75))

    END;    { Directory }

  BEGIN    { GetFileName }

    goodName := FALSE;

    WHILE NOT goodName DO
      BEGIN
        WRITELN;
        WRITE ('Account name? ');
        READLN (inName);
        IF inName = '' THEN
          Directory ('*.HRS')
        ELSE
          BEGIN
            dirRequest :=
              (POS('*', inName) <> 0) OR
              (POS('?', inName) <> 0);
            IF dirRequest THEN
              Directory (inName)
            ELSE
              BEGIN
                goodName := TRUE;
                periodPos := POS('.', inName);
                IF periodPos <> 0 THEN
                  inName := COPY(inName, 1, periodPos - 1);
              END
          END
      END;

    GetFileName := inName;

  END;    { GetFileName }


PROCEDURE InvoiceHeading (VAR printerOn: BOOLEAN;
                              client:    STRING;
                              rate:      REAL);

{ The InvoiceHeading procedure prints the
  heading for the invoice report. }

VAR
  rateString: STRING;

BEGIN    { InvoiceHeading }

  {$I-}
    WRITE (LST, '         *** Hourly Billing for: ');
  {$I+}

  IF IORESULT = 0 THEN
    BEGIN
      printerOn := TRUE;
      WRITELN (LST, UpperCase (client), ' ***');
      WRITELN (LST, StringOfChars (' ', 17), DateString);
      WRITELN (LST);
      rateString := DollarDisplay (ROUND (rate * 100), 6);
      WRITE (LST, ' Date            Hours Billed    ');
      WRITELN (LST, '@', rateString, ' / hour');
      WRITELN (LST, StringOfChars ('_', lineLength));
```

Figure 4.5: The listing of the *BillTime* program (continued)

```
            WRITELN (LST)
         END
      ELSE
         BEGIN
            printerOn := FALSE;
            WRITELN ('    *** Printer is not on. ')
         END

   END;    { InvoiceHeading }

PROCEDURE TotalLine;

   { The TotalLine procedure prints the
     bottom line of the invoice report. }

   BEGIN    { TotalLine }

      WRITELN (LST, StringOfChars ('_', lineLength));
      WRITELN (LST);
      WRITE (LST, '   TOTAL   -->   ');
      WRITELN (LST, total:13:2, DollarDisplay (totalDue, 20));
      CLOSE (accountFile)

   END;    { TotalLine }

BEGIN    { PrintBill }

   clientName := GetFileName;
   accountFileName := clientName + '.HRS';
   ASSIGN (accountFile, accountFileName);

   {$I-}
      RESET (accountFile);
   {$I+}

   IF IOResult <> 0 THEN
      BEGIN
         WRITELN;
         WRITELN ('    *** Can''t open file.');
      END

   ELSE    { If file was opened successfully }
      BEGIN
         hourlyRate := InReal('Hourly rate? ');
         WRITELN (StringOfChars ('_', lineLength));
         WRITELN;
         total := 0.0;
         totalDue := 0;
         InvoiceHeading (okToPrint, clientName, hourlyRate);

         IF okToPrint THEN
            BEGIN
               RESET (accountFile);
               WHILE NOT EOF(accountFile) DO
                  BEGIN
                     READLN (accountFile, dateLine, timeLine, hours);
                     total := total + hours;
                     WRITE (LST, dateLine, hours:10:2);
                     amountDue := hours * hourlyRate;
                     cents := ROUND(amountDue * 100);
                     totalDue := totalDue + cents;
                     WRITELN (LST, DollarDisplay (cents, 20));
                  END;
               TotalLine
            END
      END
```

Figure 4.5: The listing of the *BillTime* program (continued)

```
END;    { PrintBill }


BEGIN    { BillTime }

  { Display the date, time, and program
    description on the display screen. }

  CLRSCR;
  WRITELN (' Date: ', DateString, '  Time: ', TimeString);
  WRITELN (StringOfChars ('_', lineLength));
  WRITELN;
  WRITELN ('        Print a Client''s Invoice ');
  WRITELN (StringOfChars ('_', lineLength));

  { Print the invoice. }

  PrintBill;

END.    { BillTime }
```

Figure 4.5: The listing of the *BillTime* program (continued)

In general, the names of these variables clearly describe their purposes. For example, the four REAL variables store the following values:

- The hour amount from each account record (*hours*)

- The hourly rate provided by the user (*hourlyRate*)

- The total number of hours recorded in the account (*total*)

- The monetary amount due from a given entry in the account (*amountDue*)

The program uses long integers (*cents* and *totalDue*) for storing other monetary amounts, and for performing numeric calculations on these amounts. This data type prevents any possible loss of dollar-and-cent accuracy in the bottom-line report totals. (The *Dollar-Display* function is designed to receive a long-integer argument representing cents to create the dollar-and-cent display format.)

The following passage from the *PrintBill* procedure performs the necessary calculations and output operations for each record that the program reads from the account file:

```
WRITE (LST, dateLine, hours:10:2);
```

```
amountDue : = hours * hourlyRate;
cents : = ROUND(amountDue * 100);
totalDue : = totalDue + cents;
WRITELN (LST, DollarDisplay (cents, 20));
```

The first WRITE line in this passage begins the output line for a given account record, printing the date and the number of hours worked. Then three assignment statements perform essential arithmetic computations for this record: the first computes the amount due from a given record in the account, the second converts this amount to cents, and the third adds the amount to the current running total. Finally, the WRITELN command completes the printed output line, calling on the *DollarDisplay* function to produce the appropriate format. Here is a sample output line from this passage:

```
Fri., Mar. 18, 1988        3.50              $393.75
```

The *BillTime* program illustrates many other features that we will be returning to in subsequent chapters. Before we leave the program, however, let's look briefly at just a few additional passages.

The *InvoiceHeading* procedure contains an interesting example of a variable parameter—specifically, a Boolean variable named *printerOn:*

```
PROCEDURE InvoiceHeading ( VAR printerOn: BOOLEAN;
                               client:    STRING;
                               rate:      REAL);
```

This procedure prints the title and headings of the report, including two important items of information: the name of the client account and the rate at which the client is billed. The *PrintBill* procedure passes both of these items to *InvoiceHeading* as arguments:

```
InvoiceHeading (okToPrint, clientName, hourlyRate);
```

The purpose of the first argument, *okToPrint*, is to receive a value back from the procedure. When *InvoiceHeading* attempts to print the first line of output, it carefully disables I/O checking (using the {$I − } compiler directive). If some condition prevents the procedure from printing the output line (for example, the printer is off or not available), *InvoiceHeading* sets the variable *printerOn* to FALSE, and displays an error message on the screen:

```
printerOn : = FALSE;
WRITELN ('      * * * Printer is not on. ')
```

The value of *printerOn* is passed back to *okToPrint* in the *PrintBill* procedure. The procedure continues printing the invoice only if this value is TRUE:

```
IF okToPrint THEN
    ...
```

We'll discuss Boolean values and IF statements in detail in Chapter 5.

Finally, the *PrintBill* procedure contains an interesting example of concatenation, the operation that combines two string values. Specifically, the following passage produces an account file name by appending the extension .HRS to the end of the user-supplied account name:

```
clientName : = GetFileName;
accountFileName : = clientName + '.HRS';
```

Notice that a call to the *GetFileName* function provides the base file name. In the case of the account name SmithCo, these statements successfully produce the file name SMITHCO.HRS.

Enter the *BillTime* listing into the editor and compile the program. You'll notice that the program uses six units:

```
USES CRT, DOS, PRINTER, ChrnUnit, InUnit, StrUnit;
```

The following files must be available on disk for a successful compilation:

- TURBO.TPL, the Turbo Pascal library file
- CHRNUNIT.TPU, the compiled form of *ChrnUnit*
- INUNIT.TPU, the compiled form of *InUnit*
- STRUNIT.TPU, the compiled form of *StrUnit*

When you are ready to try performing the program, use a sample account file that you created with the *Hours* program for a test run.

The output report should be similar to the one shown earlier in this chapter.

Summary

A Turbo Pascal program is typically divided into a number of structural components, including a PROGRAM heading; a USES statement; optional CONST, TYPE, and VAR declarations; PROCEDURE and FUNCTION definitions; and finally, a main program section. The scope of identifiers, procedures, and functions is defined by the location of their declarations; global declarations are always located in the main program block, while local declarations are located inside procedure or function blocks.

Turbo Pascal gives you a useful variety of data types to work with in program applications. Understanding the characteristics of these data types will help you to write programs that are versatile, accurate, and efficient.

Procedures and functions are the building blocks of a modular program. The specific characteristics of these two kinds of routines make the Turbo Pascal language an ideal environment for developing structured programs.

This chapter has covered a lot of important material. You may want to refer back this material occasionally during your work, to review the characteristics of data types or the syntax of program parts.

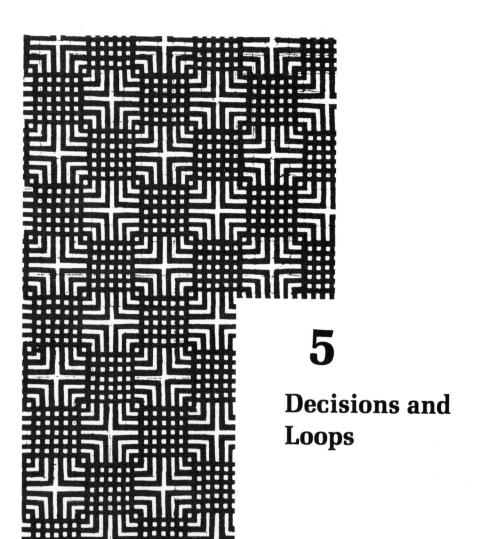

CHAPTER

5

Decisions and Loops

To control complex events, an interactive Pascal program must be able to make decisions, choose among available courses of action, and perform actions repetitively. All these activities require successful evaluation of logical conditions, in order to decide on a specific direction for the current performance or determine the duration of a particular repetition sequence. The Turbo Pascal language provides a variety of control structures for performing decisions and repetition loops; these structures are the subject of this chapter.

Turbo Pascal offers two different decision structures:

- The IF structure
- The CASE structure

These structures can express and control any variety of simple or complex decision-making processes. Using IF and CASE statements judiciously, you can translate any decision process, however complex and multifaceted, into a clearly expressed and logically implemented sequence of Pascal commands. In this chapter we'll discuss the role of these structures, and we'll look at several program examples that illustrate their power.

Repetition is the essence of many computer applications. A loop is a control structure that governs repetitive processes in a program. Like decision structures, a loop marks off a block of commands for special handling. Whereas an IF or CASE SELECT structure decides whether or not to perform a given statement or group of statements, a loop structure actually performs a block of code a number of times.

We refer to the repetitions of a loop performance as *iterations*. An essential issue in the design of any loop is how to decide when the iterations should stop. Turbo Pascal provides three distinct loop structures, each with a different scheme for controlling the iteration process:

- A FOR loop specifies the range of the iterations explicitly in advance, and provides a *control variable*: an ordinal-type variable whose value increases or decreases as the looping proceeds.

- A WHILE loop expresses a condition over which the looping will continue. The iterations stop when the condition becomes false.

- A REPEAT UNTIL loop also contains a controlling conditional expression, but in this case the looping continues until the condition becomes true.

Each of these loop structures has its own syntax and usage, which we will examine in this chapter.

Decisions and loops are normally based on the evaluated result of a logical expression; this result is a Boolean-type value of TRUE or FALSE. To develop the necessary background for understanding decision structures, we'll begin this chapter with a look at how Turbo Pascal handles logical values and expressions. We'll survey the relational and logical operations available in Turbo Pascal for use in simple and complex expressions, and we'll see how these expressions are evaluated. Then we'll examine each of the decision structures and loop structures in turn.

Finally, to illustrate all this material, we'll look at a Pascal program named *CliList*. This program continues to build on our billable-hours application. Specifically, *CliList* creates a list of all client files stored in a given directory, along with total work hours and the status of each client. We'll examine passages from this program throughout this chapter. Before we begin discussing decision and loop structures, let's see how the *CliList* program behaves.

The *CliList* Program

Up to now we have developed a library of two programs for the billable-hour application. The *Hours* program (presented and discussed in Chapter 3) creates new client files or appends new records to existing files. The *BillTime* program (discussed in Chapter 4) prints an invoice-style report from the entries stored in any specified file. We'll now add a third program to this collection: the *CliList* program. *CliList* performs the following sequence of operations:

1. Examines the current directory path and develops a list of all the client files (with .HRS extensions) stored in the directory.

2. Alphabetizes the list.

3. Opens each file in the list, one by one, and tallies up the current total billable hours recorded in the file.

4. Prints a report showing the names of the client files, the total billable hours for each file, and the status of each client (based on the date of the last entry in the client's account).

If you have used the *Hours* program to develop a collection of client files, with each file recording the billable hours you have worked for a given client, *CliList* is a quick and convenient way to determine the current status of all your files.

For example, imagine you have used this application to develop a dozen client files, as shown in this list:

```
ALTCORP   HRS
BIGCO     HRS
SMALLCO   HRS
MMMCORP   HRS
AIRPORT   HRS
TODAYCO   HRS
XYZCORP   HRS
PUBWORK   HRS
SECRETCO  HRS
NOWCORP   HRS
JONESCO   HRS
CITYJOB   HRS
```

Assuming all these files are stored together in the current directory, the *CliList* program produces printed reports like the one shown in Figure 5.1.

```
        Client Name    Billable Hours   Status
        ------ ----    -------- -----    ------

        Airport            63.75          *
        Altcorp            92.25          *
        Bigco              89.25          **
        Cityjob           190.00          ***
        Jonesco             6.75          ***
        Mmmcorp           367.75          **
        Nowcorp           741.75          ***
        Pubwork            82.25          *
        Secretco          410.25          *
        Smallco            15.25          **
        Todayco            60.50          **
        Xyzcorp           136.75          ***


        ----------------------------------------
          *** Current client account.
          **  Recent account.
          *   Inactive account.
```

Figure 5.1: Output from the *CliList* program

The report shown has three columns, labeled *Client Name*, *Hours to Date*, and *Status*. The clients are presented in alphabetical order, and in a standard capitalization format: each client name is printed with an initial uppercase letter, followed by all lowercase letters. The numeric values in the second column represent the total billable hours recorded in each file.

Finally, the third column contains one, two, or three asterisks, representing the status of the client. A key at the bottom of the report shows you how to interpret the status column:

    * * *Current client account.
     * *Recent account.
      *Inactive account.

To determine the status of a given account, the *CliList* program examines the date of the final entry recorded in the account. The current version of the program creates status categories as follows:

- If the last entry in the account was made in 1987 or 1988, the account is classified as current.

- If the last entry was made in 1985 or 1986, the account is recent.

- If the last entry was made from 1980 to 1984, the account is inactive.

All details of this printed report, including the spacing and alignment of columns, are carefully planned features of the program's output. These details are handled by routines in the *CliList* program or by tools provided for the program by the unit named *StrUnit*. (We worked with the first version of this unit in Chapter 4; we'll be adding some new routines to the unit later in this chapter.) For example, the program contains one routine that is responsible for alphabetizing the list of client names. Another routine standardizes the capitalization of each name. Yet another opens each file in turn and tallies up the total billable hours.

By the way, the *CliList* program uses a special data structure to store the list of client file names that are read from the current directory. Specifically, the structure is an array of strings named *clientArray*. The program defines this array structure globally, as follows:

```
CONST
  maxFiles = 100;

TYPE
  fileRange  = 1..maxFiles;
  clientArray = ARRAY [fileRange] OF STRING;

VAR
  clientFiles: clientArray;
```

This array can store a list of up to 100 string values. Each *element* in the array can store one string value, just like a uniquely named string variable. The advantage of an array is that the elements can be referenced by *index* numbers. For example, the first three account names in the *clientFiles* array will be stored in the following three elements:

```
clientFiles[1]
clientFiles[2]
clientFiles[3]
```

We'll study Turbo Pascal arrays in detail in Chapter 6. For now, simply keep in mind that the *clientFiles* array is the central data structure in the *CliList* program, with the potential of storing a list of up to 100 different client account names.

We'll look at the entire *CliList* program listing at the end of this chapter. First, let's begin our discussion of logical expressions.

Logical Values and Expressions

As we saw in Chapter 4, Pascal has an explicit logical data type—identified as BOOLEAN—along with standard identifiers to represent the logical constants TRUE and FALSE. A logical expression is a single or compound operation that Pascal evaluates to true or false. Turbo Pascal has two sets of operations for creating logical expressions:

- Relational operations
- Logical operations

Let's examine each of these in turn.

Relational Operations

A relational operation compares two data items and yields a BOOLEAN value as a result of the comparison. Here are the six relational operators and their meanings:

Operator	Meaning
=	Equal to
<	Less than
< =	Less than or equal to
>	Greater than
> =	Greater than or equal to
< >	Not equal to

You can use these operations with any two values of the same type. For example, let's say the integer variable *choice* contains a value of 7. The first of the following expressions gives a value of false, the second true:

    choice < = 5

    choice > 5

With string values, relational operators compare the ASCII values of corresponding characters in each string. One string is said to be "less than" another if corresponding characters have smaller ASCII code numbers. For example, all of the following expressions are true:

    'turbo' > 'TURBO'

    'ABC' < 'EFG'

    'Pascal' < 'Pascal compiler'

Note that lowercase letters have higher ASCII codes than uppercase letters. Also notice that string length becomes the determining factor in a comparison of two strings when the existing characters in the shorter string are the same as the corresponding characters in the longer. In this case, the longer string is said to be "greater than" the shorter one.

Turbo Pascal gives you some latitude in comparing values that do not precisely match in type. Specifically, you can compare integers and real numbers in the same expression. You can also compare values of type CHAR and STRING.

When we discuss *sets* in Chapter 7 we'll encounter three more relational operations that result in Boolean values; these additional operations work with sets as operands.

Logical Operations

Turbo Pascal has four logical operations. Three of them—AND, OR, and XOR—are binary operations, used to combine pairs of logical values in compound logical expressions. The fourth, NOT, is a unary operation that changes a single logical operand to its opposite value.

Given two logical values or expressions, represented by *expression1* and *expression2*, we can describe these four operations as follows:

- *expression1* AND *expression2* is true only if both *expression1* and *expression2* are true. If either is false, or if both are false, the AND operation is also false.

- *expression1* OR *expression2* is true if either *expression1* is true or *expression2* is true, or if both are true. The OR operations yields a value of false only if both *expression1* and *expression2* are false.

- *expression1* XOR *expression2* is true only if *expression1* and *expression2* have opposite values. If *expression1* and *expression2* are the same—either both true or both false—the XOR operation gives a value of false.

- NOT *expression1* evaluates to true if *expression1* is false; conversely, the NOT expression is false if *expression1* is true.

Note: Don't confuse these logical operations with Turbo Pascal's *bitwise* operations. The six bitwise operations perform low-level bit comparisons, working on INTEGER-type operands. In contrast, the logical operations always work on BOOLEAN-type values. Four of the bitwise operations have the same names as the logical operations: NOT, AND, OR, XOR. The other two are SHL and SHR.

Figure 5.2 shows the listing of a demonstration program called *TruthTbl*. This program experiments with the logical operators by combining a variety of logical values and testing the result. As its name indicates, the *TruthTbl* program displays a kind of "truth table"—a summary of the results of the logical operations:

```
AND
‾‾‾‾
TRUE AND FALSE  = FALSE
TRUE AND TRUE   = TRUE
FALSE AND FALSE = FALSE

OR
‾‾
TRUE OR FALSE  = TRUE
TRUE OR TRUE   = TRUE
FALSE OR FALSE = FALSE
```

XOR

TRUE XOR FALSE = TRUE
TRUE XOR TRUE   = FALSE
FALSE XOR FALSE = FALSE

NOT

NOT FALSE = TRUE
NOT TRUE   = FALSE

```
PROGRAM TruthTbl;

  { This program demonstrates the logical operations. }

  PROCEDURE AndTest;

    BEGIN
      WRITELN ('AND');
      WRITELN ('---');
      WRITELN ('TRUE AND FALSE  = ', TRUE AND FALSE);
      WRITELN ('TRUE AND TRUE   = ', TRUE AND TRUE);
      WRITELN ('FALSE AND FALSE = ', FALSE AND FALSE);
      WRITELN
    END;

  PROCEDURE OrTest;

    BEGIN
      WRITELN ('OR');
      WRITELN ('--');
      WRITELN ('TRUE OR FALSE  = ', TRUE OR FALSE);
      WRITELN ('TRUE OR TRUE   = ', TRUE OR TRUE);
      WRITELN ('FALSE OR FALSE = ', FALSE OR FALSE);
      WRITELN
    END;

  PROCEDURE XorTest;

    BEGIN
      WRITELN ('XOR');
      WRITELN ('---');
      WRITELN ('TRUE XOR FALSE  = ', TRUE XOR FALSE);
      WRITELN ('TRUE XOR TRUE   = ', TRUE XOR TRUE);
      WRITELN ('FALSE XOR FALSE = ', FALSE XOR FALSE);
      WRITELN
    END;

  PROCEDURE NotTest;

    BEGIN
      WRITELN ('NOT');
      WRITELN ('---');
      WRITELN ('NOT FALSE  = ', NOT FALSE);
      WRITELN ('NOT TRUE   = ', NOT TRUE);
      WRITELN
    END;
```

Figure 5.2: The listing of the *TruthTbl* program

```
BEGIN
  AndTest;
  OrTest;
  XorTest;
  NotTest

END.
```

Figure 5.2: The listing of the *TruthTbl* program (continued)

Here is an example of a logical expression using the OR operation, taken from this chapter's major program example, *CliList:*

(inChar = spaceBar) OR (inChar = escKey)

As we'll see later, this line is part of a REPEAT UNTIL loop. The purpose of this loop is to create a pause in the program performance until the user presses one of two keys: the space bar or the Escape key. Inside the loop, the user's one-character keystroke is stored in the CHAR variable *inChar.* (The identifiers *spaceBar* and *escKey* are constants established earlier in the program; as their names imply, they represent the space bar character and the Escape character, respectively.)

As a result of this condition, the looping continues and the program continues waiting for keyboard input until one of the following relational expressions is true:

inChar = spaceBar

inChar = escKey

Notice that these two expressions are enclosed in parentheses in the compound expression:

(inChar = spaceBar) OR (inChar = escKey)

The logical operators (AND, OR, XOR, and NOT) have a higher order of precedence than the relational operators (=, < >, <, >, < =, > =). The parentheses are therefore necessary to force Pascal to evaluate each of the two relational expressions (=) before evaluating the OR expression.

Significantly, Turbo Pascal's default behavior is to evaluate the operands of a logical expression in the *short-circuit* mode. We first discussed this topic in Chapter 2; we'll review the two evaluation modes briefly in the next section.

Short-Circuit Mode versus Complete Evaluation

In the short-circuit mode, evaluation of a given expression stops as soon as the final result is determined, whether or not all of the operands have been evaluated.

To see how this works, look again at the OR expression we discussed in the previous section. If the first relation, *inChar = spaceBar*, evaluates to TRUE, the value of the entire OR expression is also TRUE, regardless of the value of the second expression, *inChar = escKey*. In this case, Turbo Pascal completes its evaluation of the OR expression without evaluating the second relation.

Likewise, Turbo Pascal stops the evaluation of an AND expression if the first operand evaluates to FALSE; in this case the AND expression is also FALSE, regardless of the value of the second operand.

In some special programming contexts, you may want to change this default behavior, switching to *complete evaluation*. For example, let's say you have written an AND expression in which the two operands are calls to functions that return Boolean values:

```
logicalFun1 AND logicalFun2
```

You may want to force a performance of both functions each time this AND expression is evaluated, particularly if the functions have some essential side effect in the performance of the program. In this case, you'll switch the compiler to the complete evaluation mode. To do so, include the {B + } compiler directive in your program. Alternatively, you can pull down the Options menu, select the Compiler command, and toggle the *Boolean evaluation* option to on.

In summary, relational and logical operators are essential vocabulary for building logical expressions. These expressions in turn are the basis for performing decisions in Pascal. As we continue our discussion of Turbo Pascal's decision and loop structures in the following sections, we'll see several practical examples of relational and logical operations.

The IF Decision Structure

An IF structure selects one of two statements (or groups of statements) for performance. The structure consists of an IF clause, along with an optional ELSE clause:

IF *condition* THEN

    { *statement or group of statements*
     performed if condition *is* TRUE }

ELSE

    { *statement of group of statements*
     performed if condition *is* FALSE }

During a performance, Pascal begins by evaluating the condition in the IF clause. This condition must result in a BOOLEAN-type value, but it can take a variety of forms—it can be an expression built from any combination of logical or relational operators, or simply a BOOLEAN variable.

If the condition is TRUE, the statement or statements located between IF and ELSE are performed and the performance skips over the ELSE clause. Alternatively, if the expression is FALSE, the performance proceeds directly to the statement or statements located after the ELSE clause.

The IF and ELSE clauses can be followed by either a single statement or multiple statements. Multiple statements must be enclosed within BEGIN and END markers. (A BEGIN/END block is sometimes called a *compound statement*.) For example, consider the following passage from the *CliList* program:

```
IF listLength > 0 THEN
   BEGIN
     SortClientFiles (listLength);
     PrintClientList (listLength);
   END
ELSE
```

```
BEGIN
  WRITELN;
  WRITELN ('No .HRS files are stored in');
  WRITE ('this directory: ');
  GETDIR (0, dirString);
  WRITELN (dirString)
END
```

In this example, the decision is based on the value stored in the BYTE variable *listLength*. (This value indicates the number of .HRS files that the program has found in the current directory.) If *listLength* is greater than zero, the program calls two procedures—*SortClientFiles* to sort the list of clients, and *PrintClientFiles* to print the report. Otherwise, if *listLength* is zero, the program displays a series of messages on the screen:

```
No .HRS files are stored in
this directory: C:\CLIENTS\CURRENT
```

Notice the structure of this IF statement. Both the IF and ELSE clauses are followed by BEGIN/END blocks, enclosing groups of statements. Here is the general format of this structure:

```
IF condition THEN
  BEGIN
    { IF-clause statements }
  END
ELSE
  BEGIN
    { ELSE-clause statements }
  END;
```

Don't make the mistake of omitting the BEGIN and END markers for compound statements in an IF structure. While some structured versions of the Basic language allow you to use the IF and ELSE clauses themselves as markers between blocks of code, Pascal does not. Furthermore, do not place a semicolon between END and ELSE in the IF structure. Pascal would read this incorrect punctuation as the end of the IF statement, and the subsequent ELSE clause would result in a compile-time error.

Since the ELSE clause is optional, the simplest form of the IF structure is as follows:

IF *condition* THEN

    { *statement or statements performed*
      if condition *is* TRUE }

In this case, the program performs the statement or statements located after the IF clause only if the condition is true. If it is false, the IF statement results in no action.

IF structures can also be nested. In other words, an entire decision structure, complete with IF and ELSE clauses, may appear within the IF or ELSE clause of another structure. Nesting of IF structures can result in complex and powerful decision sequences, as we'll see in programs presented later in this book.

The CASE Decision Structure

Like the IF structure, the CASE statement divides a sequence of potential actions into individual sections of code. For any given performance of a particular CASE statement, only one of these sections at most will be selected for action. The selection is based on a series of comparison tests, all performed on an expressed target value.

The general form of the CASE structure is as follows:

CASE *selector* OF

  caseValue1:

    { *statement or statements performed if*
      selector *matches* caseValue1 }

  caseValue2:

    { *statement or statements performed if*
      selector *matches* caseValue2 }

```
{ ...
   additional caseValue and statements
   ... }
```

ELSE

```
   { statement or statements performed if
      none of the previous cases produce a match }
```

END

The structure of a CASE decision consists of the following elements:

- A CASE OF clause, supplying a target *selector* expression

- A sequence of *caseValues* to be compared with the selector, each followed by one or more statements to be performed if the selector matches the *caseValue*

- An optional ELSE statement, providing a statement or group of statements to be performed only if no match is found in the previous *caseValues*

- An END marker, identifying the end of the CASE structure

To perform the decision expressed in this structure, Pascal begins by evaluating the *selector* expression in the CASE OF clause. This value must belong to an ordinal type that has a range between $-32,768$ and $32,767$. So far in this book we have studied five data types that meet this criterion: CHAR, BOOLEAN, BYTE, SHORTINT, and INTEGER. (We'll learn more about scalar types in Chapter 7.)

The *selector* becomes the target of the comparisons with all subsequent *caseValues*. In a performance, Pascal evaluates each comparison, selects the first *caseValue* that matches the selector, and performs the statement or statements located between that *caseValue* and the next. No other statements are performed.

If none of the *caseValue* comparisons produces a match with the selector, the ELSE clause is performed instead. ELSE is an optional clause in the CASE statement; if ELSE is not present, and no *caseValue* is selected, the CASE statement results in no performed action.

The selector value in the CASE OF clause can appear as a variable or an expression, as long as the result is an ordinal value. For example, the following are both valid CASE OF clauses:

```
CASE choice OF
CASE (maxVal + 5) OF
```

All of the *caseValues* must belong to the same ordinal type as the selector value. You can express a *caseValue* in any of the following forms:

- A literal constant or a named constant
- A list of constants, separated by commas
- A *subrange* of constants, using the notation

```
constant1 .. constant2
```

Multiple statements associated with a given *caseValue* must be enclosed within BEGIN and END markers.

Figure 5.3 shows a simple program exercise you can perform to experiment with the behavior of the CASE statement. For each performance, this program displays an input prompt on the screen, eliciting a BYTE-type value:

```
Enter a BYTE value: _
```

The program stores the input value in the variable *numVar*, which becomes the selector for the subsequent CASE statement. The selector is compared with a list of constants (25, 50), a single constant (100), and a range of constants (101..200), in sequence. If one of these comparisons produces a match, the program displays a corresponding message on the screen; if not, the ELSE clause is performed.

Here is a more practical example of the CASE structure, from the *CliList* program:

```
CASE lastYear OF

  1987..1988:
    ClientStatus := '***';
```

```
    VAR
      numVar: BYTE;

    BEGIN

      WRITE ('Enter a BYTE value: ');
      READLN (numVar);
      WRITELN;

      CASE numVar OF

        25, 50:

          BEGIN
            WRITELN ('First case:');
            WRITELN ('numVar is 25 or 50.')
          END;

        100:

          BEGIN
            WRITELN ('Second case:');
            WRITELN ('numVar is 100. ')
          END;

        101..200:

          BEGIN
            WRITELN ('Third case:');
            WRITELN ('numVar is a value from 101 to 200.')
          END;

        ELSE

          BEGIN
            WRITELN ('ELSE case:');
            WRITELN ('None of the previous cases produced a match.')
          END

      END

    END
```

Figure 5.3: Using the CASE statement in a program

```
    1985..1986:
      ClientStatus : = '**';

    1980..1984:
      ClientStatus : = '*';

    ELSE
      ClientStatus : = ''

  END     { CASE lastYear }
```

This CASE statement evaluates the status of a given client account. The *lastYear* variable is an integer representing the year of the last entry in the account file. This value is compared with three ranges of integers: current years, recent years, or years in the relatively distant past.

Now we'll turn our attention to the three kinds of repetition loops available in Turbo Pascal.

FOR Loops

The FOR loop is perhaps the most familiar and commonly used repetition structure. Here is a general representation of the structure's syntax:

```
FOR controlVar : = startValue TO lastValue DO
    statement;
```

If the loop block contains multiple statements, the general format is as follows:

```
FOR controlVar : = startValue TO lastValue DO

BEGIN
  { statements performed for
    each iteration of the loop }
END;
```

The FOR statement identifies a control variable (*controlVar*) for the loop, and indicates a range of values (*startValue TO lastValue*) that the variable will receive during the iterations of the loop. The control variable must belong to an ordinal type, and *startValue* and *lastValue* must be compatible with that type. Here is an outline of the loop's performance:

1. At the beginning of the performance, the control variable receives the value of *startValue*, and the first iteration is performed.

2. Before each succeeding iteration, the control variable receives the next value in the range of *startValue..lastValue*.

3. The looping stops after the iteration corresponding to *last-Value*.

In a FOR loop that uses a TO clause, the ordinal value of *startValue* should be less than the ordinal value of *lastValue*. (If not, the loop results in no action.) Alternatively, you can use the reserved word DOWNTO to design a FOR loop that moves backward through an ordinal range:

```
FOR controlVar : = startValue DOWNTO lastValue DO
```

In this case, the value of *startValue* should be greater than *lastValue*. Before each succeeding iteration, the control variable receives the next lowest value in the range.

The control variable in a FOR loop has a special status. No statement inside the loop should attempt to change the value of this variable; doing so would interfere with the normal counting process that Pascal automatically conducts during the repetition and produce unpredictable results. However, a statement in the loop can *access* the value of the counter variable for any purpose.

Do not use a global variable declaration to define a control variable. Each control variable in a given program should be declared inside the routine that actually contains the loop. This practice avoids any possibility of interference between different control variables defined for a given program.

Although the control variable of a FOR loop typically belongs to one of the integer types, Pascal actually allows you to use other ordinal types to control the loop, including CHAR and enumerated types. We'll explore this point in Chapter 7.

The following simple FOR loop example displays the value of the control variable, along with a second value that is calculated from the counter variable; both values appear as part of an output string:

```
CONST
  tipRate = 0.15;

VAR
  i: BYTE;
```

```
BEGIN

  FOR i : = 1 TO 5 DO

    BEGIN
      WRITE ('The tip for a ', i:2);
      WRITELN (' dollar meal is $', i * tipRate:3:2)
    END

END.
```

If you run this program, you'll find that each iteration of the loop displays one output line:

```
The tip for a 1 dollar meal is $0.15
The tip for a 2 dollar meal is $0.30
The tip for a 3 dollar meal is $0.45
The tip for a 4 dollar meal is $0.60
The tip for a 5 dollar meal is $0.75
```

The output from this example shows you a lot about how a FOR loop behaves. The control variable *i* starts out with a value of 1 at the beginning of the looping process. At the end of each iteration, *i* is automatically incremented by 1, and the FOR statement tests to see if the counter is still less than the expressed maximum value, 5 in this case. If it is, the looping continues through another iteration. When the counter reaches a value that is greater than the maximum value, the looping stops.

Keep in mind that the following two conditions result in loops that perform *no* iterations at all:

- *startValue* is greater than *lastValue* in a FOR statement with a TO clause

- *startValue* is less than *lastValue* in the FOR statement with a DOWNTO clause

You can express the range values in a FOR loop as constants, variables, or expressions. For example, the following loop, excerpted from the *CliList* program, expresses the maximum value of the loop counter as the variable *printLength:*

```
FOR i : = 1 TO printLength DO
  BEGIN
    WRITE (LST,
      LeftAlign (InitialCap (clientFiles[i]), 18));
    clientFile : = clientFiles[i] + '.HRS';
    WRITE (LST, TotalAccount(clientFile, lastEntry):7:2);
    WRITELN (LST, Spaces(9), ClientStatus (lastEntry))
  END;
```

This loop, which is responsible for printing the entire list of client accounts, illustrates another crucial point about FOR loops. Notice that the counter variable *i* is used inside the loop as an index into the array *clientFile*. As a result, each new iteration of the loop accesses the next set of elements down the length of the array, and thus prints a new client address. Study this loop carefully; it is our first example of the special relationship between loop structures and arrays. We'll continue studying arrays in Chapter 6.

Finally, you can place one loop entirely inside another, to form *nested loops*. The result is a complex and powerful pattern of repetitive actions. For example, the program shown in Figure 5.4 uses a pair of nested loops to create a sales-tax table for a local tax rate of 6.5%. The resulting table has rows representing dollar increments and columns representing increments of ten cents; it is shown in Figure 5.5.

To read an amount from this table, locate the dollar amount in the first column and the additional cent amount in the top row. The intersection of the dollar row and the cent column contains the correct sales tax. For example, you can see that the 6.5% tax on $8.60 is $0.56.

The nested loops that create the main portion of this table use the control variables *dollars* and *cents:*

```
FOR dollars : = 0 TO maxDollars DO
  BEGIN
    WRITE (dollars: 2, ' ');
    FOR cents : = 0 TO 9 DO
      WRITE (((dollars + cents / 10) * taxRate):6:2);
    WRITELN
  END;
```

```
PROGRAM SalesTax;

  { This program creates a table of sales tax amounts. }

  CONST
    taxRate   = 0.065;        { the local sales tax rate }
    maxDollars = 10;          { the top dollar amount in the table }

  VAR
    cents,                    { the FOR-loop control variables }
    dollars : BYTE;

BEGIN

  WRITE ('                    *** Sales Tax  @ ');
  WRITELN ((taxRate * 100):3:1, '% *** ');
  WRITELN;

  { Display headings of ten-cent increments. }

  WRITE ('    ');
  FOR cents := 0 TO 9 DO
    WRITE ((cents / 10):6:2);
  WRITELN;
  WRITELN;

  { Display tax table. }

  FOR dollars := 0 TO maxDollars DO
    BEGIN
      WRITE (dollars: 2, '  ');
      FOR cents := 0 TO 9 DO
        WRITE (((dollars + cents / 10) * taxRate):6:2);
      WRITELN
    END;
  WRITELN

END.
```

Figure 5.4: Using nested loops in a program

```
                    *** Sales Tax  @ 6.5% ***

       0.00  0.10  0.20  0.30  0.40  0.50  0.60  0.70  0.80  0.90

   0   0.00  0.01  0.01  0.02  0.03  0.03  0.04  0.05  0.05  0.06
   1   0.06  0.07  0.08  0.08  0.09  0.10  0.10  0.11  0.12  0.12
   2   0.13  0.14  0.14  0.15  0.16  0.16  0.17  0.18  0.18  0.19
   3   0.19  0.20  0.21  0.21  0.22  0.23  0.23  0.24  0.25  0.25
   4   0.26  0.27  0.27  0.28  0.29  0.29  0.30  0.31  0.31  0.32
   5   0.32  0.33  0.34  0.34  0.35  0.36  0.36  0.37  0.38  0.38
   6   0.39  0.40  0.40  0.41  0.42  0.42  0.43  0.44  0.44  0.45
   7   0.45  0.46  0.47  0.47  0.48  0.49  0.49  0.50  0.51  0.51
   8   0.52  0.53  0.53  0.54  0.55  0.55  0.56  0.57  0.57  0.58
   9   0.58  0.59  0.60  0.60  0.61  0.62  0.62  0.63  0.64  0.64
  10   0.65  0.66  0.66  0.67  0.68  0.68  0.69  0.70  0.70  0.71
```

Figure 5.5: Output from the *SalesTax* program

The WRITE statement located inside the inner FOR loop computes and displays the sales tax. This statement adds together the dollars and cents, and multiplies the sum by the tax rate.

You can build nested loops from any combination of loop structures, including FOR loops, WHILE loops, and REPEAT UNTIL loops. In the next section we'll look at Turbo Pascal's additional loops structures.

WHILE and REPEAT UNTIL Loops

Unlike the FOR loop, the WHILE and REPEAT UNTIL loops depend on an expressed condition to determine the duration of the looping process. There are also several important differences between these two kinds of loops:

- In a WHILE loop, you place the condition at the beginning of the loop, and the iterations continue as long as the condition is TRUE. Since the condition is evaluated before each iteration, a WHILE loop results in no iterations if the condition is FALSE at the outset.

- In REPEAT UNTIL loop, the condition goes at the end of the loop, and looping continues until the condition switches to TRUE. Since the condition is evaluated after each iteration, a REPEAT UNTIL loop always performs at least one iteration.

This variety of choices allows you to express loops in a form that suits a particular application. Let's examine the syntax of these two loops and look at some examples.

The WHILE Loop Structure

Here is the syntax of the WHILE loop:

WHILE *condition* DO
  statement;

If the loop block contains multiple statements, here is the general form:

```
WHILE condition DO

   BEGIN
      { statements that will be performed
         once for each iteration of the loop }
   END;
```

The *condition* is an expression that Turbo Pascal can evaluate as TRUE or FALSE. The repetition continues as long as *condition* is TRUE. At some point in time the action inside the loop normally switches *condition* to FALSE, and the looping stops.

For example, the following WHILE statement from the *CliList* program is designed to loop through the lines of text in an .HRS account file and find the sum of all the work-hour entries stored in the account:

```
WHILE NOT EOF (targetFile) DO
   BEGIN
      READLN (targetFile, chronInfoString, hours);
      total : = total + hours
   END;
```

The condition that controls this particular loop is, in effect, the program's progress through the disk file itself. Each time the program reads one line of the file (READLN), Pascal automatically gets ready to read the succeeding line during the next loop iteration. Inside the loop, the program increments a counter variable called *total* by the number of hours read from the file:

```
total : = total + hours
```

As long as there is still another line left to read, a built-in function named EOF ("end of file") gives a value of FALSE, and the expression

```
NOT EOF(targetFile)
```

is TRUE. This condition drives the looping process forward through the file. When Pascal finally encounters the end of the file, EOF returns a value of TRUE and *NOT EOF(targetFile)* gives a value of FALSE. This event stops the looping; the final value of *total* is thus the total number of hours stored in the file.

We'll learn more about the use of READLN and EOF for reading text files Chapter 11. For now, let's concentrate on the logic of the WHILE loop itself. We can paraphrase the action of this loop as follows:

```
WHILE the end of the file has not been found
  BEGIN
      Read a line of the file, including the value hours
      Increase the value of total by hours
END;
```

When the program encounters the end of the file, the looping stops, and the performance continues at the next statement.

The REPEAT UNTIL loop results in a similar kind of performance, as we'll see in the next section.

The REPEAT UNTIL Loop Structure

The UNTIL condition is located at the bottom of a repeating loop:

```
REPEAT
  { statements that are performed once
     for each iteration of the loop }
UNTIL condition
```

This loop structure always goes through one iteration before the condition is first evaluated, and continues its iterations as long as the condition is FALSE; repetition stops when the condition becomes TRUE. Multiple statements inside a REPEAT UNTIL loop do *not* require BEGIN and END markers. The reserved words REPEAT and UNTIL serve as the delimiters for statements inside the loop.

Earlier in this chapter we saw the controlling logical expression of a particular REPEAT UNTIL loop. The loop in question reads single keystrokes of user input and continues until the user presses either the space bar or the Escape key. Let's return to this discussion. Here is the entire loop:

```
REPEAT
   inChar : = READKEY
UNTIL (inChar = spaceBar) OR (inChar = escKey);
```

READKEY is a rather important built-in Turbo Pascal function, located in the CRT unit. The function waits for the user to press a key at the keyboard, and then returns the CHAR value of the key. Unlike the READ and READLN procedures, READKEY does not "echo" the input on the screen; if you want to display the user's input, you have to include a WRITE or WRITELN statement in your program after the READKEY function is called.

We'll be looking further into the behavior of READKEY in Chapter 7. Meanwhile, notice how the *CliList* program assigns the result of the function to the variable *inChar:*

```
inChar : = READKEY
```

Then the OR condition expressed in the UNTIL clause checks to see if the result is one of two expected keystrokes:

```
(inChar = spaceBar) OR (inChar = escKey)
```

Just before this REPEAT UNTIL loop takes control, the program displays a message on the screen with the following instructions:

Press the space bar when the printer is ready,
or press <Esc> to exit without printing.

Accordingly, the program uses the result of *inChar* to determine the subsequent action. Paraphrased, this REPEAT UNTIL loop performs as follows:

```
REPEAT
   Read a keystroke, and store it in inChar
UNTIL inChar contains either the space character
   or the character corresponding to the Escape key
```

Interestingly, the identifiers *spaceBar* and *escKey* are established as symbolic constants earlier in the program:

```
CONST
  spaceBar = ' ';
  escKey = #27;
```

Turbo Pascal allows you to use the # symbol in a very convenient notation for referring to ASCII code values. For example, in this particular CONST declaration the notation #27 refers to the character represented by the ASCII code number 27; this is the character corresponding to the Escape key.

Some programmers are wary about using loop structures that automatically perform the first iteration before evaluating the controlling condition. These programmers may prefer to rely on WHILE loops rather than REPEAT UNTIL loops for most repetition programming. Nonetheless, REPEAT UNTIL is appropriate as long as you reserve its use for situations in which you always want at least one iteration to be performed.

We have already seen several examples excerpted from the *CliList* program. But before we look at the entire program listing, we have an important preliminary task to perform. *CliList* uses an expanded version of the unit named *StrUnit*, which we began building in Chapter 4. Specifically, we have to add four new functions to this unit.

Adding New Functions to *StrUnit*

Expanding the contents of a unit is a straightforward process. You begin by loading the unit's original source file into the editor. You add declarations for the new routines into the INTERFACE section, and then enter the source code for the routines into the IMPLEMENTATION section. Finally, you have to recompile the unit to disk, creating a new version of the unit's .TPU file. Let's follow through these steps for expanding *StrUnit*.

The four functions we'll add to the unit are called *LowerCase*, *InitialCap*, *Spaces*, and *LeftAlign*. The purposes of these functions are as follows:

- *LowerCase* returns an all-lowercase version of its string argument.

- *InitialCap* converts the first letter of its argument to uppercase, and the remaining letters to lowercase.

- *Spaces* returns a string consisting of a specified number of spaces.

- *LeftAlign* left justifies its string argument in an output field that is a specified number of columns wide.

The *CliList* program uses all four of these functions, directly or indirectly, to format the text of its printed report. For example, the *InitialCap* function captitalizes the first letter of each account name. (This function in turn uses the *UpperCase* and *LowerCase* functions from *StrUnit*.) The *LeftAlign* function simplifies the task of producing aligned columns in the output. (*LeftAlign* in turn uses the *Spaces* function to produce its output field.)

When you have loaded the previous version of *StrUnit* into the editor, enter the following four declarations into the IMPLEMENTATION section:

```
FUNCTION LowerCase (inString: STRING): STRING;
FUNCTION InitialCap (inString: STRING): STRING;
FUNCTION Spaces (inLength: BYTE): STRING;
FUNCTION LeftAlign (inString: STRING; fieldLength: BYTE): STRING;
```

The function declarations must appear in this order, just after the last function that we previously placed in the unit, *UpperCase*.

Next scroll down to the current end of the IMPLEMENTATION section. Just below the source code for *UpperCase*, begin entering the code for the four new functions. Their source code appears in Figure 5.6. By the way, you'll find some interesting examples of loops and decision structures in the new *StrUnit* functions.

```
FUNCTION LowerCase;

   { The LowerCase function returns a lowercase
     version of the string argument it receives. }

   VAR
     i : INTEGER;
     targetChar, lowerChar: CHAR;
     outString : STRING;
     upperCaseLetters : SET OF CHAR;

   BEGIN    { LowerCase }
     upperCaseLetters := ['A'..'Z'];
     outString := '';
     FOR i := 1 TO LENGTH(inString) DO
       BEGIN
         targetChar := inString[i];
         IF (targetChar IN upperCaseLetters) THEN
           BEGIN
             lowerChar := CHR(ORD(targetChar) + 32);
             outString := outString + lowerChar;
           END
         ELSE
           outString := outString + targetChar
       END;

   LowerCase := outString
   END;     { LowerCase }


FUNCTION InitialCap;

   { The InitialCap capitalizes the intial letter of
     a string argument, and converts the remaining
     letters to lowercase. Uses the UpperCase and
     LowerCase functions. }

   VAR
     firstLetter, remainingLetters: STRING;

   BEGIN    { InitialCap }
     firstLetter := UpperCase(inString[1]);
     remainingLetters :=
       LowerCase(COPY (inString, 2, LENGTH(inString) - 1));
     InitialCap := firstLetter + remainingLetters
   END;     { InitialCap }


FUNCTION Spaces;

   { The Spaces function returns a string of
     spaces. The inLength argument specifies the
     length of the resulting string. }

   VAR
     i: BYTE;
     tempSpace: STRING;

   BEGIN    { Spaces }
     tempSpace := '';
     FOR i := 1 TO inLength DO
       tempSpace := tempSpace + ' ';
     Spaces := tempSpace
   END;     { Spaces }
```

Figure 5.6: Adding new functions to *StrUnit*

```
FUNCTION LeftAlign;

  { The LeftAlign function returns the
    inString argument, left justified in a
    field of fieldLength columns. }

  VAR
    spacesToAdd: BYTE;

  BEGIN    { LeftAlign }
    spacesToAdd := fieldLength - LENGTH (inString);
    LeftAlign := inString + Spaces (spacesToAdd)
  END;     { LeftAlign }
```

Figure 5.6: Adding new functions to *StrUnit* (continued)

Do not disturb the final END marker on the last line of the unit. When you have finished entering the source code, save the new version of the unit to disk. Then pull down the Compile menu, toggle the Destination option to its Disk setting, and compile the unit. *StrUnit* is now ready for its role in the *CliList* program.

The Listing of the *CliList* Program

CliList appears in Figure 5.7. We have already examined many details of this program; as an overview, here are brief descriptions of the program's various routines:

- The *GetFiles* procedure investigates the current directory and creates a list of all the .HRS files. As we discussed at the beginning of this chapter, the client file names are stored in the *clientFiles* array.

- The *SortClientFiles* procedure alphabetizes the list of client names before the report is printed.

- The *PrintClientList* procedure controls the printing of the report. This procedure has three local routines that perform parts of the output task:

    - The *TotalAccount* function finds the total billable hours recorded in each file. (We examined a WHILE loop from this function.)

- The *ClientStatus* function returns a string of one, two, or three asterisks, indicating the status of a given client. (We discussed the CASE structure from this routine.)

- The *PrintExplanations* procedure prints a key at the bottom of the report, explaining the meaning of the status column.

As you look through the program listing and prepare to create your own working copy of it in the Turbo Pascal editor, you should review the various decision structures and loops that we have seen in this

```
PROGRAM CliList;

  { The CliList program prints a list of all the .HRS
    client files in the current directory, along with
    the total number of hours billed to each account.
    The program also prints the status of each account:
    current, recent, or inactive. }

USES CRT, DOS, PRINTER, StrUnit;

  { Establish the heap size, for successful use of EXEC: }
  {$M 16384, 0, 0}

CONST
  maxFiles = 100;

TYPE
  fileRange   = 1..maxFiles;
  clientArray = ARRAY [fileRange] OF STRING;

VAR
  clientFiles: clientArray;    { array of client names }
  listLength,                  { number of client names }
  i:           BYTE;
  dirString:   STRING;         { current directory identifier }


PROCEDURE GetFiles (VAR numberOfFiles: BYTE);

  { The GetFiles procedure creates an .HRS directory
    file and reads the file names into the global
    clientFiles array. GetFiles also passes back a
    BYTE value representing the number of files in
    the variable parameter numberOfFiles. }

  CONST
    fileName = 'HRSDIR.TXT';   { temporary directory file }

  VAR
    dirFile:      TEXT;
    recordNumber,
    extensionPos,
    firstSpace:   BYTE;
    dirLine:      STRING[40];
    clientName:   STRING;
```

Figure 5.7: The listing of the *CliList* program

```
      BEGIN    { GetFiles }

        { Use the EXEC command to store the list of .HRS
          file names in the temporary directory file. }

        EXEC ('\COMMAND.COM', '/C DIR *.HRS > ' + fileName);

        { Open the directory file, and prepare to read it. }

        ASSIGN (dirFile, fileName);
        RESET (dirFile);
        recordNumber := 0;

        { Read the file one line at a time, and store the
          base name of each .HRS file in the clientFiles array. }

        WHILE NOT EOF(dirFile) DO
          BEGIN
            READLN (dirFile, dirLine);
            extensionPos := POS (' HRS ', dirLine);
            IF extensionPos <> 0 THEN
              BEGIN
                INC (recordNumber);
                firstSpace := POS (' ', dirLine);
                clientName := COPY (dirLine, 1, firstSpace - 1);
                clientFiles[recordNumber] := clientName;
              END
          END;

        CLOSE (dirFile);

        { Return the number of file names in the
          variable parameter numberOfFiles. }

        numberOfFiles := recordNumber

      END;    { GetFiles }


    PROCEDURE SortClientFiles (sortLength: BYTE);

      { The SortClientFiles procedure uses the Shell sort
        algorithm to alphabetize the list of client names,
        stored in the global clientFiles array. }

      VAR
        listJump, i, j: BYTE;
        sortComplete: BOOLEAN;
        saveName: STRING;

      BEGIN    { SortClientFiles }

        listJump := 1;
        WHILE listJump <= sortLength DO
          listJump := listJump * 2;

        WHILE listJump > 1 DO
          BEGIN
            listJump := (listJump - 1) DIV 2;
            REPEAT
              sortComplete := TRUE;
```

Figure 5.7: The listing of the *CliList* program (continued)

```
                    FOR j := 1 TO sortLength - listJump DO
                      BEGIN
                        i := j + listJump;
                        IF clientFiles[j] > clientFiles[i] THEN
                          BEGIN
                            saveName := clientFiles[j];
                            clientFiles[j] := clientFiles[i];
                            clientFiles[i] := saveName;
                            sortComplete := FALSE
                          END
                      END
                  UNTIL sortComplete
              END
    END;    { SortClientFiles }



PROCEDURE PrintClientList (printLength: BYTE);

  { The PrintClientList procedure prints the sorted
    list of client names, along with two additional
    columns of information: the total work hours
    recorded in each account and the status of the
    account. }

  CONST
    spaceBar = ' ';
    escKey   = #27;
    formFeed = #12;

  VAR
    i, j:       BYTE;
    clientFile: STRING;
    lastEntry:  INTEGER;
    inChar:     CHAR;


  FUNCTION TotalAccount (targetFileName: STRING;
                         VAR lastDate:   INTEGER): REAL;

    { The TotalAccount function opens a specified account
      file, reads each entry, and computes the total number
      of work hours currently recorded in the file. This
      total is returned as the REAL result of the function. }

    CONST
      yearColumn = 16;
      yearLength = 4;

    VAR
      total,
      hours:         REAL;
      targetFile:    TEXT;
      chronInfoString: STRING[29];
      code:          INTEGER;

    BEGIN    { TotalAccount }

      total := 0.0;

      { Open the file for reading. }

      ASSIGN (targetFile, targetFileName);
      RESET (targetFile);
```

Figure 5.7: The listing of the *CliList* program (continued)

```
        { Read each entry in the file, and compute
          the total number of recorded hours. }

        WHILE NOT EOF(targetFile) DO
          BEGIN
            READLN (targetFile, chronInfoString, hours);
            total := total + hours
          END;

        CLOSE (targetFile);

        { Find the date of the last entry in the file,
          and return the four-digit year in the variable
          parameter lastDate. }

        chronInfoString :=
          COPY (chronInfoString, yearColumn, yearLength);
        VAL (chronInfoString, lastDate, code);

        TotalAccount := total

     END;    { TotalAccount }


FUNCTION ClientStatus (lastYear: INTEGER): STRING;

   { The ClientStatus function returns a string of
     asterisks, representing a client's status:

          ***  an active client
          **   a recent client
          *    an inactive client }

   BEGIN    { ClientStatus }

     CASE lastYear OF

        1987..1988:
          ClientStatus := '***';

        1985..1986:
          ClientStatus := '**';

        1980..1984:
          ClientStatus := '*';


        ELSE
          ClientStatus := ''

     END    { CASE lastYear }

   END;    { ClientStatus }


PROCEDURE PrintExplanations;

   { The PrintExplanations procedure prints notes at
     the bottom of the report, explaining the meaning
     of the status column. }
```

Figure 5.7: The listing of the *CliList* program (continued)

```
      BEGIN     { PrintExplanations }

         WRITELN (LST);
         WRITELN (LST, StringOfChars ('-', 40));
         WRITELN (LST);
         WRITELN (LST, '     *** Current client account.');
         WRITELN (LST, '     **  Recent account.');
         WRITELN (LST, '     *   Inactive account.')

      END;     { PrintExplanations }


   BEGIN     { PrintClientList }

      { Delay the start of printing until the user
        presses the space bar to signal that the
        printer is ready or the Escape key to quit. }

      WRITELN ('Press the space bar when the printer is ready, ');
      WRITE   ('or press <Esc> to exit without printing. ');
      REPEAT
        inChar := READKEY
      UNTIL (inChar = spaceBar) OR (inChar = escKey);

      WRITELN;

      IF inChar = ' ' THEN
         BEGIN
            WRITELN (LST, 'Client Name    Billable Hours   Status');
            WRITELN (LST, '------ ----     -------- -----    ------');
            WRITELN (LST);

            { Print each detail line of the output table. }

            FOR i := 1 TO printLength DO
               BEGIN
                  WRITE (LST,
                    LeftAlign (InitialCap (clientFiles[i]), 18));
                  clientFile := clientFiles[i] + '.HRS';
                  WRITE (LST, TotalAccount(clientFile, lastEntry):7:2);
                  WRITELN (LST, Spaces(9), ClientStatus (lastEntry))
               END;

            PrintExplanations;

            { Print a form-feed character. }

            WRITELN (LST, formFeed)
         END

   END;     { PrintClientList }

BEGIN     { CliList }

   CLRSCR;
   WRITELN ('Print a list of client files.');
   WRITELN ('----- - ---- -- ------ ------');
   WRITELN;

   { GetFiles reads the list of client names into
     the global clientFiles array. Then SortClientFiles
     sorts the list, and PrintClientList creates the
     printed report. }

   GetFiles (listLength);
```

Figure 5.7: The listing of the *CliList* program (continued)

```
   IF listLength > 0 THEN
      BEGIN
         SortClientFiles (listLength);
         PrintClientList (listLength);
      END
   ELSE
      BEGIN
         WRITELN;
         WRITELN ('No .HRS files are stored in');
         WRITE ('this directory: ');
         GETDIR (0, dirString);
         WRITELN (dirString)
      END
END.    { CliList }
```

Figure 5.7: The listing of the *CliList* program (continued)

chapter. As a final exercise with these structures, we'll take a look at this program's sorting routine.

The *SortClientFiles* Procedure

Among the several sorting algorithms commonly used by Pascal programmers, the Shell sort is one of the fastest and most efficient, but not necessarily the easiest to understand. Like other sorting procedures, the algorithm concentrates on a list of data values, and the goal is to rearrange the values in ascending or descending order.

The essential approach of the Shell sort is to begin by comparing and rearranging pairs of values that are a specified "jump" distance away from each other in the list. When all values at a given distance are in the correct order, the procedure decreases the jump by half and repeats the rearranging process. When the jump distance has decreased to 1 and the procedure directs its attention to comparing adjacent values in the list, the sorting process is almost complete. In short, this approach attempts to achieve the sort in as few iterations through the list as possible.

The *SortClientFiles* procedure in the *CliList* program rearranges the global *clientFiles* array within a sequence of three nested loops. The outermost WHILE loop controls the progressively decreasing jump distances:

```
WHILE listJump > 1 DO
```

Nested inside this structure is a REPEAT UNTIL loop that makes sure all the pairs of values at a given jump distance are in the right order:

```
REPEAT
  { ... }
UNTIL sortComplete
```

The innermost repetition structure is a FOR loop that actually compares pairs of elements that are located a given jump distance away from each other:

```
FOR j : = 1 TO sortLength  –  listJump DO
```

Inside this innermost loop is an IF statement that compares a given pair of account names—indexed by *i* and *j*, respectively —to see whether they are in the correct alphabetical order:

```
IF clientFiles[j] > clientFiles[i] THEN
```

For a pair of names that is out of order, the following three assignment statements perform the swap:

```
saveName : = clientFiles[j];
clientFiles[j] : = clientFiles[i];
clientFiles[i] : = saveName;
```

The *SortClientFiles* procedure is worth a closer look. Perhaps the best way to understand the Shell sort algorithm is to "walk through" the individual steps that the routine takes to sort an actual list of values. This exercise will also give you clearer insight into the relationship between the nested loop structures and the *clientFiles* array.

One additional note about *CliList:* Like the *Hours* program and the *BillTime* program, *CliList* uses Turbo Pascal's built-in EXEC procedure (located in the DOS unit) to perform a DOS command during a performance. In this case the command is

```
EXEC ('\COMMAND.COM', '/C DIR *.HRS > ' + fileName);
```

The *fileName* identifier is a string constant that contains the file name
HRSDIR.TXT. As a result, this EXEC command performs the following DOS command:

```
DIR *.HRS > HRSDIR.TXT
```

This creates the text file HRSDIR.TXT, and sends a specific directory
listing (*.HRS) to the file. The *CliList* program later reads this file to
formulate the list of client names.

In order for the EXEC command to be successful, two conditions
must be met. First, Pascal must be able locate the DOS file COM-
MAND.COM in the default root directory. Second, the necessary
heap space must be explicitly allocated in the program. Since this program does not use the heap at all, the following $M compiler directive
appears at the top of the program to specify zero bytes for the heap:

```
{$M 16384, 0, 0}
```

Look back at Chapter 2 for additional information about the $M direc-
tive. We'll study the EXEC command more formally in Chapter 7, and
discuss the heap in greater detail in Chapter 8.

Summary

The IF and SELECT CASE structures control decision-making
processes in Turbo Pascal programs. Decisions are based on logical
values and expressions that Pascal evaluates as either true or false.
You can build complex and compound logical expressions using the
relational operators (= , < , < = , > , > = , < >) and the logical operators (AND, OR, NOT, XOR, EQV, IMP).

We categorize loop structures by the mechanism that determines the
looping process. A FOR loop includes a control variable, and specifies
the range of values that the variable will take during the looping.
WHILE and REPEAT UNTIL loops, on the other hand, are controlled by an expressed condition. In a WHILE loop, the iterations
continue while the condition is true. In a REPEAT UNTIL loop, the
repetition process stops when the condition becomes true.

Exploiting the powerful relationship between loop structures and arrays, a program can perform complex data-processing tasks in very concise and efficient blocks of code. We will pursue this topic in the next chapter.

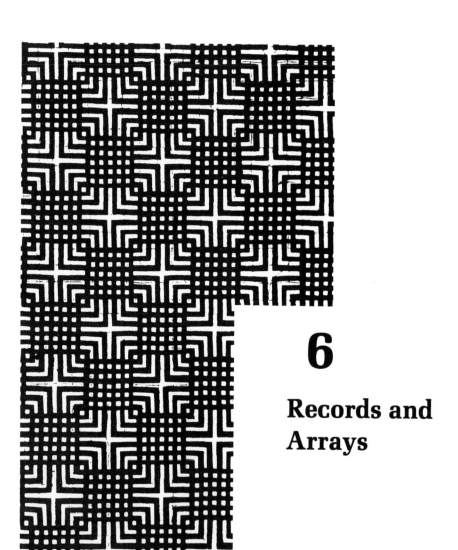

C H A P T E R

6

Records and Arrays

In this chapter we'll discuss two important types of data structures, called *records* and *arrays*. A record is a user-defined structure that represents an assortment of individual data values. The elements of a record are called *fields;* each field in a given record is defined by its own name and type. An array is a data structure that represents lists or tables of values under a single variable name. Each element of an array belongs to the same type, although you can define arrays of any type, including arrays of records.

You use TYPE and VAR declarations to define both record and array structures. A record has its own name, along with any number of named fields. An array is defined by several characteristics: an identifier, the type of data the array will hold, the number of *dimensions* it will have, and a range representing the number of values in each dimension.

Several Turbo Pascal control structures are ideally designed for working with records and arrays. For example, this chapter introduces the WITH statement, which simplifies access to record structures in Turbo Pascal. Furthermore, programs that employ arrays to store data frequently use FOR loop structures to create and manage those arrays.

These data structures and control structures are all illustrated in this chapter's sample program. The program is called *CliAddr* and is designed as an addition to our expanding library of programs for the client billable-time application. This menu-driven program creates and manages a file of client addresses. Specifically, the program allows you to append addresses to the file at any time and generate printed lists from the data—address lists and phone directories, arranged in an order that suits your particular purpose.

Before we examine the use of records and arrays, let's investigate the performance of the *CliAddr* program.

The *CliAddr* Program

A performance of *CliAddr* is controlled via a recurring menu of activities. When you first run the program, the menu appears on the screen as follows:

```
Client Address Manager

_____  _____  _____
Add an address.
Create an address directory.
Print a phone directory.
Quit.

* * Menu choice (A C P Q) —> _
```

During a given session with the program, you can select any sequence of menu options. To select an option you simply press the key corresponding to the first letter of the option: A, C, P, or Q. The program ignores any other keystrokes while the menu is displayed on the screen.

The first option allows you add a new client address to the current file. The second and third options print sorted lists of information from this file. The fourth option ends the program performance. After you complete a given activity, the menu returns to the screen.

CliAddr works with a text file named ADDRLIST.TXT. When you run the program for the first time and begin entering addresses, this file is created on disk. Until you enter at least one address, the second and third menu options are inactive. Subsequent performances may append new records to the file, or simply read the file to create address lists and phone directories.

By the way, ADDRLIST.TXT is a text file, from which the program accesses data sequentially. The text file format is suitable for this relatively simple application, because *CliAddr* reads the entire file at once and keeps all addresses in memory during a given program performance. Other, more complex, database applications are designed to read or revise individual records one at a time. Applications that require access to specific records in a database file usually create the file in a distinct format, which allows *random access* to the file. We'll discuss the differences between sequential-access and random-access files in Chapters 11 and 12.

Let's examine the three main activities of the *CliAddr* program. When you select the first menu option, *Add an address*, the program conducts an input dialog to elicit the nine items of information required for a given client-address record. Here is an example of this dialog, with the sample entry displayed in boldface type:

Enter a client address record:

____ _ ____ _____ ____

Name of client: **XYZ Corporation**
Reference number: **123**
Street address: **907 Maple Drive**
City: **Los Angeles**
USA or Foreign? (U   F): **U**
State: **CA**
Zip Code: **90047**
Phone number: **(213) 777-1234**
Head office? (Y   N): **Y**

After prompting you for the client's name, reference number, address, and city, the program asks you whether the client is located in the United States or in a foreign country. You respond by pressing the U or F key, respectively. (Any other keystroke is ignored; the prompt remains on the screen until you provide one of the two valid answers.) If you indicate that this is a foreign client, the program then asks you for a different set of information:

USA or Foreign? (U   F): **F**
State or province: **Ontario**

Country: **Canada**
Phone number: **(416) 222-3333**
Head office? (Y   N): **Y**

In addition to the client's name, address, and phone number, the program elicits a reference number, which can be any BYTE value (in the range 0 to 255). You can make use of this number in any way you like; for example, the number might be a code you devise to represent the category of work you do for the client. Finally, the program also gives you a chance to indicate whether a given address record is a head office or a branch office.

When you complete an address entry, the program gives you the chance either to save or to abandon the record:

Save this address? (Y   N) _

If you answer this question affirmatively, the program appends the address record to the end of the ADDRLIST.TXT file. If you change your mind about saving the record—for example, if you find an error in the data entry—you press the N key in response to this question, and the program abandons your record.

In either event, the program's main menu subsequently returns to the screen. The second option on the menu prints an address list containing all the records stored in the ADDRLIST.TXT file. The list is printed in a six-line label-style format. (In fact, you can use this option to print the addresses on tractor-fed strips of gummed labels.) Figure 6.1 shows an example of an address list produced by this option. Notice that each address includes a reference number, and an abbreviated code: H stands for head office, and B stands for branch office.

Before producing such a list, the program asks you to specify the order in which the addresses should be arranged. A new selection of options appears on the screen, as follows:

Print an address list.

——— —— ——— ——

Sort by:
   1. Names
   2. Reference numbers

Select 1 or 2 —>

Depending on your response to this prompt, the program sorts the address list alphabetically by the clients' names or numerically by the reference numbers. For example, you can see that the list in Figure 6.1 is arranged alphabetically.

Conveniently, the program displays the following message before printing the list:

<Space Bar> to print. <Escape> to return to menu.

The message remains on the screen until you press either the space bar to start the printing or the Esc key to abort the operation. In either event, the program returns you to the recurring menu.

```
Client Address Directory
------ ------- ---------

Airport Management Corp.          241 H
88 Airport Drive
Oliver, Ontario CANADA
(416) 444-5555


Alternate Styles Clothing Shop    201 H
55 C Mountain Mall
Los Angeles, CA 90251
(213) 888-7689


City Hall Manager                  32 H
88 Central Plaza
Melvin, CA 92111
(213) 888-6566


Jones and Madson                  130 B
6679 Inner Circle
Portland, OR 97201
(503) 909-0909


Maison Verte                       95 B
6, Rue du Village
Paris, 28000 FRANCE
(1) 42.22.12.79


Miles Market Management, Inc.       4 H
98 Oak Avenue
San Francisco, CA 94110
(415) 899-9988


Nowling and Smith, Inc.           151 B
5548 Lois Lane
Juniper, OR 97300
(503) 666-1131
```

Figure 6.1: An address directory produced by *CliAddr*

```
        Public Works Department          88 H
        66 85th Street
        El Cerrito, CA 94810
        (415) 979-9879


        Secret Whispers Flower Shop      199 H
        987 B Ocean View Mall


        Smallton and Jones, Inc.         16 H
        599 Bridge Street
        Berkeley, CA 94710
        (415) 331-9999


        XYZ Corporation                  123 B
        907 Maple Drive
        Los Angeles, CA 90047
        (213) 777-1234
```

Figure 6.1: An address directory produced by *CliAddr* (continued)

The third menu option prints a phone directory containing client names and phone numbers from the ADDRLIST.TXT file. Figure 6.2 shows an example of this directory. Again, the program gives you the opportunity to specify the order in which the phone list will be arranged. The sample output in Figure 6.2 is arranged by reference numbers.

The sorting process in this program occurs while the entire file of client addresses is stored in the computer's memory. In general, the *CliAddr* program is designed to handle a relatively small file of records that are assumed to remain constant over time; as you may have noted, the program offers no options for deleting or revising address records that are stored in the file. (In Chapter 12 we'll outline programming techniques for handling larger and more demanding database tasks.)

As we study the use of records and arrays in the Turbo Pascal language, we'll examine brief passages from the *CliAddr* program. Then, at the end of this chapter, we'll look at the entire listing.

Record Structures

A record is a collection of individual data values called fields. A record variable is thus a single identifier representing all of the field

```
Client Phone Directory
------ ----- ---------

Client                          Reference        Phone

Miles Market Management, Inc.        4        (415) 899-9988
Smallton and Jones, Inc.            16        (415) 331-9999
City Hall Manager                   32        (213) 888-6566
Public Works Department             88        (415) 979-9879
Maison Verte                        95        (1) 42.22.12.79
XYZ Corporation                    123        (213) 777-1234
Jones and Madson                   130        (503) 909-0909
Nowling and Smith, Inc.            151        (503) 666-1131
Secret Whispers Flower Shop        199        (415) 231-2131
Alternate Styles Clothing Shop     201        (213) 888-7689
Airport Management Corp.           241        (416) 444-5555
```

Figure 6.2: A phone list produced by *CliAddr*

values in a given record. Perhaps the most important characteristic of a record is that the various named fields can belong to different data types.

There are two ways to define a record variable:

- First define the record structure in a TYPE declaration, then declare the variable itself in a subsequent VAR statement.

- Define both the record structure and the variable at once in a VAR statement.

The first of these techniques is probably clearer and more frequently used, but we'll explore both techniques in this section.

Defining Record Types and Declaring Record Variables

We can represent the general form of a record-type declaration as follows:

```
TYPE
  recordType = RECORD
    fieldName1: fieldType1;
    fieldName2: fieldType2;
    fieldName3: fieldType3
    {and so on ... }
  END;
```

In this sequence, the record structure is identified as a user-defined type, *recordType*. A list of field definitions follows the reserved word RECORD. Each field in the list has its own name (*fieldName1*, *fieldName2*, and so on) and its own defined data type. Fields may belong to any standard type or user-defined type, and there is no practical limit to the number of fields in a record structure. Notice that the end of the record definition in the TYPE statement is marked by the reserved word END. Following this type definition, you can declare one or more variables belonging to the user-defined record type:

```
VAR
  recordVar: recordType;
```

Let's start with a simple example: an abbreviated version of the address record we'll find in the *CliAddr* program. The following sequence defines a record type, *addressRecord*, containing six fields, and then a record variable, *address*, belonging to the user-defined record type:

```
TYPE
  addressRecord = RECORD
    name:        STRING[30];
    refNo:       BYTE;
    headOffice:  BOOLEAN;
    street:      STRING[30];
    city:        STRING[20];
    state:       STRING[2]
  END;

VAR
  address: addressRecord;
```

Notice that the fields of the record belong to a variety of types: a BYTE value (for the reference number), a BOOLEAN value (indicating head office or branch office), and four strings of varying lengths. The record variable *address* is declared to be an *addressRecord*-type value. The variable can thus store a complete record at a time, consisting of six different values.

Alternatively, in a program that does not need to define any other record variables of this type, the *address* variable declaration can be handled all at once in a single VAR statement:

```
VAR
    address:    RECORD
       name:       STRING[30];
       refNo:      BYTE;
       headOffice: BOOLEAN;
       street:     STRING[30];
       city:       STRING[20];
       state:      STRING[2]
    END;
```

Either way you declare the variable, you use the same notation for identifying individual field values. We'll examine this notation next.

Working with Field Values

The field-value notation has two parts, as shown here in its general form:

recordVar.fieldName

The name of the record variable comes first, followed by an individual field name. The two parts are separated by a period. For example, here are the identifiers for the six defined fields in the *address* record variable:

address.name

address.refNo

address.headOffice

address.street

address.city

address.state

A program can treat a field identifier as a variable and use it in any statement that requires a variable. For instance, consider this passage:

```
WRITE ('Enter the client''s name:   ');
READLN (address.name);
```

The READLN statement accepts a string value from the keyboard, and stores the value in the field variable *address.name*.

The two-part notation for identifying each field of a record sometimes becomes a bit tedious, especially in passages that refer to many different fields:

```
WRITE ('Enter the client''s name:   ');
READLN (address.name);
WRITE ('Enter the street address:   ');
READLN (address.street);
WRITE ('Enter the city:   ');
READLN (address.city);
WRITE ('Enter the state:   ');
READLN (address.state);
WRITE ('Enter the reference number:   ');
READLN (address.refNo)
```

Fortunately, Turbo Pascal has a statement that allows you to abbreviate the field identifiers used inside a given block of commands. This statement is WITH; its general syntax is as follows:

```
WITH recordVar DO

    BEGIN
      { statements referring to
      the fields of recordVar }
    END;
```

The WITH statement identifies a particular record variable by name; inside the subsequent block of statements, you can refer to the fields of this record by the field name alone.

For example, consider this revised version of the input routine for the fields of the *address* record:

```
WITH address DO
  BEGIN
    WRITE ('Enter the client''s name:   ');
    READLN (name);
    WRITE ('Enter the street address:   ');
    READLN (street);
```

```
            WRITE ('Enter the city:    ');
            READLN (city);
            WRITE ('Enter the state:    ');
            READLN (state);
            WRITE ('Enter the reference number:    ');
            READLN (refNo)
        END
```

Inside the WITH block, you refer to the fields simply as *name*, *street*, *city*, *state*, and *refno*, rather than their full two-part names. The result of these statements is exactly the same as in the earlier example. The WITH structure simply shortens the notation and reduces the amount of typing you have to do when you enter the program into the editor.

Note that you can also perform operations on an entire record at a time, without referring to the individual fields in the record. For example, let's say you have defined two record variables of type *addressRecord*:

```
VAR
    address,
    tempAddress: addressRecord;
```

Your program can assign an entire record from one variable to another with the following statement:

```
tempAddress : = address
```

This single assignment statement copies all the field values currently stored in the *address* record into the *tempAddress* record.

Finally, Turbo Pascal supports an advanced record structure called a *variant*. We'll examine this feature in the next section.

Variant Fields

Real-life applications sometimes require flexible data structures. A fixed list of fields may not always satisfy the requirements of a given set of data. Accordingly, you may want to define a record structure containing some fields that vary according to the situation. Every record belonging to such a type contains a combination of fixed fields and selected *variant fields*.

For example, we have already seen that the *CliAddr* program allows for two varying record structures: addresses in the United States and foreign addresses. For an American address, the program elicits the state name and the zip code. In contrast, a foreign address includes a province or state name, along with the name of the country. The *CliAddr* program needs a single record structure that can accommodate this variation.

The general syntax for defining a record structure with variants is as follows:

```
TYPE
  recordType = RECORD
    fixedField: fieldType;
    fixedField: fieldType;
    fixedField: fieldType;
    {and so on... }

    CASE   tagField: fieldType OF
      constantValue1:
        (variantField: fieldType;
        variantField: fieldType;
        {and so on... } );
      constantValue2:
        (variantField: fieldType;
        variantField: fieldType;
        {and so on} );

      {constantValue... }
  END;
```

As you can see, the format of this definition is in some ways parallel to the CASE decision statement that we examined in Chapter 5. In a RECORD definition, the CASE clause defines a special *tag field*, which is actually one of the fixed fields of the record. In a given record value, the data item stored in the tag field is used to select one of several alternative lists of fields for structuring the remainder of the record.

To see how this works, let's look at the actual *addressRecord* structure defined in the *CliAddr* program:

```
TYPE
  addressRecord = RECORD
    name:         STRING[30];
```

```
        phone:          STRING[20];
        refNo:          BYTE;
        headOffice:     BOOLEAN;

        street:         STRING[30];
        city:           STRING[20];

        CASE usa:       BOOLEAN OF
          TRUE:
            (state:     STRING[2];
             zip:       STRING[5]);
          FALSE:
            (otherLoc,
             country:   STRING[15])
    END;
```

The first six fields in this record are fixed fields, defined for every record value. After these fields, the CASE clause defines a BOOLEAN tag field named *usa*. A record that stores a value of TRUE in this tag field will have the two additional fields *state* and *zip*. Alternatively, if the tag field has a value of FALSE, the final fields will be *otherLoc* and *country*.

Notice the syntax of the variant field lists. The constant value that represents a given list is followed by a colon; then the subsequent field list is enclosed in parentheses. In effect, this structure allows for two different field lists in a record belonging to the *addressRecord* type. Let's say, for example, that you define an *addressRecord* variable named *address*. Here is the complete field list for a record that contains a value of TRUE in *address.usa:*

address.name

address.phone

address.refNo

address.headOffice

address.street

address.city

address.usa

address.state

address.zip

On the other hand, if *address.usa* is FALSE, this is the field list:

address.name

address.phone

address.refNo

address.headOffice

address.street

address.city

address.usa

address.otherLoc

address.country

The notation for identifying variant fields is the same as for fixed fields. Furthermore, you can use a WITH statement to abbreviate the names of both fixed and variant fields. For example, here is the passage from *CliAddr* that sends a given address to the printer:

```
WITH addresses[i] DO
  BEGIN
    WRITE (LST, LeftAlign (name, 35), refNo:3);
    IF headOffice THEN
      WRITELN (LST, '    H')
    ELSE
      WRITELN (LST, '    B');
    WRITELN (LST, street);
    WRITE (LST, city, ', ');
    IF usa THEN
      WRITELN (LST, UpperCase (state), '    ', zip)
    ELSE
      WRITELN (LST, otherLoc, '    ', UpperCase (country));
    WRITELN (LST, phone);
    WRITELN (LST); WRITELN (LST)
  END
```

Notice the IF statement near the end of this passage; the statement uses the value of *usa* to decide whether to print the *state* and *zip* fields or the *otherLoc* and *country* fields.

The *CliAddr* program uses an *array* structure to store the entire file of address records in memory during a performance. We'll study arrays in the next section.

Arrays

The TYPE and VAR statements establish the characteristics of array variables in a Turbo Pascal program. As we briefly discussed at the beginning of this chapter, the definition of an array establishes four characteristics:

- The name of the array

- The type of values the array will store

- The number of dimensions in the array

- The range representing the length of each dimension

The location for storing one particular value in an array is called an *element* of the array. The number of elements in an array depends on the number of dimensions and the length of each dimension. Let's look at the syntax for defining arrays.

Defining Array Types and Declaring Array Variables

The typical format for defining a one-dimensional array variable is as follows:

```
TYPE
    arrayType = ARRAY [dimensionRange] OF valueType;

VAR
    arrayVar: arrayType;
```

The TYPE statement defines an array type, and the VAR statement declares an array variable belonging to the type. As with records, you can also use VAR alone to define an array variable:

```
VAR
  arrayVar: ARRAY [dimensionRange] OF valueType;
```

The *valueType* of the array is any standard type or user-defined type. Unlike a record structure, an array contains elements belonging to a single defined type.

The *dimensionRange* argument is an ordinal type, or, more typically, a subrange of an ordinal type. This type defines the *indexes* (or *subscripts*) by which you will access individual values from the array. For example, consider the following array definition, which defines a one-dimensional array variable named *numList:*

```
TYPE
  numArrayType = ARRAY [1..100] OF REAL;

VAR
  numList: numArrayType;
```

The TYPE statement defines a one-dimensional array type, with an integer index that ranges from 1 to 100. The array *numList* can therefore store a hundred REAL-type values. We represent the names of individual elements in this array by placing a single integer value in square brackets just after the array name, as follows:

```
numList[1]
numList[2]
numList[3]
...
numList[100]
```

Arrays in Pascal are always *static*. This means that the allocated length and dimensions of an array like *numList* are fixed at compile time and cannot be redefined during a program performance. (Some versions of the Basic language allow you to create *dynamic arrays*, with lengths that may be changed during performance time. Pascal does not support dynamic arrays; however, in Chapter 8 we'll study a dynamic Pascal data type called a *pointer*.)

While the most common index type for an array is an integer (SHORTINT, BYTE, INTEGER, or WORD), Pascal also allows other ordinal types to serve as indexes into arrays, including CHAR, BOOLEAN, and enumerated types. In this chapter we'll work exclusively with arrays that are indexed by integer types, but in Chapter 7 we'll see some examples of arrays indexed by other ordinal types.

To define a multidimensional array, you specify more than one *dimensionRange* between square brackets after the reserved word ARRAY; for example, here is the general form for defining a two-dimensional array:

```
TYPE
  arrayType = ARRAY [dimensionRange1, dimensionRange2] OF
    valueType;

VAR
  arrayVar: arrayType;
```

In visual terms, a *one-dimensional* array stores a *list* of values and a two-dimensional array stores a *table* of data, with rows and columns of values. Going further, a *three-dimensional* array is a structure that contains "layers" of two-dimensional tables. In practice, programmers seldom use arrays containing more than three dimensions. But if an application does require a more complex data structure, Pascal allows multidimensional arrays to the extent that there is memory available for them.

Let's look at a program exercise that uses a two-dimensional array to store a table of numbers. You might recall the *SalesTax* program that we studied as an illustration of FOR loops in Chapter 5. *SalesTax* displayed a table of sales tax amounts on the screen. The *SalesTbl* program, shown in Figure 6.3, produces a similar table, but saves it in a two-dimensional array structure.

The declarations at the top of the *SalesTbl* program set up a two-dimensional global array named *taxTable:*

```
CONST
  taxRate    = 0.065;
  maxDollars = 10;
```

```
PROGRAM SalesTbl;

  { This program creates a table of sales tax amounts,
    and stores the table in a two-dimensional array. }
  CONST
    taxRate    = 0.065;        { the local sales tax rate }
    maxDollars = 10;           { the top dollar amount in the table }

  TYPE
    taxArrayType = ARRAY [0..maxDollars, 0..99] OF REAL;

  VAR
    taxTable : taxArrayType;


  PROCEDURE FillTaxTable;

    VAR
      cents,                     { the FOR-loop control variables }
      dollars  : BYTE;

    BEGIN   { FillTaxTable }

      FOR dollars := 0 TO maxDollars DO
        FOR cents := 0 to 99 DO
          taxTable [dollars, cents] :=
            (dollars + cents/100) * taxRate

    END;    { FillTaxTable }


  BEGIN   { SalesTbl }

    FillTaxTable;
    WRITELN ('Sales tax on $5.40 is ', taxTable [5, 40] :4:2);
    WRITELN ('Sales tax on $0.85 is ', taxTable [0][85] :4:2);
    WRITELN ('Sales tax on $9.53 is ', taxTable [9, 53] :4:2);

  END.    { SalesTbl }
```

Figure 6.3: A two-dimensional array used to store a table of values

```
TYPE
  taxArrayType = ARRAY [0..maxDollars, 0..99] OF REAL;

VAR
  taxTable : taxArrayType;
```

The first dimension of *taxTable* has a length of 11 elements, with an index range from 0 to 10. The second dimension has a length of 100 elements, with an index range from 0 to 99. The array is thus designed to store a table of up to 1100 real numbers.

To identify any one of the elements in this table, write the array name along with a pair of numeric indexes enclosed in square brackets. The indexes specify the location of one particular element in the array. For example, we might represent the range of elements of the *taxTable* array as follows:

taxTable[0, 0]	taxTable[0, 1]	...	taxTable[0, 99]
taxTable[1, 0]	taxTable[1, 1]	...	taxTable[1, 99]
taxTable[2, 0]	taxTable[2, 1]	...	taxTable[2, 99]
...	...		...
taxTable[10, 0]	taxTable[10, 1]	...	taxTable[10, 99]

Each one of these array elements can hold one value: in this case, a REAL-type value.

Given this notation, you can use indexed array elements in the same way that you use simple variables in a program. For example, the following assignment statement stores a string value in element [9, 53] of the *taxTable* array:

```
taxTable [9, 53] : = 9.53 * taxRate;
```

Likewise, the following WRITELN statement displays the value stored in this element on the screen:

```
WRITELN ('Sales tax on $9.53 is ', taxTable [9, 53] :4:2);
```

In short, you can think of an array as a list or table of indexed variables. Each array element is in fact a variable that can store one value.

The *SalesTbl* program illustrates another important point about arrays: FOR loops often provide the most convenient control structures for storing values in individual array elements or reading values from array elements. For example, the following nested FOR loops generate data to store in all 1100 elements of the *taxTable* array:

```
FOR dollars : = 0 TO maxDollars DO
  FOR cents : = 0 to 99 DO
    taxTable [dollars, cents] : =
      (dollars + cents/100) * taxRate
```

In this passage, the control variables of the two FOR loops—*dollars* and *cents*, respectively—also serve as variable indexes into the *taxTable* array and as operands in the tax calculations. While this program is merely an exercise, it is a good illustration of the kind of concise and efficient code you can write using FOR loops and arrays.

The main program section of *SalesTbl* displays three examples of elements stored in the *taxTable* array:

```
WRITELN ('Sales tax on $5.40 is ', taxTable [5, 40] :4:2);
WRITELN ('Sales tax on $0.85 is ', taxTable [0][85] :4:2);
WRITELN ('Sales tax on $9.53 is ', taxTable [9, 53] :4:2);
```

These lines display the following information on the screen:

```
Sales tax on $5.40 is 0.35
Sales tax on $0.85 is 0.06
Sales tax on $9.53 is 0.62
```

Finally, you might notice that the middle WRITELN statement in this passage uses a slightly different notation to access a value from the *taxTable* array:

```
taxTable [0][85]
```

This notation is identical in effect to the more common notation that we have been using all along:

```
taxTable [0, 85]
```

You can also pass an array as an argument to a procedure or function, but Turbo Pascal imposes some restrictions on the definition of the formal parameter that receives the array. We'll discuss this subject briefly in the next section.

Passing Arrays as Arguments

When you write a procedure or function that receives an array as an argument, the array type must be predefined in a TYPE statement located before the definition of the routine itself. For example, consider the following hypothetical procedure:

```
TYPE
  byteArray = ARRAY [1..10] OF BYTE;
```

```
PROCEDURE ParamTest (a: byteArray);

  BEGIN

    { The statements of ParamTest }

  END;
```

This procedure is defined to receive an array of BYTE values as an argument. The array type, *byteArray*, is defined in the TYPE statement above the procedure. Turbo Pascal does not allow typed structures to be defined inside the parameter list. For example, the following syntax would result in a compile-time error:

```
PROCEDURE ParamTest (a: ARRAY [1..10] OF BYTE); {not allowed}
```

This rule also applies to other structured types, including records.

There is one exception to this rule: a STRING-type parameter can be defined directly in the formal parameter list:

```
PROCEDURE strTest1 (st: STRING);
```

However, if you want to specify a STRING type that has an explicit maximum length, the type must be defined above the procedure:

```
TYPE
  smallString = STRING[4];

PROCEDURE strTest2 (st: smallString);
```

In some programs you may prefer to declare a central data structure globally, rather than passing the structure as an argument to individual routines in the program. This is the design style followed in the *CliAddr* program, where the central data structure is an array of records.

When combined to form a single structure, arrays and records provide a very versatile means of storing data, as we'll see when we examine the *CliAddr* program listing. However, before we begin looking specifically at the program, we must once again enlarge our library of compiled units. *CliAddr* uses an expanded version of the unit named *InUnit*, which we began developing in Chapter 4. You'll recall that *InUnit* is designed to store a collection of special-purpose input routines. Let's examine the new routines for this unit.

New Input Routines for the *CliAddr* Program

The previous version of *InUnit* had only one routine in it, a function name *InReal*. The purpose of this routine is to elicit a real number from the keyboard and to avoid the run-time error that would normally occur if the user enters a value that Pascal cannot read as a number. The *CliAddr* program needs a similar numeric input routine to accept a BYTE value from the keyboard. We'll call this routine *InByte*.

In addition, several routines in *CliAddr* require a function that reads and validates a single keystroke, making sure that the corresponding character is in a set of valid input values. The function that accomplishes this task, named *InChar*, uses a data structure called a *set* to perform the input validation. We'll study sets, along with several additional data types, in Chapter 7. Meanwhile, we'll add the *InByte* and *InChar* functions to *InUnit* now so they will be available to the *CliAddr* program.

Here is the heading and the new INTERFACE section of *InUnit:*

```
UNIT InUnit;

   { This unit contains special input routines for accepting
     and validating data entries from the keyboard. }

   INTERFACE

     USES CRT;

     TYPE
       validSet = SET OF CHAR;
```

```
FUNCTION InReal (prompt:    STRING):  REAL;

FUNCTION InByte (prompt:    STRING):  BYTE;

FUNCTION InChar (prompt:    STRING;
                 goodChars:    validSet):CHAR;
```

Notice that in addition to the two new function declarations, the INTERFACE section now has a TYPE definition for a structure named *validSet*. This is the set structure used in the *InChar* routine.

The source code for *InByte* and *InChar* is shown in Figure 6.4. Enter these two routines just after the code for *InReal* in the IMPLEMENTATION section. Save the new version of *InUnit* to disk, and then recompile the unit, creating the compiled file named INUNIT.TPU. With this revision complete, you are ready to begin work on the *CliAddr* program.

```
FUNCTION InByte;

   { The InByte function displays an input prompt on
     the screen, eliciting a BYTE value from the keyboard.
     If the entry contains nonnumeric characters, or is
     outside the range of a BYTE value, InByte erases
     the entry from the screen and continues displaying
     the input prompt. }

VAR
   tempInteger:  INTEGER;
   goodInput:    BOOLEAN;
   saveX, saveY: BYTE;

BEGIN
  REPEAT

     { Record the current cursor position, and
       display the input prompt on the screen }

     saveX := WHEREX;
     saveY := WHEREY;

     WRITE (prompt);

     { Turn input checking off, and read an
       integer value from the keyboard. }

     {$I-}
       READLN (tempInteger);
     {$I+}

     { Check to see if the input is a valid number,
       and if the value is within the range of the
       BYTE type (0 to 255). }
```

Figure 6.4: The *InByte* and *InChar* functions for *InUnit*

```
      goodInput := (IORESULT = 0) AND
                   (tempInteger >= 0) AND
                   (tempInteger <= 255);

   { If not, erase the input value and try again. }

   IF NOT goodInput THEN
     BEGIN
       GOTOXY (saveX, saveY);
       CLREOL
     END
 UNTIL goodInput;

 InByte := tempInteger
END;

FUNCTION InChar;

 { The InChar function accepts a single key of
   input from the keyboard, and ensures that
   the input character will be IN a specified
   set of valid characters, goodChars. }


 VAR
   tempChar, codeDiscard: CHAR;

 BEGIN

   { Display the input prompt. }

   WRITE (prompt);

   REPEAT

     { Read the input character, and
       convert it to uppercase. }

     tempChar := UPCASE (READKEY);

     { If a two-character function key has
       been pressed, read the second code
       and discard it. }

     IF tempChar = #0 THEN codeDiscard := READKEY

     { Continue the input process until the input
       character tempChar is in the set goodChars. }

   UNTIL tempChar IN goodChars;

   InChar := tempChar
 END;

END.    { InUnit }
```

Figure 6.4: The *InByte* and *InChar* functions for *InUnit* (continued)

The Listing of the *CliAddr* Program

The listing of the *CliAddr* program appears in Figure 6.5. The main program calls the *Menu* procedure repeatedly to display the menu on the screen and elicit the user's choices. A CASE decision structure in the *Menu* routine calls one of two routines:

- The *NewAddress* procedure conducts the input dialog for adding a new address to the file.

- The *PrintList* procedure prints either address labels or a phone list.

As we examine the listing, we'll concentrate on the program's data requirements and on the structure that meets these requirements: an array of records.

```
PROGRAM CliAddr;

  { CliAddr is a menu-driven program designed to
    create and manage a client address file. }

  USES CRT, PRINTER, InUnit, StrUnit;

  CONST
    maxAddresses    = 250;
    addressFileName = 'ADDRLIST.TXT';
    nameSort        = '1';
    refNoSort       = '2';


  TYPE

    addressRecord = RECORD
      name:         STRING[30];
      phone:        STRING[20];
      refNo:        BYTE;
      headOffice:   BOOLEAN;

      street:       STRING[30];
      city:         STRING[20];

      CASE usa:     BOOLEAN OF
        TRUE:
          (state:   STRING[2];
           zip:     STRING[5]);
        FALSE:
          (otherLoc,
           country: STRING[15])
    END;

    indexRange   = 1..maxAddresses;
    addressArray = ARRAY [indexRange] OF addressRecord;

  VAR
    done:          BOOLEAN;
    addresses:     addressArray;
    addressFile:   TEXT;
    currentRecord: BYTE;
```

Figure 6.5: The listing of *CliAddr*

```
PROCEDURE ReadAddresses;

  { The ReadAddresses procedure opens the ADDRLIST.TXT
    file, and reads each client address into a record
    element of the addresses array. (Note that this
    address list is saved as a text file.) }

  VAR
    officeCode, usaCode: BYTE;

  BEGIN    { ReadAddresses }

    { Turn I/O checking off, and attempt to
      open the file for reading. }

    {$I-}
    RESET (addressFile);
    {$I+}

    { If the file was opened successfully, begin
      reading the address records into the array. }

    IF IORESULT = 0 THEN
      BEGIN
        WHILE NOT EOF(addressFile)
            AND (currentRecord < maxAddresses) DO
          BEGIN
            INC (currentRecord);

            { Use WITH to simplify access to each record. }

            WITH addresses[currentRecord] DO
              BEGIN
                READLN (addressFile, name);
                READLN (addressFile, officeCode, usaCode, refNo);
                headOffice := BOOLEAN(officeCode);
                usa := BOOLEAN(usaCode);
                READLN (addressFile, phone);
                READLN (addressFile, street);
                READLN (addressFile, city);
                IF usa THEN
                  BEGIN
                    READLN (addressFile, state);
                    READLN (addressFile, zip)
                  END
                ELSE
                  BEGIN
                    READLN (addressFile, otherLoc);
                    READLN (addressFile, country)
                  END
              END
          END;
        CLOSE (addressFile)
      END
  END;    { ReadAddresses }


PROCEDURE NewAddress;

  { The NewAddress procedure conducts the input
    dialog for a new address record and then gives
    the user the chance to save or abandon the input. }

  CONST
```

Figure 6.5: The listing of *CliAddr* (continued)

```
      yesNo: SET OF CHAR = ['Y', 'N'];

VAR
  usaForeign,
  isHead,
  okToSave:   CHAR;


PROCEDURE GetStateAndZip;

  { The GetStateAndZip procedure elicits the
    state and zip code for a USA address record. }

  BEGIN     { GetStateAndZip }

    WITH addresses[currentRecord] DO
      BEGIN
        WRITE ('              State: ');
        READLN (state);
        WRITE ('          Zip code: ');
        READLN (zip)
      END

  END;    { GetStateAndZip }


PROCEDURE GetCountryInfo;

  { The GetCountryInfo procedure elicits the
    state/province and country for a foreign address. }

  BEGIN     { GetCountryInfo }

    WITH addresses[currentRecord] DO
      BEGIN
        WRITE ('   State or province: ');
        READLN (otherLoc);
        WRITE ('            Country: ');
        READLN (country)
      END

  END;    { GetCountryInfo }


PROCEDURE SaveAddress;

  { The SaveAddress procedure saves a new record
    to the ADDRLIST.TXT file. }

  BEGIN     { SaveAddress }

    IF currentRecord > 1 THEN
      APPEND (addressFile)
    ELSE
      REWRITE (addressFile);
    WITH addresses[currentRecord] DO
      BEGIN
        WRITELN (addressFile, name);
        WRITELN (addressFile,
          BYTE(headOffice), ' ', BYTE(usa), ' ', refNo);
        WRITELN (addressFile, phone);
        WRITELN (addressFile, street);
        WRITELN (addressFile, city);
```

Figure 6.5: The listing of *CliAddr* (continued)

```
              IF usa THEN
                BEGIN
                   WRITELN (addressFile, state);
                   WRITELN (addressFile, zip)
                END
              ELSE
                BEGIN
                   WRITELN (addressFile, otherLoc);
                   WRITELN (addressFile, country)
                END
          END;
        CLOSE (addressFile)

  END;    { SaveAddress }


BEGIN     { NewAddress }
  WRITELN ('Enter a client address record:');
  WRITELN ('----- - ------ ------- -------');
  WRITELN;

  INC (currentRecord);
  WITH addresses[currentRecord] DO
    BEGIN
      WRITE ('      Name of client: ');
      READLN (name);
      refNo := InByte ('      Reference number: ');
      WRITE ('      Street address: ');
      READLN (street);
      WRITE ('                City: ');
      READLN (city);
      usaForeign :=
        InChar ('USA or Foreign? (U F): ', ['U', 'F']);
      WRITELN (usaForeign);

      usa := (usaForeign = 'U');
    END;

  CASE addresses[currentRecord].usa OF
    TRUE: GetStateAndZip;
    FALSE: GetCountryInfo
  END;

  WITH addresses[currentRecord] DO
    BEGIN
      WRITE ('        Phone number: ');
      READLN (phone);

      isHead :=
        InChar ('  Head office? (Y N): ', yesNo);
      headOffice := (isHead = 'Y');
      WRITELN (isHead)
    END;

  WRITELN;
  WRITELN (StringOfChars ('-', 35));
  WRITELN;
  okToSave :=
    InChar ('Save this address? (Y N): ', yesNo);
  WRITELN (okToSave);
```

Figure 6.5: The listing of *CliAddr* (continued)

```
        IF okToSave = 'Y' THEN
          SaveAddress
        ELSE
          DEC (currentRecord);
        CLRSCR

  END;      { NewAddress }


PROCEDURE SortAddresses (sortBy: CHAR);

  { The SortAddresses procedure uses the Shell sort
    algorithm to sort the address list either by
    client names or by reference numbers. The
    sortBy argument specifies the sort key. }

  VAR
    listJump, i, j:          BYTE;
    sortComplete, sortTest:  BOOLEAN;
    saveRecord:              addressRecord;

  BEGIN      { SortAddresses }
    listJump := 1;
    WHILE listJump <= currentRecord DO
      listJump := listJump * 2;

    WHILE listJump > 1 DO
      BEGIN
        listJump := (listJump - 1) DIV 2;
        REPEAT
          sortComplete := TRUE;
          FOR j := 1 TO currentRecord - listJump DO
            BEGIN
              i := j + listJump;
              IF sortBy = nameSort THEN
                sortTest
                  := addresses[j].name > addresses[i].name
              ELSE
                  sortTest
                    := addresses[j].refNo > addresses[i].refNo;
                IF sortTest THEN
                  BEGIN
                    saveRecord := addresses[j];
                    addresses[j] := addresses[i];
                    addresses[i] := saveRecord;
                    sortComplete := FALSE
                  END
            END
        UNTIL sortComplete
      END
  END;    { SortAddresses }


PROCEDURE PrintList (addressDirectory: BOOLEAN);

  { The PrintList procedure prints either an
    address list or a phone list; the
    addressDirectory argument specifies which. }

  CONST
    formFeed = #12;

  VAR
    sortSelection,
    inSpace        : CHAR;
```

Figure 6.5: The listing of *CliAddr* (continued)

```
FUNCTION Continue: BOOLEAN;

   { The Continue function accepts a signal from
     the user to indicate the next action: space bar
     to print the list; escape to return to the menu. }

   CONST
     spaceBar = ' ';
     escKey   = #27;
     prompt   =
       '<Space Bar> to print. <Escape> to return to menu.';

   VAR
     inKey: CHAR;

   BEGIN
     inKey    :=
       InChar (prompt, [spaceBar, escKey]);
     Continue := (inKey = spaceBar)
   END;


PROCEDURE PrintAddresses;

  { The PrintAddresses procedure prints an
    address directory. }

  VAR
    i: BYTE;

  BEGIN    { PrintAddresses }

    WRITELN (LST, 'Client Address Directory');
    WRITELN (LST, '------ ------- ---------');
    WRITELN (LST);

    FOR i := 1 TO currentRecord DO
      WITH addresses[i] DO
        BEGIN
          WRITE (LST, LeftAlign (name, 35), refNo:3);
          IF headOffice THEN
            WRITELN (LST, ' H')
          ELSE
            WRITELN (LST, ' B');
          WRITELN (LST, street);
          WRITE (LST, city, ', ');
          IF usa THEN
            WRITELN (LST, UpperCase (state), ' ', zip)
          ELSE
            WRITELN (LST, otherLoc, ' ', UpperCase (country));
          WRITELN (LST, phone);
          WRITELN (LST); WRITELN (LST)
        END

  END;    { PrintAddresses }


PROCEDURE PrintPhones;

  { The PrintPhones procedure prints the phone list. }

  VAR
    i: BYTE;
```

Figure 6.5: The listing of *CliAddr* (continued)

```
        BEGIN     { PrintPhones }

           WRITELN (LST, 'Client Phone Directory');
           WRITELN (LST, '------ ----- ---------');
           WRITELN (LST);
           WRITELN (LST, 'Client', Spaces (27),
                         'Reference', Spaces (10),
                         'Phone');

        WRITELN (LST);

        FOR i := 1 TO currentRecord DO
          WITH addresses[i] DO
            BEGIN
              WRITE (LST, LeftAlign (name, 35));
              WRITE (LST, refNo:3, Spaces (10));
              WRITELN (LST, phone)
            END

     END;    { PrintPhones }


  BEGIN    { PrintList }

    IF addressDirectory THEN
      BEGIN
        WRITELN ('Print an address list.');
        WRITELN ('----- -- ------- -----')
      END
    ELSE
      BEGIN
        WRITELN ('Print a phone list.');
        WRITELN ('----- - ----- -----')
      END;
    WRITELN;

    WRITELN ('Sort by:');
    WRITELN ('   1. Names');
    WRITELN ('   2. Reference numbers');
    WRITELN;
    sortSelection :=
      InChar (' Select 1 or 2 --> ', [nameSort, refNoSort]);
    WRITELN (sortSelection);
    SortAddresses (sortSelection);

    WRITELN;
    WRITELN (StringOfChars ('-', 50));
    WRITELN;

    IF Continue THEN
      BEGIN
        IF addressDirectory THEN
          PrintAddresses
        ELSE
          PrintPhones;
        WRITELN (LST, formFeed);
      END;

    CLRSCR

  END;    { PrintList }
```

Figure 6.5: The listing of *CliAddr* (continued)

```
PROCEDURE Menu (VAR exitMenu: BOOLEAN);

  { The Menu procedure displays the recurring main menu
    on the screen, and elicits the user's menu choices. }

  VAR
    choice, discardCode: CHAR;
  CONST
    menuChars: SET OF CHAR = ['A', 'C', 'P', 'Q'];
    addresses = TRUE;
    phones = FALSE;



  Procedure DisplayOption (optionString: STRING);

    { The DisplayOption procedure displays a menu option
      on the screen, with the first character displayed
      in high-intensity text. This routine uses the
      built-in TEXTCOLOR procedure, from the CRT unit. }

    BEGIN    { DisplayOption }

      TEXTCOLOR (White);
      WRITE (optionString[1]);
      TEXTCOLOR (LightGray);
      WRITELN (COPY (optionString, 2,
                  LENGTH(optionString) - 1))

    END;    { DisplayOption }

  BEGIN    { Menu }

    exitMenu := FALSE;

    GOTOXY (20, 5);
    WRITELN ('Client Address Manager');

    GOTOXY (20, 6);
    WRITELN ('------ ------- -------');

    GOTOXY (20, 7);
    DisplayOption ('Add an address.');

    GOTOXY (20, 8);
    DisplayOption ('Create an address directory.');

    GOTOXY (20, 9);
    DisplayOption ('Print a phone directory.');

    GOTOXY (20,10);
    DisplayOption ('Quit.');

    GOTOXY (20,12);

    choice :=
      InChar ('** Menu choice (A C P Q) --> ', menuChars);
```

Figure 6.5: The listing of *CliAddr* (continued)

```
        CLRSCR;
        CASE choice OF
          'A' : NewAddress;
          'C' : IF currentRecord > 0 THEN
                   PrintList (addresses);
          'P' : IF currentRecord > 0 THEN
                   PrintList (phones);
          'Q' : exitMenu := TRUE
        END

      END;    { Menu }

  BEGIN    { CliAddr }

    ASSIGN (addressFile, addressFileName);
    currentRecord := 0;
    ReadAddresses;

    CLRSCR;
    REPEAT
      Menu (done)
    UNTIL done

  END.    { CliAddr }
```

Figure 6.5: The listing of *CliAddr* (continued)

Working with an Array of Records

We have seen how the *CliAddr* program uses a TYPE statement to define a record structure named *addressRecord*. The structure contains six fixed fields, a tag field, and two pairs of variant fields corresponding to American and foreign addresses. With this structure defined, the following declarations create an array variable named *addresses*, to store the entire address list during a given performance:

```
CONST
  maxAddresses   = 250;
  { ... }

TYPE
  { ... }
  indexRange   = 1..maxAddresses;
  addressArray = ARRAY [indexRange] of addressRecord;

VAR
  { ... }
  addresses:  addressArray;
```

The current version of the program is designed to handle a maximum of 250 addresses. Notice that the TYPE statement declares a *subrange* type named *indexRange* and a user-defined structure named *address-Array*, an array of records. (We'll discover more about subrange types in Chapter 7.) Finally, the VAR statement defines the array variable *addresses*, which is the program's major global data structure.

The notation for accessing elements from an array of records is a natural extension of the other notations we have already examined in this chapter. The *n*th record in the array is named *addresses[n]*. You identify the fields of this record as follows:

addresses[n].name

addresses[n].phone

addresses[n].refNo

and so on ...

Furthermore, you can use the WITH statement to abbreviate this notation, just as with a simple record structure:

```
WITH addresses[n] DO
  BEGIN
    { statements referencing fields of
      the record addresses[n] }
  END
```

Let's look at some examples of this notation from the *CliAddr* program. At all points during a performance, *CliAddr* uses the global BYTE variable *currentRecord* to keep track of the current number of records stored in the *addresses* array. Each time the user selects the *Add an address* option from the main menu, the program increments the value stored in this variable:

```
INC (currentRecord);
```

Then, to conduct the input dialog for the new record, the program encloses a series of WRITE and READLN statements inside a WITH block. Here is the beginning of that block, from the *NewAddress* procedure:

```
WITH addresses[currentRecord] DO
    BEGIN
        WRITE ('       Name of client:   ');
        READLN (name);
        refNo : = InByte ('       Reference number:   ');
```

When the input dialog is complete, *NewAddress* calls the *Save-Address* procedure to write the new record to disk.

If the user selects the second or the third menu option—to print an address list or a phone list—the *Menu* procedure calls the *PrintList* procedure, which in turn calls either *PrintAddresses* or *PrintPhones*. These procedures use simple FOR loops to perform their respective printing operations. For example, the following seven lines from the *PrintPhones* procedure produce an entire printed phone list:

```
FOR i : = 1 TO currentRecord DO
    WITH addresses[i] DO
        BEGIN
            WRITE (LST, LeftAlign (name, 35));
            WRITE (LST, refNo:3, Spaces (10));
            WRITELN (LST, phone)
        END
```

Notice that the control variable *i* takes on values from 1 to *current-Record*. In an array index, this control variable identifies each successive record in *addresses*. Also note that the WITH statement is nested inside the FOR loop, simplifying the entire passage. A similar, but somewhat longer, loop in the *PrintAddress* procedure prints the address list.

Finally, let's take a quick look at the *SortAddresses* procedure, which is designed to sort the records in the *addresses* array either alphabetically by names or numerically by reference numbers. Like the sort routine we saw in the *CliList* program, *SortAddresses* uses the Shell sort algorithm and a trio of nested loops to rearrange the records of the array. But since there are two possible sorting keys in *CliAddr*, the routine is somewhat more complicated. The program establishes two global constants to represent the two available sorts:

```
CONST
  { ... }
  nameSort = '1';
  refNoSort = '2';
```

The *PrintList* procedure elicits one of these two character values from the user and passes the user's choice up to the *SortAddresses* routine:

```
WRITELN ('Sort by:');
WRITELN ('    1. Names');
WRITELN ('    2. Reference numbers');
WRITELN;
sortSelection : =
  InChar ('  Select 1 or 2 — >    ', [nameSort, refNoSort]);
WRITELN (sortSelection);
SortAddresses (sortSelection);
```

SortAddresses receives this argument value in the parameter variable *sortBy*. Inside the innermost sorting loop, the routine uses *sortBy* to select one of two sort-key comparisons:

```
IF sortBy = nameSort THEN
  sortTest : = addresses[j].name > addresses[i].name
ELSE
  sortTest : = addresses[j].refNo > addresses[i].refNo;
```

If the user has requested an alphabetic sort by client names, this statement compares the *name* fields of the two target records to decide whether or not to perform a swap. Otherwise, if the user has requested a numeric sort by reference numbers, the routine compares the *refNo* fields of the two records.

In either event, if *sortTest* is true, the two records must be swapped:

```
IF sortTest THEN
  BEGIN
    saveRecord : = addresses[j];
    addresses[j] : = addresses[i];
```

```
      addresses[i] : = saveRecord;
      sortComplete : = FALSE
   END
```

The first three statements in this block assign entire record values (that is, all nine fields at once) to a record variable. This passage shows why it is important to be able to reference not only the individual fields in a record, but also the entire record at once.

The *CliAddr* program is worth further study; it will help you understand several of the characteristics of three complex data structures: arrays, records, and arrays of records.

The program illustrates one additional programming feature that we will discuss in the final section of this chapter. On several different occasions, the program has to convert data values from one type to another, a process called *type-casting*. We'll see how this task is performed.

Type Casting

Turbo Pascal allows you to convert data values from one type to another, as long as the two data types involved in the operation take up exactly the same number of bytes in memory. To perform the type-casting operation, you simply reference the name of a data type—a standard or user-defined identifier—as though the name itself represented a built-in function. Here is the general form of the operation:

typeName (*value*)

This expression supplies a value of the *typeName* type, converted from the *value* argument. You can express *value* as a literal constant, an expression, or a variable in a type-casting operation.

There may be any number of reasons for performing such a conversion. For example, the *CliAddr* program needs to find some convenient way to store BOOLEAN-type values in a text file, and to read those values back again in a subsequent performance. But the Turbo Pascal READLN function cannot read BOOLEAN-type values, either from a text file or from the keyboard. For this reason, the *SaveAddress* procedure converts the BOOLEAN fields *headOffice* and *usa* into BYTE values before storing them in the address file:

```
WRITELN (addressFile,
   BYTE(headOffice), ' ', BYTE(usa), ' ', refNo);
```

If you examine the address file (named ADDRLIST.TXT on disk), you will find that these BOOLEAN values are converted to values of 0 (for FALSE) and 1 (for TRUE). For example, here is the text of an address record as stored in the file:

```
XYZ Corporation
0 1 123
(213) 777-1234
907 Maple Drive
Los Angeles
CA
90047
```

In the second line of this record you can see the values of 0 and 1, representing FALSE and TRUE, respectively.

Conversely, when the program reads these values back from the file, it uses another type-casting operation to convert the numbers back into BOOLEAN values:

```
READLN (addressFile, officeCode, usaCode, refNo);
headOffice : = BOOLEAN(officeCode);
usa : = BOOLEAN(usaCode);
```

In this case, the identifier BOOLEAN indicates the direction of the type-casting operation.

Version 5.5: Object Structures

New in Turbo Pascal 5.5 is the *object* data type that is the fulcrum of object-oriented programming. Objects look a lot like records: indeed, if you ignore their special properties, you can treat objects in the same way as records (though this would not use them to their full advantage).

Like records, objects let you group related elements inside a single "wrapper." However, the object type adds capabilities that records lack:

- In addition to data fields, an object can contain its own procedures and functions. These enable each object, if needed, to respond differently to common program commands. In object-oriented programming lingo, these embedded procedures and functions are called the object's *methods*.

- Unlike records, objects can inherit both data fields and methods from other objects. However, inherited methods can be overridden by an object's own internal methods if needed.

These are unfamiliar concepts, so let's illustrate them with a simple example. Fundamentally, you declare an object in exactly the same way as a record:

```
TYPE
  objectType = OBJECT
  fieldName1 : fieldType1;
  fieldName2 : fieldType2;
  {and so on ...}
  PROCEDURE Init (W: fieldType1; X: fieldType2; ...);
  PROCEDURE DoThis (Y: STRING);
  FUNCTION DoThat (Z: INTEGER) : INTEGER;
  {and so on ...}
  END;
```

Let's modify the *addressRecord* record type introduced earlier in the chapter to use the object type. We'll try the following:

```
TYPE
  addressRecord = OBJECT
    name:        STRING[30];
    refNo:       BYTE;
    headOffice:  BOOLEAN;
    street:      STRING[30];
    city:        STRING[20];
    state:       STRING[2]
  END;

VAR
  address: addressRecord;
```

Now, suppose that for certain customers, we want each record to keep a running balance of how much the customer owes. If we had used the record data type, we would have to start from scratch—creating a new *addressRecord* type, entering all the fields, and adding the balance field, plus creating an external procedure to update the balance information.

With objects, however, it's much simpler. Since we've already defined the name, address, and other fields, we just declare a new object that is a *descendant* of the *addressRecord* type:

```
TYPE
    addressRecord = OBJECT
        ...
    END;
        ...
    balanceRecord = OBJECT (addressRecord)
        balance: INTEGER;
        PROCEDURE InitBalance(InitBal: INTEGER);
        PROCEDURE UpdateBalance(newCharges: INTEGER;
                                    VAR balance: INTEGER);
    END;
```

Notice two things. First, we referred to the *addressRecord* object type in parentheses when we declared the *balanceRecord* type. This tells Turbo Pascal that the new type is a descendant of the already-defined type—which, in turn, is called the *ancestor* of the new type. Second, because *balanceRecord* was declared as a descendant of *addressRecord*, it *inherits* all of *addressRecord*'s fields—they don't have to be repeated in the *balanceRecord* type declaration.

Inheritance applies to an object's methods as well as its data fields. If we created a new object type as a descendant of *balanceRecord*, it would inherit the two procedures *InitBalance* and *UpdateBalance*. In our new object type, we could either leave the old procedures as is, or declare new procedures with the same names that would override the inherited ones. (The data fields of an ancestor object, however, cannot be overridden.)

This is only a sample of the immense power and programming simplicity that is made possible by object-oriented concepts. For a complete explanation of how objects work, see Chapter 16.

Summary

Real-life applications often have complex data-storage requirements. The user-defined data structures we have examined in this chapter—records and arrays (and objects, for version 5.5)—are versatile and powerful enough to meet many of the most difficult data requirements with elegance and efficiency:

- A record is a collection of named fields that can belong to diverse data types.

- An array represents a list or table (or multiple tables) of data values, all belonging to the same type.

- An object incorporates named data fields, like a record, but also includes its own procedures and functions (called "methods") that operate on the data fields.

We'll see more examples of these data structures—and learn additional techniques for handling them—in subsequent chapters. Meanwhile, in Chapter 7 we'll continue our study of Turbo Pascal's data structures and data types.

C H A P T E R

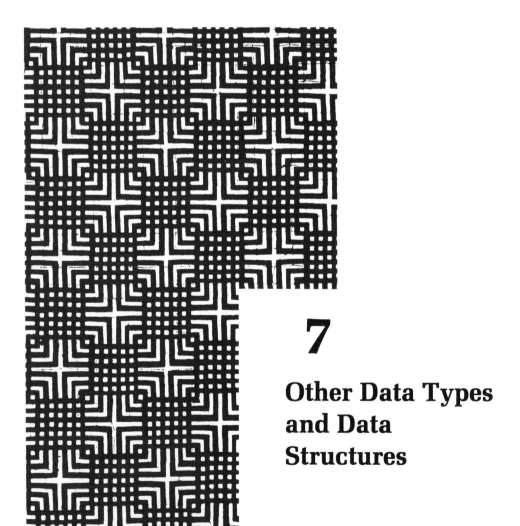

7

Other Data Types
and Data
Structures

This chapter continues our discussion of the data types available in Turbo Pascal, presenting some of the most interesting, but least employed, of all the types: sets, enumerated types, subranges, and typed constants. Along the way, this chapter's program application illustrates some advanced techniques for screen output and keyboard input.

Before we begin, here is a brief review of the data types we've worked with so far:

- Ordinal (or scalar) types are ranges of distinct ordered values. This category includes the CHAR and BOOLEAN types, and the integer types: SHORTINT, BYTE, INTEGER, WORD, and LONGINT.

- Real-number types include various ranges and precisions of floating-point numbers: REAL, SINGLE, DOUBLE, and EXTENDED. The real types and the ordinal types together are sometimes called the *simple types*, to distinguish them from structured types.

- STRING types represent sequences of characters.

- Two structured types, RECORD and ARRAY, represent collections of data values. A record contains named field values belonging to diverse data types; an array represents a list or table of uniformly typed values.

If you have written programs in any version of the Basic language, you were probably already familiar with most of these types. Basic supports data types that are equivalent to the major types and structures we've discussed so far, including integers, reals, strings, and arrays. (Some versions of Basic even support user-defined record types.)

In contrast, this chapter presents some types and structures that are associated distinctly with Pascal: sets, enumerated types, and subranges. In addition, we'll discover an interesting and useful new application for the CONST section in the course of this chapter: the technique of creating *typed constants*, or initialized variables.

To illustrate this selection of topics, we'll look at a program called *CliMenu*. As its name implies, the purpose of *CliMenu* is to draw together all of the client-account applications we have examined up to now, combining them into a single menu-driven program. This program creates a sophisticated system for eliciting and accepting the user's menu choices, and employs some carefully planned input and output techniques. We'll begin this chapter by discussing *CliMenu*'s user-interface system.

The *CliMenu* Program

The *CliMenu* program is devoted almost entirely to placing a recurring menu on the screen and accepting the user's menu choices. After receiving appropriate instructions, the program uses Turbo Pascal's EXEC command to perform one of the following four compiled programs stored on disk:

HOURS.EXE

BILLTIME.EXE

CLILIST.EXE

CLIADDR.EXE

These are compiled versions of the four programs we developed in Chapters 3, 4, 5, and 6. In order to perform *CliMenu* successfully, you must gather these these four program files together in the current directory, along with any data files that the programs use. The data files might include a collection of .HRS files (for the *Hours, BillTime,* and *CliList* programs) and the client address file, ADDRLIST.TXT (for the *CliAddr* program).

When you run *CliMenu* the program begins by displaying a menu of program choices on the screen. Here are the menu selections:

Update a client file.
Bill a client.
List accounts and totals.
Print client addresses.
Quit

As you might guess, the first four selections in the menu correspond to the *Hours, BillTime, CliList,* and *CliAddr* programs, respectively.

Beneath the selections, the menu screen gives you some simple instructions for selecting an option, as you can see in Figure 7.1. Using this menu is similar to using one of the pull-down menus in the Turbo Pascal development environment. The currently selected option on the menu is always *highlighted* in reverse-video display text, and appears in all uppercase letters. To perform a menu option, follow these two steps:

1. Move the highlight to a selected option. To do so, press either the up or down arrow (↑ or ↓) keys multiple times, until the highlight arrives at the target option (the left and right keys will also work), or the key representing the first letter of the option's name: U, B, L, P, or Q.

2. Complete the selection by pressing the Enter key.

These two steps represent the entire process that *CliMenu* controls. Interestingly enough, carrying out these two steps—that is, offering the user a relatively simple way to select a menu option—requires a few hundred lines of rather complex code. Fortunately, the program's careful use of data types and structures makes the code easy to read and easy to modify for other menu-driven applications.

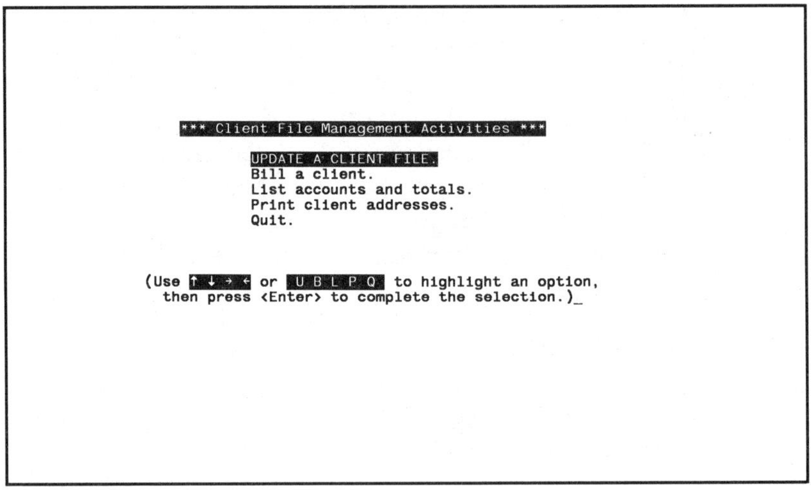

Figure 7.1: The menu screen produced by the *CliMenu* program

We'll look at the listing of the *CliMenu* program at the end of this chapter. First, let's discuss these special data types and data structures, starting with sets.

Sets

A set is a collection of individual values, all belonging to one ordinal type. Pascal defines three groups of standard operations for working with sets: set arithmetic, set comparisons, and set membership. From the programmer's point of view, probably the most important of these operations is set membership, represented by the reserved word IN. For example, a program can use the IN operation to test whether a given ordinal value is included in a particular set of values. Several of the programs we've developed in previous chapters have used this technique for input validation.

The reserved word SET defines a set type or a set variable in a program's TYPE and VAR declarations. Here is the general approach for declaring a set variable, *setVar:*

```
TYPE
    setType = SET OF ordinalType;
```

```
VAR
    setVar: setType;
```

Alternatively, you can declare variable's type directly in a VAR statement, as follows:

```
VAR
    setVar: SET OF ordinalType;
```

Only the ordinal types with ranges from 0 to 255 are available for defining sets; these include CHAR, BYTE, BOOLEAN, and enumerated types.

Once you have defined a set variable, you can use an assignment statement to store a particular set in the variable. In the notation for constructing a set, the square brackets are used as delimiters around a list of set members:

```
[setMember1, setMember2, setMember3, ...]
```

You can express set members as literal values, constants, variables, expressions, or ranges of values.

For example, the following statements declare a variable named *charSet*, defined as a SET OF CHAR:

```
TYPE
    charSetType = SET OF CHAR;

VAR
    charSet: charSetType;
```

Let's look at some examples of assignment statements that store sets in the *charSet* variable. This first example builds a set containing the members *a*, *b*, and *c*:

```
charSet := ['a', 'b', 'c'];
```

The next example builds a set containing three ranges of members:

```
charSet := ['a'..'z', 'A'..'Z', '0'..'9']
```

Assuming *enter* and *nullChar* are defined as CHAR-type variables, the following example uses a combination of variables and literal values to express set membership:

```
nullChar : = #0;
enter : = #13;
charSet : = ['U', 'B', 'L', 'P', 'Q', nullChar, enter];
```

Finally, the following example assigns an *empty set* (or *null set*) to the variable *charSet:*

```
charSet : = [];
```

By definition, the empty set contains no members, but is itself a member of every set.

Let's examine the set operations available in Turbo Pascal.

Set Operations

As we have seen, there are three functional categories of set operations in Pascal: set arithmetic, set comparisons, and set membership. A *set arithmetic* operation works with two set operands, and results in a third set. A *set comparison* operation also works with two sets, but results in a BOOLEAN-type value of TRUE or FALSE. Finally, the *set membership* operation, IN, requires two operands—an ordinal value and a set—and results in a BOOLEAN-type value.

We'll discuss each of these three categories in turn. The demonstration program shown in Figure 7.2, *SetTest*, performs a variety of experiments that illustrate the results of the set operations. (The program uses sets of lowercase letters for the examples it produces.) The output from the program appears in Figure 7.3. Note that Pascal does not allow input or output of SET-type values with the READLN or WRITELN statements. For this reason, *SetTest* contains a procedure named *PrintSet*, whose job is to display the members of a set on the screen.

```
PROGRAM SetTest;

   { This program tests the results of set operations. }

   TYPE
     lowerCaseLetters = 'a'..'z';
     charSet = SET OF lowerCaseLetters;

   VAR
     set1, set2, set3, set4, set5, set6: charSet;

   PROCEDURE PrintSet (inSet: charSet);

     VAR
       controlChar : CHAR;
       firstMember : BOOLEAN;

     BEGIN    { PrintSet }
       WRITE ('[');
       firstMember := TRUE;
       FOR controlChar := 'a' TO 'z' DO
         IF controlChar IN inSet THEN
           BEGIN
             IF NOT firstMember THEN
               WRITE (', ');
             WRITE ('''', controlChar, '''');
             firstMember := FALSE
           END;
       WRITE (']')
     END;    { PrintSet }


   BEGIN    { SetTest }

     set1 := ['a' .. 'd'];
     set2 := ['c' .. 'f'];
     set3 := ['a', 'd'];
     set4 := ['a', 'h'];
     set5 := ['a'..'e'];
     set6 := ['d', 'c', 'b', 'a'];

     WRITELN ('     Set Union (+)');
     PrintSet (set1);
     WRITE ('  +  ');
     PrintSet (set2);
     WRITELN ('  =  ');
     PrintSet (set1 + set2);
     WRITELN; WRITELN;

     WRITELN ('     Set Subtraction (-)');
     PrintSet (set1);
     WRITE ('  -  ');
     PrintSet (set2);
     WRITE ('  =  ');
     PrintSet (set1 - set2);
     WRITELN; WRITELN;

     WRITELN ('     Set Intersection (*)');
     PrintSet (set1);
     WRITE ('  *  ');
     PrintSet (set2);
     WRITE ('  =  ');
     PrintSet (set1 * set2);
     WRITELN; WRITELN;
```

Figure 7.2: The *SetTest* program

```
      WRITELN ('     Set Equality (=)');
      PrintSet (set1);
      WRITE (' = ');
      PrintSet (set6);
      WRITELN (' = ', set1 = set6);
      PrintSet (set1);
      WRITE (' = ');
      PrintSet (set5);
      WRITELN (' = ', set1 = set5);
      WRITELN;

      WRITELN ('     Subset Comparisons (<=)');
      PrintSet (set3);
      WRITE (' <= ');
      PrintSet (set5);
      WRITELN (' = ', set3 <= set5);
      PrintSet (set4);
      WRITE (' <= ');
      PrintSet (set5);
      WRITELN (' = ', set4 <= set5);
      WRITELN;

      WRITELN ('     Superset Comparisons (>=)');
      PrintSet (set5);
      WRITE (' >= ');
      PrintSet (set3);
      WRITELN (' = ', set5 >= set3);
      PrintSet (set5);
      WRITE (' >= ');
      PrintSet (set4);
      WRITELN (' = ', set5 <= set4);
      WRITELN;

      WRITELN ('     Set Membership (IN)');
      WRITE ('''d'' IN ');
      PrintSet (set5);
      WRITELN (' = ', 'd' IN set5);
      WRITE ('''D'' IN ');
      PrintSet (set5);
      WRITELN (' = ', 'D' IN set5);
      WRITELN

  END.   { SetTest }
```

Figure 7.2: The *SetTest* program (continued)

Set Arithmetic Operations

The three set arithmetic operations are union, subtraction, and intersection. Turbo Pascal uses the following symbols to represent these operations:

+   Set union

−   Set subtraction

*   Set intersection

```
        Set Union (+)
['a', 'b', 'c', 'd']  +  ['c', 'd', 'e', 'f']  =
['a', 'b', 'c', 'd', 'e', 'f']

        Set Subtraction (-)
['a', 'b', 'c', 'd']  -  ['c', 'd', 'e', 'f']  =  ['a', 'b']

        Set Intersection (*)
['a', 'b', 'c', 'd']  *  ['c', 'd', 'e', 'f']  =  ['c', 'd']

        Set Equality (=)
['a', 'b', 'c', 'd']  =  ['a', 'b', 'c', 'd']  =  TRUE
['a', 'b', 'c', 'd']  =  ['a', 'b', 'c', 'd', 'e']  =  FALSE

        Subset Comparisons (<=)
['a', 'd']  <=  ['a', 'b', 'c', 'd', 'e']  =  TRUE
['a', 'h']  <=  ['a', 'b', 'c', 'd', 'e']  =  FALSE

        Superset Comparisons (>=)
['a', 'b', 'c', 'd', 'e']  >=  ['a', 'd']  =  TRUE
['a', 'b', 'c', 'd', 'e']  >=  ['a', 'h']  =  FALSE

        Set Membership (IN)
'd' IN ['a', 'b', 'c', 'd', 'e']  =  TRUE
'D' IN ['a', 'b', 'c', 'd', 'e']  =  FALSE
```

Figure 7.3: Output from the *SetTest* program

Each of these operations requires two set operands and produces a set result. Members of both operands must belong to the same ordinal type.

The *union* operation combines the membership of two sets, *set1* and *set2:*

set1 + *set2*

The resulting set contains all the members of *set1* and all the members of *set2*, as in this example:

['a', 'b', 'c', 'd'] + ['c', 'd', 'e', 'f'] =
['a', 'b', 'c', 'd', 'e', 'f']

(Any values that are members of both *set1* and *set2* appear only once as members of the resulting set.)

The *subtraction* operation finds the difference between two sets:

set1 − *set2*

The resulting set contains all the members of *set1* that are not members of *set2:*

['a', 'b', 'c', 'd'] – ['c', 'd', 'e', 'f'] = ['a', 'b']

The *intersection* operation finds all the values that are members of both sets:

set1 * set2

The resulting set contains the membership that is a subset of both *set1* and *set2:*

['a', 'b', 'c', 'd'] * ['c', 'd', 'e', 'f'] = ['c', 'd']

Set Comparison Operations

The three set comparison operations are equality, subset, and superset. Each operation compares two sets, and results in a BOOLEAN value. The operations are represented by the following symbols in Turbo Pascal:

=	Set equality
< =	Subset
> =	Superset

The set *equality* operation results in a value of true only if the membership of two sets, *set1* and *set2*, is identical:

set1 = set2

Identical sets have the same number of members and the same values as members. For example, the following expression results in a value of true:

['a'..'d'] = ['d', 'c', 'b', 'a']

(The order of the members in a set expression is not relevant to set equality; in fact, Turbo Pascal automatically arranges the members of a set in ascending order.)

The *subset* operation determines whether all the members of a first set are also members of a second set:

set1 < = *set2*

This expression results in a value of true if all the members of *set1* are also members of *set2*. (However, *set2* may have members that are not in *set1*.) The first of the following expressions results in a value of TRUE, and the second is FALSE:

['a', 'd'] < = ['a', 'b', 'c', 'd', 'e']
['a', 'h'] < = ['a', 'b', 'c', 'd', 'e']

The *superset* operation determines whether a first set contains all the members of a second set:

set1 > = *set2*

This expression is true if *set1* contains all the members of *set2*. The first of the following examples is TRUE and the second is FALSE:

['a', 'b', 'c', 'd', 'e'] > = ['a', 'd']
['a', 'b', 'c', 'd', 'e'] > = ['a', 'h']

Set Membership

As we have seen, the reserved word IN represents the set membership operation. This operation is probably the most common reason for defining sets in a Pascal program.

Here is the general form of the membership test:

ordinalValue IN *setValue*

This expression results in a value of TRUE if *ordinalValue* is a member of *setValue*. For example, consider the following two expressions—the first is TRUE and the second is FALSE:

'd' IN ['a', 'b', 'c', 'd', 'e']
'D' IN ['a', 'b', 'c', 'd', 'e']

Note that Pascal distinguishes between lowercase and uppercase letters for testing membership in character sets.

We'll see several rather interesting examples of the IN operation when we turn to the *CliMenu* program. But first, let's continue examining data types; the next subject is the enumerated type.

Enumerated Types

The enumerated type is perhaps the most esoteric of all user-defined types. No reserved words or standard identifiers are associated with enumerated type declarations. No operations are defined specifically for the type. You cannot use READLN or WRITELN to perform input or output operations with this type. Furthermore, the identifiers you create for an enumerated type do not represent any values except themselves. Yet, an enumerated type can prove to be a very useful tool for creating clear, self-documenting application programs, as we will see in the *CliMenu* program.

An *enumerated type* is an ordered sequence of user-defined identifiers, forming an ordinal type. The format for defining such a type is as follows:

```
TYPE
    enumeratedTypeName = (name1, name2, name3, ...);
```

The names listed in the enumerated type can be used as constant values in the subsequent program block. Furthermore, you can define variables belonging to the enumerated type:

```
VAR
    enumeratedVar: enumeratedTypeName;
```

This variable can then represent any one of the ordered identifiers that belong to the enumerated type.

As with any other ordinal type, one of the important characteristics of an enumerated type is the order in which the values are sequenced. In addition to establishing the identifiers themselves, an enumerated type declaration also defines the *order* of the identifiers in the type.

Let's look at an example from the *CliMenu* program. To simplify its menu-processing tasks, the program establishes an enumerated type named *activities:*

```
TYPE
     activities = (updateClient, billClient,
                     listClients, listAddresses, quit)
```

As you might guess, each of the identifiers in this type corresponds to one of the activities offered in the menu itself.

This enumerated type becomes an integral part of the data-handling tasks associated with the menu options. For example, the program subsequently sets up an array of records for storing a variety of information about each menu option. The fields of this record structure include *fileName*, the name of the .EXE program corresponding to a given option; *row* and *column*, the fixed screen address where the option is always displayed; and *menuString*, the option string that actually appears on the screen. Here is the definition of this RECORD type:

```
activityRecord =   RECORD
    fileName:       STRING[8];
    row,
    column:         BYTE;
    menuString:     STRING[25]
END;
```

The array that contains these records is called *activity*. This array is indexed, in turn, by the enumerated type *activities:*

```
activity: ARRAY[activities] OF activityRecord
```

As a result of this elaborate arrangement, references to the individual fields describing a given menu option are very clear and readable. For example, here are the complete names of fields that describe the client-billing option:

```
activity [billClient].fileName

activity [billClient].row
```

activity [billClient].column

activity [billClient].menuString

In these expressions, the identifier *billClient*—the second value in the enumerated *activities* type—serves as the index into the *activity* array for accessing information about the second menu option.

Furthermore, the program can employ the range of *activities* values in a FOR loop, to step through the five records of the *activity* array. For example, the routine that initially displays the menu on the screen (*InitializeMenu*) begins by defining a control variable named *option*, belonging to the *activities* type:

```
VAR
   option: activities;
```

Subsequently the routine uses a FOR statement to loop through the five activities, as follows:

```
FOR option : = updateClient TO quit DO
   WITH activity[option] DO
      BEGIN
         GOTOXY (column, row);
         WRITELN (menuString)
      END;
```

The starting and ending values assigned to the control variable *option* in this loop are *updateClient* and *quit*, the first and last identifiers in the enumerated *activities* type.

There are still other ways to take advantage of an enumerated type. Specifically, Turbo Pascal has three built-in functions that work with ordinal types: ORD, SUCC, and PRED. These functions prove particularly useful in programs that use enumerated types. In addition, Turbo Pascal allows type casting to convert between integer values and enumerated type values. We'll explore these topics briefly in the next section.

Ordinal Functions and Type Casting

The ORD, SUCC, and PRED functions all take single ordinal values as their arguments. ORD returns an integer value, and SUCC and PRED return ordinal values matching the argument types. The results are as follows:

- ORD(*ordinalValue*) returns an integer value representing the position of *ordinalValue* in the defined range of the value's ordinal type.

- SUCC(*ordinalValue*) returns the successor of *ordinalValue*, from the ordinal type to which the argument belongs.

- PRED(*ordinalValue*) returns the predecessor of *ordinalValue*, from the ordinal type to which the argument belongs.

You can apply these three functions to any of the ordinal types. For example, here is a short demonstration program that illustrates the actions of ORD, SUCC, and PRED on a CHAR-type value:

```
PROGRAM OrdTest;

  BEGIN
    WRITELN (' The ORD value of "D" is ', ORD('D'), '.');
    WRITELN ('The SUCC value of "D" is "', SUCC('D'), '".');
    WRITELN ('The PRED value of "D" is "', PRED('D'), '".')
  END.
```

The output from this program is as follows:

```
The ORD   value of 'D' is 68.
The SUCC value of 'D' is 'E'.
The PRED value of 'D' is 'C'.
```

In the case of CHAR values, the ORD function supplies the ASCII code equivalent of a given character. As you can see, the code value for the character D is 68.

With enumerated types, ORD supplies the position of a given value in the list of enumerated identifiers. To illustrate, let's look again at the *activities* type from the *CliMenu* program:

```
TYPE
  activities = (updateClient, billClient,
                listClients, listAddresses, quit);
```

The ordinal values of enumerated identifiers start at 0. For example, the following expression results in a value of 1:

```
ORD(billClient)
```

Conversely, given an integer representing the ordinal position of an enumerated value, you can use *type casting* to find the value itself. (We first discussed type casting in Chapter 6.) For example, the following expression yields the enumerated value *billClient*:

```
activities(1)
```

Since the ordinal positions of an enumerated type begin at 0, this expression yields the second identifier in the enumerated *activities* list.

The *CliMenu* program contains a good example of type casting from an integer to an enumerated type. Whenever the user presses a letter-key at the keyboard representing one of the five menu options—U, B, L, P, or Q—*CliMenu* has to convert this keystroke to one of the five values of the enumerated type *activities*. To do so, the program defines a constant string value containing the five valid input characters:

```
CONST
  firstChars = 'UBLPQ';
```

The program receives the user's keystrokes in the CHAR-type variable *inChar*. In the following statement, the built-in POS function supplies the position of *inChar* in the constant string *firstChars*; then the type-casting operation converts this ordinal position to one of the five enumerated *activities* values:

```
currentSelection : =
  activities(POS(inChar, firstChars) − 1);
```

Notice that the program subtracts a value of 1 from the result of POS, to adjust the value of the character position (starting from 1) to the value of the ordinal position (starting from 0).

At the top of the program, the variable *currentSelection* is declared as a global variable of type *activities*:

```
VAR
  { ... }
  currentSelection: activities;
```

This variable, which always keeps track of the menu selection that is currently highlighted on the screen, is used for many other purposes during the course of the program. In particular, when the user presses the ↑ key the program needs to find the predecessor of the current enumerated *activities* value. The PRED function supplies the required information:

```
currentSelection : = PRED(currentSelection);
```

Conversely, when the user presses the ↓ key, the SUCC function supplies the next *activities* value down the list:

```
currentSelection : = SUCC(currentSelection);
```

We'll return later to these passages from the *CliMenu* program. But first we have two further topics to discuss: subrange types and typed constants.

Subrange Types

A *subrange type* identifies a sequence of values from within the defined range of an ordinal type. The notation for defining a subrange type explicitly is as follows:

```
TYPE
  subRangeType  = firstVal .. lastVal;
```

We have already encountered several examples of subrange types. For example, the index range of an array is typically expressed as a subrange, as in the following passage from the *CliAddr* program:

```
CONST
  maxAddresses  =   250;
  { ... }

TYPE
  { ... }
  indexRange    =   1..maxAddresses;
  addressArray  =   ARRAY [indexRange] OF addressRecord;
```

In this passage, *indexRange* is a subrange of integers, from 1 to 250.

Another example appears in the *SetTest* demonstration program, which we looked at earlier in this chapter. This program defines *lowerCaseLetters*, a subrange of the CHAR type:

```
TYPE
  lowerCaseLetters = 'a'..'z';
```

Keep in mind that you can create a subrange from any ordinal type, including an enumerated type. For example, the following definition creates a subrange of the enumerated *activities* values:

```
TYPE
  programOptions = updateClient..listAddresses;
```

The next section of this chapter examines a useful technique for initializing the values of structured variables.

Typed Constants

A *typed constant* is actually a variable that you declare and initialize in the CONST section of a program, procedure, or function. The declaration establishes three characteristics: the name of the variable, the variable's type, and the initial value the variable will have upon entry into the statement block of the program or routine. Like all variables, typed constants can be declared globally or locally.

Here is the general form of this declaration:

```
CONST
  variableName : typeName = value;
```

For example, the following CONST statement defines an integer variable named *maxVal*, and initializes its value to 100:

```
CONST
  maxVal: INTEGER = 100;
```

The effect of this statement is identical to the following passage:

```
VAR
  maxVal: INTEGER;

BEGIN
  maxVal : = 100;
  { ... }
END
```

In either case, *maxVal* is defined as a variable, the value of which can change any number of times during a program performance. In contrast, the following CONST declaration defines a named constant, *maxVal*:

```
CONST
  maxVal = 100;
```

An attempt to assign a new value to a named constant results in a compile-time error.

Signficantly, Turbo Pascal allows you use CONST to define and initialize data structures, including arrays, records, and sets. This is perhaps the most convenient use for typed constants. Let's look at some examples.

The syntax for declaring an array as a typed constant requires that you list the initial array values in the correct order, enclosed in parentheses. For example, you may recognize the following declaration from the *dateString* function in *ChrnUnit*:

```
CONST
  days: ARRAY[0..6] OF STRING[3] =
    ('Sun','Mon','Tue','Wed','Thu','Fri','Sat');
  months: ARRAY[1..12] OF STRING[3] =
    ('Jan','Feb','Mar','Apr','May','Jun',
     'Jul','Aug','Sep','Oct','Nov','Dec');
```

This CONST declaration defines the two string arrays *days* and *months*, and assigns a sequence of three-letter abbreviations to each.

To define a record as a typed constant, you supply each of the field names and initial field values in order, using the following general syntax:

```
CONST
  recordName: RECORD OF recordType =
  (fieldName1: fieldValue1; fieldName2: fieldValue2; ... )
```

In this syntax, *recordType* identifies a record structure that you have defined earlier in a TYPE declaration. (Recall that Turbo Pascal allows you to place CONST, TYPE, and VAR declarations in any order in a program.)

The *CliMenu* program contains a good illustration of a rather complex typed-constant declaration. As we have seen, *activity* is an array of records, in which each record represents all the necessary information about one particular menu option. Specifically, the record structure includes fields for the .EXE program name (*fileName*), the screen position of the option (*row* and *column*), and the text of the option as displayed in the menu itself (*menuString*). The following declaration initializes all of this information for all five menu options:

```
CONST
  { ... }
  activity: ARRAY[activities] OF activityRecord =
    ((fileName: 'HOURS'; row: 8; column: columnPos;
      menuString: 'Update a client file.'),
```

```
(fileName: 'BILLTIME'; row: 9; column: columnPos;
  menuString: 'Bill a client.'),
(fileName: 'CLILIST'; row: 10; column: columnPos;
  menuString: 'List accounts and totals.'),
(fileName: 'CLIADDR'; row: 11; column: columnPos;
  menuString: 'Print client addresses.'),
(fileName: ''; row: 12; column: columnPos;
  menuString: 'Quit.'));
```

This statement initializes all four fields of each record in turn.

Finally, *CliMenu* also uses this technique to initialize two SET-type variables, *menuChars* and *cursorScanCodes:*

```
CONST
  { ... }
  menuChars: SET OF CHAR =
          ['U', 'B', 'L', 'P', 'Q', nullChar, enter];

  cursorScanCodes: SET OF CHAR =
          [upArrow, leftArrow, rightArrow, downArrow];
```

As we'll see shortly, the program uses these two sets to validate the user's keyboard input.

In the course of studying sets, enumerated types, and typed constants, we have already examine several passages from the *CliMenu* program. Let's now take a look at the entire listing.

The Listing of the *CliMenu* Program

The *CliMenu* listing appears in Figure 7.4. We have seen how the program uses the enumerated *activities* type to represent the various menu options. As we take a closer look at the listing, we'll concentrate specifically on the keyboard input and screen output techniques implemented in the program, and the use of SET types to simplify input validation from the keyboard.

```
PROGRAM CliMenu;

  { The CliMenu program supplies menu-driven access to
    the four programs of the client-billing application:

      o Hours     (creates or updates an HRS file)
      o BillTime  (prints an invoice from an HRS file)
      o CliList   (prints a list of all HRS files)
      o CliAddr   (prints client address lists and phone lists)

    The features of the menu are cursor-key access, and
    highlighted options. This program uses the EXEC command
    to perform the four application programs, which must be
    available on disk in compiled EXE form. }

USES CRT, DOS, StrUnit;

{ Specify heap size for successful use of EXEC. }
{$M 16384, 0, 0}

TYPE
  activities = (updateClient, billClient,
                listClients, listAddresses, quit);

  { The activityRecord type contains fields of
    information about the menu options. }

  activityRecord = RECORD
    fileName:      STRING[8];      { name of EXE file. }
    row,                           { row and column }
    column:        BYTE;           {   positions of menu option }
    menuString:    STRING[25]      { menu option string }
  END;

CONST
  columnPos = 24;
  optionDisplay = ' U B L P Q ';

  { ASCII characters for null, enter, and bell }

  nullChar = #0;
  enter = #13;
  bell = #7;

  { ASCII characters for arrow keys }

  upArrow = #72;
  leftArrow = #75;
  rightArrow = #77;
  downArrow = #80;

  { The activity array contains a record of
    information about each menu option. }

  activity: ARRAY[activities] OF activityRecord =
    ((fileName: 'HOURS'; row: 8; column: columnPos;
      menuString: 'Update a client file.'),
     (fileName: 'BILLTIME'; row: 9; column: columnPos;
      menuString: 'Bill a client.'),
     (fileName: 'CLILIST'; row: 10; column: columnPos;
      menuString: 'List accounts and totals.'),
     (fileName: 'CLIADDR'; row: 11; column: columnPos;
      menuString: 'Print client addresses.'),
     (fileName: ''; row: 12; column: columnPos;
      menuString: 'Quit.'));
```

Figure 7.4: The listing of the *CliMenu* program

```
    { The menuChars set contains all the valid characters
      that the user can press in response to the menu. }

    menuChars: SET OF CHAR =
             ['U', 'B', 'L', 'P', 'Q', nullChar, enter];

    { The cursorScanCodes set contains the codes for the
      four arrow keys. }

    cursorScanCodes: SET OF CHAR =
                   [upArrow, leftArrow, rightArrow, downArrow];

VAR
  done: BOOLEAN;
  currentSelection: activities;


PROCEDURE ReverseVideo (status: BOOLEAN);

  { The ReverseVideo procedure toggles screen display
    status to reverse video or to normal, depending on
    the BOOLEAN argument value the procedure receives. }

  BEGIN     { ReverseVideo }

    IF status THEN
      BEGIN
        TEXTCOLOR (Black);
        TEXTBACKGROUND (White)
      END
    ELSE
      BEGIN
        TEXTCOLOR (White);
        TEXTBACKGROUND (Black)
      END

  END;     { ReverseVideo }


PROCEDURE HighlightSelection;

  { The HighlightSelection procedure highlights the
    current menu selection---that is, it displays the
    selection in reverse video mode, and in all
    uppercase letters. }

  BEGIN     { HighlightSelection }

    ReverseVideo (TRUE);
    WITH activity[currentSelection] DO
      BEGIN
        GOTOXY (column, row);
        WRITELN (UpperCase(menuString))
      END;
    ReverseVideo (FALSE);
    GOTOXY (60,17)

  END;     { HighlightSelection }


PROCEDURE InitializeMenu;

  { The InitializeMenu procedure displays the menu
    on the screen, and sets currentSelection to the
    first menu option. }
```

Figure 7.4: The listing of the *CliMenu* program (continued)

```
        VAR
          option: activities;

        BEGIN    { InitializeMenu }

          CLRSCR;

          { Display the menu title. }

          ReverseVideo (TRUE);
          GOTOXY (columnPos - 8, 6);
          WRITELN ('*** Client-File Management Activities ***');
          ReverseVideo (FALSE);

          { Display the menu options. }

          FOR option := updateClient TO quit DO
            WITH activity[option] DO
              BEGIN
                GOTOXY (column, row);
                WRITELN (menuString)
              END;

          { Establish the current selection, and highlight it. }

          currentSelection := updateClient;
          HighlightSelection;

          { Display the keyboard instructions. }

          GOTOXY (columnPos - 12, 16);
          WRITE ('(Use ');
          ReverseVideo (TRUE);
          WRITE (#24, ' ', #25, ' ', #26, ' ', #27);
          ReverseVideo (FALSE);
          WRITE (' or ');
          ReverseVideo (TRUE);
          WRITE (optionDisplay);
          ReverseVideo (FALSE);
          WRITE (' to highlight an option,');

          GOTOXY (columnPos - 10, 17);
          WRITE ('then press <Enter> to complete the selection.)');

        END;    { InitializeMenu }


      PROCEDURE GetSelection (VAR quitSignal: BOOLEAN);

        { The GetSelection procedure accepts a menu selection
          from the keyboard, and performs the appropriate program
          in response. }

        CONST
          firstChars = 'UBLPQ';

        VAR
          inChar: CHAR;


        PROCEDURE Continue;
```

Figure 7.4: The listing of the *CliMenu* program (continued)

```
          { The Continue procedure prompts the user to
            press the space bar to return to the menu after
            a given menu activity has been selected and
            performed. }

        VAR
          inSpace: CHAR;

        BEGIN    { Continue }

          GOTOXY (10,25);
          WRITE ('Press the space bar to return to the menu. ');
          REPEAT
            inSpace := READKEY
          UNTIL inSpace = ' ';

        END;    { Continue }


    PROCEDURE RemoveHighlight;

      { The RemoveHighlight procedure restores a
        deselected menu option to normal display,
        with uppercase and lowercase letters. }

      BEGIN    { RemoveHighlight }

        WITH activity[currentSelection] DO
          BEGIN
            GOTOXY (column, row);
            WRITELN (menuString)
          END

      END;    { RemoveHighlight }


    PROCEDURE SelectNextActivity;

      { The SelectNextActivity procedure highlights the
        next menu option down the list, responding to a
        down- or right-arrow key pressed at the keyboard. }

      BEGIN    { SelectNextActivity }

        RemoveHighlight;
        IF currentSelection = quit THEN
          currentSelection := updateClient
        ELSE
          currentSelection := SUCC(currentSelection);
        HighlightSelection

      END;    { SelectNextActivity }


    PROCEDURE SelectPreviousActivity;

      { The SelectPreviousActivity procedure highlights the
        previous menu option up the list, responding to an
        up- or left-arrow key pressed at the keyboard. }

      BEGIN    { SelectPreviousActivity }
```

Figure 7.4: The listing of the *CliMenu* program (continued)

```
            RemoveHighlight;
            IF currentSelection = updateClient THEN
              currentSelection := quit
            ELSE
              currentSelection := PRED(currentSelection);
            HighlightSelection

        END;    { SelectPreviousActivity }


   BEGIN  {GetSelection}

     quitSignal := FALSE;

     { Read keystrokes until the user presses
       a valid key in response to the menu. }

     REPEAT
       inChar := UPCASE(READKEY);
       IF NOT (inChar IN menuChars) THEN
         WRITE (bell)
     UNTIL (inChar IN menuChars);

     { Respond appropriately to the keystroke. }

     CASE inChar OF

       'U', 'B', 'L', 'P', 'Q' :

         BEGIN
           RemoveHighlight;
           currentSelection :=
               activities(POS(inChar, firstChars) - 1);
           HighlightSelection
         END;

       nullChar :

         BEGIN
           inChar := READKEY;
           IF inChar IN cursorScanCodes THEN
             CASE inChar OF
               upArrow, leftArrow: SelectPreviousActivity;
               downArrow, rightArrow: SelectNextActivity
             END
           ELSE
             WRITE (bell)
         END;

       { Perform a program when the user presses the
         enter key to confirm the current menu selection. }

       enter :

         BEGIN
           IF currentSelection = quit THEN
             quitSignal := TRUE
           ELSE
             BEGIN
               WITH activity[currentSelection] DO
                 EXEC (fileName + '.EXE', '');
```

Figure 7.4: The listing of the *CliMenu* program (continued)

```
               Continue;
               CLRSCR;
               InitializeMenu
            END
         END
   END
   END;    { GetSelection }

BEGIN    { CliMenu }

   InitializeMenu;

   { Display the recurring menu. }

   REPEAT
      GetSelection (done);
   UNTIL done;
   CLRSCR

END.    { CliMenu }
```

Figure 7.4: The listing of the *CliMenu* program (continued)

The main program section begins by making a call to the *Initialize-Menu* routine to display the menu on the screen; then the program makes repeated calls to the *GetSelection* procedure, to accept the user's menu choices:

```
Initializemenu;
REPEAT
   GetSelection (done);
UNTIL done;
```

GetSelection receives the BOOLEAN value *done* as a variable parameter, and passes back a value of TRUE if the user selects the Quit option. When this happens, the performance of the program is complete. We'll look at each of these two main procedures in turn.

The *InitializeMenu* Procedure

The *InitializeMenu* procedure displays the menu's title on the screen in reverse-video text—that is, black text against a light background. A call to the *ReverseVideo* procedure establishes the display characteristics:

```
ReverseVideo (TRUE);
GOTOXY (columnPos − 8, 6);
```

```
WRITELN ('* * * Client-File Management Activities * * *');
ReverseVideo (FALSE);
```

ReverseVideo uses Turbo Pascal's built-in TEXTCOLOR and TEXT-BACKGROUND procedures (from the CRT unit) to establish the foreground and background display colors. Passing a value of TRUE as an argument to *ReverseVideo* results in black text against a white background for subsequent output to the screen. Passing a value of FALSE restores the default light text against a black background.

Turbo Pascal's built-in GOTOXY procedure (also from the CRT unit) positions the cursor at a given row and column position on the display screen:

```
GOTOXY(column, row)
```

A subsequent WRITELN statement begins its output at the cursor position represented by *(column, row)*. After the title is on the screen, the program uses the following FOR loop to display all of the menu options at their appropriate screen positions:

```
FOR option : = updateClient TO quit DO
   WITH activity[option] DO
      BEGIN
         GOTOXY (column, row);
         WRITELN (menuString)
      END;
```

As we've seen, the control variable *option* belongs to the enumerated *activities* type. Notice the use of the WITH statement, allowing the program to refer directly to the field names of a given *activity[option]* record: *column*, *row*, and *menuString*.

The *InitializeMenu* procedure next establishes the first menu option—represented by the enumerated value *updateClient*—as the current menu selection. Recall that the global variable *currentSelection* always keeps track of the selection that is currently highlighted on the screen. A call to *HighlightSelection* actually highlights the designated current selection:

```
currentSelection : = updateClient;
HighlightSelection;
```

The *HighlightSelection* function simply switches to the reverse-video display mode and redisplays the current selection at its correct screen location:

```
ReverseVideo (TRUE);
WITH activity[currentSelection] DO
  BEGIN
    GOTOXY (column, row);
    WRITELN (UpperCase(menuString))
  END;
```

Notice that this routine also converts the highlighted menu string to all uppercase letters. The *UpperCase* function, supplied to the program by *StrUnit*, performs the case conversion.

The *InitializeMenu* procedure displays two further lines of instructions at the bottom of the screen, and then its work is complete. The *GetSelection* procedure takes control next, to receive the user's input from the keyboard.

The *GetSelection* Procedure

A REPEAT UNTIL loop located at the top of *GetSelection* uses Turbo Pascal's built-in READKEY procedure (from the CRT unit) to read the user's input from the keyboard:

```
REPEAT
  inChar : = UPCASE(READKEY);
```

The UPCASE function converts each single character of input to its uppercase equivalent if necessary. (Note that UPCASE is a built-in function that takes CHAR-type arguments. In contrast, the *UpperCase* function, from *StrUnit*, converts the case of an entire string at a time.)

Next the program checks to see if the value stored in *inChar* is a valid response to the menu. The set named *menuChars* is established as a global variable at the top of the program:

```
menuChars: SET OF CHAR =
            ['U', 'B', 'L', 'P', 'Q', nullChar, enter];
```

Given this set, the program uses the following IN operation to validate *inChar:*

```
IF NOT (inChar IN menuChars) THEN
   WRITE (bell)
```

In other words, if the *inChar* character is not a member of the *menuChars* set, the program produces an audible tone to signal the input error. (The named constant *bell* contains the ASCII value #7, which corresponds to the bell character. Writing this character produces the tone.)

The REPEAT UNTIL loop continues waiting for keystrokes until the user presses a key corresponding to a character that is a member of *menuChars:*

```
UNTIL (inChar IN menuChars);
```

When *inChar* contains a character that is a valid response to the menu, *GetSelection* uses a CASE statement to choose among the possible courses of action. The first case is selected if *inChar* contains an uppercase letter representing one of the five menu options:

```
CASE inChar OF

  'U', 'B', 'L', 'P', 'Q' :

    BEGIN
      RemoveHighlight;
      currentSelection : =
            activities(POS(inChar, firstChars) − 1);
      HighlightSelection
    END;
```

When the user presses one of these five keys, the screen highlight immediately moves to the corresponding option in the menu. The program has to perform three distinct steps to accomplish this change:

1. The highlight must be removed from the previous selection. The *RemoveHighlight* procedure (a local routine in *GetSelection*) performs this task by simply rewriting the previous option text at the appropriate screen location.

2. The program translates the user's keystroke into one of the five enumerated *activites* values and records this value as the new *currentSelection* status. We have already discussed the type-casting operation that accomplishes this:

```
currentSelection : =
        activities(POS(inChar, firstChars) – 1);
```

3. The program calls the *HighlightSelection* procedure to high-light the new option selection.

In addition to the five keystrokes that select specific menu options, the user can also press any of the four arrow keys to move the high-light up or down. To understand how the *CliMenu* program handles this activity, we need to discuss an additional feature of Turbo Pascal's READKEY function.

Advanced Use of the READKEY Function

When the user presses a key that corresponds to an ASCII charac-ter, READKEY simply returns the value of the character itself. How-ever, several groups of keys on the IBM PC keyboard perform functions that have no direct ASCII equivalent. These special keys include the function keys and the Alt and Ctrl keystroke combina-tions. The four cursor-movement keys—↑, →, ↓, and ←—are included in this special category of keys.

In response to one of these keystrokes, READKEY returns an *extended code*, consisting of two separate characters. Initially the function returns a value of 0 (sometimes called a *null character*) to indicate that a special key has been pressed. To receive the second extended code, the program must make a second call to READKEY. This second call supplies a code that indicates exactly which key the user has pressed.

Here are the extended codes that READKEY returns for the four arrow keys:

Key	Code
Up arrow (↑)	72
Left arrow (←)	75

Right arrow (→) 77

Down arrow (↓) 80

The *CliMenu* program establishes four named constants to represent these extended codes:

```
upArrow = #72;
leftArrow = #75;
rightArrow = #77;
downArrow = #80;
```

Furthermore, *cursorScanCodes* is a SET variable containing all four code characters as members:

```
cursorScanCodes: SET OF CHAR =
              [upArrow, leftArrow, rightArrow, downArrow];
```

Inside the *GetSelection* procedure, the second case block is selected when READKEY returns a null character; in response, the program performs a second call to READKEY:

```
nullChar :

  BEGIN
    inChar : = READKEY;
```

If the new *inChar* character is a member of the *cursorScanCodes* set, the program knows that the user has pressed one of the four arrow keys. A nested CASE statement makes a call to one of two functions designed to move the highlight on the screen:

```
IF inChar IN cursorScanCodes THEN
    CASE inChar OF
      upArrow, leftArrow: SelectPreviousActivity;
      downArrow, rightArrow: SelectNextActivity
    END
```

SelectPreviousActivity and *SelectNextActivity* both select a new menu option and highlight the new selection. As we saw earlier in this chapter, this process makes use of the PRED and SUCC functions.

However, the new selection is more complicated if either the first or the last option in the menu list is currently highlighted on the screen. For example, if the current selection is Quit, the *SelectNextActivity* procedure has to move the highlight to the first selection, producing a "wrap-around" effect on the menu screen:

```
IF currentSelection = quit THEN
  currentSelection : = updateClient
ELSE
  currentSelection : = SUCC(currentSelection);
```

After this selection process, a call to *HighlightSelection* moves the highlight to the newly selected option.

Finally, the user can press the Enter key to complete the selection of a highlighted menu option. The third case selection in the *GetSelection* procedure deals with this response. *CliMenu* has stored the value #13 in the named constant *enter*, which represents the carriage-return character. If *inChar* contains this character, the program first looks to see if the current selection is Quit:

```
enter :

  BEGIN
    IF currentSelection = quit THEN
      quitSignal : = TRUE
```

The value of the VAR parameter *quitSignal* is passed back to the BOOLEAN variable *done* in the main program section. When this variable contains a value of TRUE the performance ends.

However, if the highlighted selection is one of the first four menu options, the *CliMenu* program calls the EXEC procedure (from the DOS unit) to perform the corresponding .EXE file stored on disk:

```
ELSE
  BEGIN
    WITH activity[currentSelection] DO
      EXEC (fileName + '.EXE', '');
```

We've encountered the EXEC command in previous chapters. To end our discussion of the *CliMenu* program, let's look at the various forms this command can take.

The EXEC Procedure

As we have seen, EXEC makes a temporary exit to DOS to perform an .EXE or .COM program. EXEC takes two string arguments. The first is the full name of an .EXE or .COM program stored on disk (including the extension name, along with any necessary drive and path specifications). The second argument is a command-line string that will be passed to the program itself:

```
EXEC ('progName', 'commandLineString')
```

To perform an internal DOS command, you use COMMAND-.COM as the program name and the name of the internal command as the command-line string. In addition, the command-line string must begin with the special notation '/C'. We have seen several examples of this EXEC format in previous chapters; for example, the following command comes from the *Hours* program:

```
EXEC ('\COMMAND.COM', '/C DIR  ' + mask + '   /W');
```

When the program you wish to perform is a separate .EXE or .COM file, the name of the program file appears as the first argument of EXEC. The second argument may be an empty string if the program itself is not designed to take parameters. This is the case in the *CliMenu* program:

```
WITH activity[currentSelection] DO
   EXEC (fileName + 'EXE', '');
```

One additional reminder: A program has to use the $M compiler directive to set the size of the heap in order to use EXEC successfully. For example, the $M directive from the *CliMenu* program sets the heap size to zero bytes:

```
{$M 16384, 0, 0}
```

We'll discuss the purpose of the heap in Chapter 8, as we take up the topic of dynamic pointer variables.

Summary

In this chapter we have covered several new data types and data structures, including sets, enumerated types, and typed constants:

- A set is a data structure containing a group of ordinal values as members. Probably the most practical use of sets in Turbo Pascal programs is for validating input characters.

- An enumerated type is a sequence of identifiers that together form a user-defined ordinal type. Creative use of enumerated types can make a complex program easier to read and easier to revise. Like other ordinal types, enumerated values can be used as array indexes and FOR-loop controls. Furthermore, the standard functions ORD, SUCC, and PRED are all available for use with enumerated types.

- A typed constant is a variable definition that actually assigns an initial value to the variable. You write typed-constant declarations in the CONST section of a program, procedure, or function. Typed constants are particularly useful for assigning initial values to complex data structures, as we have seen illustrated in the *CliMenu* program.

With its integral use of SET-type data structures, enumerated values, and typed constants, *CliMenu* represents quintessential Turbo Pascal programming. You may want to return to this program later to review its data structures and special input and output techniques. Furthermore, you should be able use *CliMenu* as a foundation for building other menu-driven applications.

C H A P T E R

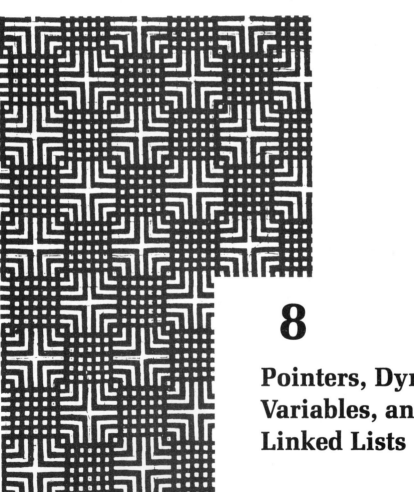

8

Pointers, Dynamic Variables, and Linked Lists

This chapter introduces you to several advanced data structures that you can build and use in Turbo Pascal programs. A *pointer* is a variable that contains the memory address of another variable or data structure. Specifically, a declared pointer variable can store the address of a *dynamic variable*, a data structure for which memory space is allocated during the actual performance of a program.

A dynamic variable is the only data structure in Pascal that does have to be identified in a VAR declaration before use in a program. Turbo Pascal stores dynamic variables in a special memory area called the *heap*. A program can create any number of dynamic variables, as long as there is space remaining in the heap.

A *linked list of records* is one of the versatile data structures that you can build with dynamic variable components. Like an array, a linked list may contain an ordered sequence of individual records. But a linked list has two characteristics that require special programming techniques:

- The length of a linked list is not defined in advance, but increases or decreases dynamically during the program performance.

- A linked list has no indexes for identifying individual record components. Rather, the records in a linked list can be accessed only through pointers that are built into the list.

Pointers, dynamic variables, and linked lists are unusual tools for a highly structured language like Pascal—a language that generally requires all variables and structures to be fully declared before use. Consider the following anomalies:

- A pointer type is generally defined to point to another structure of a specified type, called the *base type*. Uncharacteristically, Pascal allows you to declare a pointer type in advance of defining the pointer's base type.

- A pointer can refer to a dynamic variable that is *not* identified in advance in a VAR declaration.

- A linked list is a structure that has no predefined identifier representing it—only a series of pointers that contain the addresses of its components.

To explore these advanced subjects in this chapter, we'll examine a new version of a familiar program application—a revision of the *CliAddr* program, which was first presented in Chapter 6. The revised version is called the *PtrAddr* program. Like the original version of the program, *PtrAddr* is a menu-driven application designed to maintain a client address file and print address lists and phone directories from the information stored in the file. You'll recall that the *CliAddr* program organizes the information as an array of records, and uses a Shell sort to arrange the list either by client names or by reference numbers.

In contrast, the *PtrAddr* program stores the addresses in memory as a linked list of dynamic record variables. This new version of the program will give us the opportunity to examine some interesting algorithms related to linked lists—techniques for sorting the list and and for accessing records from the list in a specified order.

Before we turn to the *PtrAddr* program, however, we'll study the general characteristics of pointers, dynamic variables, linked lists, and the heap.

Introduction to Pointers and Lists

As an introductory exercise with pointers, we'll begin our discussion with a short and relatively simple program named *PtrTest*. This program creates a linked list of dynamic records in memory and then reads through the list in two directions, displaying values from the list on the screen. Unlike the *PtrAddr* program, *PtrTest* is designed merely as a demonstration, and performs no useful data-management tasks.

In the linked list that *PtrTest* creates, each record contains one CHAR-type data field, storing a letter of the alphabet from A to Z. Thus the program creates 26 dynamic records in all. The program's primary exercise is to establish links among these 26 records in two directions—from A to Z and from Z to A. In other words, each dynamic record in the list must also contain two pointer fields—one pointing to the next record in the list and another to the previous record in the list.

To demonstrate that this "double-linked" list has been successfully established, the program runs through the list in both directions and prints the value of each CHAR field on the screen. A procedure named *PrintForward* reads the list from A to Z; a procedure named *PrintBackward* reads it from Z to A. Here is the output that the program produces:

```
PrintForward:
ABCDEFGHIJKLMNOPQRSTUVWXYZ

PrintBackward:
ZYXWVUTSRQPONMLKJIHGFEDCBA
```

In performing this very simple exercise, *PtrTest* illustrates many of the essential algorithms for creating and managing linked lists.

The listing of *PtrTest* appears in Figure 8.1. The program contains three procedures in all. Before the calls to *PrintForward* and *Print-Backward*, a procedure named *SetLetterPointers* creates the linked list. As you can see, the main program section consists simply of calls to these three procedures:

```
SetLetterPointers;
PrintForward;
PrintBackward
```

We'll examine specific portions of the program as we take our first look at pointer variables.

```
PROGRAM PtrTest;

  { The PtrTest program demonstrates the essentials of pointer
    variables and linked lists. The program creates a linked
    list of 26 records. Each record in the list contains three
    fields: nextLetter is a pointer to the next record in the
    list; prevLetter is a pointer to the previous record in the
    list; and alphChar is a character from 'A' to 'Z'.}

  TYPE
    alphPtr      = ^alphRecord;
    alphRecord   = RECORD
      nextLetter,
      prevLetter: alphPtr;
      alphChar:   CHAR
    END;

  VAR
    firstLetter,        { pointer to the first record in the list }
    lastLetter,         { pointer to the last record in the list }
    newLetter,          { pointer to the most recent record }
    oldLetter: alphPtr; { pointer the the previous record }
    letter:    CHAR;


  PROCEDURE SetLetterPointers;

    { The SetLetterPointers procedure creates the linked list. }

    BEGIN    { SetLetterPointers }

      { Create the first record in the list;
        firstLetter points to this first record. }

      letter := 'A';
      NEW (newLetter);
      firstLetter := newLetter;

      { The prevLetter field of the first record in
        the list is NIL. }

      firstLetter^.prevLetter := NIL;
      firstLetter^.alphChar := letter;

      { oldLetter always points to the previously
        created record in the list. }

      oldLetter := firstLetter;

      { Create new records for each letter up to 'Z' }

      WHILE letter <> 'Z' DO

        BEGIN
          letter := SUCC (letter);
          NEW (newLetter);
          newLetter^.alphChar := letter;

          { The prevLetter field points to the previously
            created record, oldLetter. The nextLetter field
            of oldLetter points to the current record. }
```

Figure 8.1: The listing of the *PtrTest* program

```
                  newLetter^.prevLetter := oldLetter;
                  oldLetter^.nextLetter := newLetter;
                  oldLetter := newLetter
              END;

        { The nextLetter field of the last record in the
          list is NIL. }

        lastLetter := newLetter;
        lastLetter^.nextLetter := NIL

    END;    { SetLetterPointers }


PROCEDURE PrintForward;

  { The PrintForward procedure goes forward through
    the linked list and displays each alphChar field. }

  VAR
    nextPrintLetter: alphPtr;

  BEGIN    { PrintForward }

    nextPrintLetter := firstLetter;
    WHILE nextPrintLetter^.nextLetter <> NIL DO
      BEGIN
        WRITE (nextPrintLetter^.alphChar);
        nextPrintLetter := nextPrintLetter^.nextLetter
      END;
    WRITELN (nextPrintLetter^.alphChar)

  END;    { PrintForward }


PROCEDURE PrintBackward;

  { The PrintBackward procedure goes backward through
    the linked list and displays each alphChar field. }

  VAR
    prevPrintLetter: alphPtr;

  BEGIN    { PrintBackward }

    prevPrintLetter := lastLetter;

  WHILE prevPrintLetter^.prevLetter <> NIL DO
    BEGIN
      WRITE (prevPrintLetter^.alphChar);
      prevPrintLetter := prevPrintLetter^.prevLetter
    END;
  WRITELN (prevPrintLetter^.alphChar)

END;    { PrintBackward }
```

Figure 8.1: The listing of the *PtrTest* program (continued)

```
BEGIN    { PtrTest }

  { Create the linked list, then display
    the list in both directions. }

  SetLetterPointers;

  WRITELN ('PrintForward:');
  PrintForward;
  WRITELN;

  WRITELN ('PrintBackward:');
  PrintBackward;
  WRITELN;

END.     { PtrTest }
```

Figure 8.1: The listing of the *PtrTest* program (continued)

Declaring a Pointer Variable

The identifier for a pointer type is established in a TYPE declaration section, along with the definition of the pointer's base type. Here is a general format for these declarations:

```
TYPE
  pointerType  =  ^baseType;
  baseType     =  baseTypeDefinition;
```

Notice the use of the caret character (^) in the pointer type definition. In English, this line would read, "*pointerType* is a pointer to a *baseType* structure." This forward-referenced declaration is legal as long as the *baseType* structure is defined later in the same TYPE declaration section.

In a linked list, the usual base type for a pointer variable is a RECORD structure. The record can contain any combination of data fields and pointer fields, both performing distinct roles in the program:

- Data fields are designed to represent particular items of information in a given record.

- Pointer fields are designed to point to other records in the linked list.

Let's look at an example of this structure from the *PtrTest* program. The program listing begins with the following type declarations:

```
TYPE
  alphPtr    = ^alphRecord;
  alphRecord= RECORD
    nextLetter,
    prevLetter: alphPtr;
  alphChar:    CHAR
  END;
```

In this example, the *alphPtr* type is defined as a pointer to an *alph-Record*. The record structure contains three fields. The first two, *next-Letter* and *prevLetter*, are declared as *alphPtr*-type pointers—that is, they will point to other *alphRecord* structures. The third field, *alph-Char*, is a CHAR-type field, designed to store a particular data item. As you might guess, the *alphChar* field in a given record will store a letter from A to Z, and the two pointer fields establish the forward and backward links in the list of records. We'll see exactly how the program assigns values to these three fields as we continue our discussion.

Notice that the definitions of *alphPtr* and *alphRecord* are circular; the base type of the pointer is *alphRecord*, and the record structure in turn contains fields belonging to the pointer type *alphPtr*. This circular definition shows why Pascal allows a pointer type to be defined in advance of its own base type: the base type may itself contain fields belonging to the pointer type. As we will see, the pointer fields are designed to point to other dynamic records of the same type, producing an ordered sequence of records in the linked list.

The *PtrTest* program goes on to declare four pointer variables belonging to the *alphPtr* type:

```
VAR
  firstLetter,
  lastLetter,
  newLetter,
  oldLetter:  alphPtr;
```

Keep in mind the purpose of a pointer variable: it stores the memory address of a data structure. Each of these four pointer variables can store one address at a time, pointing to a particular *alphRecord*-type structure.

Significantly, the program has no explicit VAR declarations for *alphRecord* variables. All such variables will be defined dynamically, during the actual performance of the program. The only way that this program accesses an *alphRecord*-type structure is through a *alphPtr*-type pointer variable. We'll see how the program creates dynamic variables in the next section.

Creating a Dynamic Variable

First we should briefly discuss the special memory area called the heap. The purpose of the heap is to store dynamic variables. Turbo Pascal contains a variety of built-in facilities for managing the heap. By default, Turbo Pascal allocates all *remaining* memory space to the heap—that is, all memory that is not used by a program for other purposes. However, you can use the $M compiler directive to specify minimum and maximum values for the heap size:

```
{$M stackSize, minimumHeap, maximumHeap}
```

You don't really need to concern yourself very much with the heap, even when you are writing a program that works with dynamic variables. As your program creates and accesses dynamic variables, Turbo Pascal performs various heap management tasks automatically. A pointer contains the memory address of a variable stored in the heap, and thus provides a symbolic means of referencing a heap address. Your program does not need to deal explicitly with memory addresses in the heap.

A special error can occur during the performance of a program that uses the heap for dynamic variables—the memory available for the heap can become filled to capacity, leaving no room for new dynamic variables. When this happens, a subsequent attempt to create a dynamic variable results in a run-time error. The performance terminates and the following message appears at the top of the screen in the Turbo Pascal environment:

```
Heap overflow error
```

The size of the heap thus imposes a practical upper limit on the data-handling capacity of a program like *PtrAddr*, which stores the entire address database in memory at once during a program performance. Chapter 9 presents a program that will help you explore the capacity of the heap for the address-list application.

Turbo Pascal offers a number of built-in procedures and functions that you can use for working with dynamic variables in the heap. The two procedures that we'll examine in this chapter are NEW and DISPOSE. NEW allocates space for a new dynamic variable in the heap. DISPOSE performs exactly the opposite operation, releasing memory that was previously allocated for a given dynamic variable. Each of these procedures takes a single pointer variable as its argument:

- NEW (*pointerVar*) creates a new dynamic variable corresponding to the base type of *pointerVar*. The procedure stores the address of the new variable in *pointerVar*.

- DISPOSE (*pointerVar*) releases the memory allocated for a dynamic variable. After a performance of DISPOSE, *pointerVar* has no defined value.

We'll find examples of the NEW procedure in this section, as we continue looking at the *PtrTest* exercise. (We'll postpone further discussion of the DISPOSE function until we return to the *PtrAddr* program later in this chapter.)

After the NEW procedure creates a dynamic variable, Pascal recognizes two distinct notations for identifying the pointer and the corresponding dynamic variable. The variable name, *pointerVar*, refers to the pointer—that is, the memory address of the dynamic variable. A different notation refers to the dynamic variable to which the pointer variable points; the general form of this second notation is

pointerVar ^

In other words, to access the dynamic variable, you append a caret character (^) to the end of the pointer-variable name.

For example, the *PtrTest* program uses the *newLetter* pointer to create new dynamic variables, as in the following statement:

NEW (newLetter);

After this statement, the program refers to the corresponding dynamic record variable as follows:

    newLetter ^

Furthermore, the three fields of the dynamic record are

    newLetter ^.nextLetter
    newLetter ^.prevLetter
    newLetter ^.alphChar

These identifiers conform to the standard notation for representing the fields in a record variable; the field name and the record variable are separated by a period. The only difference here is the extra caret character, indicating that the record itself is a dynamic variable represented by a pointer.

You can carry this notation even further. For example, the *next-Letter* field is a pointer to another record in the linked list. Consequently, the following name would represent the character field of the next record in the linked list:

    newLetter ^.nextLetter ^.alpChar

This assumes, of course, that the program has actually built the list and assigned appropriate values to the data field and pointer fields in each record. In the next section we'll see how to assign values to dynamic variables, and how to create a linked list.

Building a Linked List

In the process of building a list, you can use assignment statements to copy the value of one pointer variable to another or to assign data values to the fields of a dynamic record variable. There is nothing new about the format of such assignment statements, but you need to pay careful attention to the distinct notations for pointers and dynamic variables. As usual, Turbo Pascal will not compile an assignment statement that attempts to assign an incompatible type value to a particular variable.

Given a dynamic record structure that includes two pointer fields, *prevPtr* and *nextPtr*, along with any number of data fields, the general steps for building a double-linked list are as follows:

1. Create a new dynamic record variable.

2. Assign appropriately typed values to the data fields of the new record.

3. Establish the *prevPtr* field as a pointer to the previous record in the list.

4. Establish the *nextPtr* field as a pointer to the next record in the list.

5. Loop back to step 1 to incorporate an additional record into the list.

6. Establish special pointers and markers for the first and last records in the list.

In the *PtrTest* program, the *SetLetterPointers* procedure builds the linked list. As we have seen, each record in the list will have three fields: a CHAR-type field (*alphChar*), storing a letter from A to Z; and two *alphPtr*-type fields (*nextLetter* and *prevLetter*), pointing to the next and the previous records in the list, respectively.

The first few statements in the *SetLetterPointers* procedure establish pointers for the first record in the list and store the letter A in this record. Then a WHILE loop creates the remaining dynamic records for the letters B through Z. Finally, two additional statements in the procedure establish pointers for the end of the list. The procedure assigns values to all three fields of each new dynamic variable.

A CHAR variable named *letter* keeps track of the letter value for each successive record. The variable is initialized as follows:

```
letter : = 'A';
```

At the top of the WHILE loop, the procedure assigns the next letter to this variable before creating each new dynamic record:

```
letter : = SUCC (letter);
```

As we have seen, the *PtrTest* program defines four different pointer variables for managing the linked list. The variables *firstLetter* and *lastLetter* are designed as special pointers to the first and last dynamic records in the list, respectively. These two pointers are created for the benefit of the routines that will later access the linked list in a particular order.

The other two pointer variables, *newLetter* and *oldLetter*, are instrumental in the process of building the linked list. First, *newLetter* always points to the most recently created dynamic variable; as we have seen, the program uses this variable in the NEW statement to allocate space for new variables. Finally, the program uses the variable *oldLetter* as a pointer to the previously created dynamic variable. Let's see how the program uses these variables.

The program begins by creating the first dynamic variable:

```
NEW (newLetter);
```

Since this will be the first record in the list, the program assigns its address to *firstLetter:*

```
firstLetter : = newLetter;
```

At this point, both *firstLetter* and *newLetter* point to the first record in the list. The program can use thus use either *firstLetter* ^ or *newletter* ^ to refer to the dynamic record itself. For example, the following statement assigns the first *letter* value to the *alphChar* field of this first record:

```
firstLetter ^.alphChar : = letter;
```

The pointer fields of the first record require special handling. Since the second dynamic record variable has not been created yet, the program has to postpone assigning an address value to the *nextLetter* field. However, the *prevLetter* field should not point to anything, because this is the first record in the list. Pascal has a special value for a pointer that points to no address, represented by the reserved word NIL:

```
firstLetter ^.prevLetter : = NIL;
```

In this case, the value of NIL marks the beginning of the list. As we'll see, this marker is essential for a successful reading of the list from Z to A.

Finally, before creating the next new dynamic variable in the list, the program points *oldLetter* to the first record:

```
oldLetter : = firstLetter;
```

At this point in the process, three pointers all point to the first dynamic record: *newLetter*, *firstLetter*, and *oldLetter*. Each of these three pointer variables has a distinct role in the subsequent steps for building the list; of the three, only *firstLetter* will retain the address of the first record in the list.

The WHILE loop next takes control of the process; the looping continues until the program has created records for each letter through Z:

```
WHILE letter < > 'Z' DO
   BEGIN
      letter : = SUCC (letter);
```

Inside the loop, the program creates each new dynamic record and assigns the value of *letter* to the record's *alphChar* field:

```
NEW (newLetter);
newLetter ^.alphChar : = letter;
```

The *prevLetter* field must point to the previously created dynamic record variable; *oldLetter* currently contains the address of this previous record:

```
newLetter ^.prevLetter : = oldLetter;
```

Furthermore, now that a new record has been created, the *nextLetter* field of *oldLetter* should point to the current record:

```
oldLetter ^.nextLetter : = newLetter;
```

Finally, the *oldLetter* pointer should be "moved forward" in the list, to point to the most recently created record, so that the next iteration of the loop will be able to refer to this record:

```
oldLetter : = newLetter
```

The looping continues until all 26 records of the list have been created. In summary, here are the steps that the program performs inside the WHILE loop:

1. Finds the succeeding value of *letter*.
2. Creates a new dynamic variable.
3. Assigns the value of *letter* to the *alphChar* field of the new record.
4. Assigns the address of the previous record (*oldLetter*) to the *prevLetter* field of the new record.
5. Points the *nextLetter* field of the previous record to the new record.
6. Assigns the address of the new record to *oldLetter*, for the benefit of the next iteration of the loop.

When the looping is complete, the *SetLetterPointers* procedure has two more tasks to perform. First, the *lastLetter* pointer must point to the final *newLetter* record that was created in the WHILE loop, the Z record:

```
lastLetter : = newLetter;
```

Then, the *nextLetter* field of *lastLetter* ^ receives a value of NIL, marking the end of the list:

```
lastLetter ^.nextLetter : = NIL
```

Master the algorithms of the *SetLetterPointers* procedure and you will have a relatively easy time understanding linked lists in a real application program like *PtrAddr*. Next we'll look at the two procedures in the *PtrTest* program that read the linked list.

Accessing Values from a Linked List

Reading the double-linked list in either direction is a simple task, thanks to several elements that the program has built into the list:

- The *firstLetter* and *lastLetter* pointers contain the addresses of the first and last records in the list, respectively.

- The *nextLetter* and *prevLetter* fields of each dynamic record always contain the addresses of the next and previous records in the list.

- The first and last records in the list contain values of NIL (in the *prevLetter* and *nextLetter* fields, respectively) to mark the beginning and end of the list.

The *PrintForward* and *PrintBackward* procedures take advantage of these elements to loop through the linked list and display its *alphChar* values on the screen. The two procedures are structured identically. We'll begin by examining *PrintForward*, then we'll take a brief look at *PrintBackward*.

To mark its own progress through the list, the *PrintForward* procedure declares a local pointer variable named *nextPrintLetter:*

```
VAR
    nextPrintLetter: alphPtr;
```

The procedure initially points *nextPrintLetter* to the first record in the list:

```
nextPrintLetter : = firstLetter;
```

Then a WHILE loop reads the records one by one until the program encounters the value of NIL in the *nextLetter* field of the final record in the list:

```
WHILE nextPrintLetter ^.nextLetter < > NIL DO
```

The first statement inside the loop simply displays the *alphChar* field of the current record:

```
WRITE (nextPrintLetter ^.alphChar);
```

Finally, the procedure assigns the value of the current record's own *nextLetter* field to the *nextPrintLetter* pointer. In effect, the following statement moves the *nextPrintLetter* pointer forward to the next record in the list, preparing for the subsequent iteration of the WHILE loop:

```
nextPrintLetter : = nextPrintLetter ^.nextLetter
```

This statement shows how important it is to distinguish carefully between the notation for a pointer (*nextPrintLetter*) and the corresponding dynamic record variable that the pointer represents (*nextPrintLetter ^*).

The *PrintBackward* procedure performs similar steps to read through the list from the last record to the first. Initially a local pointer variable named *prevPrintLetter* receives the address of the last record in the list:

```
prevPrintLetter : = lastLetter;
```

Then a WHILE loop reads each record in the list until it encounters the NIL value in the *prevLetter* field of the first record:

```
WHILE prevPrintLetter ^.prevLetter < > NIL DO
```

Finally, the following statement moves the *prevPrintLetter* pointer backward to the previous letter in the list:

```
prevPrintLetter : = prevPrintLetter ^.prevLetter
```

The *PtrTest* program is a simple demonstration of pointers and dynamic variables; nonetheless, its methods for dealing with the double-linked list are very similar to the algorithms we'll find in this chapter's actual application program, *PtrAddr*. However, the *PtrAddr* program also deals with two contingencies that are not present in *PtrTest*:

- *PtrAddr* reads address records in a random order (either from a disk file or from the keyboard), and thus requires a way to "insert" each new record into the list at the correct location, producing an ordered sequence of address records.

- *PtrAddr* offers four distinct sorting orders for printing the address records; to do so, the program keeps track of four different pointers inside each address record.

The listing for *PtrAddr* appears in Figure 8.2. We'll examine the program in the next section.

```
PROGRAM PtrAddr;

  { PtrAddr is a menu-driven program designed to
    create and manage a client address file. This
    version of the program uses a linked list to
    store the file in memory, and illustrates
    pointer types. }

USES CRT, PRINTER, InUnit, StrUnit;

CONST
  addressFileName = 'ADDRLIST.TXT';
  numRecords: INTEGER = 0;

TYPE
  addressPointer = ^addressRecord;
  addressRecord  = RECORD
    nextName,
    prevName,
    nextRefNo,
    prevRefNo:      addressPointer;

    name:           STRING[30];
    phone:          STRING[20];
    refNo:          BYTE;
    headOffice:     BOOLEAN;

    street:         STRING[30];
    city:           STRING[20];

    CASE usa:       BOOLEAN OF
      TRUE:
        (state:     STRING[2];
         zip:       STRING[5]);
      FALSE:
        (otherLoc,
         country:   STRING[15])
  END;

CONST
  firstName: addressPointer = NIL;

VAR

  { Four independent address pointers, designating
    the first record in each sorting order. }

  firstRefNo,
  lastName,
  lastRefNo,
  newRecord:      addressPointer;
```

Figure 8.2: The listing of the *PtrAddr* program

```
            done:       Boolean;
            addressFile: TEXT;


    PROCEDURE SetPointers;

      { The SetPointers procedure establishes the pointers
        of the linked list. It sets the four record
        pointer fields in each new address record---whether
        the record is read from the ADDRLIST.TXT file or
        from the user at the keyboard. }

      VAR
        current,
        previous: addressPointer;
        locFound: BOOLEAN;


      PROCEDURE FindNamePointers;

        { The FindNamePointers procedure establishes the pointers
          for two sorting orders: alphabetical order and reverse
          alphabetical order by the name field. }

        BEGIN    { FindNamePointers }

          IF newRecord^.name < firstName^.name THEN

            { Make the new record the first record in
              the alphabetical sorting order. }

            BEGIN
              newRecord^.nextName := firstName;
              newRecord^.prevName := NIL;
              firstName^.prevName := newRecord;
              firstName := newRecord;
            END
          ELSE

              { Otherwise, find the correct alphabetical
                location for the new record. }

            BEGIN
              locFound := FALSE;
              previous := firstName;
              current := firstName;
              WHILE (NOT locFound) AND (current^.nextName <> NIL) DO
                BEGIN
                  current := current^.nextName;
                  IF newRecord^.name < current^.name THEN
                    BEGIN
                      locFound := TRUE;
                      previous^.nextName := newRecord;
                      newRecord^.prevName := previous;
                      newRecord^.nextName := current;
                      current^.prevName := newRecord
                    END
                  ELSE
                    previous := current
                END;

              { If the correct position has not been found
                yet, then make this new record the last
                record in the alphabetical sorting order. }
```

Figure 8.2: The listing of the *PtrAddr* program (continued)

```
                    IF (NOT locFound) THEN
                      BEGIN
                        newRecord^.prevName := current;
                        current^.nextName := newRecord;
                        newRecord^.nextName := NIL;
                        lastName := newRecord
                      END
                  END

          END;    { FindNamePointers }


      PROCEDURE FindRefNoPointers;

        { The FindRefNoPointers procedure establishes the pointers
          for two sorting orders: numerical order and reverse
          numerical order by the refNo field. }

        BEGIN    { FindRefNoPointers }

        IF newRecord^.refNo < firstRefNo^.refNo THEN

          { Make the new record the first record in
            the numerical sorting order. }

          BEGIN
            newRecord^.nextRefNo  := firstRefNo;
            newRecord^.prevRefNo  := NIL;
            firstRefNo^.prevRefNo := newRecord;
            firstRefNo := newRecord;
          END
        ELSE

          { Otherwise, find the correct numerical
            location for the new record. }

          BEGIN
            locFound := FALSE;
            previous := firstRefNo;
            current := firstRefNo;
            WHILE (NOT locFound) AND (current^.nextRefNo <> NIL) DO
              BEGIN
                current := current^.nextRefNo;
                IF newRecord^.refNo < current^.refNo THEN
                  BEGIN
                    locFound := TRUE;
                    previous^.nextRefNo := newRecord;
                    newRecord^.prevRefNo := previous;
                    newRecord^.nextRefNo := current;
                    current^.prevRefNo := newRecord
                  END
                ELSE
                  previous := current
              END;

          { If the correct position has not been found
            yet, then make this new record the last
            record in the numerical sorting order. }

          IF (NOT locFound) THEN
```

Figure 8.2: The listing of the *PtrAddr* program (continued)

```
                BEGIN
                  newRecord^.prevRefNo := current;
                  current^.nextRefNo := newRecord;
                  newRecord^.nextRefNo := NIL;
                  lastRefNo := newRecord
                END
           END

     END;   { FindRefNoPointers }


   BEGIN    { SetPointers }

     { If this record is the first record in the
       linked list, set all four independent
       starting pointers to this record, and set
       all four pointers in this record to NIL. }

     IF firstName = NIL THEN
        BEGIN
          firstName := newRecord;
          lastName := newRecord;
          firstRefNo := newRecord;
          lastRefNo := newRecord;
          WITH newRecord^ DO
             BEGIN
               nextName := NIL;
               prevName := NIL;
               nextRefNo := NIL;
               prevRefNo := NIL
             END
        END
     ELSE

        { Otherwise, if this is not the first record
          in the linked list, find the correct location
          for this record in all four sorting orders. }

        BEGIN
          FindNamePointers;
          FindRefNoPointers
        END

   END;   { SetPointers }


PROCEDURE ReadAddresses;

   { The ReadAddresses procedure opens the ADDRLIST.TXT
     file, and reads each client address into a record
     element of the linked list. (Note that this
     address list is saved as a text file on disk.) }

   VAR
     officeCode,
     usaCode:  BYTE;

   BEGIN    { ReadAddresses }
```

Figure 8.2: The listing of the *PtrAddr* program (continued)

```
    {$I-}
      RESET (addressFile);
    {$I+}

    IF IORESULT = 0 THEN
      BEGIN
        WHILE NOT EOF(addressFile) DO
          BEGIN
            NEW (newRecord);
            INC (numRecords);
            WITH newRecord^ DO
              BEGIN
                READLN (addressFile, name);
                READLN (addressFile, officeCode, usaCode, refNo);
                headOffice := BOOLEAN(officeCode);
                usa := BOOLEAN(usaCode);
                READLN (addressFile, phone);
                READLN (addressFile, street);
                READLN (addressFile, city);
                IF usa THEN
                  BEGIN
                    READLN (addressFile, state);
                    READLN (addressFile, zip)
                  END
                ELSE
                  BEGIN
                    READLN (addressFile, otherLoc);
                    READLN (addressFile, country)
                  END     { ELSE }
              END;    { WITH newRecord^ }

            { Set the record pointers
              for this new record. }

            SetPointers

          END;    { WHILE NOT EOF }

        CLOSE (addressFile)
      END    { IF IORESULT = 0 }

  END;    { ReadAddresses }


PROCEDURE NewAddress;

  { The NewAddress procedure conducts the input
    dialog for a new address record and then gives
    the user the chance to save or abandon the input. }

  CONST
    yesNo: SET OF CHAR = ['Y', 'N'];

  VAR
    usaForeign,
    isHead,
    okToSave:  CHAR;
    inAddress: addressPointer;
```

Figure 8.2: The listing of the *PtrAddr* program (continued)

```
PROCEDURE GetStateAndZip;

  { The GetStateAndZip procedure elicits the
    state and zip code for a USE  address record. }

  BEGIN     { GetStateAndZip }

    WITH inAddress^ DO
      BEGIN
        WRITE ('              State: ');
        READLN (state);
        WRITE ('           Zip code: ');
        READLN (zip)
      END

  END;    { GetStateAndZip }


PROCEDURE GetCountryInfo;

  { The GetCountryInfo procedure elicits the
    state/province and country for a foreign address. }

  BEGIN     { GetCountryInfo }

    WITH inAddress^ DO
      BEGIN
        WRITE ('   State or province: ');
        READLN (otherLoc);
        WRITE ('             Country: ');
        READLN (country)
      END

  END;    { GetCountryInfo }


PROCEDURE SaveAddress;

  { The SaveAddress procedure saves a new record
    to the ADDRLIST.TXT file. }

  BEGIN     { SaveAddress }

    IF numRecords > 1 THEN
      APPEND (addressFile)
    ELSE
      REWRITE (addressFile);

    WITH inAddress^ DO
      BEGIN
        WRITELN (addressFile, name);
        WRITELN (addressFile,
          BYTE(headOffice), ' ', BYTE(usa), ' ', refNo);
        WRITELN (addressFile, phone);
        WRITELN (addressFile, street);
        WRITELN (addressFile, city);
        IF usa THEN
          BEGIN
            WRITELN (addressFile, state);
            WRITELN (addressFile, zip)
          END
```

Figure 8.2: The listing of the *PtrAddr* program (continued)

```
                    ELSE
                       BEGIN
                          WRITELN (addressFile, otherLoc);
                          WRITELN (addressFile, country)
                       END
                 END;
              CLOSE (addressFile)

          END;    { SaveAddress }


       BEGIN    { NewAddress }

          NEW (inAddress);
          WRITELN ('Enter a client address record:');
          WRITELN ('----- - ------ ------- -------');
          WRITELN;

          WITH inAddress^ DO
             BEGIN
                WRITE ('      Name of client: ');
                READLN (name);
                refNo := InByte ('     Reference number: ');
                WRITE ('      Street address: ');
                READLN (street);
                WRITE ('               City: ');
                READLN (city);
                usaForeign := InChar ('USA or Foreign? (U F): ', ['U', 'F']);
                WRITELN (usaForeign);

                usa := (usaForeign = 'U');
             END;

          CASE inAddress^.usa OF
             TRUE: GetStateAndZip;
             FALSE: GetCountryInfo
          END;

          WITH inAddress^ DO
             BEGIN
                WRITE ('          Phone number: ');
                READLN (phone);

                isHead :=
                   InChar ('  Head office? (Y N): ', yesNo);
                headOffice := (isHead = 'Y');
                WRITELN (isHead)
             END;

          WRITELN;
          WRITELN (StringOfChars ('-', 30));
          WRITELN;
          okToSave :=
             InChar ('Save this address? (Y N): ', yesNo);
          WRITELN (okToSave);

          IF okToSave = 'Y' THEN

             { Save the address. }
```

Figure 8.2: The listing of the *PtrAddr* program (continued)

```
      BEGIN
        INC (numRecords);
        SaveAddress;
        newRecord := inAddress;
        SetPointers
      END

    ELSE

      { Abandon the address, and dispose
        of the dynamic pointer variable. }

      DISPOSE (inAddress);

    CLRSCR

  END;     { NewAddress }


PROCEDURE PrintList (addressDirectory: BOOLEAN);

  { The PrintList procedure prints either an
    address list or a phone list; the
    addressDirectory argument specifies which. }

  CONST
    formFeed    = #12;

    nameAtoZ     = '1';
    nameZtoA     = '2';
    refNoAscend  = '3';
    refNoDescend = '4';
    sortSet: SET OF CHAR =
            [nameAtoZ, nameZtoA, refNoAscend, refNoDescend];

  VAR
    sortSelection: CHAR;
    firstAddress:  addressPointer;


  FUNCTION Continue: BOOLEAN;

    { The Continue function accepts a signal from
      the user to indicate the next action: space bar
      to print the list; escape to return to the menu. }

    CONST
      spaceBar = ' ';
      escKey   = #27;
      prompt   =
        '<Space Bar> to print. <Escape> to return to menu.';

    VAR
      inKey: CHAR;

    BEGIN     { Continue }

      inKey    :=
        InChar (prompt, [spaceBar, escKey]);
      Continue := (inKey = spaceBar)

    END;     { Continue }
```

Figure 8.2: The listing of the *PtrAddr* program (continued)

```
      PROCEDURE PrintAddresses (address:   addressPointer;
                               whichSort: CHAR);

      { The PrintAddresses procedure prints an address
        directory. The argument passed to the address
        parameter is a pointer to the record that should
        be printed first. The whichSort paramter indicates
        the sorting key and the direction of the sort. }

      VAR
        i: BYTE;

      BEGIN     { PrintAddresses }

        WRITELN (LST, 'Client Address Directory');
        WRITELN (LST, '------ ------- ---------');
        WRITELN (LST);

        WHILE address <> NIL DO
          BEGIN
            WITH address^ DO
              BEGIN
                WRITE (LST, LeftAlign (name, 35), refNo:3);
                IF headOffice THEN
                  WRITELN (LST, ' H')
                ELSE
                  WRITELN (LST, ' B');
                WRITELN (LST, street);
                WRITE (LST, city, ', ');
                IF usa THEN
                  WRITELN (LST, UpperCase (state), ' ', zip)
                ELSE
                  WRITELN (LST, otherLoc, ' ', UpperCase (country));
                WRITELN (LST, phone);
                WRITELN (LST); WRITELN (LST)
              END;

            { Find the next address, using the appropriate
              pointer in the current record. }

            CASE whichSort OF
              nameAtoZ: address := address^.nextName;
              nameZtoA: address := address^.prevName;
              refNoAscend: address := address^.nextRefNo;
              refNoDescend: address := address^.prevRefNo;
            END

          END

      END;    { PrintAddresses }


   PROCEDURE PrintPhones (address: addressPointer;
                          whichSort: CHAR);

      { The PrintPhones procedure prints a phone directory.
        The argument passed to the address parameter is a
        pointer to the record that should be printed first.
        The whichSort parameter indicates the sorting key
        and the direction of the sort. }

      VAR
        i: BYTE;
```

Figure 8.2: The listing of the *PtrAddr* program (continued)

```
        BEGIN    { PrintPhones }
          WRITELN (LST, 'Client Phone Directory');
          WRITELN (LST, '------ ----- ---------');
          WRITELN (LST);
          WRITELN (LST, 'Client', Spaces (27),
                        'Reference', Spaces (10),
                        'Phone');

          WRITELN (LST);

          WHILE address <> NIL DO
            BEGIN
              WITH address^ DO
                BEGIN
                  WRITE (LST, LeftAlign (name, 35));
                  WRITE (LST, refNo:3, Spaces (10));
                  WRITELN (LST, phone)
                END;

              { Find the next address, using the appropriate
                pointer in the current record. }

              CASE whichSort OF
                nameAtoZ: address := address^.nextName;
                nameZtoA: address := address^.prevName;
                refNoAscend: address := address^.nextRefNo;
                refNoDescend: address := address^.prevRefNo;
              END

            END

        END;    { PrintPhones }


      BEGIN    { PrintList }

        IF addressDirectory THEN
          BEGIN
            WRITELN ('Print an address list.');
            WRITELN ('----- -- ------- -----')
          END
        ELSE
          BEGIN
            WRITELN ('Print a phone list.');
            WRITELN ('----- - -----'-----')
          END;
        WRITELN;

        WRITELN ('Sort by:');
        WRITELN ('    1. Names (A to Z)');
        WRITELN ('    2. Names (Z to A)');
        WRITELN ('    3. Reference numbers (ascending)');
        WRITELN ('    4. Reference numbers (descending)');
        WRITELN;
        sortSelection :=
          InChar ('  Select (1 2 3 4) --> ', sortSet);

        WRITELN (sortSelection);

        CASE sortSelection OF
          nameAtoZ:      firstAddress := firstName;
          nameZtoA:      firstAddress := lastName;
          refNoAscend:   firstAddress := firstRefNo;
          refNoDescend:  firstAddress := lastRefNo
        END;
```

Figure 8.2: The listing of the *PtrAddr* program (continued)

```
            WRITELN (StringOfChars ('-', 50));
            WRITELN;

            IF Continue THEN
              BEGIN
                IF addressDirectory THEN
                  PrintAddresses (firstAddress, sortSelection)
                ELSE
                  PrintPhones (firstAddress, sortSelection);
                WRITELN (LST, formFeed)
              END;

          CLRSCR

        END;    { PrintList }


    PROCEDURE Menu (VAR exitMenu: BOOLEAN);

      { The Menu procedure displays the recurring main menu
        on the screen, and elicits the user's menu choices. }

      VAR
        choice,
        discardCode: CHAR;

      CONST
        menuChars: SET OF CHAR = ['A', 'C', 'P', 'Q'];
        addresses = TRUE;
        phones    = FALSE;


      Procedure DisplayOption (optionString: STRING);

        { The DisplayOption procedure displays a menu option
          on the screen, with the first character displayed
          in high-intensity text. This routine uses the
          built-in TEXTCOLOR procedure, from the CRT unit. }

        BEGIN    { DisplayOption }

          TEXTCOLOR (White);
          WRITE (optionString[1]);
          TEXTCOLOR (LightGray);
          WRITELN (COPY (optionString, 2,
                       LENGTH(optionString) - 1))
        END;    { DisplayOption }


      BEGIN    { Menu }

        exitMenu := FALSE;

        GOTOXY (20, 5);
        WRITELN ('Client Address Manager');

        GOTOXY (20, 6);
        WRITELN ('------ ------- -------');

        GOTOXY (20, 7);
        DisplayOption ('Add an address.');
```

Figure 8.2: The listing of the *PtrAddr* program (continued)

```
        GOTOXY (20, 8);
        DisplayOption ('Create an address directory.');

        GOTOXY (20, 9);
        DisplayOption ('Print a phone directory.');

        GOTOXY (20,10);
        DisplayOption ('Quit.');

        GOTOXY (20,12);

        choice :=
          InChar ('** Menu choice (A C P Q) --> ', menuChars);

        CLRSCR;
        CASE choice OF
          'A' : NewAddress;
          'C' : IF numRecords > 0 THEN
                   PrintList (addresses);
          'P' : IF numRecords > 0 THEN
                   PrintList (phones);
          'Q' : exitMenu := TRUE
        END

      END;    { Menu }


BEGIN    { PtrAddr }

  ASSIGN (addressFile, addressFileName);
  ReadAddresses;

  CLRSCR;
  REPEAT
    Menu (done)
  UNTIL done

END.    { PtrAddr }
```

Figure 8.2: The listing of the *PtrAddr* program (continued)

The *PtrAddr* Program

Like the *CliAddr* program presented in Chapter 6, *PtrAddr* presents a recurring menu on the screen with the following four options:

Add an address.
Create an address directory.
Print a phone directory.
Quit.

PtrAddr also works with the same data file of address records as *CliAddr;* the name of the file on disk is ADDRLIST.TXT. In other words, the two programs are completely compatible—you can use either one to read the same ADDRLIST.TXT file and to produce address lists and phone lists from the information in the file.

When you select the first menu option, *PtrAddr* conducts the familiar input dialog, eliciting information about a given client, such as the client's name, reference number, address, city, state, ZIP code, and phone number.

To print an address list or a phone list, you select either the second or third menu option. The *PtrAddr* is somewhat more versatile than the *CliAddr* program in responding to these options. You'll recall that *CliAddr* offers you only two sorting options for a printed list: alphabetical order by the client names or numerical order by the reference numbers. *PtrAddr*, on the other hand, offers four different sorting orders for either an address list or a phone list:

Sort by:
1. Names (A to Z)
2. Names (Z to A)
3. Reference numbers (ascending)
4. Reference numbers (descending)

As you can see, the two new sorting options allow you to print a list in reverse alphabetical order by client names or in descending numeric order by the reference numbers. To select one of these options, you simply press the corresponding digit on the keyboard: 1, 2, 3, or 4.

Because *PtrAddr* stores the addresses in memory as a linked list of dynamic record variables, the technique for sorting the list is completely different from the method used in the *CliAddr* program. *CliAddr* stores the addresses as an array of records, and calls on a sorting routine to rearrange the records before each different printing operation. If the user prints three lists during a given performance, the program has to sort the addresses three times.

PtrAddr, on the other hand, simply adjusts the values of a selected group of pointers each time the program reads a new address into memory. As a result, the linked list is always ready to be printed in any of the four available orders. Let's investigate the *PtrAddr* program listing and see how this is done.

Inside the *PtrAddr* Program

At the top of the listing are declarations for the pointer type and the record structure that the program defines for the dynamic record variables:

```
TYPE
  addressPointer =   ^addressRecord;
  addressRecord =   RECORD
    nextName,
    prevName,
    nextRefNo,
    prevRefNo:        addressPointer;

    name:             STRING[30];
    phone:            STRING[20];
    refNo:            BYTE;
    headOffice:       BOOLEAN;

    street:           STRING[30];
    city:             STRING[20];

    CASE usa:         BOOLEAN OF
      TRUE:
        (state:       STRING[2];
         zip:         STRING[5]);
      FALSE:
        (otherLoc,
         country:     STRING[15])
  END;
```

The *addressPointer* type is defined as a pointer to an *addressRecord* structure. The record structure in turn contains four pointer fields: *nextName*, *prevName*, *nextRefNo*, and *prevRefNo*.

The program goes on to declare five global pointer variables belonging to the *addressPointer* type. The first of these, *firstName*, is declared in a CONST section and initialized to a value of NIL:

```
CONST
  firstName: addressPointer = NIL;
```

We'll see why this initialization is important as we continue looking at the program. The remaining four pointer variables are declared in a VAR section:

```
VAR
    firstRefNo,
    lastName,
    lastRefNo,
    newRecord:          addressPointer;
```

As you might guess, the program uses the *newRecord* pointer in a NEW statement each time the user adds a new address to the file. The remaining four pointers keep track of the first record in each of the four sorting orders:

- *firstName* points to the first record in the alphabetical sort.
- *lastName* points to the first record in the reverse-alphabetical sort.
- *firstRefNo* points to the first record in the ascending numeric sort.
- *lastRefNo* points to the first record in the descending numeric sort.

Likewise, the program uses the four pointer fields in a given dynamic *addressRecord* variable to point to the next record in each of the four sorting orders. Each time a new record is created, the program thus has several tasks to perform:

1. Find the new record's correct place in each of the four sorting orders.

2. Assign appropriate addresses to the four pointer fields in the new record; each pointer should point to the next record in a given sorting order.

3. Assign the address of the new record to the pointer fields in appropriate existing records; in other words, find the record that comes just before the new record in each sorting order, and point that record's pointer fields to the new record.

4. If the new record is at the top or bottom of the list in any of the four sorting orders, adjust the *firstName*, *lastName*, *firstRefNo*, or *lastRefNo* pointers accordingly.

All of these rather detailed tasks are performed by a procedure named *SetPointers*. This routine is called from two locations in the program. The *ReadAddresses* procedure calls *SetPointers* after reading each new address from the ADDRLIST.TXT file. Likewise, the *NewAddress* procedure calls *SetPointers* after accepting the fields of a new address record from the user at the keyboard. In each case, the global pointer variable *newRecord* contains the address of the newly created dynamic record variable. Both *ReadAddresses* and *New-Address* store the information about a given client in the appropriate fields of *newRecord* ^ before calling *SetPointers*.

Let's see how *SetPointers* incorporates *newRecord* ^ into the linked list.

Inserting New Records into the List

SetPointers contains two local procedures, named *FindNamePointers* and *FindRefNoPointers*. As their names imply, these two routines take care of setting the pointers for the alphabetic and numeric sorts. In general, *SetPointers* calls both routines for each new record, except for the very first dynamic record that the program creates. For the first record, *SetPointers* performs some important initializations and then returns control to the calling routine.

You'll recall that the *firstName* pointer is initialized to NIL in a CONST declaration at the beginning of the program listing. At the beginning of any call to *SetPointers*, the program looks to see if this pointer still has the value NIL; if so, the program can assume that the current *newRecord* is the first record in the linked list:

```
IF firstName = NIL THEN
```

In this case, each of the four special pointers that indicate the first record in each of the sorting orders should initially point to the new record:

```
firstName : = newRecord;
lastName : = newRecord;
```

```
firstRefNo : = newRecord;
lastRefNo : = newRecord;
```

Furthermore, the pointer fields inside the new dynamic record must all be set to NIL, since there is currently no other record in the list to point to:

```
WITH newRecord ^ DO
  BEGIN
    nextName : = NIL;
    prevName : = NIL;
    nextRefNo : = NIL;
    prevRefNo : = NIL
  END
```

However, if the current *newRecord* ^ is not the first dynamic record in the list, the *SetPointers* procedure makes calls to its two local routines to insert the record properly into each of the sorting orders:

```
ELSE
  BEGIN
    FindNamePointers;
    FindRefNoPointers
  END
```

These two routines are identical in structure, but deal with different sets of pointers. We'll examine *FindNamePointers* here as an example of the process of setting the pointers.

The initial task of the *FindNamePointers* procedure is to determine whether the new record should take the place of the record that is currently first in the alphabetical sorting order. To find out whether or not this is the case, the program compares the *name* fields of *newRecord* ^ and the current *firstName* ^ record:

```
IF newRecord ^.name < firstName ^.name THEN
```

If the new record's *name* field is higher in the alphabet, the new record's *nextName* field should point to the former *firstName* ^ record, and the new record's *prevName* pointer should be NIL:

```
newRecord ^.nextName : = firstName;
newRecord ^.prevName : = NIL;
```

The former *firstName* ^ record now loses its status as the first record in the sorting order. Its own *prevName* field should now point to the new record, as should the *firstName* pointer itself:

```
firstName ^.prevName : = newRecord;
firstName : = newRecord;
```

However, if *newRecord* ^ does not properly come before the current *firstName* ^ record in alphabetical order, the program must next search record by record through the linked list to find the correct place for the new record. Three local variables serve as tools in this search. The BOOLEAN variable *locFound* indicates whether the search has been successful; the routine initializes this variable to FALSE:

```
locFound : = FALSE;
```

In addition, the routine makes use of two local *addressPointer*-type variables to mark its place in the search through the list. The *previous* pointer contains the address of the previous record in the list, and the *current* pointer contains the address of the record that the program is currently examining. Both of these variables initially point to the first record in the list, *firstName* ^:

```
previous : = firstName;
current : = firstName;
```

A WHILE loop performs the search through the list. The looping continues until the correct location for *newRecord* ^ is found (*locFound* becomes TRUE), or until the routine encounters the end of the list (the *nextName* field of the *current* ^ record is NIL):

```
WHILE (NOT locFound) AND (current ^.nextName < > NIL) DO
```

The first statement inside the loop moves the *current* pointer forward in the list by one record:

```
current : = current ^.nextName;
```

An IF statement then compares the *name* fields of *newRecord* ^ and *current* ^:

```
IF newRecord ^.name < current ^.name THEN
```

If the *name* field of the new record comes first alphabetically, the correct location for the new record has been found:

```
BEGIN
  locFound : = TRUE;
```

The previous record's *nextName* field should now point to the new record, and the new record's *prevName* field should point back to the previous record:

```
previous ^.nextName : = newRecord;
newRecord ^.prevName : = previous;
```

Likewise, the new record's *nextName* field should point to the current record, and the current record's *prevName* field should point to the new record:

```
newRecord ^.nextName : = current;
current ^.prevName : = newRecord
```

With these four pointers established, the new record has been inserted in its proper place in the alphabetical sequence.

However, if the current iteration of the WHILE loop has not found the correct place of the new record, the *previous* pointer must be moved forward in the list in preparation for the next iteration:

```
previous : = current
```

If the looping ends without ever locating the correct place in the list for the new record, the program can assume that the new record's name field comes last in the alphabetical sequence, after any of the existing records. In this case a different set of pointers must properly established:

```
IF (NOT locFound) THEN
  BEGIN
```

First, the *prevName* pointer in the new record should point back to the record that was previously last in the list. This record is represented by the *current* pointer. The *nextName* pointer of the current record should point forward to the new record:

```
newRecord ^.prevName : = current;
current ^.nextName : = newRecord;
```

Finally, the *nextName* field of the new record should be NIL, marking the end of the list, and the *lastName* pointer should now point to the new record:

```
newRecord ^.nextName : = NIL;
lastName : = newRecord
```

The process of placing a new record in the ordered sequence of the linked list seems complex and detailed. However, Turbo Pascal works very efficiently with a linked list of dynamic variables; the placement of each new record occurs very quickly. (A program presented in Chapter 9 will help you judge the speed of the linked-list algorithms.) Furthermore, when the program is ready to print the list, all four sorting orders are already established; the list never has to be re-sorted during the performance. In the next section we'll look briefly at the program's rather elegant technique for moving through the list in the *PrintList* procedure.

Moving Through the List

When the user requests a printed list of addresses or phone numbers, the *PtrAddr* program calls the *PrintList* procedure to display the submenu of sorting orders on the screen. *PrintList* establishes a group of four constant CHAR values to represent the four sorting orders:

```
CONST
{ ... }
nameAtoZ          = '1';
nameZtoA          = '2';
refNoAscend       = '3';
refNoDescend      = '4';
```

The routine accepts the user's sorting choice as one of these four digit characters and stores the choice in the variable *sortSelection*.

Given this selection, *PrintList* begins by determining the first record that should be printed in the list. A CASE statement assigns the address of the first record to the local pointer variable *firstAddress*, selecting one of the four pointers that were established in the *Set-Pointers* procedure:

```
CASE sortSelection OF
    nameAtoZ:      firstAddress : = firstName;
    nameZtoA:      firstAddress : = lastName;
    refNoAscend:   firstAddress : = firstRefNo;
    refNoDescend: firstAddress : = lastRefNo
END;
```

Finally, *PrintList* calls one of two procedures—*PrintAddresses* or *PrintPhones*—to print the list. In either case, *PrintList* sends two items of information to the print routine: the address of the first record that should be printed and the digit character that represents the selected sorting order:

```
PrintAddresses (firstAddress, sortSelection)
PrintPhones (firstAddress, sortSelection)
```

These two routines have similar structures, but print different list formats. We'll look at *PrintAddresses* to see exactly how the program handles the list.

PrintAddresses has two parameter variables:

```
PROCEDURE PrintAddresses (address: addressPointer;
                         whichSort: CHAR);
```

The *address* parameter is an *addressPointer*-type variable that receives the address of the selected first record; *whichSort* is a CHAR-type variable that receives a character from '1' to '4', representing the selected sorting order.

A WHILE loop moves through the ordered sequence of records in the list, starting from the first record represented by *address* ^:

```
WHILE address < > NIL DO
    BEGIN
        WITH address ^ DO
```

Inside this WITH block, the routine prints appropriate fields from the selected *address* ^ record. Then, at the end of each iteration of the WHILE loop, the following CASE statement locates the next record in the ordered sequence:

```
CASE whichSort OF
  nameAtoZ: address : = address ^.nextName;
  nameZtoA: address : = address ^.prevName;
  refNoAscend: address : = address ^.nextRefNo;
  refNoDescend: address : = address ^.prevRefNo;
END
```

In other words, the program selects the appropriate pointer from field inside the current *address* ^ record to locate the next record in the list. The looping continues until the *address* pointer has a value of NIL, indicating that the program has found the end of the list.

We have one further topic to discuss before we complete our work with the *PtrAddr* program. Near the beginning of this chapter we talked briefly about Turbo Pascal's built-in DISPOSE procedure. Let's look at an example of DISPOSE from *PtrAddr*.

Using the DISPOSE Procedure

As we have seen, DISPOSE releases the heap space taken up by a dynamic variable. DISPOSE takes a pointer variable as its argument:

```
DISPOSE (pointerVar)
```

As a result of this procedure, the dynamic variable *pointerVar* ^ is released from memory; the value of the pointer variable *pointerVar* is subsequently undefined.

The purpose of using DISPOSE in a program like *PtrAddr* is to avoid wasting heap space on a dynamic variable that the program does not need any more. For example, the *NewAddress* procedure creates a dynamic variable for storing a new client record that the user enters from the keyboard. After eliciting all the data fields of the record, *NewAddress* gives the user a chance to abandon the input record rather than storing it in the file. If the user takes advantage of this opportunity, the procedure releases the dynamic record from memory before returning control to the main program.

NewAddress uses the local pointer variable *inAddress* for creating a new dynamic variable:

```
NEW (inAddress);
```

The routine subsequently elicits data values from the keyboard, and stores these values in the various fields of the *inAddress* ^ record:

```
WITH inAddress ^ DO
  BEGIN
    { Conduct the input dialog ... }
```

At the end of the input dialog, the routine asks the user to confirm that the address should be saved:

```
okToSave : =
  InChar ('Save this address? (Y N): ', yesNo);
WRITELN (okToSave);
```

If the user answers affirmatively, *NewAddress* saves the record to disk via a call to the *SaveAddress* procedure. Then the routine assigns the address of the new record to *newRecord* and calls the *SetPointer* procedure to insert the new record in the list:

```
IF okToSave = 'Y' THEN

  BEGIN
    INC (numRecords);
    SaveAddress;
    newRecord : = inAddress;
    SetPointers
  END
```

However, if the user opts to abandon the record, *NewAddress* calls the DISPOSE procedure to release the record from memory:

```
ELSE

  DISPOSE (inAddress);
```

Since *inAddress* is always the most recently allocated dynamic variable, this DISPOSE operation does not create any "holes" in the heap memory. The next time *PtrAddr* creates a new dynamic variable, the released memory will automatically be reused.

Version 5.5: Dynamic Allocation With Objects

Version 5.5 extends Turbo Pascal's dynamic allocation capabilities to handle objects. Because this involves several new concepts, an in-depth explanation is given in Chapter 16. Here, we'll simply highlight the basics.

One of the most powerful tools in object-oriented programming is called *late binding*. Late binding means that you can compile a program but postpone some decisions about how it will work until you actually run it. This is particularly useful when you don't know in advance what sorts of objects you'll be called on to handle. Such "surprise" objects are handled through *virtual methods*, a concept borrowed from C++ and Smalltalk.

For example, suppose that you have created a family tree of related customer objects—"local customer," "overseas customer," "government agency customer," and so forth. You might need to have a different billing procedure for each customer type, but you will not know at compile time which types your billing program will have to handle on a particular day.

Declaring *SendBill* as a virtual method lets the program call *SendBill* without knowing the customer type at compile time. When the program is actually run, it selects the appropriate version of *SendBill* based on the type of customer object the bill is going to. You declare a method as a virtual method simply by adding the new keyword VIRTUAL in the initial declaration:

```
PROCEDURE SendBill; VIRTUAL;
```

Any object that uses virtual methods has to be initialized with a new type of procedure called a *constructor*. This is extremely important, since calling an uninitialized virtual-method object can crash the system.

Fortunately, it's easy to set up a constructor. As with other object methods, you put its heading inside the object declaration and spell out its details separately. A simple example would be:

```
TYPE
  customer = OBJECT
    name:      STRING[30];
    IDnumber: INTEGER;
  END;

  localCustomer = OBJECT(customer)
    city:      STRING[15];
    CONSTRUCTOR Init(InitName: STRING[30]; InitID: INTEGER;
                                      InitCity: STRING[15]);
    PROCEDURE Sendbill; VIRTUAL;
  END;
```

You must call the constructor for *localCustomer* before you try to activate the virtual method *SendBill*. (Remember that *localCustomer* inherits the *name* and *IDnumber* fields from the *customer* object type from which it is a descendant.)

Turbo Pascal's NEW procedure has also been extended to support dynamic allocation with objects. In standard Pascal, as noted earlier in this chapter, NEW is used to set aside space in RAM for a particular kind of variable and create a pointer to the variable's address in memory. Now, you can also use it to set up pointers to object variables and initialize their virtual methods and data fields. It's done this way:

```
VAR
  PBill: ^Bill;      [ declare pointer type for "bill" object ]
  ...

  NEW (PBill, Init(0000));      { allocate & initialize bill vbl. }
```

Destructors work in tandem with the DISPOSE procedure to clean up memory that is no longer needed by dynamically-allocated objects (since objects can be a little more complicated than simpler data types). You lay out the details of a particular object's destructor routine in the same way as the object's constructor, and call the destructor with DISPOSE when the memory allocated for the object is no longer needed:

```
DESTRUCTOR Bill.Done
  BEGIN
```

```
        ...
    END;

        ...
    DISPOSE(PBill, Done);
```

For complete details of how Turbo Pascal handles virtual methods and dynamic allocation of objects, please see Chapter 16.

Summary

A pointer variable in Pascal stores the memory address of another variable. The built-in NEW procedure allocates space for a new dynamic variable in the heap and assigns the memory address of the new variable to a pointer. A dynamic variable is the only structure in Pascal that does not have to be identified in a VAR declaration before use in a program.

You can use dynamic record variables to create a linked list of data records. Handling this rather unusual data structure requires careful attention to detail as you design your program. However, Turbo Pascal works very efficiently with linked lists. Furthermore, the length of a linked list is not defined in advance and is limited only by the amount of memory available for the heap.

The *CliAddr* and *PtrAddr* programs present you with an excellent opportunity to compare two very different data-storage schemes. Studying these two programs and comparing their respective algorithms will help you understand the difference between an array of records and a linked list of dynamic records.

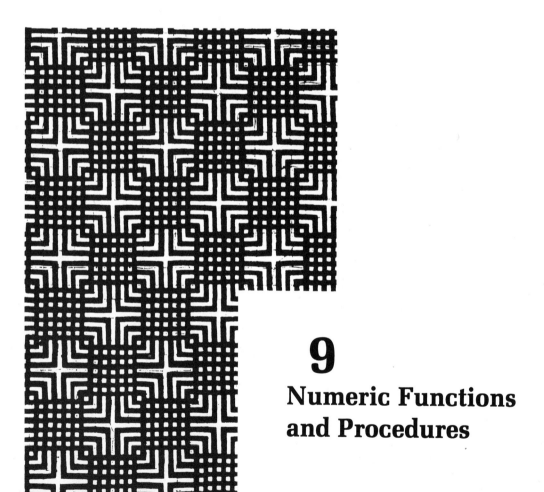

C H A P T E R

9

**Numeric Functions
and Procedures**

In this chapter we'll focus on Turbo Pascal's standard numeric functions and procedures. All of the routines we'll look at in this chapter can be found in Turbo Pascal's standard SYSTEM unit. (You'll recall that this unit is automatically linked to every program you write.) Some of the routines work with real types, others with integer types; still others convert values from real to integer types.

This chapter presents two programs for you to run and explore. The first, a menu-driven program called *NumDemo*, is a simple exercise designed to demonstrate several categories of numeric functions. The program produces output tables from the exponential functions, the trigonometric functions, the integer functions, and some miscellaneous arithmetic functions. Examining these tables, you'll learn how these functions work and what types of values they return.

The second program, called *RandAddr*, is a tool designed to test the performance of the *PtrAddr* program, presented in Chapter 8. You'll recall that *PtrAddr* is a revision of the *CliAddr* program from Chapter 6; it maintains a file of client address records, but uses a linked list of dynamic records (rather than an array) to store the records in memory during a performance.

In this chapter, the *RandAddr* program produces a simulated client address list, containing randomly generated data. The program demonstrates the use of Turbo Pascal's random-number generator, the

RANDOM function. It also illustrates one general technique for creating realistic test data to judge the performance of an application program. Specifically, *RandAddr* allows you to test the sorting speed and record capacity of the linked-list algorithms.

We'll begin this chapter by looking at the categories of numeric functions.

Numeric Functions by Categories

The *NumDemo* program is listed in Figure 9.1. The program contains individual procedures for demonstrating each of four categories of numeric functions. You call on these procedures by selecting options from the program's recurring menu:

Standard Numeric Functions

    1. Exponential
    2. Trigonometric
    3. Integer
    4. Arithmetic
    5. Quit

* * * Menu choice: _

We'll examine each of these categories in order. If you want to experiment further with these functions, you can revise individual routines in *NumDemo* to generate different ranges of returned values.

The EXP and LN Functions

Turbo Pascal supplies an exponential and a logarithmic function, each of which takes a single REAL argument, *n*.

- EXP(*n*) returns the value of e raised to the power *n*, where e is the base for natural logarithms. This natural constant is equal to approximately 2.71828.

```
PROGRAM NumDemo;

  { This program contains demonstrations for a
    selection of Turbo Pascal's standard numeric
    functions and procedures. }

  USES CRT, InUnit, StrUnit;

  VAR
    done: BOOLEAN;
    arg:  REAL;

  PROCEDURE ExpLnDemo;

    { The ExpLnDemo function demonstrates
      the EXP and LN functions. }

    VAR
      i:   SHORTINT;

    BEGIN     { ExpLnDemo }

      WRITE (Spaces (6), 'n');
      WRITE (Spaces (6), 'EXP (n)');
      WRITELN (Spaces (4), 'LN (n)');
      WRITELN;
      FOR i := -6 TO 7 DO
        BEGIN
          arg := i / 2;
          WRITE (arg: 10: 4, EXP (arg): 10: 4);
          IF i <= 0 THEN
            WRITELN ('          -')
          ELSE
            WRITELN (LN (arg): 10: 4);
        END

    END;     { ExpLnDemo }

  PROCEDURE TrigDemo;

    { The TrigDemo procedure demonstrates the
      trigonometric functions, including SIN,
      COS, ARCTAN, and PI. }

    VAR
      i: SHORTINT;

    BEGIN     { TrigDemo }

      WRITE (Spaces (4), 'n');
      WRITE (Spaces (7), 'SIN (n*PI)');
      WRITE (Spaces (4), 'COS (n*PI)');
      WRITELN (Spaces (2), 'ARCTAN (n)');
      WRITELN;

      FOR i := -8 TO 8 DO
        BEGIN
          arg := PI * i / 8;
          WRITE (i / 8: 7: 4);
          WRITE (SIN (arg): 13: 4);
          WRITE (COS (arg): 13: 4);
          WRITELN (ARCTAN (i / 8): 13: 4)
        END

    END;     { TrigDemo }
```

Figure 9.1: The listing of the *NumDemo* program

```
PROCEDURE IntDemo;

  { The IntDemo procedure demonstrates
    integer functions: INT, ROUND, and TRUNC.
    This routine also illustrates the FRAC
    function. }

  VAR
    i: SHORTINT;

  BEGIN    { IntDemo }

    WRITE ('  n');
    WRITE (Spaces (6), 'INT (n)');
    WRITE (Spaces (3), 'ROUND (n)');
    WRITE (Spaces (2), 'TRUNC (n)');
    WRITELN (Spaces (3), 'FRAC (n)');
    WRITELN;

    FOR i := -10 TO 10 DO
      BEGIN
        arg := i / 4;
        WRITE (arg: 5: 2);
        WRITE (INT (arg): 10: 1);
        WRITE (ROUND (arg): 10);
        WRITE (TRUNC (arg): 10);
        WRITELN (FRAC (arg): 13: 2)
      END

  END;    { IntDemo }


PROCEDURE ArithDemo;

  { The ArithDemo procedure demonstrates
    miscellaneous functions: ABS, SQR, and SQRT. }

  VAR
    i: SHORTINT;

  BEGIN    { ArithDemo }

    WRITE ('  n');
    WRITE (Spaces (6), 'ABS (n)');
    WRITE (Spaces (3), 'SQR (n)');
    WRITELN (Spaces (2), 'SQRT (n)');
    WRITELN;

    FOR i := -10 TO 10 DO
      BEGIN
        WRITE (i: 3);
        WRITE (ABS (i): 10);
        WRITE (SQR (i): 10);

        IF i < 0 THEN
          WRITELN ('         - ')
        ELSE
          WRITELN (SQRT (i): 12: 4)
      END

  END;    { ArithDemo }
```

Figure 9.1: The listing of the *NumDemo* program (continued)

```
PROCEDURE Menu (VAR exitMenu: BOOLEAN);

   { The Menu procedure displays the menu on the screen and
     responds appropriately to the user's menu choices. The
     VAR parameter exitMenu passes back a value of TRUE when
     the user selects the Quit option. }

   CONST
     col = 25;

   VAR
     choice:    CHAR;
     contSignal: STRING;

   BEGIN     { Menu }

      CLRSCR;
      exitMenu := FALSE;

      GOTOXY (col - 5, 5);
      WRITELN ('Standard Numeric Functions');
      GOTOXY (col, 7); WRITELN ('1. Exponential');
      GOTOXY (col, 8); WRITELN ('2. Trigonometric');
      GOTOXY (col, 9); WRITELN ('3. Integer');
      GOTOXY (col, 10); WRITELN ('4. Arithmetic');
      GOTOXY (col, 11); WRITELN ('5. Quit');
      WRITELN; GOTOXY (col - 5, 13);

      choice := InChar ('   *** Menu choice: ',
                         ['1'..'5']);

      CLRSCR;
      CASE choice OF
        '1': ExpLnDemo;
        '2': TrigDemo;
        '3': IntDemo;
        '4': ArithDemo;
        '5': exitMenu := TRUE
      END;

      IF choice <> '5' THEN
        BEGIN
          WRITELN;
          contSignal :=
            inChar (' Press <Space Bar> to continue.',
                       [' '])
        END;

      CLRSCR

   END;    { Menu }


BEGIN     { NumDemo }

   REPEAT
     Menu (done)
   UNTIL done

END.    { NumDemo }
```

Figure 9.1: The listing of the *NumDemo* program (continued)

- LN(*n*) gives the natural logarithm of a positive argument. The natural logarithm is the power of e that produces *n*. (An argument less than or equal to zero is illegal, producing a run-time error.)

Like all floating-point numeric functions we'll discuss in this chapter, EXP and LN produce floating-point values of the EXTENDED type on a system that includes an 8087 coprocessor chip. (To take advantage of this feature, use the {$N + } compiler directive.)

The *NumDemo* procedure produces the table of EXP and LN values shown in Figure 9.2. Examining the first column of this table, you can see that an argument of 1 gives the base value of the EXP function, e. An argument of .5 gives the square root of e, and negative arguments yield inverse roots or powers. An argument of zero produces a result of 1, since the result of any number raised to the 0 power is defined to be 1.

The second column of this table shows results from the LN function. Notice that a fractional argument produces a negative logarithm, and an argument of 1 returns a value of 0. Arguments greater than 1 produce positive logarithms. As we've seen, the argument of LN must be greater than zero.

Turbo Pascal does not support an exponential operation, for finding powers or roots of a base value. (In other languages such as Basic,

```
        n      EXP (n)    LN (n)

    -3.0000     0.0498      -
    -2.5000     0.0821      -
    -2.0000     0.1353      -
    -1.5000     0.2231      -
    -1.0000     0.3679      -
    -0.5000     0.6065      -
     0.0000     1.0000      -
     0.5000     1.6487   -0.6931
     1.0000     2.7183    0.0000
     1.5000     4.4817    0.4055
     2.0000     7.3891    0.6931
     2.5000    12.1825    0.9163
     3.0000    20.0855    1.0986
     3.5000    33.1155    1.2528
```

Figure 9.2: Values calculated by the EXP and LN functions

this operation is usually represented by the caret character, ^ .) In place of this missing operation, you can use a formula that employs the LN and EXP functions. In general, the following formula gives the value of x^n:

EXP (LN (*x*) * *n*)

For example, the following demonstration program finds powers and roots of the base value 5:

```
VAR
  base,
  i:     BYTE;

BEGIN
  base : = 5;
   WRITELN ('        power of   ', base,
                '     root of   ', base);
  WRITELN;
  FOR i : = 1 TO 5 DO
    WRITELN
            (i: 2,
             EXP (LN (base) * i): 10: 1,
             EXP (LN (base) / i): 12: 4)
  END.
```

Here is the program's output:

```
    power of 5   root of 5

1          5.0   5.0000
2         25.0   2.2361
3        125.0   1.7100
4        625.0   1.4953
5       3125.0   1.3797
```

The first column gives powers of 5 (squared, cubed, and so on), and the second column gives roots of 5 (square root, cube root, and so on).

The Trigonometric Functions

Three trigonometric functions are available in Turbo Pascal. Two of them take angle arguments, *a*, expressed in radians; the third takes a numeric argument, *n*, and returns an angle expressed in radians:

- SIN(*a*) gives the sine of *a*.

- COS(*a*) gives the cosine of *a*.

- ARCTAN(*n*) gives the arctangent, the angle whose tangent is equal to *n*.

Notice that angles are expressed in radians in the trigonometric functions. An angle of 360 degrees is equal to 2π radians, 180 degrees equals π radians, 90 degrees equals $\pi/2$ radians, and so on. All four functions produce REAL results.

The *NumDemo* program produces the table shown in Figure 9.3 to illustrate the trigonometric functions. The first two columns give values of SIN and COS for arguments ranging from $-\pi$ to $+\pi$. If you study the resulting values, you'll notice the cyclical "wave" behavior of these two functions. Both SIN and COS yield values ranging from -1 to $+1$, but in different cycles. In the range from $-\pi$ to $+\pi$, the sine and cosine waves meet in two places: at $-3\pi/4$ and $\pi/4$.

The third column shows results from the ARCTAN function, for arguments from -1 to 1. Note that the arctangent of 1 is $\pi/4$. For this reason, the expression 4 * ATN(1) is sometimes used to produce an approximation of π. However, Turbo Pascal conveniently includes the standard function PI, which returns the value of π and which the *Num-Demo* program employs in the trigonometric function expressions.

The Integer Functions

Turbo Pascal provides three functions that produce an integer value from a real number. Each function follows its own specific rules for either truncating or rounding numbers to a nearby integer. Here is how they behave:

- The INT function simply truncates the decimal portion of its argument and gives a result of type REAL.

```
         n        SIN (n*PI)   COS (n*PI)   ARCTAN (n)

      -1.0000      -0.0000      -1.0000      -0.7854
      -0.8750      -0.3827      -0.9239      -0.7188
      -0.7500      -0.7071      -0.7071      -0.6435
      -0.6250      -0.9239      -0.3827      -0.5586
      -0.5000      -1.0000       0.0000      -0.4636
      -0.3750      -0.9239       0.3827      -0.3588
      -0.2500      -0.7071       0.7071      -0.2450
      -0.1250      -0.3827       0.9239      -0.1244
       0.0000       0.0000       1.0000       0.0000
       0.1250       0.3827       0.9239       0.1244
       0.2500       0.7071       0.7071       0.2450
       0.3750       0.9239       0.3827       0.3588
       0.5000       1.0000       0.0000       0.4636
       0.6250       0.9239      -0.3827       0.5586
       0.7500       0.7071      -0.7071       0.6435
       0.8750       0.3827      -0.9239       0.7188
       1.0000       0.0000      -1.0000       0.7854
```

Figure 9.3: Values calculated by the SIN, COS, and ARCTAN functions

- The ROUND(n) function rounds its argument up or down to the nearest integer. When the decimal portion of the argument is less than .5, ROUND rounds the absolute value down; and when the decimal portion is greater than or equal to .5, the ROUND function rounds up.

- The TRUNC function truncates the decimal portion of the number, producing an INTEGER result. (Notice that TRUNC and INT produce the same numbers, but different data types.)

The *NumDemo* program produces the table of integer functions shown in Figure 9.4. This table gives you the opportunity to compare the various rules followed by the three functions. This table also illustrates results from the FRAC function, which gives the decimal portion of a real number.

Arithmetic Functions

The final table produced by the *NumDemo* program appears in Figure 9.5. It illustrates three miscellaneous arithmetic functions

n	INT (n)	ROUND (n)	TRUNC (n)	FRAC (n)
-2.50	-2.0	-3	-2	-0.50
-2.25	-2.0	-2	-2	-0.25
-2.00	-2.0	-2	-2	0.00
-1.75	-1.0	-2	-1	-0.75
-1.50	-1.0	-2	-1	-0.50
-1.25	-1.0	-1	-1	-0.25
-1.00	-1.0	-1	-1	0.00
-0.75	0.0	-1	0	-0.75
-0.50	0.0	-1	0	-0.50
-0.25	0.0	0	0	-0.25
0.00	0.0	0	0	0.00
0.25	0.0	0	0	0.25
0.50	0.0	1	0	0.50
0.75	0.0	1	0	0.75
1.00	1.0	1	1	0.00
1.25	1.0	1	1	0.25
1.50	1.0	2	1	0.50
1.75	1.0	2	1	0.75
2.00	2.0	2	2	0.00
2.25	2.0	2	2	0.25
2.50	2.0	3	2	0.50

Figure 9.4: Values calculated using the integer functions

named ABS, SQR, and SQRT. Here is what these three functions do:

- ABS(n) returns the absolute value of n. If n is positive or zero, the result of ABS is the same as n. If n is negative, ABS returns the unsigned, or positive, equivalent of n.

- SQR(n) gives the value of n squared.

- SQRT(n) gives the square root of n. Negative arguments are not allowed.

The next section describes a potential problem that you must watch out for when you are working with integer applications.

Type Casting and Numeric Conversions

We discussed type casting in Chapter 7; this convenient feature provides a technique for converting a value from one type to another. Type casting can prove essential in some situations involving operations with integers. For example, let's say you want to find the average of four integers, a, b, c, and d, as in the following passage:

```
VAR
   a, b, c, d : INTEGER;
```

n	ABS (n)	SQR (n)	SQRT (n)
-10	10	100	-
-9	9	81	-
-8	8	64	-
-7	7	49	-
-6	6	36	-
-5	5	25	-
-4	4	16	-
-3	3	9	-
-2	2	4	-
-1	1	1	-
0	0	0	0.0000
1	1	1	1.0000
2	2	4	1.4142
3	3	9	1.7321
4	4	16	2.0000
5	5	25	2.2361
6	6	36	2.4495
7	7	49	2.6458
8	8	64	2.8284
9	9	81	3.0000
10	10	100	3.1623

Figure 9.5: Values calculated using the ABS, SQR, and SQRT functions

```
BEGIN

   a : = 32765;
   b : = 11111;
   c : = 22222;
   d : = 30000;

   WRITELN ((a + b + c + d) / 4.0: 8: 1)

END.
```

The WRITELN statement finds the sum of the four integers, and divides by 4.0 in an attempt to find the average. Unfortunately, a phenomenon called *overflow* occurs in the intermediate sum operation. The four integers combine to produce a value that is outside the legal range of integers in Pascal. (You'll recall that the largest legal integer value is 32767.) As a result, Pascal miscalculates the final value, and the WRITELN statement calculates an average of 7640.5. Clearly this is not the correct answer.

As a solution to this problem, we can use type casting to force Turbo Pascal into performing the intermediate sum in a numeric format that can actually handle the result, specifically LONGINT. Consider this revised version of the WRITELN statement:

```
WRITELN ((LONGINT(a) + b + c + d) / 4.0: 8: 1)
```

Note that when any one of the four integer values is converted to the LONGINT type, Pascal performs the entire sum operation in this type. The final calculation results in the correct value: 24024.5.

To guard against the problem of overflow in integer applications, you should always perform a spot check of the numeric results of a program to make sure they are reasonable.

Next we turn to Turbo Pascal's random-number generator and the RANDOMIZE procedure.

The RANDOM Function

The RANDOM function is Turbo Pascal's random-number generator. You can use it to produce an unpredictable sequence of real or integer values, using the following syntax:

```
RANDOM(n)
```

RANDOM takes an optional integer argument, *n*. Without the argument, each call to RANDOM yields a number between 0 and 1. With the *n* argument, RANDOM produces a random integer from 0 to *n*. For example, the FOR loop in the following passage makes three sets of calls to RANDOM, illustrating the function both with and without an argument:

```
VAR
  i: BYTE;

BEGIN

  RANDOMIZE;

  WRITELN ('  RANDOM     RANDOM(100)  RANDOM(1000)');
  WRITELN;
```

```
FOR i : = 1 TO 5 DO
  WRITELN (RANDOM: 10: 8,
             RANDOM(100): 12,
             RANDOM (1000): 14);

  WRITELN

END.
```

Here is one set of results from a performance of this program:

RANDOM	RANDOM(100)	RANDOM(1000)
0.25507248	55	978
0.77725405	39	602
0.72975895	91	65
0.95623537	5	827
0.34311198	32	734

RANDOM is useful for conducting random events in game programs or for producing random data in simulations. Actually, the numbers supplied by RANDOM are not random at all, but rather are the result of a particular sequence of numeric calculations. The trick to using the RANDOM function successfully is to start out at a random point within these calculations. This process, called "setting the seed" of the random-number generator, is performed by the RANDOMIZE procedure. This procedure, which takes no argument, is also illustrated in the short program we've just examined.

As we've discussed, random numbers are important for creating simulated sets of information to test the performance of a data-processing program. For example, the *RandAddr* program serves as a data-file simulator for the *PtrAddr* application. This program ses a new unit of procedures called *RandUnit*, shown in Figure 9.6. We'll discuss *RandUnit* briefly in the next section before turning to the *RandAddr* program.

The Functions of *RandUnit*

RandUnit contains three functions, which supply randomly generated data values of three different types: integers, strings, and

BOOLEAN-type values. The names of the functions are *RandInt*, *RandStr*, and *RandBoolean*, respectively.

The *RandInt* function gives a random integer that is inside a specified range of integers, *min* and *max:*

RandInt (*min, max*)

For example, the expression *RandInt (5, 25)* results in a random integer selected from within a range of 5 to 25.

The *RandStr* function supplies a string of randomly selected uppercase letters. You specify the length of the string in the argument *strLen:*

RandStr (*strLen*)

```
UNIT RandUnit;

    { RandUnit contains three functions that generate
      random data values of various types: integer,
      string, or logical. }

    INTERFACE

        FUNCTION RandInt (min, max: INTEGER): INTEGER;

        FUNCTION RandStr (strLen: BYTE): STRING;

        FUNCTION RandBoolean: BOOLEAN;


    IMPLEMENTATION

        FUNCTION RandInt;

            { The RandInt function supplies a random integer
              within the range of the specified arguments min and
              max. For example, RandInt (10, 20) gives a random
              integer between 10 and 20. }

            CONST
              minInt = -32767;

            VAR
              randRange: WORD;

            BEGIN
              IF min < minInt THEN min := minInt;
              randRange := max - min + 1;
              RandInt := RANDOM(randRange) + min
            END;
```

Figure 9.6: The listing of *RandUnit*

```
FUNCTION RandStr;

    { The RandStr function gives a string of random uppercase
      letters. The length of the string is specified by
      the argument strLen. }

    VAR
      A, Z, i: BYTE;
      tempStr: STRING;

    BEGIN
      A := ORD('A');
      Z := ORD('Z');
      tempStr := '';
      FOR i := 1 TO strLen DO
        tempStr := tempStr + CHR (RandInt (A, Z));
      RandStr := tempStr
    END;


FUNCTION RandBoolean;

    { The RandBoolean function supplies a randomly
      selected BOOLEAN value, TRUE or FALSE. }

    BEGIN
      RandBoolean := BOOLEAN (RandInt (0, 1))
    END;

END.
```

Figure 9.6: The listing of *RandUnit* (continued)

Finally, the *RandBoolean* function simply returns a randomly selected value of TRUE or FALSE. *RandBoolean* takes no argument.

Here is a short program that demonstrates the results of these three functions:

```
USES RandUnit;

VAR
  i: BYTE;

BEGIN
  RANDOMIZE;
  FOR i : = 1 TO 5 DO
    WRITELN (RandInt (100, 200), ' ',
             RandStr(10), ' ',
             RandBoolean)
END.
```

This program generates three columns of random data. The first column contains integers from 100 to 200; the second column contains strings with 10 characters each; and the third column contains BOOLEAN values. Here is the result of one performance:

```
148    MSTMLLDNKB    TRUE
169    TRIYKNEQRK    TRUE
159    JRRILEFHCB    FALSE
186    JRQYVUYDNE    TRUE
196    PVBOXQMJKL    FALSE
```

A program can use these three functions to generate large quantities of random data very quickly. The advantage of this simulated data is that you can test the performance of a program without having to supply the input values yourself. We'll see an example of this testing technique as we examine the *RandAddr* program in the next section.

The *RandAddr* Program

The *PtrAddr* program, presented in Chapter 8, creates a linked list of records to store and sort a collection of client address records. There are two possible input sources for these records; the program first reads existing records from a text file, then gives you the opportunity to add new records from the keyboard.

You'll recall that the record structure for this list contains four pointer fields, along with nine fields that describe a given client. Each time you enter a new address record from the keyboard, the program creates a new dynamic record to store the address. The program also assigns values to the four pointer fields, placing each new record in its proper place within four established sorting orders:

- Alphabetical by client name
- Reverse alphabetical by client name
- Ascending order by reference numbers
- Descending order by reference numbers

To test the performance of a complex program like *PtrAddr*, you should give the program as large a set of input data as possible. Not only must you be certain that the program's algorithms work the way you expect them to, but you would also like to know how the program behaves under the burden of a large data set. For example, you might want to explore the following two questions:

- How many dynamic address records can the program create before a heap overflow error occurs?
- How long does the sort take for a large number of records?

While you are developing and testing a program like *PtrAddr*, you may not want to supply the test data yourself. Sometimes realistic data is simply not available, or is available in too small a quantity to test the application adequately. Inventing your own test data takes a lot of time and may result in biased input that does not truly test the program. In this situation you have to find some way to generate plausible data for the application to work with.

One solution to this problem is to create a test version of the program that generates its own random data. The program can then use the simulated data for a run through the program's algorithms. This is precisely the role of the *RandAddr* program. Specifically, *RandAddr* uses the functions in *RandUnit* to generate a specified number of address records. The program creates dynamic records and builds a linked list to sort the addresses in each of the four sorting orders. Finally, to document its own action, the program creates a text file that shows you the data it has generated, along with evidence that the four sorting orders have been correctly established.

When you run *RandAddr*, the program displays a sequence of integers on the screen indicating the number of records it has generated. Then, when the entire linked list of simulated address records is in memory, the program informs you that it is creating the documentation file RANDTEST.TXT. For example, the current version of the program generates only eight records; the following messages appear on the screen during the performance:

```
Creating and sorting 8 records:
   1   2   3   4   5   6   7   8

Creating file RANDTEST.TXT
```

Figure 9.7 shows an example of the RANDTEST.TXT file, created by the program. You can see that the program has successfully sorted the linked list by all four of the established sorting criteria.

Increasing the size of the simulated data set for subsequent performance tests is very easy, as we'll see when we examine the listing. The *RandAddr* program is shown in Figure 9.8.

```
Sort by names, A to Z:

ANGQEILVIQ    212
HQYFZZIDXH    122
KHJTNBCFQS    246
MXROQTYLQL    108
PTMXRPBBFP    208
QHHSTEEKKS    43
UTKOHXSROM    37
XSEQOHRDYQ    249


Sort by names, Z to A:

XSEQOHRDYQ    249
UTKOHXSROM    37
QHHSTEEKKS    43
PTMXRPBBFP    208
MXROQTYLQL    108
KHJTNBCFQS    246
HQYFZZIDXH    122
ANGQEILVIQ    212


Sort by numbers, ascending:

UTKOHXSROM    37
QHHSTEEKKS    43
MXROQTYLQL    108
HQYFZZIDXH    122
PTMXRPBBFP    208
ANGQEILVIQ    212
KHJTNBCFQS    246
XSEQOHRDYQ    249


Sort by numbers, descending:

XSEQOHRDYQ    249
KHJTNBCFQS    246
ANGQEILVIQ    212
PTMXRPBBFP    208
HQYFZZIDXH    122
MXROQTYLQL    108
QHHSTEEKKS    43
UTKOHXSROM    37
```

Figure 9.7: A RANDTEST.TXT file created by the *RandAddr* program

```
PROGRAM RandAddr;

  { The RandAddr program simulates data for testing the
    algorithms of the PtrAddr program. The program's main
    output is a text file named RANDTEST.TXT; this file
    contains lists of names and reference numbers generated
    by the program, sorted in four different ways. }

  USES CRT, RandUnit;

  CONST
    recsToCreate = 8;
    numRecords:  INTEGER = 0;

  TYPE
    addressPointer = ^addressRecord;
    addressRecord = RECORD
      nextName:   addressPointer;
      prevName:   addressPointer;
      nextRefNo:  addressPointer;
      prevRefNo:  addressPointer;

      name:       STRING[30];
      phone:      STRING[20];
      refNo:      BYTE;
      headOffice: BOOLEAN;

      street:     STRING[30];
      city:       STRING[20];

      CASE usa: BOOLEAN OF
        TRUE:  (state:    STRING[2];
                zip:      STRING[5]);
        FALSE: (otherLoc,
                country:  STRING[15])
    END;

  CONST
    firstName: addressPointer = NIL;

  VAR
    firstRefNo,
    lastName,
    lastRefNo,
    newRecord:      addressPointer;

  PROCEDURE SetPointers;

    { The SetPointers procedure establishes the pointers
      of the linked list. It sets the four record
      pointer fields in each new address record. }

    VAR
      current,
      previous: addressPointer;
      locFound: BOOLEAN;


    PROCEDURE FindNamePointers;

      { The FindNamePointers procedure establishes the pointers
        for two sorting orders: alphabetical order and reverse
        alphabetical order by the simulated data of the
        name field. }
```

Figure 9.8: The listing of the *RandAddr* program

```
       BEGIN    { FindNamePointers }

       IF newRecord^.name < firstName^.name THEN
          BEGIN
            newRecord^.nextName := firstName;
            newRecord^.prevName := NIL;
            firstName^.prevName := newRecord;
            firstName := newRecord;
          END
       ELSE
          BEGIN
            locFound := FALSE;
            previous := firstName;
            current := firstName;
            WHILE (NOT locFound) AND (current^.nextName <> NIL) DO
               BEGIN
                 current := current^.nextName;
                 IF newRecord^.name < current^.name THEN
                    BEGIN
                      locFound := TRUE;
                      previous^.nextName := newRecord;
                      newRecord^.prevName := previous;
                      newRecord^.nextName := current;
                      current^.prevName := newRecord
                    END
                 ELSE
                      previous := current
               END;

            IF (NOT locFound) THEN
               BEGIN
                 newRecord^.prevName := current;
                 current^.nextName := newRecord;
                 newRecord^.nextName := NIL;
                 lastName := newRecord
               END
          END
     END;    { FindNamePointers }



PROCEDURE FindRefNoPointers;

    { The FindRefNoPointers procedure establishes the pointers
      for two sorting orders: numerical order and reverse
      numerical order by the simulated refNo field. }

    BEGIN    { FindRefNoPointers }

    IF newRecord^.refNo < firstRefNo^.refNo THEN
       BEGIN
         newRecord^.nextRefNo := firstRefNo;
         newRecord^.prevRefNo := NIL;
         firstRefNo^.prevRefNo := newRecord;
         firstRefNo := newRecord;
       END
    ELSE
       BEGIN
         locFound := FALSE;
         previous := firstRefNo;
         current := firstRefNo;
         WHILE (NOT locFound) AND (current^.nextRefNo <> NIL) DO
```

Figure 9.8: The listing of the *RandAddr* program (continued)

```
                    BEGIN
                      current := current^.nextRefNo;
                      IF newRecord^.refNo < current^.refNo THEN
                        BEGIN
                          locFound := TRUE;
                          previous^.nextRefNo := newRecord;
                          newRecord^.prevRefNo := previous;
                          newRecord^.nextRefNo := current;
                          current^.prevRefNo := newRecord
                        END
                      ELSE
                        previous := current
                    END;

                 IF (NOT locFound) THEN
                    BEGIN
                      newRecord^.prevRefNo := current;
                      current^.nextRefNo := newRecord;
                      newRecord^.nextRefNo := NIL;
                      lastRefNo := newRecord
                    END
               END
       END;     { FindRefNoPointers }


   BEGIN    { SetPointers }

     IF firstName = NIL THEN
        BEGIN
          firstName := newRecord;
          lastName := newRecord;
          firstRefNo := newRecord;
          lastRefNo := newRecord;
          WITH newRecord^ DO
            BEGIN
              nextName := NIL;
              prevName := NIL;
              nextRefNo := NIL;
              prevRefNo := NIL
            END
        END
     ELSE
        BEGIN
          FindNamePointers;
          FindRefNoPointers
        END

   END;     { SetPointers }



   PROCEDURE CreateAddressPointers;

     { The CreateAddressPointers procedure creates simulated
       data for each new dynamic record. The routines of the
       RandUnit unit are used for creating the data: RandStr,
       RandInt, and RandBoolean. }

     BEGIN    { CreateAddressPointers }
```

Figure 9.8: The listing of the *RandAddr* program (continued)

```
            WRITE ('Creating and sorting ');
            WRITELN (recsToCreate, ' records:');
            REPEAT
              NEW (newRecord);
              INC (numRecords);
              WRITE (numRecords: 4);
              WITH newRecord^ DO
                BEGIN
                  name := RandStr (10);
                  refNo := RandInt (1, 255);
                  headOffice := RandBoolean;
                  usa := RandBoolean;
                  phone := RandStr (20);
                  street := RandStr (30);
                  city := RandStr (20);
                  IF usa THEN
                    BEGIN
                      state := RandStr (2);
                      zip := RandStr (5);
                    END
                  ELSE
                    BEGIN
                      otherLoc := RandStr (15);
                      country := RandStr (15)
                    END    { ELSE }
                END;    { WITH newRecord^ }
              SetPointers
            UNTIL (numRecords = recsToCreate)

          END;    { CreateAddressPointers }



    PROCEDURE PrintList;

      { The PrintList procedure creates four sorted lists of the
        simulated data, and stores the lists in the text file
        RANDTEST.TXT. The lists contain two columns, with the
        simulated name strings and the simulated reference
        numbers. }

      CONST
        testFileName = 'RANDTEST.TXT';

      TYPE
        sortTypes = (nameAtoZ, nameZtoA, refNoAscend, refNoDescend);

      VAR
        nextRecord: addressPointer;
        whichSort:  sortTypes;
        testFile:   TEXT;

      BEGIN    { PrintList }

        ASSIGN (testFile, testFileName);
        REWRITE (testFile);
        WRITELN; WRITELN;
        WRITELN ('Creating file ', testFileName, '.');
```

Figure 9.8: The listing of the *RandAddr* program (continued)

```
        FOR whichSort := nameAtoZ to refNoDescend DO
          BEGIN
            CASE whichSort OF
              nameAtoZ:
                BEGIN
                  nextRecord := firstName;
                  WRITELN (testFile, 'Sort by names, A to Z:')
                END;
              nameZtoA:
                BEGIN
                  nextRecord := lastName;
                  WRITELN (testFile, 'Sort by names, Z to A:')
                END;
              refNoAscend:
                BEGIN
                  nextRecord := firstRefNo;
                  WRITELN (testFile, 'Sort by numbers, ascending:')
                END;
              refNoDescend:
                BEGIN
                  nextRecord := lastRefNo;
                  WRITELN (testFile, 'Sort by numbers, descending:')
                END
            END;
            WRITELN (testFile);

            WHILE nextRecord <> NIL DO
              WITH nextRecord^ DO
                BEGIN
                  WRITELN (testFile, name, '   ', refNo);
                  CASE whichSort OF
                    nameAtoZ:      nextRecord := nextName;
                    nameZtoA:      nextRecord := prevName;
                    refNoAscend:   nextRecord := nextRefNo;
                    refNoDescend:  nextRecord := prevRefNo
                  END
                END;
            WRITELN (testFile); WRITELN (testFile)
          END;

      CLOSE (testFile)

    END;    { PrintList }


  BEGIN    { RandAddr }

    RANDOMIZE;
    CLRSCR;
    CreateAddressPointers;
    PrintList

  END.    { RandAddr }
```

Figure 9.8: The listing of the *RandAddr* program (continued)

Inside the *RandAddr* Program

The CONST statement located at the beginning of the *RandAddr* program defines a constant named *recsToCreate:*

```
CONST
  recsToCreate = 8;
```

This constant value controls the size of the simulated data set. As we have seen, only eight address records are generated for the linked list in this current version of the program. However, you can expand the program performance by changing the value of *recsToCreate*. Try changing this value to 500, 1000, and 2000 for subsequent performances of the program, and notice what happens to the sorting speed as the program creates each new dynamic record.

You'll probably want to disable the *PrintList* procedure before generating such large data sets, however. To do so, simply enclose the procedure call within comment delimiters in the main program section:

```
{ PrintList }
```

You will eventually learn the program's maximum record capacity, which depends partly on the amount of memory available in your system.

The *RandAddr* program contains three major procedures:

- *SetPointers* establishes the pointers for each new record that the program adds to the linked list. This routine, which is basically unchanged from its original version in the *PtrAddr* program, has two local procedures, *FindNamePointers* and *FindRefNoPointers*.

- The *CreateAddressPointers* routine creates the simulated address records. This routine takes the place of the input routines in the original *PtrAddr* program (*ReadAddresses* and *NewAddress*).

- The *PrintList* procedure creates the program's text-file output. This routine takes the place of the various output routines in the original program, including *SaveAddress* and *PrintList*.

You may want to look back at Chapter 8 to review the structure of the *PtrAddr* program. A performance of *RandAddr* requires no input from you at the keyboard, and offers you no menu choices. (For this reason, the *Menu* procedure is not needed in *RandAddr*.)

Let's look briefly at how *RandAddr* generates the address records. Within a REPEAT UNTIL loop, the *CreateAddressPointers* procedure creates each new dynamic record and increments the current record count:

```
NEW (newRecord);
INC (numRecords);
```

Then the routine uses the various random functions from *RandUnit* to assign a value to each field of the new record, as in this excerpt:

```
WITH newRecord ^ DO
  BEGIN
    name : = RandStr (10);
    refNo : = RandInt (1, 255);
    headOffice : = RandBoolean;
    usa : = RandBoolean;
    phone : = RandStr (20);
    street : = RandStr (30);
    city : = RandStr (20);
```

Finally, the program calls the *SetPointers* procedure to establish this new record's pointers to other records in the linked list. The REPEAT UNTIL loop continues creating new dynamic records until the record count (*numRecords*) is equal to the fixed number of records specified by *recsToCreate*:

```
UNTIL (numRecords = recsToCreate)
```

The program also displays the current record number on the screen after each new dynamic record is created:

```
WRITE (numRecords: 4);
```

The time lapse between the appearance of one record number and the next indicates how long the *SetPointers* routine is taking to establish pointers for the new record. If you increase the value of *recsToCreate* you'll notice that each performance of *SetPointers* takes a progressively longer time as the size of the linked list increases.

Summary

The Turbo Pascal SYSTEM unit supplies a useful library of standard numeric functions, which can be divided into the following categories:

- Exponential and logarithmic functions
- Trigonometric functions
- Integer functions
- Arithmetic functions
- A random-number generator

We'll come across additional examples of these functions as we continue our survey of Turbo Pascal. Meanwhile, Chapter 10 presents a survey of the standard string functions and procedures, an equally impressive library of programming tools.

C H A P T E R

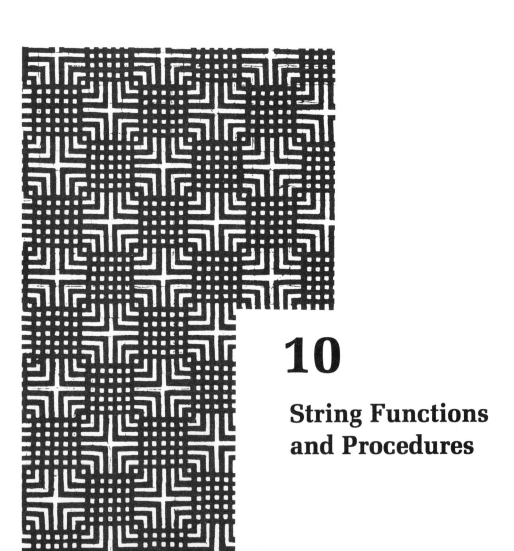

10

String Functions and Procedures

In this chapter we'll discuss several groups of functions and procedures that work with string values. The main focus of the chapter will be the standard string routines in Turbo Pascal's SYSTEM unit. In addition, we'll take a closer look at the functions we have been storing in the compiled unit named *StrUnit*. We first created *StrUnit* in Chapter 4, for use in the *BillTime* program; then we expanded the unit in Chapter 5 for use in the *CliList* program. In this chapter we'll add a final group of new functions to the unit, and we'll review the uses for each routine in turn.

Here are the categories of string routines that we'll study in this chapter:

- Functions that isolate a *substring* portion of a larger string argument, including the standard COPY function and three new *StrUnit* functions named *Left*, *Right*, and *FirstChar*.

- Functions that return an uppercase or lowercase version of a string: the standard UPCASE function and the *UpperCase*, *LowerCase*, and *InitCap* functions from *StrUnit*.

- Routines that change the content of a string: the standard procedures INSERT and DELETE and the *StrUnit* functions *DollarDisplay*, *RightJustify*, and *LeftAlign*.

- Routines that build strings of repeated characters, including *StringOfChars* and *Spaces*, both from *StrUnit*.

- Functions that supply information about the content of a string, including the standard functions LENGTH and POS.

- Functions that convert between strings and numeric-type values: STR and VAL.

Along with this large variety of routines, we'll also discuss two important Turbo Pascal functions designed for use in compiled .EXE programs: PARAMSTR and PARAMCOUNT. We can take advantage of these functions to create command-style programs that accept parameters from the DOS prompt. Specifically, PARAMSTR returns an array of user-supplied string parameters, while PARAMCOUNT specifies the number of parameters that have been supplied. Using these functions, a command-style Pascal program can react appropriately to specific parameter information that the user enters from the keyboard at the time the program is performed.

To illustrate both the traditional string functions and the PARAMCOUNT and PARAMSTR functions, this chapter presents a sample program called *AddrCom*. This program is yet another revision of the address-file management program we have discussed in earlier chapters. The previous versions—including *CliAddr* (Chapter 6) and *PtrAddr* (Chapter 8)—allow the user to enter new client addresses into a file and print phone lists and address lists from this file. Both of these programs display menus on the screen to elicit the user's choices among the available activities.

In contrast, *AddrCom* is designed to accept option parameters directly from the DOS command line. As we'll see, the program gains access to these options from the PARAMSTR function, and then uses other string routines to analyze the parameters and convert them to a usable form.

But before we look at *AddrCom*, let's review the standard Turbo Pascal string routines and the functions of *StrUnit*.

String Functions

Most of the standard string-handling routines are designed as functions, although a few of them—including INSERT and DELETE—are procedures. The routines require various types of string and numeric arguments. Except for LENGTH and POS, all of the functions return string values. We'll begin our discussion with the functions that supply substrings.

Substring Functions

Given a string argument, *inStr*, and two integer arguments, *pos* and *numChars*, Turbo Pascal's standard COPY function employs the following syntax:

```
COPY (inStr, pos, numChars)
```

This function returns a substring of characters from inside the string *inStr*. The substring begins with the character at position *pos* in *inStr* and continues forward for *numChars* characters.

For example, consider the following simple demonstration:

```
VAR
   product,
   language: STRING;
BEGIN
   product : = 'The Turbo Pascal Compiler';
   language : = COPY (product, 11, 6);
   WRITELN (language)
END.
```

The COPY function in this program isolates the six-character substring that begins at the 11th character position in the string variable *product*. The result of the expression is 'Pascal'.

You may be familiar with the equivalent function, MID$, available in many versions of the Basic language. In addition, many versions of Basic include two useful functions that extract substrings from the beginning or end of a string: LEFT$ and RIGHT$. Turbo Pascal does not have these two functions; but we can easily create them using the COPY command. We'll add these two functions to *StrUnit*, along with a third function named *FirstChar*. As its name suggests, *First-Char* supplies the first character of a string argument.

To incorporate these three functions into *StrUnit*, begin by adding their headings to the end of the INTERFACE section of the unit:

```
FUNCTION FirstChar (inString: STRING): CHAR;
FUNCTION Left (inString: STRING; numChars: BYTE): STRING;
FUNCTION Right (inString: STRING; numChars: BYTE): STRING;
```

Figure 10.1 shows the complete INTERFACE section of *StrUnit* in its final form. The implementations of *FirstChar*, *Left*, and *Right* are shown in Figure 10.2. To complete *StrUnit*, you should enter these three short functions into the IMPLEMENTATION section.

```
UNIT StrUnit;

   { This unit supplies a variety of string
     functions and procedures. }

   INTERFACE

     CONST
       maxScreenColumn = 80;

     TYPE
       screenRange = 1..maxScreenColumn;
       screenLine  = STRING[maxScreenColumn];

     FUNCTION StringOfChars (displayChar: CHAR;
                             lineLength:  screenRange): screenLine;

     FUNCTION RightJustify (inString:    STRING;
                            fieldLength: BYTE):  STRING;

     FUNCTION DollarDisplay (inAmount: LONGINT;
                             width:    BYTE):   STRING;

     FUNCTION UpperCase (inString: STRING): STRING;

     FUNCTION LowerCase (inString: STRING): STRING;

     FUNCTION InitialCap (inString: STRING): STRING;

     FUNCTION Spaces (inLength: BYTE): STRING;

     FUNCTION LeftAlign (inString: STRING; fieldLength: BYTE): STRING;

     FUNCTION FirstChar (inString: STRING): CHAR;

     FUNCTION Left (inString: STRING; numChars: BYTE): STRING;

     FUNCTION Right (inString: STRING; numChars: BYTE): STRING;
```

Figure 10.1: The INTERFACE section of *StrUnit*

```
FUNCTION FirstChar;

   { The FirstChar function returns the
     first character of the string it
     receives as an argument. }

   BEGIN    { FirstChar }

     FirstChar := inString[1]

   END;    { FirstChar }


FUNCTION Left;

   { The Left function returns the first
     numChar characters of the inString
     argument. }

   BEGIN    { Left }

     Left := COPY (inString, 1, numChars)

   END;    { Left }


FUNCTION Right;

   { The Right function returns the last
     numChar characters of the inString
     argument. }

   VAR
     index: BYTE;

   BEGIN    { Right }

     IF numChars >= LENGTH (inString) THEN
       RIGHT := inString
     ELSE
       BEGIN
         index := LENGTH (inString) - numChars + 1;
         Right := COPY (inString, index, numChars)
       END

   END;    { Right }
```

Figure 10.2: The implementation of *FirstChar*, *Left*, and *Right*

These three functions behave as follows:

- *FirstChar* (*inString*) returns the first character of *inString*.

- *Left* (*inString*, *numChars*) returns the first *numChars* characters of *inString*.

- *Right* (*inString*, *numChars*) returns the final *numChars* characters of *inString*.

In either the *Left* and *Right* function, if *numChars* is greater than the number of characters in *inString*, the function returns the entire length of *inString*.

Here is a short program that demonstrates the use of these three new *StrUnit* functions:

```
USES StrUnit;
VAR
   product: STRING;
BEGIN
   product : = 'Turbo Pascal Compiler';
   WRITELN (Left (product, 5));
   WRITELN (Right (product, 8));
   WRITELN (FirstChar (Right (product, 8)))
END.
```

The WRITELN statements in this program display the following three strings on the screen:

```
Turbo
Compiler
C
```

You can see that the *Left* function has yielded the first five characters of the *product* string, and the *Right* function has returned the last eight characters.

The *FirstChar* function, which supplies the first character of a string, is useful in special situations. Normally, you can simply use the following notation to find the first character of a string:

```
inStr[1]
```

However, this notation is possible only when a string is represented by a variable name. If you are working with a string that is returned by a function, you would normally have to assign the return value to a temporary variable and then extract the first character, as in this example:

```
temp : = Right (product, 8);
WRITELN (temp[1])
```

The *FirstChar* function abbreviates this passage to

```
WRITELN (FirstChar (Right (product, 8)))
```

We'll see a practical example of the *FirstChar* function when we turn to the *AddrCom* program.

Alphabetic Case Functions

Turbo Pascal has one function that deals with alphabetic case conversions: UPCHAR. This function receives a character argument and returns a character result:

```
UPCHAR (inChar)
```

This returns the uppercase equivalent of the *inChar* argument. If the argument is already an uppercase letter, or if the argument is a non-alphabetic character, UPCHAR simply returns the original value of *inChar*.

StrUnit provides three additional case-related functions, *UpperCase*, *LowerCase*, and *InitialCap*, all of which deal with string arguments rather than single characters. Given a string argument, *inString*, here is how these functions behave:

- *UpperCase (inString)* returns an all-uppercase version of the argument.

- *LowerCase (inString)* returns an all-lowercase version of the argument.

- *InitialCap (inString)* returns a new version of the string argument in which the first letter is capitalized and remaining letters are all converted to lowercase.

These functions have no effect on nonalphabetic characters in the argument string.

The following short program demonstrates the use of these three functions:

```
USES StrUnit;

VAR
   product: STRING;
```

```
BEGIN
  product : = 'Turbo Pascal Compiler';

  WRITELN (UpperCase (product));
  WRITELN (LowerCase (product));
  WRITELN (InitialCap (product))
END.
```

The three WRITELN statements in this program produce the follow-ing lines of screen output:

```
TURBO PASCAL COMPILER
turbo pascal compiler
Turbo pascal compiler
```

Routines That Change Strings

Turbo Pascal supplies two procedures that change the length and the content of a string variable: INSERT and DELETE. In each of these procedures the target string is a VAR argument; after a call to the procedure, the variable contains the new string value. Here is a sum-mary of these two procedures:

- INSERT (*insertStr*, *targetStr*, *pos*) inserts the value of *insert-Str* starting at the character position *pos* in *targetStr*. As a result, the dynamic length of the target string increases by the number of characters in *insertStr*.

- DELETE (*targetStr*, *pos*, *numChars*) deletes *numChars* char-acters from the value of *targetStr*, starting from the character position *pos*. As a result, the dynamic length of the target string decreases by *numChars*.

Here is a short demonstration program that shows how these two procedures work:

```
VAR
  product: STRING;

BEGIN
  product : = 'Turbo Pascal Compiler';
```

```
    INSERT ('5.0 ', product, 14);
    WRITELN (product);

    DELETE (product, 7, 11);
    WRITELN (product)
END.
```

The program produces two lines of screen output as follows:

```
Turbo Pascal 5.0 Compiler
Turbo Compiler
```

The first output line illustrates an insertion, and the second illustrates a deletion.

We have also seen many examples of concatenation in the programs of this book. Concatenation is the process of combining two strings to form a third. (See Chapter 4 for a review of this subject.)

StrUnit has three functions that build on the INSERT procedure and the concatenation operation: *RightJustify*, *DollarDisplay*, and *LeftAlign*. We have seen the results of all three of these functions in the column-oriented reports produced by programs like *BillTime*, *Cli-List*, and *CliAddr*. Here is a review of these functions:

- *RightJustify* (*inString*, *fieldLength*) returns a string *fieldLength* characters long, in which *inString* is right-aligned. The new string is padded on the left by space characters.

- *DollarDisplay* (*inAmount*, *width*) returns a dollar-and-cent string (for example, $1,234,567.89). The *inAmount* argument is a long integer representing cents (for example, 123456789). The resulting string will be right-aligned in a field of *width* characters.

- *LeftAlign* (*inString*, *fieldLength*) returns a string *fieldLength* characters long, in which *inString* is left- aligned. The new string is padded on the right by space characters.

Studying the implementations of these three functions, you'll see several interesting examples of concatenation and the INSERT function. For example, the following statement from *DollarDisplay* inserts a comma at a calculated position in the string argument:

```
INSERT (',', inString, inLength - commaMarker);
```

To see examples of output from *DollarDisplay* and the two alignment functions, look back at the programs presented in Chapters 4, 5, and 6.

Repeating-Character Functions

Many versions of Basic have two functions that return sequences of repeated characters. For example, the SPACE$ function supplies a string consisting of a specified number of spaces, and the STRING$ function returns a string consisting of a specified number of repeated characters. Turbo Pascal does not have these functions, but we have included equivalent functions in *StrUnit—Spaces* and *StringOfChars*, respectively:

- *Spaces* (*inLength*) returns a string of *inLength* spaces.

- *StringOfChars* (*displayChar*, *inLength*) returns a string of *inLength* characters. The repeating character is represented by *displayChar*.

Here is a short demonstration of these two functions:

```
USES StrUnit;
BEGIN
  WRITELN (StringOfChars (' - ', 21));
  WRITELN ('Turbo', Spaces (10), 'Pascal');
  WRITELN (StringOfChars (' - ', 21))
END.
```

The output from this program is as follows:

```
_____
Turbo        Pascal
_____
```

You'll find many more examples of *Spaces* and *StringOfChars* in programs presented throughout this book.

By the way, Turbo Pascal has a built-in function named FILL-CHAR that can be used to fill a string variable with a specified character. However, this function is less convenient to use than *Spaces* or *StringOfChars*.

Information Functions

The standard LENGTH function supplies the length of a string, and the POS function returns a number representing the position of one string inside another. Both functions return integer values. LENGTH takes a single string argument, while POS takes two string arguments and an optional integer argument:

- LENGTH(*inStr*) gives the length, in characters, of *inStr*. For example, if *lastName* contains the string "Washington", the following expression gives a value of 10:

    LENGTH(lastName)

- POS(*subStr*, *targetStr*) returns the position of *subStr* inside *targetStr*. If *subStr* is not in *targetStr*, POS returns a value of 0.

The *Hours* program uses POS to search for wild-card characters in an input file name. For example, the following expression returns an integer greater than zero if the string *inName* contains the character *:

    POS('*', inName)

In this example, POS serves simply to test for the presence of the asterisk character in the input string; the actual position of the character is irrelevant. Here is relevant passage from the *Hours* program:

```
dirRequest : =
  (POS ('*', inName) < > 0)
  OR (POS ('?', inName) < > 0);
IF dirRequest THEN
  Directory (inName)
ELSE
  goodName : = TRUE;
```

The value of *dirRequest* is FALSE if both POS functions return values of zero; this means that neither wild-card character is present. But if *inName* contains either an asterisk or a question mark, one of the POS functions will return a nonzero integer, and Turbo Pascal will read this number as a logical value of TRUE.

You might also recall an example of the POS function in the *CliMenu* program. The POS function here becomes a tool for converting a one-letter keystroke into a value belonging to the enumerated type *activities:*

```
CONST
  firstChars = 'UBLPQ';
  { ... }
  CASE inChar OF
    'U', 'B', 'L', 'P', 'Q' :
        { ... }
      currentSelection : =
          activities(POS(inChar, firstChars) - 1);
```

In this example, POS finds the position of the input character *inChar* in 'UBLPQ', the string of characters representing menu options. The program then uses a type-casting operation to convert the integer result into one of the enumerated *activities* values.

Type Conversion Functions

Finally, Turbo Pascal supplies procedures that convert numeric values to strings or string values to numbers. These functions are STR and VAL, respectively:

- STR (*inNum*, *strVar*) supplies the string equivalent of the numeric value *inNum;* the result is returned in the string variable *strVar*.

- VAL (*inStr*, *numVar*, *codeVar*) finds the numeric equivalent of the string value *inStr*, and stores the result in the numeric variable *numVar*. The *inStr* argument must contain a string that Turbo Pascal can successfully convert to a numeric value. If not, the procedure stores the position of the first unusable character in the *codeVar* variable.

The *DollarDisplay* function uses STR to convert its numeric argument into a string:

```
STR (inAmount, inString);
```

Once the number is in string form, *DollarDisplay* can begin inserting commas, a dollar sign, and a decimal point at appropriate positions in the string.

This concludes our review of standard string routines and the functions of *StrUnit*. Next we'll look at PARAMSTR and PARAM-COUNT, and we'll discuss strategies for using these functions.

Programming for Command-Line Parameters

PARAMSTR is the Turbo Pascal function that passes along user-supplied parameters to a stand-alone program. Before we examine this function, we should briefly discuss some general design questions: What kind of Turbo Pascal program can profitably make use of the PARAMSTR function, and what will this technique mean to a person who uses the program?

Designing Stand-Alone Programs

As we discussed in Chapter 1, the Destination command (in Turbo Pascal's Compile menu) is a toggle that determines the destination of the object code from a compilation. Under the default status of this command, the compiler stores object code only in the computer's memory:

```
Destination     Memory
```

Once you leave the development environment, any code that you have stored only in memory will be lost.

Toggling the Destination command to its Disk status results in a stand-alone program that can be performed directly from DOS. For example, let's say you switch to this status and then compile the program called *CliAddr*. As a result of the compilation, Turbo Pascal creates a file named ADDRMENU.EXE on disk. Using this program file, you can run the application outside the Turbo Pascal environment. You simply enter the following command at the DOS prompt:

```
A>ADDRMENU
```

In general, the program performance will proceed just as it did when you ran the program inside the Turbo Pascal environment. Since *CliAddr* is designed as a menu-driven application, the program's menu will appear on the screen as soon as the performance begins.

An important factor in the design of any stand-alone program is the *user interface*—that is, the approach the program takes in eliciting choices and data from the user at the keyboard. Displaying a menu on the screen is one common approach, as we have seen in several examples in this book. A rather different approach is to require the user to enter specific information at the prompt along with the name of the program. This is the way most of the DOS utility commands are designed.

For example, if you've ever used the MODE command to establish the characteristics of a serial printer, you probably remember entering a string of parameters something like this:

```
MODE COM1: 9600, N, 8, 1, P
```

MODE does not supply a menu of options; rather, DOS expects you to enter the options at the time you invoke the command. Before you try to use the MODE command, you must find out what the available options are and determine the correct responses for configuring your particular printer. If you enter an inappropriate option, or if you supply the parameters in the wrong order, DOS will probably supply an error message, and the MODE command will not work properly.

This command-style interface is perhaps not as friendly as other approaches; it demands more of the user. But the command approach is nonetheless ideal for some applications. In programs that offer a relatively simple set of options, a command-style interface may prove much more convenient to use than any other design.

Once you decide that the command-style approach is an appropriate design for a Turbo Pascal program you are writing, the PARAMSTR and PARAMCOUNT functions provide a very simple way of capturing the parameters from the command line. Let's discuss the syntax and usage of these functions.

Using **PARAMSTR** and **PARAMCOUNT**

PARAMSTR returns an array of string values, one for each parameter that the user enters from the DOS prompt. The following expression supplies the *n*th parameter in the list:

PARAMSTR(*n*)

The result of PARAMCOUNT indicates the number of parameters that the user has supplied for a given performance. This function allows you to build a FOR loop that examines each parameter in turn. PARAMCOUNT takes no arguments. For example, consider the following passage:

```
VAR
   i:          BYTE;
   nextParam: STRING;

BEGIN
   WRITELN ('Processing ', PARAMCOUNT, ' parameters.');

   FOR i : = 1 TO PARAMCOUNT DO
     BEGIN
       nextParam : = PARAMSTR(i);
       { Process each nextParam in turn ... }
     END
END.
```

This program begins by displaying a message that indicates the number of parameters that were received from the DOS prompt, as in this example:

Processing 5 parameters.

Then a FOR loop reads each parameter string in turn—from PARAMSTR(i)—and goes on to process the parameter in some way.

The PARAMSTR function supplies all the parameters that the user enters on the DOS command line after the program name. The function reads a space character or a tab character as the delimiter between one parameter and the next. For example, imagine a stand-alone compiled program named *Sample*, stored on disk as SAMPLE.EXE. Let's say a user has run this program by entering the following command from DOS:

```
A>SAMPLE  a  b  cd  19  88
```

Inside *Sample*, the PARAMSTR function supplies the following five parameters:

PARAMSTR(1) is the value 'a'

PARAMSTR(2) is the value 'b'

PARAMSTR(3) is the value 'cd'

PARAMSTR(4) is the value '19'

PARAMSTR(5) is the value '88'

PARAMSTR ignores the program name and any spaces located between the program name and the first character of the parameter string. Otherwise, PARAMSTR does not make any changes in the punctuation or alphabetic case of the command line.

Obviously a program that uses PARAMSTR must be prepared to examine the parameter strings closely and analyze each element of information that the user supplies. The program defines the parameter requirements—what information should be supplied on the command line and in what order. If the user supplies valid parameters, the program should respond accordingly. The program should also be designed to react in a reasonable manner if the user supplies some unexpected and invalid parameters.

While you are developing such a program inside the Turbo Pascal environment, you'll want some way to test the program's reaction to a variety of valid and invalid parameter lines. This is the purpose of the Parameters command in Turbo Pascal's Options menu. When you select this command, an input box appears on the screen; you can enter any combination of test parameter strings into this box. In a subsequent program performance inside the Turbo Pascal development environment, the PARAMSTR function will return the string you have entered into the Parameter line input box.

In summary, PARAMSTR actually works in two different ways, depending on whether you are still developing your program or you have already completed the final product. When you are testing your program inside the Turbo Pascal environment, PARAMSTR returns the value you have entered in the Parameters input box. Once you have compiled the program and saved the compiled code as an EXE file on disk, PARAMSTR returns the parameters entered from the DOS command line.

Now let's turn to this chapter's sample application, *AddrCom*.

The *AddrCom* Program

Like the *CliAddr* and *PtrAddr* programs before it, *AddrCom* produces address lists or phone lists from the ADDRLIST.TXT file stored on disk. (Unlike the previous versions of the program, however, the *AddrCom* program does not include an option for adding new records to the ADDRLIST file.)

The *AddrCom* program expects three parameters to be entered from the DOS command line. We can represent these parameters as follows:

ADDRCOM *listOption   sortKey   sortOrder*

The three parameters may appear as single letters or as words, separated from each other by spaces or tabs. Case is not significant to *AddrCom;* the program accepts the parameters in uppercase, lowercase, or any combination.

The first parameter, *listOption*, specifies whether the program should produce an address list or a phone list. This parameter can be supplied in the following ways:

- An entry of *a* or *address* results in an address list.

- An entry of *p* or *phone* results in a phone list.

The second parameter, *sortKey* specifies either the client names or the reference numbers as the sort key; it should be supplied as follows:

- An entry of *n* or *names* sorts the list by client names.
- An entry of *r* or *refno* sorts the list by reference numbers.

Finally, the third parameter, *sortOrder*, specifies an ascending or descending sort; this parameter should appear in one of the following ways:

- An entry of *a* or *ascending* sorts in ascending order.
- An entry of *d* or *descending* sorts in descending order.

Actually, the *AddrCom* program looks only at the first character of each parameter, so you can supply any appropriate abbreviations that make sense to you, provided that they begin with the correct letter. In response to these three parameters, *AddrCom* prints either an address list or a phone list, sorted by the selected key and in the specified order.

In summary, the *AddrCom* program allows a great deal of variety in the way the three parameters are expressed. They may appear in uppercase or lowercase letters, and they may be expressed as single letters or entire words. For example, any of the following parameter combinations results in an address list sorted by reference numbers in descending order:

ADDRCOM a r d

ADDRCOM A R D

ADDRCOM Address Refno Descending

ADDRCOM addresses reference descending

The program prints the address lists and phone lists in the same format as provided by the *CliAddr* program (see Figures 6.1 and 6.2 for examples). Before starting to print, the *AddrCom* program displays one of two messages on the screen. If you have selected an address list, the following lines appear:

Print an address list.

─── ── ─── ──

<Space Bar> to print. <Escape> to return to DOS.

If you have selected a phone line, you will see the following message:

Print a phone list.

——— – ——— ———

<Space Bar> to print. <Escape> to return to DOS.

In either case, you can start the printing by pressing the space bar or cancel the operation by pressing Esc.

If you supply inappropriate parameters, *AddrCom* responds by displaying a screenful of information that explains how the program works. This help screen is shown in Figure 10.3. Once the screen appears, the program performance terminates, and you are returned to the DOS prompt. After reading the explanation, you can always try running the program again.

Actually, this help screen appears in response to any of the following errors:

- A missing parameter

- Invalid separators between the parameters (note that commas alone do not serve as separators)

- Invalid letter codes for one or more parameters are not valid

- No parameter strings provided

The listing of the *AddrCom* program appears in Figure 10.4. The routines that analyze, validate, and act on the parameter strings are

```
-----------------------------------------------------------
    The ADDRCOM program prints sorted address or phone
    lists from  the client  file  named  ADDRLIST.TXT.
    The program takes three arguments, separated by spaces:

First argument:
            'a' or 'address':     Produce an  address  list.
            'p' or 'phone':       Produce  a   phone   list.

Second argument:
            'n' or 'names':       Sort  the  list  by names.
            'r' or 'ref':         Sort by reference numbers.

Third argument:
            'a' or 'ascending':   Sort  in  ascending order.
            'd' or 'descending':  Sort in descending order.
-----------------------------------------------------------
```

Figure 10.3: The help screen from the *AddrCom* program

```
PROGRAM AddrCom;

  { AddrCom is a command-driven version of the PtrAddr
    program. This program prints address lists and
    phone lists from the client address file, ADDRLIST.TXT. }

  USES CRT, PRINTER, InUnit, StrUnit;

  CONST
    addressFileName = 'ADDRLIST.TXT';
    numRecords: INTEGER = 0;


  TYPE
    addressPointer = ^addressRecord;
    addressRecord = RECORD
      nextName,
      prevName,
      nextRefNo,
      prevRefNo: addressPointer;

      name:       STRING[30];
      phone:      STRING[20];
      refNo:      BYTE;
      headOffice: BOOLEAN;

      street:     STRING[30];
      city:       STRING[20];

      CASE usa: BOOLEAN OF
        TRUE:  (state:  STRING[2];
                zip:    STRING[5]);
        FALSE: (otherLoc,
                country:  STRING[15])
    END;

    sortOptions = (nameAtoZ, nameZtoA,
                   refNoAscend, refNoDescend);

    argString = STRING[3];


  CONST
    firstName: addressPointer = NIL;

  VAR
    firstRefNo,
    lastName,
    lastRefNo,
    newRecord:   addressPointer;
    addressFile: TEXT;
    args:        argString;


PROCEDURE SetPointers;

  { The SetPointers procedure establishes the pointers
    of the linked list. It sets the four record pointer
    fields in each new address record read from the
    ADDRLIST.TXT file. }

  VAR
    current,
    previous: addressPointer;
    locFound: BOOLEAN;
```

Figure 10.4: The listing of the *AddrCom* program

```
PROCEDURE FindNamePointers;

  { The FindNamePointers procedure establishes the pointers
    for two sorting orders: alphabetical order and reverse
    alphabetical order by the name field. }

  BEGIN    { FindNamePointers }

  IF newRecord^.name < firstName^.name THEN
    BEGIN
      newRecord^.nextName := firstName;
      newRecord^.prevName := NIL;
      firstName^.prevName := newRecord;
      firstName := newRecord;
    END
  ELSE
    BEGIN
      locFound := FALSE;
      previous := firstName;
      current := firstName;
      WHILE (NOT locFound) AND (current^.nextName <> NIL) DO
        BEGIN
          current := current^.nextName;
          IF newRecord^.name < current^.name THEN
            BEGIN
              locFound := TRUE;
              previous^.nextName := newRecord;
              newRecord^.prevName := previous;
              newRecord^.nextName := current;
              current^.prevName := newRecord
            END
          ELSE
            previous := current
        END;

      IF (NOT locFound) THEN
        BEGIN
          newRecord^.prevName := current;
          current^.nextName := newRecord;
          newRecord^.nextName := NIL;
          lastName := newRecord
        END
    END

  END;    { FindNamePointers }



PROCEDURE FindRefNoPointers;

  { The FindRefNoPointers procedure establishes the pointers
    for two sorting orders: numerical order and reverse
    numerical order by the refNo field. }

  BEGIN    { FindRefNoPointers }

  IF newRecord^.refNo < firstRefNo^.refNo THEN
    BEGIN
      newRecord^.nextRefNo := firstRefNo;
      newRecord^.prevRefNo := NIL;
      firstRefNo^.prevRefNo := newRecord;
      firstRefNo := newRecord;
    END
```

Figure 10.4: The listing of the *AddrCom* program (continued)

```
                ELSE
                  BEGIN
                    locFound := FALSE;
                    previous := firstRefNo;
                    current := firstRefNo;
                    WHILE (NOT locFound) AND (current^.nextRefNo <> NIL) DO
                      BEGIN
                        current := current^.nextRefNo;
                        IF newRecord^.refNo < current^.refNo THEN
                          BEGIN
                            locFound := TRUE;
                            previous^.nextRefNo := newRecord;
                            newRecord^.prevRefNo := previous;
                            newRecord^.nextRefNo := current;
                            current^.prevRefNo := newRecord
                          END
                        ELSE
                          previous := current
                      END;

                    IF (NOT locFound) THEN
                      BEGIN
                        newRecord^.prevRefNo := current;
                        current^.nextRefNo := newRecord;
                        newRecord^.nextRefNo := NIL;
                        lastRefNo := newRecord
                      END
                  END
          END;     { FindRefNoPointers }


      BEGIN     { SetPointers }

        IF firstName = NIL THEN
          BEGIN
            firstName := newRecord;
            lastName := newRecord;
            firstRefNo := newRecord;
            lastRefNo := newRecord;
            WITH newRecord^ DO
              BEGIN
                nextName := NIL;
                prevName := NIL;
                nextRefNo := NIL;
                prevRefNo := NIL
              END
          END
        ELSE
          BEGIN
            FindNamePointers;
            FindRefNoPointers
          END
      END;     { SetPointers }


  PROCEDURE ReadAddresses;

    { The ReadAddresses procedure opens the ADDRLIST.TXT
      file and creates a new dynamic record variable for
      each address read from the file. }

    VAR
      officeCode, usaCode: BYTE;
```

Figure 10.4: The listing of the *AddrCom* program (continued)

```
     BEGIN     { ReadAddresses }

       {$I-}
         RESET (addressFile);
       {$I+}

       IF IORESULT = 0 THEN
         BEGIN
           WHILE NOT EOF(addressFile) DO
             BEGIN
               NEW (newRecord);
               INC (numRecords);
               WITH newRecord^ DO
                 BEGIN
                   READLN (addressFile, name);
                   READLN (addressFile, officeCode, usaCode, refNo);
                   headOffice := BOOLEAN(officeCode);
                   usa := BOOLEAN(usaCode);
                   READLN (addressFile, phone);
                   READLN (addressFile, street);
                   READLN (addressFile, city);
                   IF usa THEN
                     BEGIN
                       READLN (addressFile, state);
                       READLN (addressFile, zip)
                     END
                   ELSE
                     BEGIN
                       READLN (addressFile, otherLoc);
                       READLN (addressFile, country)
                     END    { ELSE }
                 END;    { WITH newRecord^ }
               SetPointers
             END;    { WHILE NOT EOF }
           CLOSE (addressFile)
         END    { IF IORESULT = 0 }

     END;    { ReadAddresses }




PROCEDURE PrintList (addressDirectory: BOOLEAN;
                     sortSelection:    sortOptions);

  { The PrintList procedure prints either an
    address list or a phone list; the
    addressDirectory argument specifies which
    list to print, and sortSelection specifies
    the sorting option. }

  CONST
    formFeed = #12;


  VAR
    firstAddress: addressPointer;


  FUNCTION Continue: BOOLEAN;

    { The Continue function accepts a signal from
      the user to indicate the next action: space bar
      to print the list, Escape to return to the menu. }
```

Figure 10.4: The listing of the *AddrCom* program (continued)

```
        CONST
          spaceBar = ' ';
          escKey   = #27;
          prompt   =
            '<Space Bar> to print. <Escape> to return to DOS.';

        VAR
          inKey: CHAR;

        BEGIN    { Continue }

          inkey    :=
            InChar (prompt, [spaceBar, escKey]);
          Continue := (inKey = spaceBar);
          WRITELN

        END;    { Continue }


  PROCEDURE PrintAddresses (address:   addressPointer;
                            whichSort: sortOptions);

    { The PrintAddresses procedure prints an address
      directory. The argument passed to the address
      parameter is a pointer to the record that should
      be printed first. The whichSort parameter indicates
      the sorting key and the direction of the sort. }

    VAR
      i: BYTE;

    BEGIN    { PrintAddresses }

      WRITELN (LST, 'Client Address Directory');
      WRITELN (LST, '------ ------- ---------');
      WRITELN (LST);

      WHILE address <> NIL DO
        BEGIN
          WITH address^ DO
            BEGIN
              WRITE (LST, LeftAlign (name, 35), refNo:3);
              IF headOffice THEN
                WRITELN (LST, ' H')
              ELSE
                WRITELN (LST, ' B');
              WRITELN (LST, street);
              WRITE (LST, city, ', ');
              IF usa THEN
                WRITELN (LST, UpperCase (state), ' ', zip)
              ELSE
                WRITELN (LST, otherLoc, ' ', UpperCase (country));
              WRITELN (LST, phone);
              WRITELN (LST)
            END;

          CASE whichSort OF
            nameAtoZ:     address := address^.nextName;
            nameZtoA:     address := address^.prevName;
            refNoAscend:  address := address^.nextRefNo;
            refNoDescend: address := address^.prevRefNo;
          END
        END
      END
```

Figure 10.4: The listing of the *AddrCom* program (continued)

```
        END;    { PrintAddresses }


    PROCEDURE PrintPhones (address: addressPointer;
                           whichSort: sortOptions);

      { The PrintPhones procedure prints a phone list.
        The argument passed to the address parameter
        is a pointer to the record that should be
        printed first. The whichSort parameter indicates
        the sorting key and the direction of the sort. }

      VAR
        i: BYTE;

      BEGIN    { PrintPhones }

        WRITELN (LST, 'Client Phone Directory');
        WRITELN (LST, '------ ----- ---------');
        WRITELN (LST);
        WRITELN (LST, 'Client', Spaces (27),
                      'Reference', Spaces (10),
                      'Phone');

        WRITELN (LST);

        WHILE address <> NIL DO
          BEGIN
            WITH address^ DO
              BEGIN
                WRITE (LST, LeftAlign (name, 35));
                WRITE (LST, refNo:3, Spaces (10));
                WRITELN (LST, phone)
              END;

            CASE whichSort OF
              nameAtoZ:      address := address^.nextName;
              nameZtoA:      address := address^.prevName;
              refNoAscend:   address := address^.nextRefNo;
              refNoDescend:  address := address^.prevRefNo;
            END
          END

      END;    { PrintPhones }


    BEGIN    { PrintList }

      WRITELN;
      IF addressDirectory THEN
        BEGIN
          WRITELN ('Print an address list.');
          WRITELN ('----- -- ------- -----')
        END
      ELSE
        BEGIN
          WRITELN ('Print a phone list.');
          WRITELN ('----- - ----- -----')
        END;

      CASE sortSelection OF
        nameAtoZ:       firstAddress := firstName;
        nameZtoA:       firstAddress := lastName;
```

Figure 10.4: The listing of the *AddrCom* program (continued)

```
              refNoAscend:   firstAddress := firstRefNo;
              refNoDescend:  firstAddress := lastRefNo
           END;

          IF Continue THEN
            BEGIN
              IF addressDirectory THEN
                PrintAddresses (firstAddress, sortSelection)
              ELSE
                PrintPhones (firstAddress, sortSelection);
              WRITELN (LST, formFeed);
            END

    END;    { PrintList }


PROCEDURE Explain;

  { The Explain procedure displays instructions
    for using this program. }

  CONST
    indent = 13;

  BEGIN     { Explain }

    WRITELN (StringOfChars ('-', 62));

    WRITE   ('  The ADDRCOM program prints ');
    WRITELN ('sorted address or phone');
    WRITE   ('  lists from the client ');
    WRITELN ('file  named  ADDRLIST.TXT.');
    WRITE   ('  The program takes three arguments, ');
    WRITELN ('separated by spaces:');
    WRITELN;
    WRITELN ('First argument:');
    WRITE (Spaces (indent), '''a'' or ''address'':     ');
    WRITELN ('Produce an address list.');
    WRITE (Spaces (indent), '''p'' or ''phone'':      ');
    WRITELN ('Produce a phone list.');
    WRITELN;
    WRITELN ('Second argument:');
    WRITE (Spaces (indent), '''n'' or ''names'':      ');
    WRITELN ('Sort the list by names.');
    WRITE (Spaces (indent), '''r'' or ''ref'':        ');
    WRITELN ('Sort by reference numbers.');
    WRITELN;
    WRITELN ('Third argument:');
    WRITE (Spaces (indent), '''a'' or ''ascending'':  ');
    WRITELN ('Sort in ascending order.');
    WRITE (Spaces (indent), '''d'' or ''descending'': ');
    WRITELN ('Sort in descending order.');
    WRITELN;
    WRITELN (StringOfChars ('-', 62))

  END;    { Explain }


FUNCTION CheckArguments (VAR userArgs: argString): BOOLEAN;

  { The CheckArguments function reads the three
    user-supplied arguments and determines
    whether they are valid. If so, the function
    returns a value of TRUE, and the three
    argument characters are returned in the VAR
    parameter userArgs. }
```

Figure 10.4: The listing of the *AddrCom* program (continued)

```
    TYPE
      testSet = SET OF CHAR;

    CONST
      setArray: ARRAY [1..3] OF testSet =
      (['A', 'P'], ['N', 'R'], ['A', 'D']);

    VAR
      ok: BOOLEAN;
      i:  BYTE;
      temp: CHAR;

    BEGIN    { CheckArguments }

      ok := TRUE;
      userArgs := '';

      IF PARAMCOUNT = 3 THEN
        FOR i := 1 TO 3 DO
          BEGIN
            temp := UPCASE (FirstChar (PARAMSTR(i)));
            ok := ok AND (temp IN setArray[i]);
            IF ok THEN
              userArgs := userArgs + temp
          END
      ELSE
        ok := FALSE;

      CheckArguments := ok

    END;    { CheckArguments }


PROCEDURE DoCommand (arguments: argString);

  { The DoCommand procedure processes the user's
    requests by calling on the printing routine,
    and passing on the correct sorting instructions. }

  VAR
    printAddresses: BOOLEAN;
    whichSort:      sortOptions;

  BEGIN    { DoCommand }

    { First decide which list to print. }

    IF (Left (arguments, 1) = 'A') THEN
      printAddresses := TRUE
    ELSE
      printAddresses := FALSE;

    { Next determine how to sort the list. }

    IF (COPY (arguments, 2, 1) = 'N') THEN
      BEGIN
        IF (Right (arguments, 1) = 'A') THEN
          whichSort := nameAtoZ
        ELSE
          whichSort := nameZtoA
      END
```

Figure 10.4: The listing of the *AddrCom* program (continued)

```
        ELSE
          BEGIN
            IF (Right (arguments, 1) = 'A') THEN
              whichSort := refNoAscend
            ELSE
              whichSort := refNoDescend
          END;

        PrintList (printAddresses, whichSort)

    END;    { DoCommand }


BEGIN    { AddrCom }

  { If all three parameter values passed to
    the program are valid, open the address
    file, read its contents, and print the
    requested list. }

  IF CheckArguments (args) THEN
    BEGIN
      ASSIGN (addressFile, addressFileName);
      ReadAddresses;
      DoCommand (args)
    END

  { Otherwise, simply display the program's
    help screen. }

  ELSE
    Explain

END.    { AddrCom }
```

Figure 10.4: The listing of the *AddrCom* program (continued)

located in three places in the program: the main program section, the *CheckArguments* function, and the *DoCommand* procedure. We'll focus on these three sections of the program as we turn our attention to the listing of *AddrCom*. (Except for a few adjustments, the remainder of the program is very similar to the *PtrAddr* program, which we examined in Chapter 8.)

Inside the *AddrCom* Program

The main program section of *AddrCom* begins by calling the *CheckArguments* function. This function reads the three DOS-line parameter values and passes them back as a string of three uppercase letters, stored in the variable *args*:

```
IF CheckArguments (args) THEN
```

The *CheckArguments* function returns a BOOLEAN value, indicating whether or not the user has supplied three valid arguments.

If *CheckArguments* returns a value of FALSE, indicating that the user's arguments are invalid, the main program calls the *Explain* procedure to display the program's help messages on the screen:

```
ELSE
  Explain
```

On the other hand, if *CheckArguments* is TRUE, the program opens the address file and read the addresses into a linked list structure. Finally, the main program calls on the *DoCommand* procedure to respond appropriately to the user-supplied parameters:

```
DoCommand (args)
```

In the next two sections we'll examine the *CheckArguments* function and the *DoCommand* procedure in turn.

The *CheckArguments* Function

To simplify the process of validating the user-supplied parameter strings, *CheckArguments* declares and initializes an array of sets. The array contains a set corresponding to the valid options for each of the three program parameters:

```
TYPE
  testSet = SET OF CHAR;
CONST
  setArray: ARRAY [1..3] OF testSet =
  (['A', 'P'], ['N', 'R'], ['A', 'D']);
```

Even though *AddrCom* allows whole words as parameters, we'll see that the program really only pays attention to the first character of each parameter string. For this reason, the three sets in *setArray* contain single characters representing responses expected for the first, second, and third parameters.

In addition to this data structure, the function declares a local BOOLEAN variable, *ok:*

```
VAR
  ok: BOOLEAN;
```

As the function reads and tests the three parameter strings, the value in this variable indicates whether or not the parameters are valid. If any one condition switches *ok* to a value of FALSE, the *CheckArgument* function also returns a value of FALSE.

The first test concerns the number of parameters that the user has supplied. If this number is anything other than 3, the function does not even bother to read the parameters, but immediately returns a value of FALSE:

```
IF PARAMCOUNT = 3 THEN
  { read and check the
     user-supplied parameters }
ELSE
  ok : = FALSE;
CheckArguments : = ok
```

However, if PARAMCOUNT returns a value of 3, the function begins investigating the three parameters. For each parameter, *Check-Argument* performs five processing tasks:

1. Reads the parameter string (PARAMSTR).

2. Isolates the first character of the string (*FirstChar*).

3. Converts the character to uppercase (UPCASE).

4. Tests the character for membership in the appropriate set of valid parameter options (IN).

5. Concatenates the character to the string *userArgs*, but only if the character is a valid parameter.

A single FOR loop performs all these tasks very economically:

```
FOR i : = 1 TO 3 DO
  BEGIN
    temp : = UPCASE (FirstChar (PARAMSTR(i)));
    ok : = ok AND (temp IN setArray[i]);
    IF ok THEN
      userArgs : = userArgs + temp
  END
```

The first assignment statement inside the loop reads the parameter string, extracts its first character, converts the character to uppercase, and assigns the result to the CHAR variable *temp*. The second statement tests for the membership of *temp* in the appropriate validation set. Finally, if *temp* passes the validation test, the last statement in the loop concatenates *temp* to *userArgs*.

CheckArguments sends the three-character string value represented by *userArgs* back to the main program section. From there the string value is sent to the *DoCommand* procedure.

The *DoCommand* Procedure

DoCommand receives the three-character string in the variable *arguments*, and uses the *Left*, COPY, and *Right* functions to gain access to the first, second, and third characters in the string. To pass information on to the rest of the program, *DoCommand* assigns values to two variables:

- The *printAddresses* variable is a BOOLEAN variable that indicates which list the program will print. If the value is TRUE, the program prints an address list; if FALSE, a phone list.

- The *whichSort* variable is a value belonging to an enumerated type named *sortOptions*. The elements of this type represent the four different combinations of sorting keys and sorting orders:

```
sortOptions = (nameAtoZ, nameZtoA,
               refNoAscend, refNoDescend);
```

A series of decisions in *DoCommand* select values for these two variables. The routine begins by assigning a BOOLEAN value to *printAddresses*, according to the first character in *arguments:*

```
IF (Left (arguments, 1) = 'A') THEN
  printAddresses : = TRUE
ELSE
  printAddresses : = FALSE;
```

Then a series of nested decisions look at the second and third characters in *arguments* and determine the correct enumerated value for *whichSort:*

```
IF (COPY (arguments, 2, 1) = 'N') THEN
  BEGIN
    IF (Right (arguments, 1) = 'A') THEN
      whichSort : = nameAtoZ
    ELSE
      whichSort : = nameZtoA
  END
ELSE
  BEGIN
    IF (Right (arguments, 1) = 'A') THEN
      whichSort : = refNoAscend
    ELSE
      whichSort : = refNoDescend
  END;
```

Finally, these two values—*printAddresses* and *whichSort*—are sent as arguments to the *PrintList* procedure:

```
PrintList (printAddresses, whichSort)
```

As you might recall, the work of *PrintList* is organized into two procedures, *PrintAddresses* and *PrintPhones*. The choice between these two procedures is based on the value of *printAddresses*. Likewise, the choice among the four established paths through the linked list depends on the value of *whichSort*.

In short, you can see that the process of analyzing and acting on the information in the command-line parameters can be complex and detailed. Nonetheless, the resulting program achieves a style of user-interface that is simple, direct, and effective.

Summary

We have discussed several categories of standard string routines, along with the collection of functions stored in *StrUnit:*

- The COPY, *Left*, and *Right* functions supply substring portions of a string.

- The UPCASE, *UpperCase*, and *LowerCase* functions give upper- and lowercase versions of a string.

- The INSERT, DELETE, *RightJustify*, *DollarDisplay*, and *LeftAlign* routines make carefully defined changes in their string arguments.

- The *Spaces* and *StringOfChars* functions build strings of repeating characters.

- The LENGTH function yields the length of a string, and the POS function gives the position of one string inside another.

- The STR and VAL procedures convert values between numeric and string formats.

Many of these routines are important elements in this chapter's sample program application, which uses the PARAMSTR function to access user-supplied command parameters. A program of this type must carefully analyze the command-line strings; the built-in string functions are the appropriate tools for this job.

C H A P T E R

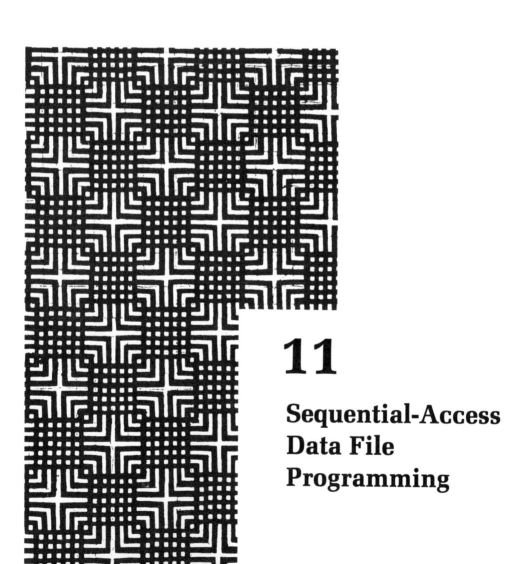

11

**Sequential-Access
Data File
Programming**

As the programs in previous chapters have shown, data-file programming is an essential skill for developing successful business applications. The tools for organizing, saving, and retrieving disk-based data files are among the most important features of any programming language, including Turbo Pascal. In this chapter we begin our discussion of data-file programming.

The term *file* generally refers to a collection of data stored on disk. In Turbo Pascal, however, a file is actually another data structure that you declare in a VAR statement. To work with a disk file, you establish an association between a defined file variable and a specific file name on disk. When you subsequently open the file for a particular operation, you can use the familiar READ procedure to read data from the file, or the WRITE procedure to write data to the file. We'll examine these commands and techniques in this chapter and the next.

Interestingly enough, even the simplest Turbo Pascal programs work with file structures. Whenever a program performs screen output or keyboard input operations, a file structure is implicitly involved. To simplify these most common of I/O operations, Turbo Pascal automatically opens two text files named INPUT and OUTPUT at the beginning of each program performance. Thanks to these predefined file variables, the READ procedure accepts data from the keyboard by default, and the WRITE procedure sends data to the display screen.

As we have seen, text files can be defined for other hardware devices as well. For example, to simplify WRITE operations to the printer, the PRINTER unit defines a text file named LST and associates that file with the device LPT1.

Nonetheless, when we use the term *file* we usually mean a disk file. Broadly speaking, there are three kinds of files in Turbo Pascal, each managed using a distinct vocabulary of built-in procedures and functions:

- A *typed file* contains elements belonging to a specified data type—either a simple type such as an integer or a structured type such as a record. Each element in a typed file can be accessed directly, by number; we therefore use the term *direct access* or *random access* to describe the operations of reading and modifying such a file.

- A *text file* belongs to the type TEXT, a predefined file type in Turbo Pascal. Text files are stored on disk as lines of ASCII characters, and can only be read or written sequentially—that is, from the beginning to the end of the file. The term *sequential access* thus describes operations with a text file.

- An *untyped file* is designed for low-level access to disk data. The component type of an untyped file is not specified.

In this chapter we'll study text files and the techniques of sequential data access. We'll also look briefly at untyped files. Then in Chapter 12 we'll discuss typed files and the random-access mode. In the course of these two chapters, we'll examine Turbo Pascal's built-in procedures and functions devoted to handling each of the two access modes.

A sequential disk file is designed to be read from beginning to end each time it is opened. In other words, there is no way to jump directly to a particular record located in the middle of the file. For this reason, sequential files are best used in applications that perform tasks on an entire data set, rather than on individual records in a data set.

A program that writes information to a sequential file can either create a new file on disk or append information to an existing file. We've already seen examples of sequential file applications in almost every chapter of this book—for instance, the .HRS client files created by the *Hours* program (Chapter 3), and the ADDRLIST.TXT file created by the *CliAddr* program (Chapter 6). Programs we have developed to read these files have always performed tasks on entire data sets stored in the files; the *BillTime* program (Chapter 4), for example, reads an entire .HRS file and prints a report from its contents. Likewise, the *AddrCom* program (Chapter 10) reads the ADDRLIST-.TXT file and prints either an address list or a phone list from the records in the file.

The basic steps for reading or writing a sequential file are simple:

1. Define a TEXT file variable, and associate the variable with a file name on disk.

2. Open the file, either for reading or for writing.

3. Read data from the file, or write data to the file.

4. Close the file when the process is complete.

To illustrate the techniques for performing these steps, this chapter presents at a program named *CliChart*. The program creates a simple horizontal bar chart depicting the relative number of billable hours recorded in a set of client files. *CliChart* stores the chart on disk as a text file, which you can subsequently incorporate into a word-processed document. Before turning to the details of sequential-file programming, let's begin with a quick look at what the *CliChart* program does.

The *CliChart* Program

CliChart borrows a number of procedures and functions from the *CliList* program, presented in Chapter 5. You'll recall that *CliList* examines all the .HRS files stored in the current disk directory and prints a summary report supplying the client names and total billable hours recorded in each file.

The *CliChart* program uses modified versions of several routines from *CliList*. For example, *GetFiles* investigates the directory and forms a list of clients represented by .HRS files, *TotalAccount* finds the total number of hours in each account, and *SortClientFiles* sorts the list of clients. But the program's output is different from that of *CliList*. Rather than sending a report to the printer, *CliChart* stores a bar chart on disk in a form that can be used in word-processed memos or letters.

CliChart contains several interesting examples of sequential-file programming techniques. Specifically, the program is designed to conduct the following file activities:

1. Generate a text file named HRSDIR.TXT, a DOS directory listing of all the .HRS files available on disk.

2. Read the names of the .HRS files from HRSDIR.TXT.

3. Open each one of the .HRS files in turn and read its contents.

4. Create a file named HRSCHART.TXT to store the bar chart depicting relative billable hours.

We'll examine each of these activities in detail later in this chapter. For now, let's look at an example of the program's output.

The program begins by reading information from all the .HRS files stored in the current directory. Then, while the program is creating the chart file, the following message appears on the display screen:

```
Creating HRSCHART.TXT on disk.
    (This is a text file that can be read
    into a word-processed memo or report.)
```

Once the DOS prompt reappears on the screen, the program's performance is complete. You will subsequently find the file HRSCHART.TXT in the current directory. From DOS, you can use the TYPE command to examine the contents of the file. Figure 11.1 shows an example. Notice that the output includes the name of each client, the total number of billable hours recorded to date, and the chart itself—a line of asterisks representing the total hours.

One of the advantages of sequential files is that they consist exclusively of ASCII characters. In general, this means that you can use such files to transfer information between one program and another on your computer. Since HRSCHART.TXT is stored as a sequential text file, you can easily include the file in a word-processed document.

```
       Airport      64.2   *********
       Altcorp      92.5   *************
       Bigco        99.2   *************
       Cityjob     190.7   **************************
       Jonesco      19.0   ***
       Mmmcorp     295.7   ****************************************
       Nowcorp     220.7   ******************************
       Pubwork      82.2   ***********
       Secretco    268.8   ************************************
       Smallco      30.2   ****
       Todayco      70.5   **********
       Xyzcorp     144.7   *******************
```

Figure 11.1: A sample HRSCHART.TXT file created by *CliChart*

For example, in the WordStar word-processing program the command Ctrl-K-R reads a file from disk into the current document. If you issue this command and then supply the name of the file you wish to include, WordStar reads the file from disk and makes a copy of it in your current text. Most word processors have commands equivalent to this one.

Figure 11.2 shows an example of a memo that includes the chart from the HRSCHART.TXT file. As you can see, the file serves as an effective medium for transferring data from a Turbo Pascal program to a word-processing environment. But this is only one example of data transfer using sequential files. Sequential files that conform to certain standard data formats (for example, formats with acronyms like SYLK and DIF) are often used for other kinds of data transfer: between spreadsheets, database management programs, and programming languages.

We'll return to the *CliChart* program and examine its listing after we have discussed the techniques for handling sequential text files in Turbo Pascal.

Working with Sequential Files

In this section we'll examine the steps for declaring, opening, reading, writing, and closing a text file for sequential access. Here is a preview of the built-in Turbo Pascal tools that accomplish these various tasks:

- A VAR declaration defines the TEXT-type file variable.

```
Date: April 4, 1988
To:   All Managers
From: M.M.H.

RE:   Billable hours for the first quarter.

    The following chart gives you a quick overall picture of our
billable activities this quarter:

        Client      Hours
        ------      -----
        Airport      64.2  *********
        Altcorp      92.5  *************
        Bigco        99.2  *************
        Cityjob     190.7  **************************
        Jonesco      19.0  ***
        Mmmcorp     295.7  ****************************************
        Nowcorp     220.7  ******************************
        Pubwork      82.2  ***********
        Secretco    268.8  *************************************
        Smallco      30.2  ****
        Todayco      70.5  **********
        Xyzcorp     144.7  ********************

I'm pleased to see that we have some promising new clients, and
that we are maintaining strong relationships with our old
clients.

    We'll have a staff meeting on Thursday (4/7) to discuss
current activities and new client prospects. Keep up the good
work.

                    M.M.H.
```

Figure 11.2: The HRSCHART.TXT file incorporated into a word-processed document

- The ASSIGN statement associates the file variable with a specific file name on disk.

- The REWRITE statement creates a new file and opens it for writing operations. Alternatively, the APPEND statement opens an existing file so that you can append new text at the end of the file. You can subsequently use the WRITE and WRITELN procedures to write data values and lines of text to the file.

- The RESET statement opens an existing file so that you can use READ and READLN to read data values and lines of text from the file. (A text file can be opened for only one operation at a time: writing, appending, or reading.)

- The {$I − } and {$I + } compiler directives turn I/O error-checking off and on, allowing you to control Turbo Pascal's reaction to an anticipated file error. Specifically, you can turn error checking off to avoid the run-time error that would occur if you tried to open a nonexistent file for reading or appending. The built-in IORESULT function tells you whether or not an error has occurred.

- The EOF function returns a BOOLEAN-type value indicating whether or not the program has arrived at the end of a file during a reading operation.

- The CLOSE statement closes a file that has been opened for reading or writing.

We'll review each of these tools in turn.

Establishing a TEXT File Variable

The word TEXT is Turbo Pascal's standard type identifier for defining text file variables. The general format for defining such variables is simple:

```
VAR
    fileVar: TEXT;
```

Like any other variable, a TEXT variable can be defined locally or globally; but unlike other structures, the length of a file variable is not specified.

You can define any number of file variables for a given program. In order to use a file variable for accessing data from a text file, you have to associate the variable with the name of a particular disk file. You use the built-in ASSIGN procedure to perform this task. ASSIGN takes two arguments, a file variable and a string representing a file name:

```
ASSIGN (fileVar, diskFileName)
```

For example, consider the following passage from the *CliChart* program:

```
CONST
    chartFileName = 'HRSCHART.TXT';
```

```
VAR
  chartFile: TEXT;

BEGIN
  ASSIGN (chartFile, chartFileName);
  { ... }
```

This passage establishes a file variable named *chartFile* to represent the disk file HRSCHART.TXT. As you can see, the program uses a named constant, *chartFileName*, to store the actual file name. The VAR declaration defines the variable *chartFile*, and the ASSIGN statement associates the variable with the file name HRSCHART.TXT.

After these steps, the program is ready to open the file.

Opening the File

A given text file can be opened for reading or for writing, but not for both operations at once. Turbo Pascal actually supplies three different commands for opening a text file; each command takes a file variable as its argument:

- REWRITE (*fileVar*) creates a new file for a writing operation.

- APPEND (*fileVar*) opens an existing file for writing new text to the end of the file.

- RESET (*fileVar*) opens an existing file for reading. An ASSIGN statement must precede each of these statements to associate *fileVar* with a named file on disk.

For example, here is how the *CliChart* program creates a new chart file:

```
ASSIGN (chartFile, chartFileName);
REWRITE (chartFile);
```

In this case, if a file named HRSCHART.TXT (represented here by *chartFileName*) already exists on disk, the REWRITE command overwrites it. In other words, the previous version of the file is lost.

In contrast, the APPEND and RESET commands both assume the existence of the named file on disk. If the file cannot be located, both of these commands normally result in run-time errors. As we have seen in previous chapters, the {$I − } compiler directive turns I/O error-checking off and prevents a run-time error in the event that the file is missing.

```
{$I − }
  RESET (fileVar);
{$I + }

IF IORESULT = 0 THEN
   { read the file }
ELSE
   { an I/O error has occurred }
```

In this passage, the built-in IORESULT function returns a value of zero if the RESET command was performed successfully.

The WRITE, WRITELN, READ, and READLN statements have special syntax and usage rules for text files, as we'll see in the following sections.

Writing Data to a TEXT File

Given a file variable representing a text file that is open for writing, the WRITE and WRITELN take the following syntax:

```
WRITE (fileVar, dataList)
WRITELN (fileVar, dataList)
```

The first argument, *fileVar*, is the name of the file variable to which the program will write the data. Subsequent arguments are the actual data values that the program will send to the file.

We have seen the differences between the WRITE and WRITELN procedures for screen output; these differences are equally true for file output. A WRITE statement allows a subsequent command to send additional data values to the current line. WRITELN ends the current line by sending carriage-return and line-feed characters after the final data value is sent to the file.

The list of data values in the WRITE and WRITELN statements can include characters, strings, or numeric values. For example, the following passage from the *CliChart* program creates a single line of the chart file:

```
WRITE (chartFile,
    LeftAlign (InitialCap (name), 11));
WRITE (chartFile, totalHours:7:1);
lengthOfChart : = ROUND(totalHours * scaleFactor);
WRITE (chartFile, '      ');
WRITELN (chartFile,
            StringOfChars (chartChar, lengthOfChart))
```

The first WRITE statement sends the client's name to the file. (Notice how the program uses the *LeftAlign* and *InitialCap* functions from *StrUnit* to format the name.) The second WRITE statement sends a real number to the file, represented by the variable *totalHours*. WRITE and WRITELN automatically convert numeric data values to strings of digit characters for storage in text files.

Finally, the third WRITE statement in this passage sends a short string of spaces to the file, and the WRITELN statement sends a string of asterisks representing the total hours recorded for the current client. (Note the use of the *StringOfChars* function from *StrUnit*.) Here is an example of a line of text produced by these WRITE and WRITELN statements:

```
Pubwork        82.2    * * * * * * * * * *
```

We'll examine this passage again later, in our discussion of the *Cli-Chart* program.

You can also use WRITE and WRITELN to send BOOLEAN-type values to a text data file. Turbo Pascal converts these values to one of two strings: 'TRUE' or 'FALSE'. However, the READ and READLN statements cannot, in turn, read these string values back as BOOLEAN values. You might recall that the *CliAddr* program (Chapter 6) illustrates a technique for solving this problem. The program uses type casting to convert BOOLEAN values to numbers for storage in a file and to convert the numbers back into BOOLEAN values when the file is read again.

Reading Data from a TEXT File

Like WRITE and WRITELN, the READ and READLN procedures both take a file variable as the first argument:

READ (*fileVar, variableList*)
READLN (*fileVar, variableList*)

The *fileVar* argument represents a file that is open for reading. The
subsequent list of identifiers are the variables in which the operation
will store values read from the file.

The READ statement reads one or more data values from the open
file and leaves the file pointer on the current line, so that subsequent
READ statements can read additional data from the same line.
The READLN statement reads one or more data values from the current line and then skips to the beginning of the next line in the file for a
subsequent input operation.

Even though a text file contains only ASCII characters, a READ or
READLN statement can read appropriate data values into both string
and numeric variables. For example, consider the following passage
from the *TotalAccount* function, designed to read an .HRS file:

```
VAR
   total, hours: REAL;
   targetFile: TEXT;
   chronInfoString: STRING[29];


BEGIN      { TotalAccount }

   ASSIGN (targetFile, targetFileName);
   RESET (targetFile);

       { ... }
   READLN (targetFile, chronInfoString, hours);
```

The READLN statement at the end of this passage reads two data values
from each line of an open .HRS file: a string (*chronInfoStrin*) and a real
number (*hours*). Notice how the program defines the string variable
chronInfoString. Given this variable, the READLN statement reads the
first 29 characters of a given line into *chronInfoString* and then reads
the remaining characters on the line as a numeric value *hours*.

Here is an example of the kind of text line this statement reads:

Thu., Jan. 7, 1988   5:34 pm 82.25

The first 29 characters of this line consist of date and time information (*chronInfoString*), and the final data value is a number (*hours*). As we will see later, the *TotalAccount* function is interested only in the numeric value, but has to read the string value first.

Any one of three characters can serve as a *delimiter* between one numeric value and the next inside a text file:

- A space character

- A tab character

- A carriage return character

When reading a sequence of numeric values from a text file, the READ procedure recognizes these characters as separators between one value and the next. However, an attempt to read a string of non-numeric characters into a numeric variable results in a run-time error, just as it does during a keyboard input operation.

Typically, a program uses a structured loop to read through the data items stored in a sequential file. Each iteration of the loop might read one data item or one line of data items. If you know in advance how many items or lines are stored in the file, you can use a FOR loop to read the data. A more typical approach, however, is to use Turbo Pascal's EOF (end of file) function to determine the extent of the looping. This function takes one argument, a file variable:

EOF (*fileVar*)

EOF returns a logical value of true or false, indicating whether a program has reached the end of the file. The function typically appears as the controlling condition of a WHILE loop, as in this passage from the *TotalAccount* function:

```
WHILE NOT EOF(targetFile) DO
   BEGIN
      READLN (targetFile, chronInfoString, hours);
      total : = total + hours
   END;
```

During the reading of a sequential file, Turbo Pascal keeps track at the current position in the file. As long as there is another data value available to be read, the expression NOT EOF(*targetFile*) returns a value of true, and the action of the WHILE loop continues. But when the reading reaches the end of the file, the result of NOT EOF becomes false, and this condition stops the looping.

Finally, a program must close a file when a reading or writing operation is complete; we'll look at this operation next.

Closing a TEXT File

The CLOSE procedure properly closes a disk file after a series of READ or WRITE commands. CLOSE takes the name of the file variable as its argument:

CLOSE (*fileVar*)

For example, here is how the *CliChart* program closes the chart file when the chart is complete:

CLOSE (chartFile)

This statement closes the external disk file, but it does not end the association between the file variable and the file name. In other words, the program can use a subsequent RESET, REWRITE, or APPEND statement to reopen the same file without first performing a new ASSIGN operation.

Let's turn now to the listing of the *CliChart* program for some additional examples of sequential file operations.

Inside the *CliChart* Program

The listing of *CliChart* appears in Figure 11.3. The main program section makes calls to three procedures: *GetFiles* develops the list of client file names; *SortClientFiles* alphabetizes the list; and *CreateChart* creates the bar chart and stores it in a text file on disk.

The *GetFiles* procedure begins by instructing DOS to create a directory file. The following EXEC command accomplishes this task:

```
EXEC ('\COMMAND.COM', '/C DIR *.HRS > ' + fileName);
```

The DOS command issued by this EXEC statement is DIR, but the output of the command is redirected to a disk file:

```
DIR *.HRS > HRSDIR.TXT
```

```
PROGRAM CliChart;

{ The CliChart program prepares a horizontal bar chart
  showing relative hours recorded in the .HRS files that
  the program finds in the current directory. The chart
  is stored in the text file named HRSCHART.TXT. }

{ Establish heap min and max,
  for successful use of EXEC. }
{$M 16384, 0, 0}

USES CRT, DOS, StrUnit;

CONST
  maxClients = 100;

TYPE
  clientRecord = RECORD
    name:        STRING;
    totalHours:  REAL
  END;

VAR
  clientFiles: ARRAY [1..maxClients] OF clientRecord;
  listLength,
  i:           BYTE;
  chartFactor: REAL;


PROCEDURE GetFiles (VAR numberOfFiles: BYTE;
                    VAR scaleFactor:   REAL);

  { The GetFiles procedure forms a list of all the .HRS
    files in the current directory. The file names and
    the total hours in each file are stored in the global
    array of records clientFiles. GetFiles also computes
    the scaleFactor that the program uses to create the
    bar chart. }

  CONST
    fileName   = 'HRSDIR.TXT';
    chartWidth = 40;
    largestTotal: REAL = 0.0;

  VAR
    dirFile: TEXT;
    recNum, extensionPos, firstSpace: BYTE;
    dirLine: STRING[40];
    clientName: STRING;
```

Figure 11.3: The listing of the *CliChart* program

```
FUNCTION MaxReal (value1, value2: REAL): REAL;

  { The MaxReal function determines which of
    its two argument values is larger. }

  VAR
    temp: REAL;

  BEGIN    { MaxReal }

    IF value1 > value2 THEN
      temp := value1
    ELSE
      temp := value2;
    MaxReal := temp

  END;    { MaxReal }


FUNCTION TotalAccount (targetFileName: STRING): REAL;

  { The TotalAccount function opens an .HRS file, reads
    all its entries, and finds the total number of
    hours recorded in the file. }

  VAR
    total, hours: REAL;
    targetFile: TEXT;
    chronInfoString: STRING[29];

  BEGIN    { TotalAccount }

    total := 0.0;
    ASSIGN (targetFile, targetFileName);
    RESET (targetFile);

    WHILE NOT EOF(targetFile) DO
      BEGIN
        READLN (targetFile, chronInfoString, hours);
        total := total + hours
      END;

    CLOSE (targetFile);
    TotalAccount := total

  END;    { TotalAccount }


BEGIN    { GetFiles }

  { Uses an EXEC command to create HRSDIR.TXT, a
    directory listing of all the .HRS files.
    Open the file for reading.  }

  EXEC ('\COMMAND.COM', '/C DIR *.HRS > ' + fileName);
  ASSIGN (dirFile, fileName);
  RESET (dirFile);
  recNum := 0;
```

Figure 11.3: The listing of the *CliChart* program (continued)

```
      { Read each line in HRSDIR.TXT, and extract the
        file names. }
      WHILE NOT EOF(dirFile) DO
        BEGIN
          READLN (dirFile, dirLine);
          extensionPos := POS (' HRS ', dirLine);
          IF extensionPos <> 0 THEN
            BEGIN
              INC (recNum);
              firstSpace := POS (' ', dirLine);
              clientName := LEFT (dirLine, firstSpace - 1);
              WITH clientFiles[recNum] DO
                BEGIN
                  name := clientName;

                  { Call TotalAccount to compute the
                    number of hours in a given account. }

                  totalHours := TotalAccount
                                    (clientName + '.HRS');

                  { Find the largest total hours amount
                    in any of the HRS files. }

                  largestTotal :=
                    MaxReal (largestTotal, totalHours)
                END
            END
        END;

      CLOSE (dirFile);

      { Use largestTotal and chartWidth to compute
        a scale factor for creating the line chart. }

      scaleFactor := chartWidth / largestTotal;
      numberOfFiles := recNum

    END;    { GetFiles }


PROCEDURE SortClientFiles (sortLength: BYTE);

  { The SortClientFiles procedure uses the Shell sort
    algorithm to sort the array of records, clientFiles,
    by the name field. }

  VAR
    listJump, i, j: BYTE;
    sortComplete: BOOLEAN;
    saveRecord: clientRecord;

  BEGIN     { SortClientFiles }

    listJump := 1;
    WHILE listJump <= sortLength DO
      listJump := listJump * 2;

    WHILE listJump > 1 DO
      BEGIN
```

Figure 11.3: The listing of the *CliChart* program (continued)

```
            listJump := (listJump - 1) DIV 2;
            REPEAT
              sortComplete := TRUE;
              FOR j := 1 TO sortLength - listJump DO
                BEGIN
                  i := j + listJump;
                  IF clientFiles[j].name > clientFiles[i].name THEN
                    BEGIN
                      saveRecord := clientFiles[j];
                      clientFiles[j] := clientFiles[i];
                      clientFiles[i] := saveRecord;
                      sortComplete := FALSE
                    END
                END
            UNTIL sortComplete
          END

    END;    { SortClientFiles }


PROCEDURE CreateChart (printLength: BYTE;
                       scaleFactor: REAL);

  { The CreateChart procedure creates the chart file
    named HRSCHART.TXT. The chart contains one line of
    text for each record in the clientFiles array. }

  CONST
    chartFileName = 'HRSCHART.TXT';
    chartChar     = '*';

  VAR
    i, j:        BYTE;
    inChar:      CHAR;
    chartFile:   TEXT;
    lengthOfChart: BYTE;

  BEGIN    { CreateChart }

    ASSIGN (chartFile, chartFileName);
    REWRITE (chartFile);

    FOR i := 1 TO printLength DO
      WITH clientFiles[i] DO
        BEGIN
          WRITE (chartFile,
            LeftAlign (InitialCap (name), 11));
          WRITE (chartFile, totalHours:7:1);
          lengthOfChart := ROUND(totalHours * scaleFactor);
          WRITE (chartFile, '   ');
          WRITELN (chartFile,
                   StringOfChars (chartChar, lengthOfChart))
        END;

    CLOSE (chartFile)

  END;    { CreateChart }
```

Figure 11.3: The listing of the *CliChart* program (continued)

This command stores the directory selection (*.HRS) in the file HRS-DIR.TXT. (The constant *fileName* is used to represent the string 'HRSDIR.TXT'.) Figure 11.4 shows how the file might appear when this operation is complete.

```
BEGIN     { CliChart }

  CLRSCR;
  WRITELN ('Create a chart of client files.');
  WRITELN ('------ - ----- -- ------ ------');
  WRITELN;

  { Create the array of records, clientFiles,
    and sort the array by the name field. }

  GetFiles (listLength, chartFactor);
  SortClientFiles (listLength);

  WRITELN ('Creating HRSCHART.TXT on disk.');
  WRITELN ('   (This is a text file that can be read');
  WRITELN ('    into a word processed memo or report.)');
  WRITELN;

  CreateChart (listLength, chartFactor);

END.    { CliChart }
```

Figure 11.3: The listing of the *CliChart* program (continued)

```
        Volume in drive C has no label
        Directory of  C:

        XYZCORP  HRS     350   3-11-88   8:54a
        BIGCO    HRS     225   3-12-88  11:27a
        SMALLCO  HRS      37   3-13-88  10:22a
        CITYJOB  HRS     430   3-14-88   9:15a
        PUBWORK  HRS     186   3-16-88  10:23a
        SECRETCO HRS     948   3-18-88   8:05a
        MMMCORP  HRS     836   3-20-88  10:24a
        TODAYCO  HRS     167   3-21-88  11:27a
        JONESCO  HRS      67   3-22-88   9:24a
        ALTCORP  HRS     221   3-23-88   8:25a
        AIRPORT  HRS     148   3-25-88  10:25a
        NOWCORP  HRS     480   3-27-88   9:29a
          12 File(s)  15521792 bytes free
```

Figure 11.4: Sample contents from the HRSDIR.TXT file

In short, the EXEC command is simply a convenient way for the *GetFiles* procedure to gain access to the list of .HRS file names. To read this list of names, the procedure subsequently opens the HRS-DIR.TXT file for reading:

```
ASSIGN (dirFile, fileName);
RESET (dirFile);
```

The program loops through the file, reading each line as a string of text stored in the variable *dirLine:*

```
WHILE NOT EOF(dirFile) DO
BEGIN
   READLN (dirFile, dirLine);
```

But the only lines that are really of interest to the procedure are the ones that contain the extension name .HRS. The following statement uses the POS function to search for this extension name in each line:

```
extensionPos : = POS ('   HRS   ', dirLine);
```

If a given line contains the extension, the program increments a counter variable, *recNum*, and isolates the file name in the string variable *clientName:*

```
IF extensionPos < > 0 THEN
   BEGIN
      INC (recNum);
      firstSpace : = POS ('   ', dirLine);
      clientName : = LEFT (dirLine, firstSpace − 1);
```

The central data structure in the *CliChart* program is an array of records named *clientFiles*. Each record in this array has two fields: *name*, for the name of a given client; and *totalHours*, for the number of hours logged into that client's account. The program stores the *clientName* string in the *name* field:

```
WITH clientFiles[recNum] DO
   BEGIN
      name : = clientName;
```

Then the program calls the *TotalAccount* function to count up the total number of hours stored in the current account. This value is stored in the *totalHours* field of the current record element:

```
totalHours : = TotalAccount
                  (clientName + '.HRS');
```

You'll recall that *TotalAccount* opens a given file, reads each entry, and accumulates the total billable hours in the variable *total:*

```
ASSIGN (targetFile, targetFileName);
RESET (targetFile);

WHILE NOT EOF(targetFile) DO
  BEGIN
    READLN (targetFile, chronInfoString, hours);
    total : = total + hours
  END;
```

Finally, as the *GetFiles* procedure loops through the client accounts, it keeps track of the largest total billable hour amount among all the client files:

```
largestTotal : =
  MaxReal (largestTotal, totalHours)
```

(The *MaxReal* function simply returns the larger of its two REAL-type arguments.) Later, after closing the HRSDIR.TXT file, the program uses this maximum total amount to compute a special scale factor:

```
scaleFactor : = chartWidth / largestTotal;
numberOfFiles : = recNum
```

As we'll see shortly, the program uses this scale factor to translate each account total into a bar length that is proportional to the available chart width. (The named constant *chartWidth* receives a value of 40 at the beginning of the *GetFiles* procedure.)

Finally the program is ready to create the HRSCHART.TXT file. A REWRITE statement creates the file on disk, and a FOR loop writes each line of text to the file:

```
ASSIGN (chartFile, chartFileName);
REWRITE (chartFile);

FOR i : = 1 TO printLength DO
```

In the series of statements that create each line of the bar chart, the *scaleFactor* is used to compute the correct number of asterisks for representing each client's total hours:

```
lengthOfChart : = ROUND(totalHours * scaleFactor);
```

Given this value, the *StringOfChars* function (from *StrUnit*) then conveniently supplies the actual string of asterisks:

```
WRITE (chartFile, '      ');
WRITELN (chartFile,
              StringOfChars (chartChar, lengthOfChart))
```

The named constant *chartChar* contains the single character *. If you want the program to use some other character for the bar charts, you can simply revise the following CONST declaration at the top of the *Create-Chart* procedure:

```
CONST
    { ... }
    chartChar = '*';
```

In the final section of this chapter we'll look briefly at untyped files and use the HRSCHART.TXT file again in a short demonstration program.

Untyped Files

We noted at the beginning of this chapter that Turbo Pascal recognizes three categories of files: *typed*, *text*, and *untyped*. We have already seen several text file applications, and we'll discuss typed files in Chapter 12. The third kind of file—untyped—is not used very often in application programs, but can prove useful in utility programs that perform specific file operations, such as copying files.

The general syntax for declaring an untyped file variable is as follows:

```
VAR
    unTypedFile: FILE;
```

The declaration does not indicate the type of values or records that the file contains; this is why we call the structure an untyped file.

You can open any existing disk file as an untyped file and read blocks of data from the file into a variable. Alternatively, you can create a new untyped file and write blocks of data to the file. Turbo Pascal has two built-in procedures that are designed specifically for operations with untyped files: BLOCKREAD and BLOCKWRITE.

The BLOCKREAD procedure reads a block of data from an untyped file into a defined data structure. The command takes four arguments:

BLOCKREAD (*unTypedFile*, *varName*, *maxSize*, *actualSize*)

The first argument, *unTypedFile*, is the untyped file variable. The second argument, *varName*, is the name of the variable designated to receive the data that is read from the file. The third argument, *maxSize*, specifies the maximum size of the block that you want the procedure to read from the file. Finally, the last argument, *actualSize*, is a VAR integer variable that receives a numeric value from the procedure; this value represents the size of the block that BLOCKREAD has actually read from the file.

The BLOCKWRITE procedure takes four equivalent arguments:

BLOCKWRITE (*unTypedFile*, *varName*, *maxSize*, *actualSize*)

In this case, *varName* is the name of a variable containing the data that BLOCKWRITE will write to the untyped file.

The short program shown in Figure 11.5 is provided only as an illustration of the techniques for handling untyped files. The program, named *UnTypedF*, opens HRSCHART.TXT as an untyped file, reads a block of one-byte values from the file, and displays the values on the screen. The result of the program appears in Figure 11.6. Each byte value in this display is an ASCII code number representing a single character stored in HRSCHART.TXT. Looking carefully at the output, you can see illustrated a fact of programming that is often difficult to visualize: elements that are invisible on the screen, such as spaces and carriage returns, are stored in a file as actual ASCII values. Thus we can see several predictable sequences of characters in the output shown in Figure 11.6, including

```
PROGRAM UnTypedF;
  { This program demonstrates the use of untyped files. }

  CONST
    fileName = 'HRSCHART.TXT';
    maxSize = 1000;

  VAR
    unTypedFile: FILE;
    asciiCodes:  ARRAY [1..maxSize] OF BYTE;
    actualSize,
    i:           INTEGER;

  BEGIN
    ASSIGN (unTypedFile, fileName); .
    RESET (unTypedFile, 1);
    BLOCKREAD (unTypedFile, asciiCodes, maxSize, actualSize);
    CLOSE (unTypedFile);

    FOR i := 1 TO actualSize DO
      WRITE (asciiCodes[i]: 4);

    WRITELN
  END.
```

Figure 11.5: The listing of *UnTypedF*, demonstrating untyped files

- Strings of spaces (ASCII 32)

- Strings of asterisks from the bar chart (ASCII 42)

- Carriage-return/line-feed combinations (ASCII 13 and 10)

The *UnTypedF* program begins by defining two named constants: *fileName* is a string constant containing the name of the disk file, and *maxSize* is set at 1000, the largest number of bytes that the program will read. Next the program defines the untyped file variable and an array of bytes for receiving the data read from the file:

```
VAR
  unTypedFile: FILE;
  asciiCodes:  ARRAY [1..maxSize] OF BYTE;
```

To open the file for reading, the program follows the usual sequence of ASSIGN and RESET statements, with one small difference:

```
ASSIGN (unTypedFile, fileName);
RESET (unTypedFile, 1);
```

For an untyped file, the RESET procedure takes an additional argument, *recordSize*, indicating the length, in bytes, of the individual

```
 65 105 114 112 111 114 116   32   32   32   32   32   32   32   54   52
 46   50   32   32   32   42   42   42   42   42   42   42   42   42   13   10
 65 108 116   99 111 114 112   32   32   32   32   32   32   32   57   50
 46   53   32   32   32   42   42   42   42   42   42   42   42   42   42   42
 42   42   13   10   66 105 103   99 111   32   32   32   32   32   32   32
 32   32   57   57   46   50   32   32   32   42   42   42   42   42   42   42
 42   42   42   42   42   42   13   10   67 105 116 121 106 111   98   32
 32   32   32   32   32   49   57   48   46   55   32   32   32   42   42   42
 42   42   42   42   42   42   42   42   42   42   42   42   42   42   42   42
 42   42   42   42   42   42   42   13   10   74 111 110 101 115   99 111
 32   32   32   32   32   32   32   49   57   46   48   32   32   32   42   42
 42   13   10   77 109 109   99 111 114 112   32   32   32   32   32   32
 50   57   53   46   55   32   32   32   42   42   42   42   42   42   42   42
 42   42   42   42   42   42   42   42   42   42   42   42   42   42   42   42
 42   42   42   42   42   42   42   42   42   42   42   42   42   42   42   42
 13   10   78 111 119   99 111 114 112   32   32   32   32   32   32   50
 50   48   46   55   32   32   32   42   42   42   42   42   42   42   42   42
 42   42   42   42   42   42   42   42   42   42   42   42   42   42   42   42
 42   42   42   42   42   13   10   80 117   98 119 111 114 107   32   32
 32   32   32   32   32   56   50   46   50   32   32   32   42   42   42   42
 42   42   42   42   42   42   42   13   10   83 101   99 114 101 116   99
111   32   32   32   32   32   50   54   56   46   56   32   32   32   42   42
 42   42   42   42   42   42   42   42   42   42   42   42   42   42   42   42
 42   42   13   10   83 109   97 108 108   99 111   32   32   32   32   32
 32   32   51   48   46   50   32   32   42   42   42   42   13   10   84
111 100   97 121   99 111   32   32   32   32   32   32   32   55   48   46
 53   32   32   32   42   42   42   42   42   42   42   42   42   42   13   10
 88 121 122   99 111 114 112   32   32   32   32   32   32   49   52   52
 46   55   32   32   32   42   42   42   42   42   42   42   42   42   42   42
 42   42   42   42   42   42   42   42   42   13   10
```

Figure 11.6: Output from the *UnTypedF* program

data values that BLOCKREAD will read from the file. The REWRITE and RESET procedures also take this extra parameter for an untyped file. If you omit *recordSize*, the default length is 128 bytes.

The *UnTypedF* program specifies a record size of 1; as a result, the BLOCKREAD command reads one-byte values into the array of bytes, *asciiCodes*. Here is the BLOCKREAD command that reads the file:

```
BLOCKREAD (unTypedFile, asciiCodes, maxSize, actualSize);
```

If the chart file contains a thousand characters or fewer, this one command reads the entire file into the *asciiCodes* array. (If the file contains more characters, only the first thousand are read.) In the *actualSize* variable BLOCKREAD stores the actual number of bytes that were read from the file. Given this value, the following FOR loop displays all the character codes on the screen:

```
FOR i : = 1 TO actualSize DO
    WRITE (asciiCodes[i]: 4);
```

For additional work with untyped files, you might want to revise the *UnTypedF* program as follows:

1. Elicit a target file name from the keyboard, so that the user can examine the byte-by-byte contents of other files.

2. Enclose the BLOCKREAD command in a loop, so that the program will read more than the first thousand bytes. (The looping should end when a performance of BLOCKREAD reads no bytes of data—that is, when *actualSize* equals zero.)

3. Use the BLOCKWRITE command to store the data in another file.

Summary

Turbo Pascal provides a predefined file type, TEXT, for creating sequential-access files of ASCII characters. A sequential file contains a collection of data values or lines of text, designed to be processed from beginning to end each time the file is opened. There is no way to go directly to individual data items stored within the file.

To work with a text file, a program defines a TEXT-type file variable and then uses the ASSIGN procedure to associate the variable with a specific disk file name. A program can open a text file in one of three ways:

- The REWRITE procedure creates a new file for writing.

- The RESET procedure opens an existing file for reading.

- The APPEND procedure opens an existing file for an append operation.

When a file is open for reading, a program can use the READ or READLN command to read individual data values or entire lines of text from the file. In a WHILE loop designed to read a file, the EOF function is useful for determining the end of the file. When a file is open for writing, the WRITE command sends individual data values to the file, or the WRITELN command sends an entire line of data to the file.

An untyped file has no specified component type. Turbo Pascal supplies two special procedures, BLOCKREAD and BLOCK-WRITE, for reading and writing untyped files. These operations are best reserved for special-purpose utility programs.

In Chapter 12 we'll discuss typed files and the *random-access* mode of handling disk files.

C H A P T E R

12

**Random-Access
Data File
Programming**

In Chapter 11 we discussed two of the three kinds of files supported in Turbo Pascal: text files and untyped files. In this chapter we'll examine the third—typed files—and we'll explore the techniques of random-access data-file programming.

A typed file contains a sequence of individually accessible components, all belonging to the same data type or data structure. For example, a database application might typically employ a typed file of RECORD-type components for managing a structured collection of information. (In fact, we often refer informally to each data component of a typed file as a *record*, even when the components actually belong to some other data type.) Because individual record positions in a typed file are directly accessible for reading or writing operations, we use the term *random access* to describe the use of typed files.

As we saw in Chapter 11, a file can itself be a variable in Turbo Pascal. The declaration for a typed file variable uses the reserved words FILE OF, in the following general format:

```
VAR
typedFileVar: FILE OF componentType;
```

The *componentType* in this declaration refers to any standard or user-defined data type, except for another FILE type.

Typed files have several important features that contrast with the characteristics of text files. Here is a preview of these differences:

- An open typed file is available for both writing and reading operations at once.

- Turbo Pascal uses its own internal data formats for storing typed file components on disk. (Unlike a text file, a typed file is not stored in a line-by-line ASCII text format.)

- A program that works with a typed file can use Turbo Pascal's built-in SEEK procedure to gain access to a particular record at any specified location inside the file. The program can subsequently read the record into memory or write a new record at the same location.

The SEEK command is the key to random-access file programming in Turbo Pascal, enabling typed files to meet the requirements of complex database applications. For example, in this chapter we'll look at a program named *CliProf* that manages a database of client "profiles." Each record in the file contains an assortment of information about one client, including the client's name, the type of business, the amount of work billed to the client in the past, and so on. Since this client-profile database is defined as a typed file, the *CliProf* program can use SEEK to go directly to any record in the file at any time. In short, the program can access profile records in any random order.

As we explore the random-access mode in this chapter, we'll discuss several subjects related to typed files, including the process of defining a typed file; the commands and functions that Turbo Pascal supplies for working with such files; and the most convenient programming techniques for accessing the data stored in a typed file. Broadly, here are the steps for creating, reading, and writing a typed file in a random-access data file application:

1. Define the file's component type, and declare the file variable as a FILE-type structure (the TYPE and VAR declarations).

2. Establish an association between the file variable and a file name on disk (the ASSIGN procedure).

3. Open a new file or an existing file on disk (the RESET or REWRITE procedure). In either case, the file is open for both writing and reading operations at once.

4. Specify a particular record position in the file as the target of a subsequent read or write operation (SEEK). Read the record into memory (READ), or write a new record to the selected file position (WRITE).

5. Close the file when all the read and write operations are complete (the CLOSE command).

Because typed files are potentially so powerful, they also make extra demands on you as a programmer. One significant problem in a random-access file application is keeping track of record numbers. In order to take full advantage of a random-access file, a program needs a systematic scheme for locating records that are stored in the file.

For example, let's say your client-profile database has a record for company X; this record contains all the information that you need to know about your client. Unfortunately, the record is sandwiched in among other records inside the file, in an unpredictable order. (Records are typically stored in a database chronologically—that is, in the order of data entry over time—rather than alphabetically or numerically.) Unless you know the record number for company X within the file, you cannot gain access to the information that the record contains.

A typical scheme for solving this problem is to set up an *index* into the database. For the client-profile database an index might consist of an alphabetized list of all the client names stored in the database. Along with the client names, a program would also keep a list of the corresponding record numbers. So, to find a given client record, your program begins by searching through the alphabetized index list for the client's name. When the name is found, your program reads the corresponding record number from the index entry. Then, to access the client record, the program goes directly to the target location in the database: the location identified by the indexed record number.

The *CliProf* program maintains an index for the client-profile database. The program stores the database and the index as separate file structures on disk, under the names PROFILE.DAT and PRO-FILE.NDX, respectively. The program includes both a sorting routine to keep the index alphabetized, and a search routine to find individual client names within the alphabetized index list.

Interestingly enough, this elaborate scheme for locating records is completely invisible to a person who is using the program. The program is menu-driven and simple to use. Most important of all, the program's indexing system relieves the user of having to keep track of record numbers manually.

Before we turn our attention to the Turbo Pascal's random-access file commands, let's take a look at the specific database activities performed by the *CliProf* program.

Managing a Client-Profile Database

The *CliProf* program offers you three different operations relating to the client-profile database. You can add records to the database, display an existing record on the screen, or revise the information in an existing record. Here are the options as described in the recurring menu:

Add a client profile.
Display a client profile.
Revise a client profile.
Quit.

CliProf sets up a menu system that is similar to the one presented by the *CliMenu* program (Chapter 7). The current menu selection is indicated by a reverse-video highlight on the screen. To move the highlight to a different option, press the first letter of the target option (A, D, R, or Q), or press the ↑ or ↓ key. To perform the highlighted option, press the Enter key.

You can select the menu options in any order or any combination during a given program performance. (The only exception is that the program disables the *Display* and *Revise* options until the database contains at least one record.) At the beginning of each performance, the program opens the database and determines the current number of records in the file. This number is displayed on the screen at the top of the menu, as shown here:

(Currently 28 records in database.)

When you select the *Add* operation, the program leads you through an input dialog, eliciting information for a new client profile record. Here is an example of the dialog:

Add a client profile.

—— — —— ——

Client's name? **XYZ Corporation**
Reference number? **27**
Type of business? **Wholesale**
Contact Person? **Jane Davidson**
Phone number? **(213) 765-4321**
Billable hours last year? **40**

As you can see, this application example contains only a sampling of the many fields you might want to include in a real-life client database.

Once you have entered data values for each of the fields, the program asks you to confirm that you want to save the record. If you respond affirmatively, the record is saved to disk:

Save this record? **Y**
Saving record #29

The program uses the list of client names as a key field in the indexing system for the database. For this reason, each client name must be unique. The program does not allow you to add a new record that has the same name as an existing record. If you try to do so, the program displays an error message:

Client's name? **XYZ Corporation**
This client is already in the database.

The second menu option lets you examine any record in the database. To tell the program which record you want to see, you simply supply the target client name:

Display a client profile.

—— — —— ——

Client's name? **Biggers Company**

The program quickly searches for the record, and displays it on the screen:

Biggers Company
_____

Reference number: 18
Type of business: Consulting
Date of record: Wed., Apr. 6, 1988
Contact person: Jeff Biggers
Phone number: (619) 876-5432
Last year's hours: 25.0

Notice that the record structure includes a field that you do not have to supply yourself: the date on which the record was originally entered into the database. (The program automatically includes this field in each record.) You can take as much time as you want to examine the record. At the bottom of the screen the program displays the following instruction for returning to the main menu:

Press the space bar to return to the menu.

If you request a client record that does not exist in the database, the following error message appears on the screen:

Can't find this client in the database.

This message applies to both the *Display* option and the *Revise* option.

The program's third menu option allows you to make changes in any existing record. Once you have identified a target record and the program has located it, the record appears on the screen. The program then conducts an input dialog during which you can change any combination of three fields: the contact person, the phone number, and the total billable hours for the previous year. Here is a sample of the dialog conducted by this option:

Biggers Company
_____

Reference number: 18
Type of business: Consulting
Date of record: Wed., Apr. 6, 1988

Contact person: Jeff Biggers
Phone number: (619) 876-5432
Last year's hours: 25.0

Change the contact person? **Yes**
New contact person: **Mary Biggers**

Change the phone number? **Yes**
New phone number: **(213) 901-2345**

Change last year's billable hours? **Yes**
New billable-hours amount? **32**

An expanded version of the *CliProf* program might offer a variety of other options—for example, producing printed reports from the database, deleting records, indexing the database by fields other than the client names, and so on. Any one of these options would easily fit into the application as a new program module.

By the way, the performance of the program begins by opening the database file, PROFILE.DAT, and the index file, PROFILE.NDX. In the event that the program finds the database file but not the index file, the following error message appears on the screen:

PROFILE.DAT exists, but PROFILE.NDX does not.
    ... Can't continue.

Since the program depends on finding both files, the current version of *CliProf* simply terminates its own performance if the index file is missing (for example, if the file has been inadvertently deleted from the disk). After you have worked with the program for a while, a useful programming exercise would be to add a routine that builds a new index if PROFILE.NDX is missing.

As we'll see later in this chapter, the *CliProf* program contains many interesting examples of random-access file programming techniques. But *CliProf* is too detailed and complex to serve as an ideal starting point for our study of typed files. Instead, we'll begin our discussion by examining a simpler program named *RandFile*, listed in Figure 12.1. This program is merely an exercise—it performs no useful database tasks—but it is designed to illustrate the standard procedures and functions that Turbo

Pascal provides for random-access file programming. We'll look at relevant passages from the *RandFile* program as we discuss random-access file management in the next section.

```
PROGRAM RandFile;

  { The RandFile program illustrates the use of SEEK, FILEPOS,
    FILESIZE, READ, and WRITE for typed files, in a random-access
    file demonstration. The program creates a file represented
    by the file variable randFileVar. After storing a sequence of
    records in the file, the program makes random seaches for a
    selection of records and displays the results on the screen. }

CONST
  randFileName = 'RANDFILE.DAT';
  maxRecords   = 26;

{ The record structure consists of a CHAR field
  and a BYTE field. }

TYPE
  fileRecordType = RECORD
    ordChar:       CHAR;
    ordByte:       BYTE;
  END;

{ The variable randFileVar represents a file of records. }

VAR
  randFileVar: FILE OF fileRecordType;
  fileRecord:  fileRecordType;


PROCEDURE FillFile;

  { The FillFile procedure stores maxRecords records in
    the typed file represented by randFileVar. }

  CONST
    letter: CHAR = 'A';

  VAR
    i: BYTE;

  BEGIN     { FillFile }

    { Associate the file variable with the disk file
      name, and then create the file. }

    ASSIGN (randFileVar, randFileName);
    REWRITE (randFileVar);

    FOR i := 1 TO maxRecords DO

      { Store field values in the record ... }

      BEGIN

          WITH fileRecord DO
            BEGIN
              ordChar := letter;
              ordByte := i
            END;
```

Figure 12.1: The listing of the *RandFile* program

```
                { ... and write the record to the file. }

                WRITE (randFileVar, fileRecord);
                letter := SUCC (letter)
            END;

        CLOSE (randFileVar)

    END;      { FillFile }



PROCEDURE RandRead;

    { The RandRead procedure reads randomly selected
      records from the randFileVar file and displays
      their field values on the screen. }

    CONST
        doneRecord: fileRecordType =
          (ordChar: ' '; ordByte: 0);
        maxRead = 5;

    VAR
        i,
        targetRecordNum: BYTE;

    BEGIN     { RandRead }

        { Open the existing file. (The ASSIGN operation
          has already been performed.) }

        RESET (randFileVar);
        i := 0;

        REPEAT

            { Select a random file number, from 0 to the number
              of records stored in the file. }

            targetRecordNum :=
              RANDOM (FILESIZE (randFileVar) - 1);

            { SEEK the target record, and read it into memory. }

            SEEK (randFileVar, targetRecordNum);
            READ (randFileVar, fileRecord);

            { SEEK the target record again, since the READ
              operation moved the record pointer forward. }

            SEEK (randFileVar, targetRecordNum);

            WITH fileRecord DO

                { Display the record on the screen, but only
                  if this record has not been selected before. }
```

Figure 12.1: The listing of the *RandFile* program (continued)

```
                    IF ordChar <> ' ' THEN
                      BEGIN
                        WRITELN ('Record #', FILEPOS (randFileVar));
                        WRITELN ('  Char field: ', ordChar);
                        WRITELN ('  Byte field: ', ordByte);

                        { Once the record has been selected, overwrite
                          it with the value of doneRecord. }

                        WRITE (randFileVar, doneRecord);
                        INC (i);
                        WRITELN
                      END;

              { Display maxRead records on the screen. }

              UNTIL i = maxRead;

              CLOSE (randFileVar)

           END;    { RandRead }


   BEGIN    { RandFile }

       RANDOMIZE;
       FillFile;
       RandRead

   END.    { RandFile }
```

Figure 12.1: The listing of the *RandFile* program (continued)

Random-Access File Management

The action of *RandFile* is simple: The program creates a typed file and stores 26 records sequentially in the file. Then, to demonstrate the random-access mode, the program reads a group of records from selected locations in the file. Each record in the file contains two fields: a character field (with values from A to Z) and a BYTE field (with values from 1 to 26). During a performance, the program reads five randomly selected records from the file and displays the records on the screen. For example, here is the result from one such performance:

```
Record #0
  Char field: A
  Byte field: 1
```

Record #9
  Char field: J
  Byte field: 10

Record #19
  Char field: T
  Byte field: 20

Record #5
  Char field: F
  Byte field: 6

Record #2
  Char field: C
  Byte field: 3

The *RandFile* program contains examples of all the built-in routines we'll be looking at in this section, including several procedures we have already discussed in Chapter 11 (ASSIGN, REWRITE, RESET, READ, and WRITE) and a selection of procedures and functions that are designed specifically for random-access operations (SEEK, FILEPOS, and FILESIZE).

In the next section we'll see how to define a typed file variable and how to open a random-access file.

Defining and Opening a Typed File

As we noted at the beginning of this chapter, a typed file variable is defined as a file of a particular standard type or user-defined type:

```
VAR
   typedFileVar: FILE OF componentType;
```

For example, the *RandFile* program defines a typed file named *randFileVar*, as follows:

```
TYPE
  fileRecordType = RECORD
    ordChar:      CHAR;
    ordByte:      BYTE;
  END;
```

```
VAR
   randFileVar: FILE OF fileRecordType;
```

First the TYPE statement defines a record type named *fileRecord-Type*, and then the VAR statement declares the file variable *rand-FileVar*, specifying the component type.

Just as with text files, the first statement you must perform before attempting to open a typed file is the ASSIGN procedure, which associates the file variable with a disk file name. The *RandFile* program creates a global constant named *randFileName*, which contains the file name:

```
CONST
   randFileName = 'RANDFILE.DAT';
```

The *FillFile* procedure is designed to create the file and store a sequence of records in it. The first statement in this procedure is

```
ASSIGN (randFileVar, randFileName);
```

After the ASSIGN statement, you can use the REWRITE procedure to create and open a new file, or the RESET procedure to open an existing file. If you use REWRITE, any previous version of the file is deleted from disk. On the other hand, if you use RESET the file must exist on disk, or a run-time error results. (As we have seen, the {$I – } compiler directive prevents a run-time error by turning off Turbo Pascal's usual I/O checking. We'll find yet another example of this technique in the *CliProf* program.)

A typed file is always open for both writing and reading, regardless of whether you use REWRITE or RESET to open the file. The APPEND procedure is not available for typed files, nor is it needed. We'll see why shortly.

The built-in FILESIZE function supplies another operation that a program often performs as soon as an existing typed file is opened. FILESIZE returns the current number of components in the typed file. The function takes the name of a file variable as its single argument:

```
FILESIZE (typedFileVar)
```

If the file is new (that is, opened with the REWRITE procedure), FILESIZE gives a value of zero. Once the program begins writing records to the file, *FILESIZE* supplies the current number of records in the file. For example, in the *RandFile* program the following expression supplies the current number of records in the typed file represented by the variable *randFileVar:*

FILESIZE (randFileVar)

In the next section we'll see how to access individual records in a typed file.

Using the SEEK Procedure

You can refer to each record or component of a typed file by number. The first record in the file is always numbered 0, and subsequent records are 1, 2, 3, and so on. For example, the output from the *RandFile* program shows that record 0 is the first record in the file:

Record #0
    Char field: A
    Byte field: 1

The program uses the following expression to calculate the number of the last record in the file represented by *typeFileVar*

FILESIZE (typedFileVar) − 1

Because the numbering system starts with zero, the last record number is one less than the total number of records in the file.

The SEEK procedure selects a particular file record by number for a subsequent read or write operation. SEEK takes two arguments—the name of the file variable and the target record number:

SEEK (*typedFileVar, recordNumber*)

The record represented by *recordNumber* becomes the *current record* (or the *current component*) in the file. We sometimes say that SEEK moves the file's *record pointer* to a new numbered record. (However, don't confuse this informal terminology with the Pascal data structure known as a pointer variable.)

For example, the following two statements move the pointer to the first record and the last record, respectively, in a typed file represented by *typeFileVar:*

```
SEEK (typedFileVar, 0);
SEEK (typedFileVar, (FILESIZE (typedFileVar) − 1);
```

As another example, the following statement from the *RandFile* program selects a record represented by the variable *targetRecordNum:*

```
SEEK (randFileVar, targetRecordNum)
```

Turbo Pascal supplies a useful built-in function, FILEPOS, that gives the current record number in a typed file. Like FILESIZE, this function takes a typed file variable as its argument:

```
FILEPOS (typedFileVar)
```

When you first open a typed file, FILEPOS always gives a value of zero. Another way of saying this is that Turbo Pascal always sets the file pointer at the first record in a newly opened file.

Finally, Pascal allows you to move the record pointer to the numbered position located one record past the last record currently stored in the file. The following SEEK statement accomplishes this move:

```
SEEK (typedFileVar, FILESIZE (typedFileVar))
```

For example, if the file currently contains ten records, numbered 0 to 9, this SEEK statement moves the file pointer to the position numbered 10, located just after the last record. At this point the EOF function returns a value of TRUE, and a subsequent WRITE statement will append a new record at the end of the typed file. We'll return to this point shortly.

In the next two sections we'll discuss the writing and reading operations for a typed file.

Writing a Record to a Typed File

The WRITE procedure writes one or more records to an open typed file, starting at the current record position. The procedure takes at least two arguments: the name of the typed file variable and a variable that matches the file's defined component type:

```
WRITE (typedFileVar, recordVar)
```

After writing the record, the WRITE procedure also moves the record pointer forward by one position.

Alternatively, a single WRITE statement can send multiple records to the file:

```
WRITE (typedFileVar, recordVar1, recordVar2, ...)
```

In this case, the record pointer is moved forward after each individual record is written to the file.

A program that has the task of creating a new typed file can use a loop to write an initial sequence of records to the file. For example, consider the following passage from the *RandFile* program:

```
FOR i : = 1 TO maxRecords DO
   BEGIN

      { Store field values in the
         fileRecord structure ... }

      WRITE (randFileVar, fileRecord);
      { ... }
   END;
```

At the beginning of each iteration, the program stores unique field values in the *fileRecord* structure. Then each performance of the WRITE procedure sends a new record to the file, and moves the record pointer forward for the next write operation. No SEEK statement is needed here, because WRITE carries the record pointer forward in a sequential manner.

In contrast, a program that revises an existing record normally uses the SEEK procedure to position the record pointer appropriately before writing the record to the file. For example, the *RandFile* program uses the following two statements to write a "marker" value back to a record that has already been displayed on the screen:

```
SEEK (randFileVar, targetRecordNum);
   { ... }
WRITE (randFileVar, doneRecord);
```

RandFile selects random records for display on the screen. To avoid displaying a given record more than once, the program writes the record value represented by *doneRecord* as a marker for any record that has already been selected.

Finally, keep in mind that a program can always append a new record to the end of a file by moving the record pointer past the last record currently stored in the file and then writing the new record:

```
SEEK (typedFileVar, FILESIZE (typedFileVar));
WRITE (recordVar)
```

We'll see additional examples of the WRITE statement in the *Cli-Prof* program. Next we'll examine the process of reading a record.

Reading a Record from a Typed File

The READ procedure reads one or more records from an open typed file, starting at the current record position. Like WRITE, the procedure takes at least two arguments—first the name of the typed file variable, and then a variable that matches the file's defined component type:

```
READ (typedFileVar, recordVar)
```

After reading the record, READ moves the record pointer forward by one position.

A single READ statement can read multiple records from the file:

```
READ (typedFileVar, recordVar1, recordVar2, ...)
```

In this case, the record pointer is moved forward after each individual record is read from the file. After the read operation, the record values are available to the program in the named record variables: *record-Var1*, *recordVar2*, and so on.

A program can read all of the records in a text file sequentially, using a WHILE loop and the EOF function:

```
WHILE NOT EOF(typedFileVar) DO
  BEGIN
    READ (typedFileVar, recordVar);

    { Process each record in turn... }

  END;
```

In this passage, each performance of the READ procedure reads the current record and then moves the record pointer forward for the next read operation. For this reason, no SEEK statement is required in a sequential reading of the file. When the record pointer moves past the last existing record, the EOF function returns a value of TRUE, terminating the action of the WHILE loop.

More typically, however, an appliction takes advantage of a typed file to gain direct access to individual records. In this case, a program begins by performing the SEEK procedure to position the record pointer and then performs the READ procedure. For example, consider the following passage from the *RandFile* program:

```
targetRecordNum : =
  RANDOM (FILESIZE (randFileVar) − 1);

SEEK (randFileVar, targetRecordNum);
READ (randFileVar, fileRecord);
```

This routine uses the built-in RANDOM function to select a random integer from 0 up to the last record position in the file; the integer is stored in the variable *targetRecordNum*. A performance of the SEEK procedure then moves the record pointer to the position represented by *targetRecordNum*, and the READ procedure reads the record into memory. Finally, the program displays the record's two fields on the screen.

Now we're ready to move on to a more realistic and practical example of a random-access file application: the *CliProf* program.

Inside the *CliProf* Program

The listing of *CliProf* appears in Figure 12.2. The listing begins with a large collection of global constants, type definitions, and variable declarations. Among these are two user-defined record types, defining the base structures for the main database file and the index.

The record structure for the profile database file contains seven fields:

```
TYPE
   nameString =    STRING[30];
   profileRecord = RECORD
      name:          nameString;
      refNo:         BYTE;
      businessType:  STRING[15];
      recordDate:    STRING[20];
      contactPerson: STRING[20];
      phoneNumber:   STRING[15];
      hoursLastYear: REAL
   END;
```

Six of these fields represent the data items that the program reads as input from the keyboard: the client's name, reference number, type of business, contact person, and phone number; and the total hours billed to the client in the previous year. The remaining field represents the entry date for a given record, a data item supplied by the program itself.

The program's VAR section defines two variables that use this record structure as a base type. First, *profile* is a record of type *profileRecord:*

```
VAR
   profile:     profileRecord;
```

The program uses this record variable to store individual records that are read from or sent to the profile database. Finally, the name of the variable that represents the database file is *profileFile;* it is defined as a typed file of records:

```
profileFile: FILE OF profileRecord;
```

```
PROGRAM CliProf;

{ The CliProf program maintains a database of client profiles.
  The database itself is stored on disk in a file named
  PROFILE.DAT. An accompanying file named PROFILE.NDX serves
  as an index into this database. CliProf is menu-driven, and
  allows the user to add a new record, display a record, or
  revise an existing record. }

USES CRT, ChrnUnit, InUnit, StrUnit;

{ The profileRecord type defines the structure of the
  database records. }

TYPE
  nameString   = STRING[30];
  profileRecord = RECORD
    name:         nameString;
    refNo:        BYTE;
    businessType: STRING[15];
    recordDate:   STRING[20];
    contactPerson: STRING[20];
    phoneNumber:  STRING[15];
    hoursLastYear: REAL
  END;

  { The indexRecord type defines the structure of the
    index, as it is stored in memory during a performance. }

  indexRecord =   RECORD
    clientName:    nameString;
    recordNumber: INTEGER
  END;

  activities    = (add, display, revise, quit);
  activityRange = add..quit;

  { The activityRecord type contains fields of
    information describing the program's menu options. }

  activityRecord = RECORD
    row, column:  BYTE;
    menuString:   STRING[25]
  END;

CONST
  maxRecords    = 250;
  columnPos     = 24;
  optionDisplay = ' A D R Q ';

  profileName   = 'PROFILE.DAT';
  indexFileName = 'PROFILE.NDX';

  { The activity array contains a record of
    information about each menu option. }

  activity: ARRAY[activityRange] OF activityRecord =
    ((row: 10; column: columnPos;
      menuString: 'Add a client profile.'),
     (row: 11; column: columnPos;
      menuString: 'Display a client profile.'),
     (row: 12; column: columnPos;
      menuString: 'Revise a client profile.'),
     (row: 13; column: columnPos;
      menuString: 'Quit.'));
```

Figure 12.2: The listing of the *CliProf* program

```
          { ASCII characters for null, enter, and bell. }

          nullChar  = #0;
          enter     = #13;
          bell      = #7;

          { ASCII characters for the arrow keys. }

          upArrow    = #72;
          leftArrow  = #75;
          rightArrow = #77;
          downArrow  = #80;

          { The menuChars set contains all the valid characters
            that the user can press in response to the menu. }

          menuChars:      SET OF CHAR =
                          ['A', 'D', 'R', 'Q', nullChar, enter];

          { The cursorScanCodes set contains the extended
            codes for the four arrow keys. }

          cursorScanCodes: SET OF CHAR =
                          [upArrow, leftArrow, rightArrow, downArrow];

     VAR

          { The profile record stores the current record in memory
            during a performance, and the index array stores the
            entire index in memory. }

          profile:       profileRecord;
          index:         ARRAY [1..maxRecords] OF indexRecord;

          { The primary database file is represented as a typed
            file named profileFile, and the index file is a
            TEXT file named indexFile. }

          profileFile: FILE of profileRecord;
          indexFile:   TEXT;

          { The fileLength variable always indicates the current
            number of records in the database file. }

          fileLength: INTEGER;

          done, ready:      BOOLEAN;
          currentSelection: activities;



     PROCEDURE ReverseVideo (status: BOOLEAN);

          { The ReverseVideo procedure toggles screen display
            status to reverse video or to normal, depending on
            the BOOLEAN argument value the procedure receives. }

          BEGIN     { ReverseVideo }
```

Figure 12.2: The listing of the *CliProf* program (continued)

```
            IF status THEN
               BEGIN
                  TEXTCOLOR (Black);
                  TEXTBACKGROUND (LightGray)
               END
            ELSE
               BEGIN
                  TEXTCOLOR (White);
                  TEXTBACKGROUND (Black)
               END

         END;    { ReverseVideo }


PROCEDURE HighlightSelection;

   { The HighlightSelection procedure highlights the
     current menu selection--that is, it displays the
     selection in reverse video mode, and in all
     uppercase letters. }

   BEGIN    { HighlightSelection }

      ReverseVideo (TRUE);
      WITH activity[currentSelection] DO
         BEGIN
            GOTOXY (column, row);
            WRITELN (UpperCase(menuString))
         END;
      ReverseVideo (FALSE);
      GOTOXY (60,17)

   END;    { HighlightSelection }


PROCEDURE InitializeMenu;

   { The InitializeMenu procedure displays the menu
     on the screen, and sets currentSelection to the
     first menu option. }

   VAR
      option: activities;

   BEGIN    { InitializeMenu }

      CLRSCR;

      { Display the menu title. }

      ReverseVideo (TRUE);
      GOTOXY (columnPos - 7, 6);
      WRITELN ('*** Client-Profile Database Manager ***');
      ReverseVideo (FALSE);

      { Display the menu options. }

      GOTOXY (columnPos - 12, 16);
      WRITE ('(Use ');
```

Figure 12.2: The listing of the *CliProf* program (continued)

```
                   ReverseVideo (TRUE);
                   WRITE (#24, ' ', #25, ' ', #26, ' ', #27);
                   ReverseVideo (FALSE);
                   WRITE (' or ');
                   ReverseVideo (TRUE);
                   WRITE (optionDisplay);
                   ReverseVideo (FALSE);
                   WRITE (' to highlight an option,');

                   { Establish the current selection, and highlight it. }

                   GOTOXY (columnPos - 10, 17);
                   WRITE ('then press <Enter> to complete the selection.)');

                   { Display the keyboard instructions. }

                   FOR option := add TO quit DO
                     WITH activity[option] DO
                       BEGIN
                         GOTOXY (column, row);
                         WRITELN (menuString)
                       END;

                   GOTOXY (columnPos - 5, 8);
                   WRITE ('(Currently ', fileLength);
                   IF fileLength = 1 THEN
                     WRITE (' record ')
                   ELSE
                     WRITE (' records ');
                   WRITELN ('in database.)');

                   currentSelection := add;
                   HighlightSelection;

                 END;    { InitializeMenu }

                 FUNCTION SearchIndex (targetName: nameString): INTEGER;

                   { The SearchIndex function uses the binary search
                     algorithm to search through the index for a target
                     client name. If the name is in the list, the function
                     returns the corresponding database record number
                     from the index array. Otherwise, the function returns
                     a value of -1. }

                   VAR
                     found, notThere: BOOLEAN;
                     first, last,
                     midPoint,
                     targetRecord:    INTEGER;

                   BEGIN    { SearchIndex }

                     found := FALSE;
                     notThere := FALSE;
                     first := 1;
                     last := fileLength;
                     targetRecord := -1;

                     { Divide the index continually in half, in an
                       effort to locate the target record. }
```

Figure 12.2: The listing of the *CliProf* program (continued)

```
        REPEAT
          midPoint := (first + last) DIV 2;
          WITH index[midPoint] DO
            BEGIN
              IF clientName = targetName THEN
                BEGIN
                  found := TRUE;
                  targetRecord := recordNumber
                END
              ELSE
                BEGIN
                  IF clientName < targetName THEN
                    first := midPoint + 1
                  ELSE
                    last := midPoint - 1
                END
            END;
          notThere := (last < first)
        UNTIL (found OR notThere);

        SearchIndex := targetRecord

    END;    { SearchIndex }


PROCEDURE SortIndex (sortLength: BYTE);

    { The SortIndex procedure uses the Shell sort
      algorithm to sort the index array by the
      clientName field of each record in the array. }

    VAR
      listJump, i, j: BYTE;
      sortComplete:   BOOLEAN;
      saveRecord:     indexRecord;

    BEGIN     { SortIndex }

      listJump := 1;
      WHILE listJump <= sortLength DO
        listJump := listJump * 2;

      WHILE listJump > 1 DO
        BEGIN
          listJump := (listJump - 1) DIV 2;
          REPEAT
            sortComplete := TRUE;
            FOR j := 1 TO sortLength - listJump DO
              BEGIN
                i := j + listJump;
                IF index[j].clientName > index[i].clientName THEN
                  BEGIN
                    saveRecord := index[j];
                    index[j] := index[i];
                    index[i] := saveRecord;
                    sortComplete := FALSE
                  END
              END
          UNTIL sortComplete
        END

    END;    { SortIndex }
```

Figure 12.2: The listing of the *CliProf* program (continued)

```
PROCEDURE AddClient;

  { The AddClient procedure conducts an input dialog for
    a new client record. If the user confirms, the procedure
    then appends the record to the end of the database file. }

  VAR
    searchName: nameString;
    okRecord:   BOOLEAN;
    answer:     CHAR;

  BEGIN    { AddClient }
    WRITELN ('Add a client profile.');
    WRITELN ('--- - ------ --------');
    WRITELN;
    WITH profile DO
      BEGIN
        WRITE ('Client''s name? ');
        READLN (name);
        searchName := LeftAlign (UpperCase (name), 30);

        { Make sure this client name does not already
          exist. }

        IF (SearchIndex (searchName) >= 0) THEN
          BEGIN
            WRITELN;
            WRITELN ('This client is already in the database.')
              END
        ELSE

          { Conduct the input dialog to elicit each field
            of the new record. }

          BEGIN
            refNo := inByte ('Reference number? ');
            WRITE ('Type of business? ');
            READLN (businessType);
            WRITE ('Contact person? ');
            READLN (contactPerson);
            WRITE ('Phone Number? ');
            READLN (phoneNumber);
            hoursLastYear := inReal ('Billable hours last year? ');
            recordDate := DateString;

            WRITELN;
            WRITELN;
            answer := inChar ('Save this record? ', ['Y', 'N']);
            okRecord := (answer = 'Y');
            WRITELN (answer);

            IF okRecord THEN
              BEGIN

                { Move the file pointer to the current
                  end of the database, increment the number
                  of records, and write the new record to
                  the database. }

                SEEK (profileFile, fileLength);
                INC (fileLength);
                WRITELN ('Saving record #', fileLength);
                WRITE (profileFile, profile);
```

Figure 12.2: The listing of the *CliProf* program (continued)

```
                        { Update the index. }

                        WITH index[fileLength] DO
                          BEGIN
                            clientName := searchName;
                            recordNumber := fileLength - 1
                          END;
                        SortIndex (fileLength)
                          END
                        ELSE
                          WRITELN ('Abandoning this record input...');
                      END
               END

     END;     { AddClient }


  PROCEDURE GetClient (VAR whichRecord: INTEGER);

    { The GetClient procedure is called by AddClient and
      ReviseClient. It elicits a client name, searches for
      the name inside the database index, reads the corresponding
      record from the database file, and displays the record
      on the screen. GetClient also passes back the record
      number in the VAR parameter whichRecord. }

    VAR
      inName: nameString;

    BEGIN     { GetClient }

      WRITE ('Client''s name? ');
      READLN (inName);
      inName := LeftAlign (UpperCase (inName), 30);

      { Search for the name in the index. }

      whichRecord := SearchIndex (inName);

      { If the client exists, read its record from the file. }

      IF whichRecord >= 0 THEN
        BEGIN
          SEEK (profileFile, whichRecord);
          READ (profileFile, profile);
          CLRSCR; WRITELN; WRITELN;

          { Display the field values of the target record ... }

          WITH profile DO
            BEGIN
              WRITELN (name);
              WRITELN (StringOfChars ('-', LENGTH (name)));
              WRITELN ('Reference number: ', refNo);
              WRITELN ('Type of business: ', businessType);
              WRITELN ('Date of record:   ', recordDate);
              WRITELN ('Contact person:   ', contactPerson);
              WRITELN ('Phone number:     ', phoneNumber);
              WRITELN ('Last year''s hours: ', hoursLastYear:7:2)
            END
        END
      ELSE
```

Figure 12.2: The listing of the *CliProf* program (continued)

```
                  { ... or display an error message if the record
                        does not exist. }

                  BEGIN
                    WRITELN; WRITELN;
                    WRITELN ('Can''t find this client in the database.');
                    WRITELN
                  END

          END;     { GetClient }


      PROCEDURE DisplayClient;

        { The DisplayClient procedure calls GetClient to
          display a client record on the screen. }

        VAR
          location: INTEGER;

        BEGIN     { DisplayClient }

          WRITELN ('Display a client profile.');
          WRITELN ('------- - ------ --------');
          WRITELN;
          GetClient (location)

        END;     { DisplayClient }


      PROCEDURE ReviseClient;

        { The ReviseClient procedure guides the user through the
          process of revising the data in a client record. If
          the user confirms, the procedure then writes the revised
          record to the database file, PROFILE.DAT. }

        TYPE
          changeType    = (contact, phone, hours);
          changeRange   = contact..hours;
          promptStrings = RECORD
            question,
            inPrompt:     STRING
          END;

        CONST

          { The prompts array contains all the questions that
            this procedure asks during the input dialog. }

          prompts: ARRAY [changeRange] OF promptStrings =
            ((question: 'Change the contact person? ';
              inPrompt: 'New contact person: '),
             (question: 'Change the phone number? ';
              inPrompt: 'New phone number: '),
             (question: 'Change last year''s billable hours? ';
              inPrompt: 'New billable-hours amount: '));

        VAR
          currentChange: changeType;
          location:      INTEGER;
          changed:       BOOLEAN;
```

Figure 12.2: The listing of the *CliProf* program (continued)

```
    BEGIN    { ReviseClient }

        WRITELN ('Revise a client profile.');
        WRITELN ('------ - ------ --------');
        WRITELN;
        GetClient (location);
        changed := FALSE;

        IF location >= 0 THEN
          BEGIN
            WRITELN;
            FOR currentChange := contact TO hours DO
              BEGIN
                WITH prompts[currentChange] DO
                  IF InChar (question, ['Y', 'N']) = 'Y' THEN
                    BEGIN
                      WRITELN ('Yes');
                      WRITE (inPrompt);
                      WITH profile DO
                        CASE currentChange OF
                          contact: READLN (contactPerson);
                          phone:   READLN (phoneNumber);
                          hours:   hoursLastYear := inReal ('')
                        END;    { CASE currentChange }
                      changed := TRUE
                    END
                  ELSE
                    WRITELN ('No');
                WRITELN
              END;

          IF changed THEN
            BEGIN
              WRITELN;
              IF InChar ('Save revised record? ',
                         ['Y', 'N']) = 'Y' THEN
                BEGIN
                  WRITELN ('Yes');
                  WRITELN ('Saving the record...');
                  profile.recordDate := DateString;
                  SEEK (profileFile, location);
                  WRITE (profileFile, profile)
                END
              ELSE
                BEGIN
                  WRITELN ('No');
                  WRITELN ('Abandoning the revision...')
                END    { ELSE }
            END    { IF changed }
        END    { IF location >= 0 }

    END;    { ReviseClient }


PROCEDURE GetSelection (VAR quitSignal: BOOLEAN);

    { The GetSelection procedure accepts a menu selection
      from the keyboard, and calls the appropriate routine. }

    CONST
      options: ARRAY [1..4] OF activities =
        (add, display, revise, quit);
      firstChars = 'ADRQ';
```

Figure 12.2: The listing of the *CliProf* program (continued)

```
VAR
  inChar: CHAR;

PROCEDURE Continue;

  { The Continue procedure prompts the user to
    press the space bar to return to the menu after
    a given menu activity has been performed. }

  VAR
    inSpace: CHAR;

  BEGIN    { Continue }

    GOTOXY (10,25);
    WRITE ('Press the space bar to return to the menu. ');
    REPEAT
      inSpace := READKEY
    UNTIL inSpace = ' ';

  END;    { Continue }


PROCEDURE RemoveHighlight;

  { The RemoveHighlight procedure restores a deselected
    menu option to normal display. }

  BEGIN    { RemoveHighlight }

    WITH activity[currentSelection] DO
      BEGIN
        GOTOXY (column, row);
        WRITELN (menuString)
      END

  END;    { RemoveHighlight }

PROCEDURE SelectNextActivity;

  { The SelectNextActivity procedure highlights the next
    menu option down the list, responding to an arrow key. }

  BEGIN    { SelectNextActivity }

    RemoveHighlight;
    IF currentSelection = quit THEN
      currentSelection := add
    ELSE
      currentSelection := SUCC(currentSelection);
    HighlightSelection

  END;    { SelectNextActivity }


PROCEDURE SelectPreviousActivity;

  { The SelectPreviousActivity procedure highlights the
    previous menu option up the list, in response
    to an arrow key. }

  BEGIN    { SelectPreviousActivity }
```

Figure 12.2: The listing of the *CliProf* program (continued)

```
                    RemoveHighlight;
                    IF currentSelection = add THEN
                      currentSelection := quit
                    ELSE
                      currentSelection := PRED(currentSelection);
                    HighlightSelection

                  END;    { SelectPreviousActivity }


              BEGIN  {GetSelection}

                quitSignal := FALSE;

                { Read keystrokes until the user presses a valid
                  key in response to the menu. }

                REPEAT
                  inChar := UPCASE(READKEY);
                  IF NOT (inChar IN menuChars) THEN
                    WRITE (bell)
                UNTIL (inChar IN menuChars);

                { Respond appropriately to the keystroke. }

                CASE inChar OF

                  'A', 'D', 'R', 'Q' :

                    BEGIN
                      RemoveHighlight;
                      currentSelection :=
                          options[POS(inChar, firstChars)];
                      HighlightSelection
                    END;

                  nullChar :

                    BEGIN
                      inChar := READKEY;
                      IF inChar IN cursorScanCodes THEN
                        CASE inChar OF
                          upArrow, leftArrow: SelectPreviousActivity;
                          downArrow, rightArrow: SelectNextActivity
                        END
                      ELSE
                        WRITE (bell)
                    END;

                  { Call the appropriate procedure when the user
                    presses the enter key to confirm the current
                    menu selection. }

                  enter :

                    BEGIN
                      IF currentSelection = quit THEN
                        quitSignal := TRUE
                      ELSE
                        BEGIN
                          CLRSCR;
                          CASE currentSelection OF
```

Figure 12.2: The listing of the *CliProf* program (continued)

```
                    add:
                      BEGIN
                        AddClient;
                        Continue
                      END;

                    display:
                      IF fileLength > 0 THEN
                        BEGIN
                          DisplayClient;
                          Continue
                        END;

                    revise:
                      IF fileLength > 0 THEN
                        BEGIN
                          ReviseClient;
                          Continue
                        END;
                END;
                CLRSCR;
                InitializeMenu
              END
            END
          END

      END;    { GetSelection }



    PROCEDURE OpenFiles (VAR filesOk: BOOLEAN);

      { The OpenFiles procedure opens both the database file
        and the index file. The procedure sends back a BOOLEAN
        value in the VAR parameter filesOk. If this value is
        false, the database file exists but the index cannot
        be located. In this case, the current version of the
        program cannot continue. }

      VAR
        i: INTEGER;

      BEGIN    { OpenFiles }

        ASSIGN (profileFile, profileName);
        ASSIGN (indexFile, indexFileName);
        filesOk := TRUE;

        { Try opening the database file. If it does not
          exist, create it. }

        {$I-}
          RESET (profileFile);
        {$I+}
        IF IORESULT <> 0 THEN REWRITE (profileFile);
        fileLength := FILESIZE (profileFile);

        { If the database file already exists, try opening
          the index file. If it does not exist, and the
          database does, set fileOk to false. }
```

Figure 12.2: The listing of the *CliProf* program (continued)

```
            IF fileLength > 0 THEN
              BEGIN
                {$I-}
                  RESET (indexFile);
                {$I+}
                IF IORESULT = 0 THEN

                    { Read the index file into the index array. }

                    BEGIN
                      FOR i := 1 TO fileLength DO
                        WITH index[i] DO
                          READLN (indexFile, clientName, recordNumber);
                      CLOSE (indexFile);
                    END
                ELSE    { IF IORESULT <> 0 }
                  BEGIN
                    filesOk := FALSE;
                    WRITE ('PROFILE.DAT exists, ');
                    WRITELN ('but PROFILE.NDX does not.');
                    WRITELN ('    ... Can''t continue.');
                    CLOSE (profileFile)
                  END
              END

    END;    { OpenFiles }


  PROCEDURE SaveIndex;

    { The SaveIndex procedure saves the index file
      to disk at the end of a program performance. }

    VAR
      i: INTEGER;

    BEGIN    { SaveIndex }

      REWRITE (indexFile);
      FOR i := 1 TO fileLength DO
        WITH index[i] DO
          WRITELN (indexFile, clientName, recordNumber);
      CLOSE (indexFile)

    END;    { SaveIndex }


BEGIN    { CliProf }

  CLRSCR;

  { Attempt to open the database file and the index
    file, and determine whether the performance can
    continue. If ready is true, the files are OK. }

  OpenFiles (ready);

  IF ready THEN
    BEGIN
```

Figure 12.2: The listing of the *CliProf* program (continued)

```
        { Display the menu, and get the user's choices. }

        InitializeMenu;
        REPEAT
          GetSelection (done)
        UNTIL done;
        CLRSCR;

        { Close the database file, and save the index
          if at least one record exists. }

        CLOSE (profileFile);
        IF fileLength > 0 THEN SaveIndex
      END

  END.    { CliProf }
```

Figure 12.2: The listing of the *CliProf* program (continued)

The disk name corresponding to this file is stored in the named constant *profileName:*

```
CONST
  { ... }
  profileName = 'PROFILE.DAT'
```

The index structure type is a record that contains two fields:

```
indexRecord = RECORD
  clientName: nameString;
  recordNumber: INTEGER
END;
```

The first field represents the name of a given client, and the second is an integer indicating the client's record position in the main database file. To store the index in memory during a performance, the program declares an array of records:

```
index:      ARRAY [1..maxRecords] OF indexRecord;
```

The value of *maxRecords* is defined in the CONST section:

```
maxRecords      = 250;
```

As you can see, the current version of the program limits the size of the database to 250 records. To increase the number of records the program can handle, you can simply revise this constant declaration.

During a program performance the program always keeps the entire index in memory, but it stores only one actual profile record in memory at a time.

Since the program reads and writes the index file sequentially, the structure is defined as a TEXT-type file:

```
indexFile:      TEXT;
```

(Since the index is stored as a text file, you can examine the index file from DOS, using the TYPE utility.) The disk name for the index file is also established as a named constant:

```
indexFileName = 'PROFILE.NDX';
```

The main program section of *CliProf* begins with a call to the *OpenFiles* procedure, which opens both the profile database and the index file. First, the routine uses a pair of ASSIGN statements to associate the file variables with their respective file names on disk:

```
ASSIGN (profileFile, profileName);
ASSIGN (indexFile, indexFileName);
```

Then the program makes an attempt to open the existing profile database:

```
{$I – }
  RESET (profileFile);
{$I + }
```

If this attempt fails, IORESULT returns a value other than zero. In this case, the program assumes that the database file simply does not exist yet, and creates it:

```
IF IORESULT < > 0 THEN REWRITE (profileFile);
```

In either event, a call to the built-in FILESIZE function determines the number of records currently stored in the database:

```
fileLength : = FILESIZE (profileFile);
```

This value, *fileLength,* is an important global variable that is used throughout the program to help manage both the database and the index.

Assuming there is at least one record in the database, the program next attempts to open the index file:

```
IF fileLength > 0 THEN
   BEGIN
     {$I – }
       RESET (indexFile);
     {$I + }
```

If this operation is successful, the program reads the entire index into the *index* array, and then closes the index file again:

```
IF IORESULT = 0 THEN

   BEGIN
     FOR i : = 1 TO fileLength DO
       WITH index[i] DO
         READLN (indexFile, clientName, recordNumber);
       CLOSE (indexFile);
   END
```

The index file remains closed now until the end of the program performance. Each time the program accepts a new profile record from the keyboard, it also stores an additional record in the *index* array and calls on the *SortIndex* procedure to alphabetize the index by the *clientName* fields. Then, at the very end of a performance, the *SaveIndex* procedure rewrites the entire index to disk. We'll encounter the index again later in our discussion of the program.

After opening the two files, the main program section calls the *InitializeMenu* procedure to display the menu on the screen. Then the *GetSelection* procedure elicits the user's menu choices and makes calls to the appropriate procedures to carry out the options. The main program calls this procedure repeatedly until the user selects the Quit option:

```
REPEAT
   GetSelection (done)
UNTIL done;
```

Three main procedures control the input dialogs and screen displays for the three menu activities: *AddClient* appends a new client record to the database, *DisplayClient* displays a client profile on the screen, and *ReviseClient* writes a revised client record to the database. The latter two procedures both call on the *GetClient* procedure to locate, read, and display a given client record.

GetClient elicits a target client name from the user at the keyboard, and then relies on the function named *SearchIndex* to find the corresponding record in the database. *SearchIndex* searches efficiently for a given name in the records of the index array, and returns the corresponding record number from the *recordNumber* field. The searching algorithm is called a *binary search;* given an alphabetized list, this algorithm finds a target string very quickly, even if the list is long.

Let's say the *SearchIndex* function finds a given client name in the array element *index[i].clientName*. The corresponding record number is in the field *index[i].recordNumber;* this number represents the correct place to look for this client record in the PROFILE.DAT database. *SearchIndex* supplies this record number as its return value. (If the client name is not found in the index list, the function returns a value of − 1.)

The selection process is illustrated in the following passage from the *GetClient* procedure:

```
WRITE ('Client''s name? ');
READLN (inName);

{ ... }

whichRecord : = SearchIndex (inName);

IF whichRecord > = 0 THEN
   BEGIN
      SEEK (profileFile, whichRecord);
      READ (profileFile, profile);
```

IF *SearchIndex* returns a value that is greater than or equal to zero, the program performs the SEEK procedure to position the database record pointer at the target record and the READ procedure to read the record into the *profile* variable. Then a series of WRITELN statements display the record on the screen:

```
WITH profile DO
  BEGIN
    WRITELN (name);
    WRITELN (StringOfChars (' – ', LENGTH (name)));
    WRITELN ('Reference number:', refNo);
    WRITELN ('Type of business:  ', businessType);
    WRITELN ('Date of record:    ', recordDate);
    WRITELN ('Contact person:    ', contactPerson);
    WRITELN ('Phone number:      ', phoneNumber);
    WRITELN ('Last year''s hours: ', hoursLastYear:7:2)
  END
```

However, if *SearchIndex* returns a value of -1, indicating that the search for the client name was not successful, the program displays an error message on the screen:

```
ELSE

BEGIN
  WRITELN; WRITELN;
  WRITELN ('Can''t find this client in the database.');
  WRITELN
END
```

When the *GetClient* procedure relinquishes control, the *CliProf* program displays the recurring menu once again on the screen.

We have seen how the program searches for and reads individual records from the profile database. Now we'll look briefly at the two routines that write records: *AddClient* and *ReviseClient*.

Appending a New Record

To append a new record to the end of the client-profile database, the *AddClient* begins by eliciting the new client's name from the user:

```
WITH profile DO
  BEGIN
```

```
WRITE ('Client''s name? ');
READLN (name)
```

The program standardizes the input string stored in *name*, converting it to all capital letters and inserting it within a string of standard length:

```
searchName : = LeftAlign (UpperCase (name), 30);
```

The program uses this same standard format for storing client names inside the PROFILE.NDX file. This double-conversion process allows the program to locate client names even if the user enters them with inconsistent capitalization.

A call to *SearchIndex* determines whether this client name is already in the database. If so, *AddClient* rejects the new entry:

```
IF (SearchIndex (searchName) > = 0 THEN
  BEGIN
    WRITELN;
    WRITELN ('This client is already in the database.')
  END
```

However, if this is truly a new client, the program conducts the input dialog for the remaining fields of the *profile* record, and asks the user to confirm that the record actually should be entered into the database.

Once all the fields are stored in the *profile* record, *AddClient* is ready to append the record to the end of the database file, *profileFile*. First, a call to the SEEK procedure positions the record pointer at the end of the file:

```
SEEK (profileFile, fileLength);
```

Keep in mind that the global *fileLength* variable always stores the current number of records in the file. (As we have seen, this number is one greater than the position of the last record in the file.) Since the program is now adding a new record, the value of *fileLength* is next increased by 1:

```
INC (fileLength);
```

As the program informs the user that the record is being appended, the WRITE procedure writes the new record to the file:

```
WRITELN ('Saving record #', fileLength);
WRITE (profileFile, profile);
```

Whenever the program adds a new record to the database, *Add-Client* must also update the index. The process is simple. First, the new client name and record number are stored in the next available element of the *index* array:

```
WITH index[fileLength] DO
  BEGIN
    clientName : = searchName;
    recordNumber : = fileLength - 1
  END;
```

Finally, the *SortIndex* procedure sorts the index, so that any subsequent binary searches can be conducted successfully:

```
SortIndex (fileLength)
```

Revising an Existing Record

To revise an existing record, the *ReviseClient* procedure begins by calling on the *GetClient* procedure to elicit the target client name. If the name is located in the database, *GetClient* displays the record on the screen, and returns the record number in the variable *location:*

```
GetClient (location);
```

ReviseClient then conducts the dialog for the three revisable fields of the record: *contactPerson*, *phoneNumber*, and *hoursLastYear*. If the user changes any combination of these fields, the procedure prepares to write the revised record back to the database.

First, the *recordDate* field must be updated, reflecting the date of the new record entry:

```
profile.recordDate : = DateString;
```

(You'll recall that the *DateString* procedure is located in *ChrnUnit*, the first unit we developed in this book.) Next, the *ReviseClient* procedure uses SEEK to position the record pointer at the appropriate position for rewriting the record:

```
SEEK (profileFile, location);
```

Finally, the routine writes the revised record to the file:

```
WRITE (profileFile, profile)
```

When the user finally selects the *Quit* option from the main menu, the *CliProf* program closes the database file and calls the *SaveIndex* procedure to rewrite the index file to disk:

```
CLOSE (profileFile);
IF fileLength > 0 THEN SaveIndex
```

SaveIndex uses the REWRITE command to open the index file, discarding any previous version of the file:

```
REWRITE (indexFile);
```

Finally, a simple FOR loop saves the entire index to disk:

```
FOR i : = 1 TO fileLength DO
   WITH index[i] DO
      WRITELN (indexFile, clientName, recordNumber);
```

As you can see, each line of the index file contains a client's name and the corresponding record number in the main database file. Since *CliProf* always keeps the index in alphabetical order by client names, the saved index is already sorted and ready for the next program performance.

Summary

Typed files and the random-access file mode are ideal for applications that require direct access to individual records within a database.

A typed file is defined as a FILE OF a specified data type. Turbo Pascal has a distinct set of commands and functions for handling random-access files:

- The FILESIZE function returns the current number of records in an open typed file.

- The SEEK procedure moves the record pointer to a specified location within the file.

- The FILEPOS function indicates the current position of the record pointer in the file.

- The WRITE command writes a record to the current position of the record pointer in an open typed file.

- The READ command reads a record from the current position of the pointer in an open typed file. Subsequently, the record's field values are available in the designated field variables.

An important task for managing a random-access file is keeping track of the locations of records within the file. One efficient scheme for accomplishing this is to create an index structure. The structure should contain two fields: the entries from a key field in the database (for example, client names) and a list of corresponding record numbers. If a program keeps this index sorted, the binary search algorithm can locate any individual key entry very quickly.

PART

Advanced Programming Techniques

III

C H A P T E R

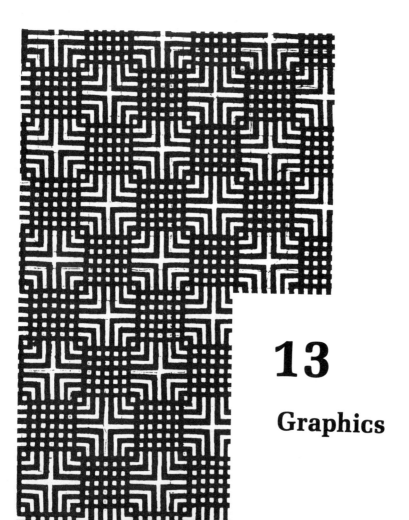

13

Graphics

With the appropriate display hardware installed in your computer system, you can use Turbo Pascal's impressive library of graphics routines to place images and special text fonts on the screen. This chapter gives you a brief first look at this library, and presents a program exercise that demonstrates several of the graphics routines in action.

Actually, version 5.0 of Turbo Pascal includes two separate graphics packages in the standard units named GRAPH and GRAPH3. The GRAPH3 unit is an implementation of the "turtle graphics" library from version 3.0 of the language and is included primarily for compatibility.

The GRAPH unit is the subject of this chapter. It contains over 60 different procedures and functions that you can use on any of the common configurations of graphics display hardware. Learning to use a package as large as the GRAPH unit requires some considerable amount of time and effort. This chapter is merely a first look—a sampling of some of the major tools you'll find in this versatile package. From here, you can begin exploring other tools in the package and writing your own graphics programs.

All of the programs presented up to now in this book have operated on the *text screen*, the standard row/column grid arrangement designed for displaying ASCII characters. In the text mode, the smallest controllable screen elements are the rectangles of space that display single ASCII characters. As we have seen, the most important routines for displaying information on the text screen are WRITE and

WRITELN. In addition, the GOTOXY procedure (from the CRT unit) positions the cursor at a specified character location on the text screen, allowing a subsequent WRITE statement to display a character at that location.

The tools in the GRAPH unit, together with appropriate graphics hardware, offer much greater levels of screen control. A single display element on a graphics screen is called a *pixel* (a picture element). A pixel is a small dot that can be turned on or off and displayed in any of a selection of available colors. On each graphics screen there are hundreds of pixels across and down the screen; the exact number depends on the resolution of the hardware in your system.

In general, you need two hardware components in order to use the Turbo Pascal graphics routines:

- A graphics display controller board installed inside your computer

- A color monitor (or other display device) that can be plugged into the controller board

Some of the standard graphics display boards available for the IBM PC are the *Color/Graphics Adapter* (CGA), the *Enhanced Graphics Adapter* (EGA), the *Video Graphics Array* adapter (VGA), and the *Multicolor Graphics Array* adapter (MCGA). The Turbo Pascal package includes a collection of special *drivers*, which provide low-level software compatibility with these and other hardware configurations. The drivers are stored on disk in files that have extensions of .BGI:

ATT.BGI

CGA.BGI

EGAVGA.BGI

HERC.BGI

IBM8514.BGI

PC3270.BGI

To perform a program that uses the routines of the GRAPH unit, Turbo Pascal must be able to find and load the appropriate graphics driver for your hardware.

The GRAPH unit routines covered in this chapter allow you to accomplish the following general tasks:

- Determine what kind of hardware is present, initialize a particular graphics mode, and find the dimensions of the current screen.
- Display shapes on the screen, including points, lines, circles, rectangles, and boxes.
- Fill in designated areas on the screen with patterns or colors.
- Draw business graphs, including pie charts and bar charts.
- Display various styles of text on the screen, using special font files available with Turbo Pascal.

Let's begin looking at these selected routines.

Procedures and Functions in the GRAPH Unit

As we examine the GRAPH unit, we'll look at graphics screen examples produced by a demonstration program called *GrphDemo*. This program, listed in Figure 13.1, creates a sequence of five screens, illustrating techniques for a variety of programming tasks. The program finds the tools for these tasks in the GRAPH unit:

```
PROGRAM GrphDemo;
   USES CRT, GRAPH;
```

Although you will see the output screens from this demonstration program in the pages of this chapter, the best way to see the effects of Turbo Pascal's graphics routines is to run demonstration programs on your own computer. As you enter and compile *GrphDemo*, keep in mind that Turbo Pascal will need to find several different files on disk in order to run the program. These files include

```
PROGRAM GrphDemo;

  { The GraphDemo program produces five graphics screens,
    illustrating various procedures and functions in the
    GRAPH unit. }

USES CRT, GRAPH;

VAR
  driverVar,
  modeVar:   integer;



PROCEDURE GraphTitle (inTitle: STRING);

  { The GraphTitle procedure places a centered title at the
    top of the screen, using the gothic font. }

  BEGIN     { GraphTitle }

    SETTEXTJUSTIFY (CENTERTEXT, TOPTEXT);
    SETTEXTSTYLE (TRIPLEXFONT, HORIZDIR, 4);
    OUTTEXTXY (GETMAXX DIV 2, 1, inTitle)

  END;      { GraphTitle }



PROCEDURE GraphContinue;

  { The GraphContinue procedure places a message at the
    bottom of the screen and waits for the user to
    press the space bar. }

  CONST
    message = 'Press the space bar to continue.';

  VAR
    inKey: CHAR;

  BEGIN     { GraphContinue }

    SETTEXTJUSTIFY (CENTERTEXT, TOPTEXT);
    SETTEXTSTYLE (GOTHICFONT, HORIZDIR, 3);
    OUTTEXTXY (GETMAXX DIV 2, GETMAXY - 40, message);
    REPEAT
      inKey := READKEY
    UNTIL inKey = ' ';
    CLEARDEVICE

  END;      { GraphContinue }



PROCEDURE DrawSine;

  { The DrawSine procedure draws a graph of the sine
    curve, illustrating the PUTPIXEL and LINE procedures. }

  CONST
    maxLength = 200;
    maxHeight = 40;
```

Figure 13.1: The listing of the *GrphDemo* program

```
      VAR
        centerX,
        centerY,
        startX,
        endX,
        i,
        plotHeight: INTEGER;
        angle: REAL;

      BEGIN     { DrawSine }

        GraphTitle ('The Sine Function');

        centerX := GETMAXX DIV 2;
        centerY := GETMAXY DIV 2;
        startX := centerX - maxLength;
        endX := centerX + maxLength;

        FOR i := startX TO endX DO
          BEGIN
            angle := ((i - centerX) / (maxLength / 2)) * PI;
            plotHeight := centerY - TRUNC (maxHeight * SIN(angle));
            PUTPIXEL (i, plotHeight, 1)
          END;

        LINE (startX - 10, centerY, endX + 10, centerY);
        LINE (centerX, centerY - maxHeight, centerX, centerY + maxHeight);

        GraphContinue

      END;     { DrawSine }



    PROCEDURE DrawCircles;

      { The DrawCircles procedure draws a design of
        circles, illustrating the CIRCLE procedure. }

      VAR
        orientation,
        radius:      INTEGER;

      BEGIN     { DrawCircles }

        GraphTitle ('Circles');

        FOR orientation := -1 TO 1 DO
          FOR radius := 1 to 4 DO
            CIRCLE (GETMAXX DIV 2 + orientation * 100,
                    GETMAXY DIV 2,
                    radius * 30 + ABS (orientation) * 20);

        GraphContinue

      END;     { DrawCircles }


    PROCEDURE DrawPie;

      { The DrawPie procedure draws a simulated pie
        chart, illustrating the PIESLICE and
        SETFILLSTYLE procedures. }
```

Figure 13.1: The listing of the *GrphDemo* program (continued)

```
    CONST
      items = 5;
      sampleData: ARRAY [1..items] OF REAL=
        (7.5, 3.0, 4.5, 9.0, 6.0);

    VAR
      i,
      portion,
      startAngle,
      endAngle:    WORD;
      total:       REAL;

    BEGIN    { DrawPie }

      GraphTitle ('Pie Chart');

      total := 0.0;
      FOR i := 1 TO items DO
        total := total + sampleData [i];

      startAngle := 0;
      FOR i := 1 TO items DO
        BEGIN
          portion := TRUNC (360.0 * (sampleData[i] / total));
          IF i = items THEN
            endAngle := 359
          ELSE
            endAngle := startAngle + portion;

          SETFILLSTYLE (5 + i, 0);
          PIESLICE (GETMAXX DIV 2, GETMAXY DIV 2,
                    startAngle, endAngle, 150);

          startAngle := endAngle
        END;

      GraphContinue

    END;    { DrawPie }


  PROCEDURE DrawBars;

    { The DrawBars procedure draws a simulated
      three-dimensional stacked bar chart,
      illustrating the use of the BAR3D and
      SETFILLSTYLE procedures. }

    CONST
      items = 9;
      sampleData: ARRAY [1..items, 1..2] OF BYTE =
        ((19, 10), (25, 25), (37, 10), (18, 5),
         (18, 25), (35, 43), (43, 58), (32, 55), (43, 32));

    VAR
      x1, x2, y1, y2, y3,
      depth: INTEGER;
      i:     BYTE;

    BEGIN    { DrawBars }

      GraphTitle ('Bar Chart');
```

Figure 13.1: The listing of the *GrphDemo* program (continued)

```
              x1 := 50;
              depth := 9;

              FOR i := 1 TO items DO
                BEGIN
                  y1 := GETMAXY - 50;
                  y2 := y1 - sampleData [i, 1];
                  y3 := y2 - sampleData [i, 2];
                  INC (x1, 50);
                  x2 := x1 + 36;

                  SETFILLSTYLE (6, 0);
                  BAR3D (x1, y1, x2, y2, depth, FALSE);
                  SETFILLSTYLE (7, 0);
                  BAR3D (x1, y2, x2, y3, depth, TRUE)
                END;

            GraphContinue

        END;    { DrawBars }


    PROCEDURE DrawShapes;

      { The DrawShapes procedure draws a rectangle, an
        ellipse, and a triangle, illustrating the use of
        the RECTANGLE, ELLIPSE, and DRAWPOLY procedures. }


      CONST
        polyPoints: ARRAY [1..8] OF WORD =
          (200, 60, 50, 140, 250, 140, 200, 60);

      BEGIN     { DrawBars }

        GraphTitle ('Miscellaneous Shapes');

        RECTANGLE (30, 50, GETMAXX - 30, 150);
        ELLIPSE (GETMAXX DIV 2 + 100, GETMAXY DIV 2, 0, 359, 160, 20);
        DRAWPOLY (4, polyPoints);

        GraphContinue

      END;    { DrawBars }


BEGIN     { GrphDemo }

  driverVar := 0;
  INITGRAPH (driverVar, modeVar, '');

  DrawSine;
  DrawCircles;
  DrawPie;
  DrawBars;
  DrawShapes;

  CLOSEGRAPH

END.   { GrphDemo }
```

Figure 13.1: The listing of the *GrphDemo* program (continued)

- The compiled graphics unit, GRAPH.TPU. (You'll recall that the GRAPH unit is not incorporated into Turbo Pascal's library file, TURBO.TPL.)

- The appropriate driver for your graphics configuration. As we have seen, the drivers have extensions of .BGI.

- Font files, which supply the instructions for drawing text characters on the graphics screen. These files have extensions of .CHR. The *GrphDemo* program produces examples of fonts named Triplex and Gothic; these fonts are stored in the files GOTH.CHR and TRIP.CHR, respectively. (Two other font files available are LITT.CHR, called the *small font* and SANS.CHR, a *sans-serif* font.) We'll see how to use these fonts a little later in this chapter.

Let's begin our discussion by looking at the INITGRAPH procedure, which initializes the graphics hardware.

Initializing a Graphics Mode

The INITGRAPH procedure takes three arguments:

INITGRAPH (*driverVar, modeVar, driverPath*)

The *driverVar* argument is an integer code representing the current hardware configuration, and thus specifying the graphics driver that Turbo Pascal should use for the performance. The *modeVar* argument selects one of the various graphics modes available for a given hardware configuration. These first two arguments are expressed as VAR parameters inside the INITGRAPH procedure; consequently, you must send these arguments to the routine as variables.

Finally, the *driverPath* argument is a string value specifying the path location where the driver files are stored on disk. If you supply an empty string for this argument, Turbo Pascal looks in the current directory for the drivers.

Turbo Pascal uses certain fixed code values to represent hardware configurations for the *driverVar* parameter and graphics modes for the *modeVar* parameter. However, we'll see later that INITGRAPH does not necessarily require that a program commit to a particular graphics hardware system in advance; as a result you do not usually need to worry about *driverVar* codes. Nonetheless, here is a sample of the codes for the four graphics adapters listed earlier in this chapter:

Adapter	Code
CGA	1
MCGA	2
EGA	3
VGA	9

Each graphics adapter offers a variety of graphics modes. Each mode, in turn, has three characteristics:

- The screen resolution—that is, the number of horizontal and vertical pixel addresses that make up the graphics screen
- The number of colors available for the screen
- The number of graphics *pages* that can be stored in memory at once, allowing a program to switch between one image display and another

For example, there are three modes available for the Color Graphics Adapter board (CGA), represented by codes 0, 1, and 2:

- Mode 0 has a resolution of 320 horizontal by 200 vertical pixel addresses, and has four colors (black, red, yellow, and green).
- Mode 1 has the same resolution as mode 0, but with a different selection of colors (black, cyan, magenta, and white).
- Mode 2 is a high-resolution mode, with 640 horizontal by 200 vertical pixel addresses, in black and white only.

Here is a program excerpt that selects graphics mode 2 on a system that has a CGA board:

```
USES GRAPH;

VAR
  driverVar,
  modeVar:    INTEGER;
```

```
BEGIN
  driverVar : = 1;
  modeVar : = 2;
  INITGRAPH (driverVar, modeVar, '');
  { ... }
END.
```

The three CGA modes each provide only one graphics page. Other graphics adapters offer higher resolutions, greater selections of colors, and additional memory space for multiple graphics pages.

Conveniently, the INITGRAPH procedure allows you to write graphics programs that will run on any graphics hardware system. You do not need to know in advance which graphics adapter board will be available, and you do not have to select a particular *driverVar* code. In short, if you supply a value of zero for the *driverVar* argument, INITGRAPH automatically examines the current graphics hardware and determines which driver should be used. The procedure also automatically selects the graphics mode with the highest resolution available on the current hardware.

This feature is called the *auto-detect* mode of the INITGRAPH procedure. Here is a short program, named *InitTest*, that demonstrates the auto-detect mode:

```
PROGRAM InitTest;

  USES GRAPH;

  VAR
    driverVar,
    modeVar:      INTEGER;

  BEGIN
    driverVar : = 0;
    INITGRAPH (driverVar,  modeVar, '');
    WRITELN ('Driver = ',  driverVar);
    WRITELN ('Mode = ',  modeVar);
    WRITELN;
    WRITELN ('Lower-right corner of the screen:');
    WRITELN ('    X-coordinate: ', GETMAXX);
    WRITELN ('    Y-coordinate: ', GETMAXY)
  END.
```

In this program the INITGRAPH procedure initializes the graphics system and automatically detects the hardware status. Then the program displays information on the screen describing the adapter and the selected graphics mode. For example, here is the information the program provides for a system that contains a CGA board:

```
Driver = 1
Mode = 2

Lower-right corner of the screen:
      X-coordinate: 639
      Y-coordinate: 199
```

Notice that INITGRAPH has automatically selected the high-resolution graphics mode.

At the bottom of its output, the *InitTest* program displays the coordinates of the pixel address located at the far lower-right corner of the screen in the selected mode. To determine this address, the program employs two important functions available in the GRAPH unit—GETMAXX and GETMAXY:

```
WRITELN ('     X-coordinate: ', GETMAXX);
WRITELN ('     Y-coordinate: ', GETMAXY)
```

As their names imply, these two functions give the maximum horizontal and vertical screen address coordinates in the current graphics mode. Most procedures and functions in the GRAPH unit use an addressing system based on coordinate pairs. We can represent such a pair as

(x, y)

where x is the horizontal address coordinate and y is the vertical coordinate. By default, the "origin" for the graphics address system, the address (0,0), is located at the upper-left corner of the screen in any graphics mode. The horizontal coordinate increases as you move across the screen to the right, and the vertical coordinate increases as you move down the screen.

Returning now to the *GrphDemo* program, you can see that the main program section uses the INITGRAPH procedure's auto-detect mode to establish the driver and mode for the program:

```
driverVar : = 0;
INITGRAPH (driverVar, modeVar, '');
```

Subsequently, the program makes calls to the five procedures that produce five different graphics demonstration screens:

```
DrawSine;
DrawCircles;
DrawPie;
DrawBars;
DrawShapes;
```

As we examine these procedures, we'll see that the program often uses the GETMAXX and GETMAXY functions to determine the dimensions of the current screen. Furthermore, the program uses statements such as the following to find the address of the pixel located approximately in the center of the screen:

```
centerX : = GETMAXX DIV 2;
centerY : = GETMAXY DIV 2;
```

In the next section we'll look at the first of the demonstration procedures, *DrawSine*, which illustrates two built-in procedures named PUTPIXEL and LINE.

Plotting Points and Drawing Lines

The command for plotting individual points on the screen is PUT-PIXEL. This procedure takes three arguments—a pair of address coordinates, and an integer color code:

```
PUTPIXEL (x, y, colorCode)
```

The range of legal values for *colorCode* depends on the current graphics mode. For example, in mode 0 for the CGA board, *colorCode* can be 0, 1, 2, or 3, representing one of the four colors available in the mode: black, red, yellow, or green. Here is an example of PUTPIXEL in this mode:

```
USES GRAPH;

  VAR
    driverVar,
    modeVar:      INTEGER;

BEGIN
  driverVar : = 1;
  modeVar : = 0;
  INITGRAPH (driverVar, modeVar, '');
  PUTPIXEL (GETMAXX DIV 2, GETMAXY DIV 2, 3)
END.
```

This program simply places one colored pixel at the approximate center of the screen. If you try running this short program, you'll find that the pixel is almost too small to see unless you look very closely at the screen. A program that uses PUTPIXEL to plot individual points on the screen will normally issue many such commands in sequence, creating an image or graph out of many adjacent pixels.

An example of this plotting process appears in the *DrawSine* procedure. This procedure creates the sine curve graph shown in Figure 13.2. Like all the output of the *GrphDemo* program, this screen is produced in black and white on the high-resolution CGA screen, with 640 by 200 pixel addresses.

The *DrawSine* procedure uses a FOR loop to produce the sine wave, calculating the position for each pixel individually:

```
FOR i : = startX TO endX DO
  BEGIN
    angle : = ((i – centerX) / (maxLength / 2)) * PI;
    plotHeight : = centerY – TRUNC (maxHeight * SIN(angle));
    PUTPIXEL (i, plotHeight, 1)
  END;
```

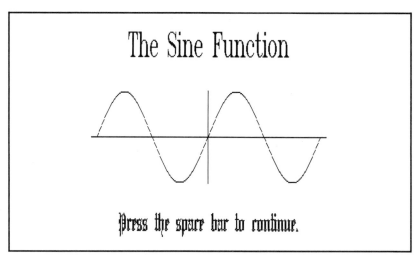

Figure 13.2: A demonstration of PUTPIXEL, LINE, and the text procedures

Inside the loop, the program converts the horizontal address coordinate *i* to an angle from -2π to $+2\pi$, and then converts the SIN value of this angle to a corresponding vertical coordinate, *plotHeight*. Finally, a call to the PUTPIXEL procedure plots each point on the screen:

```
PUTPIXEL (i, plotHeight, 1)
```

On the high-resolution CGA screen, the color code 1 represents white.

The X- and Y-axes of this graph are produced by Turbo Pascal's built-in LINE procedure. The LINE command takes a pair of address coordinates as arguments:

```
LINE (x1, y1, x2, y2)
```

The first address (*x1, y1*) represents the starting point of the resulting line; the second address (*x2, y2*) is the ending point. Lines can be drawn horizontally, vertically, or diagonally across the screen. For example, the following command draws a diagonal line from (5,10) to (200,100):

```
LINE (5, 10, 200, 100)
```

In the *DrawSine* procedure, the arguments of the two LINE commands are all calculated from constants and variables established earlier in the procedure:

```
LINE (startX - 10, centerY, endX + 10, centerY);
LINE (centerX, centerY - maxHeight, centerX, centerY +
   maxHeight);
```

The first of these statements draws the horizontal X-axis, and the second draws the Y-axis.

You'll notice that the sine-graph screen also contains two lines of text. The title, *The Sine Function*, appears in Triplex font. The message at the bottom of the screen, *Press the space bar to continue*, is displayed in Gothic font—a bit incongruously, perhaps, but nonetheless demonstrating the versatility of Turbo Pascal's font files. In the next section we'll see how the program gains access to these two text fonts and displays the lines of text on the screen.

Displaying Text on the Graphics Screen

Several procedures in the GRAPH unit are designed to display text on the graphics screen; among them are the following three routines that appear in the *GrphDemo* program:

- SETTEXTJUSTIFY determines how the text will be oriented around a given point on the screen.

- SETTEXTSTYLE specifies the text font, the text direction (horizontal or vertical), and the size of the text.

- OUTTEXTXY gives an address location for the text and supplies the text string itself.

The exact result of OUTTEXTXY depends on the settings established by the SETTEXTJUSTIFY and SETTEXTSTYLE procedures.

The first of these routines, SETTEXTJUSTIFY, takes two integer arguments:

```
SETTEXTJUSTIFY (horizontalCode, verticalCode)
```

The two arguments are codes for the horizontal and vertical orientation of the subsequent text output, relative to the pixel address specified in the OUTTEXTXY command. The valid values for these two codes are 0, 1, and 2:

- A *horizontalCode* of 0 means that the specified pixel address will be located immediately to the left of the resulting text output. A *verticalCode* of 0 means that the pixel address will be located below the resulting text.

- A *horizontalCode* of 1 means that the text will be centered horizontally around the specified pixel address. A *verticalCode* of 1 means that the text will be centered vertically around the pixel address.

- A *horizontalCode* of 2 means that the specified pixel address will be located at the right of the resulting text output. A *verticalCode* of 2 means that the pixel address will be located above the resulting text.

For convenience and clarity, the GRAPH unit defines named constants that contain the code values for each argument. The constant names for the *horizontalCode* argument are LEFTTEXT, CENTERTEXT, and RIGHTTEXT, respectively. The names for the *verticalCode* argument are BOTTOMTEXT, CENTERTEXT, and TOPTEXT.

Using these constants, the following statement specifies that the subsequent text output will be centered horizontally around a specified pixel address and placed vertically just below the address:

```
SETTEXTJUSTIFY (CENTERTEXT, TOPTEXT);
```

This statement appears in the *GraphTitle* procedure in the *GrphDemo* program. *GraphTitle* accepts a string parameter from any of the routines in the program, and displays the string as a title at the top of the screen. Thanks to the call to the SETTEXTJUSTIFY procedure, the title is centered horizontally. We'll see exactly how this happens shortly.

The SETTEXTSTYLE procedure takes three integer arguments, as follows:

```
SETTEXTSTYLE (fontCode, directionCode, size)
```

The *fontCode* argument selects one of the special graphics fonts available in Turbo Pascal. Here are the fonts and their corresponding code numbers:

Font	Code
Default	0
Triplex	1
Small	2
Sans-serif	3
Gothic	4

The definition for the first of these fonts is included in the GRAPH unit, but the other four fonts are defined in CHR files. Turbo Pascal must be able to find the appropriate CHR file on disk in order to produce the font on the screen. The GRAPH unit defines named constants to represent codes for the five graphics fonts: DEFAULTFONT, TRIPLEXFONT, SMALLFONT, SANSSERIFFONT, and GOTHICFONT.

The second argument of the SETTEXTSTYLE procedure, *directionCode*, specifies the direction of the text. A code value of 0 produces horizontal text, and a value of 1 produces vertical text. Named constants defined for these two settings are HORIZDIR and VERTDIR, respectively. Finally, the third argument, *size*, determines the size of the text. The normal size setting is 1, but you can supply values from 2 to 10 to produce larger text.

The following call to SETTEXTSTYLE in the *GraphTitle* procedure selects the Triplex font for the title. The text is displayed horizontally, and is four times the normal size:

SETTEXTSTYLE (TRIPLEXFONT, HORIZDIR, 4);

You can see the result of these settings in the titles of all of the output screens produced by the *GrphDemo* program.

The OUTTEXTXY procedure displays a string of text at a specified location on the screen, following the settings of SETTEXTJUSTIFY and SETTEXTSTYLE. OUTTEXTXY takes three arguments, two integer address coordinates and a string of text:

OUTTEXTXY (*x, y, displayString*)

The address (*x, y*) determines the effect of the SETTEXTJUŞTIFY command. For example, here is the call to OUTTEXTXY in the *GraphTitle* procedure:

```
OUTTEXTXY (GETMAXX DIV 2, 1, inTitle)
```

The address specified in this statement is at the center of the screen horizontally, and near the top of the screen vertically. Thanks to the CENTERTEXT and TOPTEXT arguments sent to the SETTEXT-JUSTIFY procedure, the title is centered horizontally at the top of the screen around this address.

You might also want to take a look at the *GraphContinue* procedure in the *GrphDemo* program. This procedure makes additional calls to the SETTEXTJUSTIFY, SETTEXTSTYLE, and OUT-TEXTXY procedures to place the message at the bottom of the screen. Then *GraphContinue* waits for a space character to be entered from the keyboard; when the correct character value is read, the procedure issues the following command:

```
CLEARDEVICE
```

This GRAPH unit procedure clears the graphics screen and reestablishes default graphics settings.

In the next section we'll look at the CIRCLE procedure, which draws circles on the screen.

Drawing Circles

The arguments of the CIRCLE procedure are a coordinate address representing the center of the circle, and a radius length expressed in pixels:

```
CIRCLE (x, y, radius)
```

For example, the following statement draws a circle with a radius of 20 pixels in the approximate center of the screen:

```
CIRCLE (GETMAXX DIV 2, GETMAXY DIV 2, 20)
```

In the *GrphDemo* program, the procedure named *DrawCircles* produces the display shown in Figure 13.3. A pair of nested FOR loops in the procedure draws a dozen circles with various center points and radii:

```
FOR orientation : =  − 1 TO 1 DO
   FOR radius : = 1 to 4 DO
      CIRCLE (GETMAXX DIV 2 + orientation * 100,
                 GETMAXY DIV 2,
                 radius * 30 + ABS (orientation) * 20);
```

The GRAPH unit also has two procedures that draw wedges and ellipses on the screen, named PIESLICE and ELLIPSE, respectively. We'll examine PIESLICE in the next section and ELLIPSE later in the chapter.

Drawing Pie Charts

A wedge is the portion of a circle located between two radius lines. The familiar business graph known as a *pie chart* consists of a complete circle of concentric wedges. Each wedge in the chart represents a numeric amount. For example, in a pie chart representing total expenses, each wedge might represent an individual expense category; the size of a given wedge corresponds to the amount of a particular expense in relation to all the expenses.

The GRAPH unit has a simple command named PIESLICE, which draws wedges on the screen; you can use this command to create a pie chart from a list of numeric data values. In the *GrphDemo* program, the *DrawPie* procedure creates an example of such a chart from a short list of sample data values. The chart screen appears in Figure 13.4. As you can see, each wedge in the chart is filled in with a distinct pattern, resulting in a chart that attracts attention and is easy to read. The built-in SETFILLSTYLE procedure specifies the fill pattern for each wedge of the chart. Let's see how the PIESLICE and SETFILLSTYLE procedures work.

PIESLICE takes five arguments, all of them integer values:

PIESLICE (*x, y, startAngle, endAngle, radius*)

The first two arguments are the coordinates a pixel address, the center of the circle to which the wedge belongs. The next two arguments,

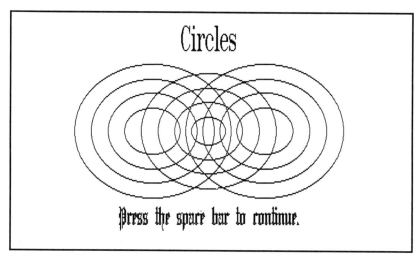

Figure 13.3: A demonstration of the CIRCLE procedure

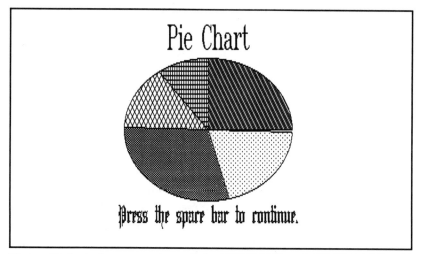

Figure 13.4: A demonstration of the PIESLICE and SETFILLSTYLE
procedures

startAngle and *endAngle*, are values from 0 to 359, representing the
angles, in degrees, of the two radius lines that form the wedge. (The
radius that extends directly to the right from the center point represents an angle of zero.) Finally, the *radius* argument is the length, in
pixels, of the circle's radius.

The *DrawPie* routine simulates a business pie chart from a list of numeric values stored in the array *sampleData*. This array is built in the CONST section of the procedure:

```
CONST
  items = 5;
  sampleData: ARRAY [1..items] OF REAL =
    (7.5, 3.0, 4.5, 9.0, 6.0);
```

To create the chart from these values, the procedure must first find the total of all the numeric values in the list and then perform the following sequence of steps for each value of *sampleData[i]* in the list:

1. Divide *sampleData[i]* by the total of all the values in the list.

2. Multiply this fractional result by 360, to find the wedge angle that will correctly represent the value.

3. Draw the wedge, using the ending angle of the previous wedge as the starting angle of the current wedge.

4. Fill in the wedge with a distinct pattern.

Let's look briefly at the statements that perform these steps. First, the variable *total* is initialized to zero, and a FOR loop finds the total of the values in the list:

```
total : = 0.0;
FOR i : = 1 TO items DO
  total : = total + sampleData[i];
```

Then the variable *startAngle* is initialized to zero:

```
startAngle : = 0;
```

As the procedure draws the wedges, this variable serves as a marker for the starting point of each new wedge. Next, a FOR loop goes through the list of values, one at a time. An assignment statement at the top of the loop calculates the value *portion*, the wedge angle representing the current data value:

```
FOR i : = 1 TO items DO
  BEGIN
```

```
portion : = TRUNC (360.0 * (sampleData[i] / total));
```

Then the routine adds *portion* to the current value of *startAngle* to find *endAngle*, the second radius of the wedge:

```
endAngle : = startAngle + portion;
```

A call to the PIESLICE procedure draws the wedge, using the center point of the current graphics mode as the center of the circle:

```
PIESLICE (GETMAXX DIV 2, GETMAXY DIV 2,
          startAngle, endAngle, 150);
```

Finally, the ending angle of the current wedge becomes the starting angle of the next wedge:

```
startAngle : = endAngle
```

The loop continues in this way through the entire list of values.

Just before drawing each wedge, the *DrawPie* procedure calls the SETFILLSTYLE procedure to establish a new fill pattern for the wedge. SETFILLSTYLE takes two arguments, both integers:

```
SETFILLSTYLE (patternCode, colorCode)
```

The first argument is a value from 0 to 11, representing one of twelve predefined patterns available for use by procedures in the GRAPH unit. The second argument is a color code for one of the colors offered in the current graphics mode.

As you can see in Figure 13.4, the patterns are made up of a variety of lines, dots, and cross-hatch designs. The *DrawPie* procedure selects patterns 6 through 10 for the pie chart:

```
FOR i : = 1 TO items DO
   { ... }
   SETFILLSTYLE (5 + i, 0);
```

This SETFILLSTYLE statement specifies the pattern that PIESLICE uses for the next wedge. We'll encounter the SETFILLSTYLE procedure again in the next section, as we examine the routine that creates a three-dimensional bar chart.

Creating Bar Charts

The GRAPH unit actually has two procedures that you can use for creating bar charts. The BAR procedure creates simple filled-in rectangles that you can use as the bars of a chart. The BAR3D procedure, which we'll examine in this section, creates fancier three-dimensional bars.

BAR3D takes six arguments, as follows:

BAR3D (*x1, y1, x2, y2, depth, topBar*)

The first four arguments form two pixel addresses, representing the lower-left corner (*x1, y1*) and the upper-right corner (*x2, y2*) of the resulting bar. The *depth* argument is the depth in pixels—the third dimension of the bar. Finally, the *topBar* argument is a BOOLEAN value indicating whether or not the bar should be finished off with a rectangular top. If you are creating a stacked bar chart—in which one bar fits squarely on top of another, displaying two quantities of information for each bar—you will want to draw a top on only the uppermost bar in the stack.

The *DrawBars* procedure in the *GrphDemo* program produces a stacked bar chart, as shown in Figure 13.5. Like the *DrawPie* procedure before it, *DrawBars* creates its graph from a set of sample data values initialized in a CONST statement:

```
CONST
  items = 9;
  sampleData: ARRAY [1..items, 1..2] OF BYTE =
    ((19, 10), (25, 25), (37, 10), (18, 5),
     (18, 25), (35, 43), (43, 58), (32, 55), (43, 32));
```

As you can see, the data is stored as a two-dimensional array of BYTE values.

Inside the procedure, a FOR loop produces each stack of bars. The routine begins by calculating three height values, *y1*, *y2*, and *y3*:

```
FOR i := 1 TO items DO
  BEGIN
    y1 := GETMAXY − 50;
    y2 := y1 − sampleData [i, 1];
    y3 := y2 − sampleData [i, 2];
```

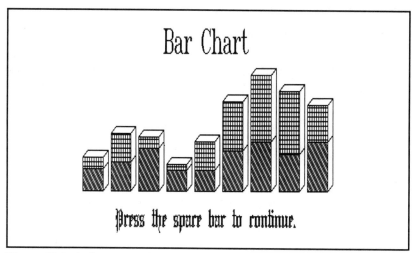

Figure 13.5: A demonstration of the BAR3D procedure

The value of *y1* is the standard starting point for all the stacks; *y2* is the vertical address representing the top of the first bar in a stack; and *y3* is the top of the second bar. To calculate the values for *y2* and *y3*, the routine subtracts the appropriate *sampleData* values from the current vertical address. (The vertical address coordinates decrease as the routine builds each bar up toward the top of the screen.)

The *DrawBar* procedure calculates the horizontal address of each bar in even increments of 50 pixels. The width of each bar is 36 pixels, and the depth is 9 pixels:

```
depth : = 9;
{ ... }
INC (x1, 50);
x2 : = x1 + 36;
```

Given these five address coordinates (three *y* values and two *x* values), the routine makes two calls to BAR3D to create each bar in a stack:

```
BAR3D (x1, y1, x2, y2, depth, FALSE);
BAR3D (x1, y2, x2, y3, depth, TRUE)
```

Only the second of the two bars needs a top, as indicated by the final BOOLEAN arguments.

Before each call to BAR3D, the routine calls SETFILLSTYLE to select a fill pattern. The first bar is filled with pattern 6, and the second is filled with pattern 7:

```
SETFILLSTYLE (6, 0);
SETFILLSTYLE (7, 0);
```

Although the *DrawPie* and *DrawBars* procedures draw charts from random sets of sample data, you can use almost identical algorithms to draw pie charts and three-dimensional bar charts from actual input data. As you can see, Turbo Pascal's PIESLICE, BAR3D, and SET-FILLSTYLE make charting tasks quite simple.

We'll look at three final graphics tools before we end this brief survey of the GRAPH unit. These three routines draw additional varieties of geometric shapes on the screen.

Drawing Miscellaneous Shapes on the Screen

As you can see in Figure 13.6, the *DrawShapes* procedure from *GrphDemo* demonstrates the RECTANGLE, ELLIPSE, and DRAWPOLY routines.

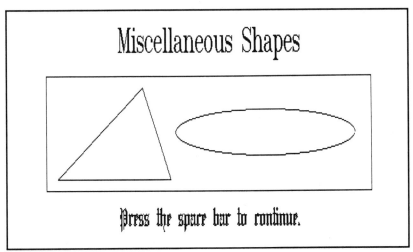

Figure 13.6: A demonstration of the ELLIPSE, DRAWPOLY, and REC-TANGLE procedures

The RECTANGLE procedure takes four integer arguments, representing two corner addresses of the resulting rectangle:

RECTANGLE (*x1, y1, x2, y2*)

Here is the statement that draws the rectangle shown in Figure 13.6:

RECTANGLE (30, 50, GETMAXX − 30, 150);

The ELLIPSE procedure takes six integer arguments, as follows:

ELLIPSE (*x, y, startAngle, endAngle, horizRadius, vertRadius*)

You can think of an elipse as a circle that has been stretched horizontally or vertically. The *x* and *y* coordinates represent the center of the ellipse. The *startAngle* and *endAngle* arguments represent the portion of the ellipse that will actually be drawn. (You should set these arguments at 0 and 359 for a full ellipse.) Finally, the *horizRadius* represents the horizontal length, in pixels, from the center of the ellipse to the side of the ellipse; *vertRadius* is the length from the center to the top of the ellipse.

Here is the statement that creates the ellipse shown in Figure 13.6:

ELLIPSE (GETMAXX DIV 2 + 100, GETMAXY DIV 2, 0, 359, 160, 20)

Notice that the ellipse is stretched horizontally when *horizRadius* is greater than *vertRadius*.

Finally, the DRAWPOLY procedure draws any polygonal shape, given a series of addresses representing corners of the shape:

DRAWPOLY (*numCorners, addressList*)

The first argument, *numCorners*, is the number of corner addresses specified for the shape. The second argument is a data structure that contains the coordinate addresses of each corner. If you want to draw a closed polygon with *n* sides, *addressList* must contain *n + 1* addresses, and the last address must be the same as the first one.

The *DrawShapes* procedure sets up an array of WORD values to define the triangle that appears in Figure 13.6; the name of the array is *polyPoints:*

```
CONST
   polyPoints: ARRAY [1..8] OF WORD =
      (200, 60, 50, 140, 250, 140, 200, 60);
```

To draw the triangle, the routine simply provides this array as the second argument of the DRAWPOLY procedure:

```
DRAWPOLY (4, polyPoints);
```

DRAWPOLY is useful for creating any shape that consists of lines drawn between pairs of pixel addresses.

Summary

The GRAPH unit provides procedures that you can use to produce impressive graphics on the screen, given any standard graphics display hardware.

The INITGRAPH command's *auto-detect* mode determines what kind of graphics hardware is present in a given computer system and loads the appropriate graphics driver from disk. Once this is done, you can choose from a variety of procedures devoted to plotting points and drawing shapes. In these commands, an address is represented by a coordinate pair, (x, y). For example, PUTPIXEL plots a single point at a designated address. Several procedures draw shapes on the screen; these include LINE, RECTANGLE, CIRCLE, ELLIPSE, and POLYDRAW.

In addition, three procedures, PIESLICE, BAR, and BAR3D, are useful for producing business charts. Along with these routines, you can use the SETFILLSTYLE procedure to specify fill patterns and colors.

Finally, the GRAPH unit contains a group of commands that you can use to display text on the screen in a variety of fonts. The SETTEXTJUSTIFY and SETTEXTSTYLE procedures establish the characteristics of the text, and the OUTTEXTXY procedure displays a string of text on the screen.

We have looked at only a very small selection of all the procedures and functions contained in Turbo Pascal's GRAPH unit. This library of graphics routines is worth exploring further if you plan to write graphics programs in Pascal.

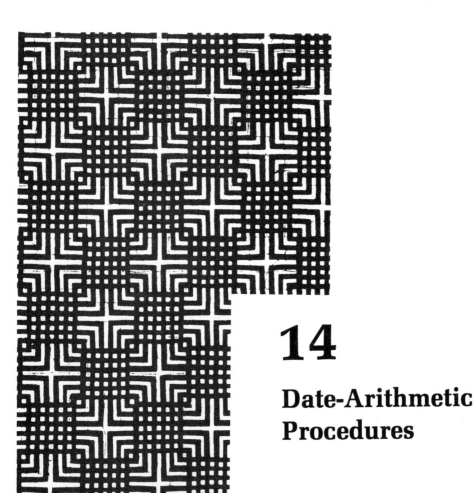

C H A P T E R

14

Date-Arithmetic Procedures

Business application programs often require techniques for performing accurate chronological operations with dates. In this chapter we'll examine a variety of date operations, and we'll develop a library of routines for performing them. In particular, we'll discuss three essential date-arithmetic operations, designed to

- Calculate the difference, in days, between two dates
- Find the date that is a specified number of days in the past or future from a given reference date
- Determine the day of the week corresponding to any specified date in the past or future

A complete package of date-handling procedures should also include input and output routines—for example, specialized functions that can

- Accept and validate dates entered from the keyboard
- Produce date display strings in various appropriate output formats

A wide variety of business applications—depreciation routines, loan calculations, accounts-receivable operations, scheduling applications, and more—require date procedures like these.

Unlike some other programming environments—such as spreadsheets and database management packages—the Pascal language does not include built-in functions for performing date operations. In fact, Turbo Pascal has only two built-in date routines, SETDATE and GETDATE, both included in the DOS unit. The SETDATE procedure allows you to change the current date setting of the system calendar:

SETDATE (*year, month, day, weekday*)

Conversely, the GETDATE procedure supplies the current date from the system calendar:

GETDATE (*year, month, day, weekday*)

The components of the system date are returned in the GETDATE procedure's four parameters. We've also added one routine to this collection already, in the unit named *ChrnUnit:* the *DateString* procedure supplies a string representing the current date.

As we set out to build a more complete library of date routines, we'll have the opportunity to review Turbo Pascal's large variety of integer data types. Selecting an appropriate integer type to represent dates is an important first step in the process of designing date routines. Specifically, in this chapter we'll use LONGINT-type values to represent individual twentieth-century dates. As we saw in Chapter 4, the LONGINT type supports a very large range of values (from about −2 billion to +2 billion). We'll find that LONGINT is more suitable than any other integer type for representing dates.

The usual technique for performing date-arithmetic operations involves converting dates into scalar values. A scalar date is simply an integer that represents a number of elapsed days since a selected starting point in calendar time. In this chapter we'll develop a scalar date system that takes January 1, 1901 as its starting point. In other words, this date is day 1 in the system; subsequent dates are then represented as the number of elapsed days since January 1, 1901. For example, here are some scalar-date equivalents in this particular system:

Date	Scalar Date
Jan. 1, 1911	3653

Jan. 1, 1931	10958
Jan. 1, 1951	18263
Jan. 1, 1971	25568
Jan. 1, 1991	32873

As you can see from the last of these examples, scalar date equivalents eventually reach values that are outside the range of the INTEGER type (− 32768 to 32767).

We might at first be tempted to use the WORD type to represent scalar dates. Since this integer type has a range from 0 to 65535, we could clearly represent all twentieth-century dates as WORD values. However, the fact that this type supports only positive numbers proves a liability in some date operations, as we'll see later in this chapter. For complete accuracy in all operations, the best choice turns out to be the LONGINT type.

Given a function that supplies the scalar equivalent of any date, date-arithmetic operations become quite simple. For example, computing the difference in days between two dates is simply a matter of subtracting one scalar date from another. Furthermore, to find a date that is a number of days forward in time from a given reference date, we simply add the specified number of days to the scalar equivalent of the reference date. This operation, which yields a new scalar date, also requires a procedure for converting a scalar date value back into a date display string.

In the first section of this chapter, we'll examine a group of functions that together make up a complete date-handling package. We'll see how these routines work, and we'll study examples of their output. The most important of these routines are

- A date input function that reads a date string from the keyboard and converts the input to a scalar date value, first making sure that the string represents a valid date

- A conversion function that computes the scalar equivalent of a date expressed as month, day, and year arguments

- A conversion function that produces a date display string from a scalar date

- A function that yields the scalar equivalent of today's date

- A function that finds the day of the week of any scalar date in the system

We will store all of these routines in the unit that we began building at the beginning of this book, *ChrnUnit*. Once the new version of *ChrnUnit* is compiled, it will become a powerful library of date routines.

After studying these routines, we'll turn briefly to a business example that demonstrates all of them in action. This application example, a program called *LateCli*, produces late-payment notices to facilitate a company's accounts-receivable operations.

Let's begin, then, by examining the collection of date functions in *ChrnUnit*.

A Library of Date Routines

The INTERFACE section of *ChrnUnit* appears in Figure 14.1, and the IMPLEMENTATION section is shown in Figure 14.2. Glancing quickly at the listings, you'll notice three functions in the group that return LONGINT-type values. These three routines produce scalar dates:

- The *InDate* function reads a date string from the keyboard and converts it to a scalar date.

- The *ScalarDate* function determines the scalar date equivalent of any date.

- The *TodaysDate* function supplies the scalar equivalent of the current date.

Other functions in the package supply strings and integer values:

- The *ChronString* function produces a complete date display string from a given date. The date must be supplied in four separate WORD arguments—*year, month, day,* and *weekday*—in the style of Turbo Pascal's built-in GETDATE procedure. This function produces a string in the following format:

    Fri., Apr. 15, 1988

```
UNIT ChrnUnit;

  { This unit supplies ten chronological functions:

      ChronString returns a string representing any date.
      DateString returns a string representing today's date.
      TimeString returns a string representing the current time.
      DaysInMonth supplies the number of days in a given month.
      DaysInYear supplies the number of days in a given year.
      ScalarDate converts date components to a scalar date.
      InDate accepts a valid date from the keyboard.
      TodaysDate supplies the scalar date of today's date.
      DayOfWeek returns the numeric day of the week for any date.
      ScalarToString converts a scalar date to a string.

      Note that these functions work with any date from
      January 1, 1901 to December 31, 1999.  }

  INTERFACE

    USES DOS, CRT;

    FUNCTION ChronString (year, month,
                          day, weekday: WORD): STRING;

    FUNCTION DateString: STRING;

    FUNCTION TimeString: STRING;

    FUNCTION DaysInMonth (month,
                          year:  WORD): BYTE;

    FUNCTION DaysInYear (year: WORD): WORD;

    FUNCTION ScalarDate (month,
                         day,
                         year:  WORD): LONGINT;

    FUNCTION InDate (prompt: STRING): LONGINT;

    FUNCTION TodaysDate: LONGINT;

    FUNCTION DayOfWeek (scDate: LONGINT): BYTE;

    FUNCTION ScalarToString (scDate: LONGINT): STRING;
```

Figure 14.1: The INTERFACE section of the *ChrnUnit* unit

Actually, most of the code for this function has been extracted from its original location inside the *DateString* function.

- The *DateString* function supplies a string representing the current date from the system calendar. Although this function has been reorganized from its original version, it produces the same result as before.

```
IMPLEMENTATION

FUNCTION ChronString;

  { The ChronString function converts four numeric
    date components---year, month, day, weekday---into a
    date string, in the format Day., Mo. dd, yyyy. }

  CONST

    { Set up arrays for the three-character
      day and month strings. }

    days: ARRAY[0..6] OF STRING[3] =
      ('Sun','Mon','Tue','Wed','Thu','Fri','Sat');
    months: ARRAY[1..12] OF STRING[3] =
      ('Jan','Feb','Mar','Apr','May','Jun',
       'Jul','Aug','Sep','Oct','Nov','Dec');

  VAR
    yearStr, monthStr, dayStr, weekdayStr: STRING;

  BEGIN    { ChronString }

    { Convert numeric date values to strings. }

    STR (year, yearStr);
    STR (day, dayStr);
    IF LENGTH(dayStr) = 1 THEN
      dayStr := ' ' + dayStr;

    { Get the appropriate day and month strings. }

    weekdayStr := days[weekday] + '., ';
    monthStr := months[month] + '. ';

    { Concatenate to produce final result. }

    ChronString := weekdayStr + monthStr +
                   dayStr + ', ' + yearStr

  END;    { ChronString }


FUNCTION DateString;

  { The DateString function converts the numeric
    values supplied by the GETDATE procedure into a
    date string, in the format 'Day., Mo. dd, yyyy'. }

  VAR
    year, month, day, weekday: WORD;

  BEGIN    { DateString }

    GETDATE(year, month, day, weekday);
    DateString := ChronString (year, month, day, weekday)

  END;    { DateString }
```

Figure 14.2: The IMPLEMENTATION section of the *ChrnUnit* unit

```
FUNCTION TimeString;

  { The TimeString function converts the numeric
    values supplied by the GETTIME procedure into a
    time string in the format hh:mm am/pm. }

  VAR
    hour, minute, second, hundredth: WORD;
    ampm: STRING[2];
    hourStr, minuteStr: STRING;

  BEGIN    { TimeString }

    GETTIME (hour, minute, second, hundredth);

    { Convert 24-hour time into am/pm format. }

    IF hour > 11 THEN
      BEGIN
        ampm := 'pm';
        IF hour > 12 THEN DEC (hour, 12)
      END
    ELSE
      BEGIN
        ampm := 'am';
        IF hour = 0 THEN hour := 12
      END;

    { Convert numeric time elements into strings. }

    STR (hour, hourStr);
    STR (minute, minuteStr);
    IF LENGTH(hourStr) = 1 THEN
      hourStr := ' ' + hourStr;
    IF LENGTH(minuteStr) = 1 THEN
      minuteStr := '0' + minuteStr;

    { Concatenate to produce final result. }

    TimeString := hourStr + ':' + minuteStr + ' ' + ampm

  END;    { TimeString }


FUNCTION DaysInMonth;

  { The DaysInMonth function returns the number of
    days in a specified month. To account for the
    varying number of days in February, this function
    takes two parameters: the month and the year. }

  VAR
    temp: BYTE;

  BEGIN    { DaysInMonth }

    CASE month OF

      { The months with 31 days. }
```

Figure 14.2: The IMPLEMENTATION section of the *ChrnUnit* unit
(continued)

```
         1, 3, 5, 7, 8, 10, 12:
           temp := 31;

         { The months with 30 days. }

         4, 6, 9, 11:
           temp := 30;

         { February. }

         2:
           IF ((year MOD 4) = 0) THEN
             temp := 29
           ELSE
             temp := 28
       END;

     DaysInMonth := temp

   END;    { DaysInMonth }


FUNCTION DaysInYear;

   { The DaysInYear function supplies the number of
     days in a specified year. }

   VAR
     temp: WORD;

   BEGIN    { DaysInYear }

     { 366 days for leap years; 365 for others. }

     IF ((year MOD 4) = 0) THEN
       temp := 366
     ELSE
       temp := 365;

     DaysInYear := temp

   END;    { DaysInYear }


FUNCTION ScalarDate;

   { The ScalarDate function returns a scalar equivalent
     of a valid twentieth-century date. In this scalar
     system, January 1, 1901 is day 1. The last valid date
     is December 31, 1999, which is day 36,159. }

   VAR
     temp: LONGINT;
     i:    BYTE;

   BEGIN    { ScalarDate }

     { Add the days of the years,
       up to the previous year. }
```

Figure 14.2: The IMPLEMENTATION section of the *ChrnUnit* unit
(continued)

```
        temp := 0;
        FOR i := 1 to (year - 1) DO
          INC (temp, DaysInYear (i));

        { Add the days of the months,
          up to the previous month. }

        FOR i := 1 TO (month - 1) DO
          INC (temp, DaysInMonth (i, year));

        { Add the days of the current month. }

        INC (temp, day);

        ScalarDate := temp

    END;     { ScalarDate }



FUNCTION InDate;

    { The InDate function reads a valid date from the
      keyboard in the MM DD YY format. The function accepts
      slashes, hyphens, periods, or spaces as separators
      between the elements of a date. }

    CONST
      numChars = 4;
      divisionChars: ARRAY [1..numChars] OF CHAR =
                   ('/', '-', '.', ' ');

    VAR
      xSave, ySave,
      charIndex,
      firstDiv, secondDiv:         BYTE;
      month, day, year,
      monthCode, dayCode, yearCode: WORD;
      inDateString,
      monthStr, dayStr, yearStr:   STRING;
      good:                        BOCLEAN;
      targetChar:                  CHAR;


      FUNCTION Pos2 (inChar: CHAR;
                     inStr:  STRING): BYTE;

        { The Pos2 function finds the second position
          of inChar in inStr. }

        VAR
          firstPos,
          secondPos:    BYTE;
          secondString: STRING;

        BEGIN     { Pos2 }
```

Figure 14.2: The IMPLEMENTATION section of the *ChrnUnit* unit
(continued)

```
           firstPos := POS (inChar, inStr);
           secondString :=
             COPY (inStr, firstPos + 1, LENGTH(inStr) - firstPos);
           secondPos :=
             POS (inChar, secondString) + firstPos;
           Pos2 := secondPos

       END;    { Pos2 }


BEGIN     { InDate }

  { Loop until a valid date has been entered. }

  REPEAT
    xSave := WHEREX;
    ySave := WHEREY;
    WRITE (prompt);
    READLN (inDateString);

    { Find the positions of the separator characters. }

    charIndex := 1;
    REPEAT
      targetChar := divisionChars [charIndex];
      firstDiv := POS (targetChar, inDateString);
      secondDiv := Pos2 (targetChar, inDateString);
      good := (firstDiv > 0) AND (secondDiv > 0);
      IF (NOT good) THEN
        INC (charIndex)
    UNTIL good OR (charIndex > numChars);

    { Separate the three elements of the date,
      month, day, and year. }

    IF good THEN
      BEGIN
        monthStr := COPY (inDateString, 1, firstDiv - 1);
        dayStr   := COPY (inDateString, firstDiv + 1,
                              secondDiv - firstDiv -1);
        yearStr  := COPY (inDateString, secondDiv + 1,
                    LENGTH (inDateString) - secondDiv);
        VAL (monthStr, month, monthCode);
        VAL (dayStr, day, dayCode);
        VAL (yearStr, year, yearCode);

        { Test the validity of the date. }

        IF (monthCode + dayCode + yearCode = 0) THEN
          BEGIN
            IF year > 99 THEN year := year MOD 100;
            good := (1 <= month) AND (month <= 12);
            good := good AND (year > 0);
            good := good AND
                    (day <= DaysInMonth (month, year))
          END
        ELSE
          good := FALSE;
      END;

  { Repeat the prompt if the input is not valid. }
```

Figure 14.2: The IMPLEMENTATION section of the *ChrnUnit* unit
       (continued)

```
            IF NOT good THEN
               BEGIN
                  GOTOXY (xSave, ySave);
                  CLREOL
               END
            UNTIL good;

            { Convert the date to a scalar value. }

            InDate := ScalarDate (month, day, year)

         END;    { InDate }


      FUNCTION TodaysDate;

         { The TodaysDate function supplies the scalar date of
           today's date. }

         VAR
            year, month, day, weekday: WORD;

         BEGIN    { TodaysDate }

            GETDATE(year, month, day, weekday);
            TodaysDate := ScalarDate (month, day, (year MOD 100))
         END;    { TodaysDate }


      FUNCTION DayOfWeek;

         { The DayOfWeek function supplies an integer from
           0 to 6, representing the day of the week of a given
           scalar date. A value of 0 represents Sunday. }


         BEGIN    { DayOfWeek }

            { Formula based on the fact that
              January 1, 1901---the first day in this
              scalar date system---was a Tuesday. }

            DayOfWeek := ((scDate + 1) MOD 7)

         END;    { DayOfWeek }


      FUNCTION ScalarToString;

         { The ScalarToString function converts a scalar date
           into a date string in the format Day., Mo., dd, yyyy }

         VAR
            remainder:    LONGINT;
            year, month,
            day, weekday: WORD;

         BEGIN
            remainder := scDate;

            { Determine the current year. }
```

Figure 14.2: The IMPLEMENTATION section of the *ChrnUnit* unit (continued)

```
            year := 1;
            WHILE (remainder > DaysInYear (year)) DO
              BEGIN
                DEC (remainder, DaysInYear (year));
                INC (year)
              END;

            { Determine the current month. }

            month := 1;
            WHILE (remainder > DaysInMonth (month, year)) DO
              BEGIN
                DEC (remainder, DaysInMonth (month, year));
                INC (month)
              END;

            { The day of the month is the number still
              left in the remainder variable. }

            day := remainder;
            weekday := DayOfWeek (scDate);

            { Create the date string. }

            ScalarToString :=
              ChronString ((year + 1900), month, day, weekday)

          END;

      END.    { ChrnUnit }
```

Figure 14.2: The IMPLEMENTATION section of the *ChrnUnit* unit (continued)

- The *DaysInMonth* and *DaysInYear* functions supply the correct number of days in a given month or year.

- The *DayOfWeek* function determines the day of the week of a specified scalar date. The result of this function is an integer from 0 to 6, representing days from Sunday through Saturday.

- The *ScalarToString* function supplies a date string from a scalar date argument. (Note the difference between this function and the *ChronString* function, which produces a date string from four separate date-component arguments.)

The library of routines stored in *ChrnUnit* is designed to work with dates ranging from Janary 1, 1901, through December 31, 1999. However, with a few revisions the package could be extended to handle dates outside the twentieth-century. In the following sections we'll discuss each of the routines in turn.

A Date Input Routine: The *InDate* Function

Any successful date input routine should be able to both accept dates in a variety of input formats, and recognize and reject invalid dates. Let's see how these two features are implemented in the *InDate* function.

A call to the *InDate* function takes a single string argument; this string becomes the prompt in the input operation that the function subsequently performs. For example, consider the following statement:

invoiceDate : = InDate ('Invoice date? ');

As a result of this statement, the *InDate* function displays the following prompt on the screen and waits for the user to enter a date:

Invoice date? _

The function expects dates to be entered in the general format MM/DD/YY. You can enter the three elements of a date—the month, the day, and the year—as one- or two-digit numbers. For example, you could enter the date January 12, 1988 as follows:

Invoice date? **1/12/88**

InDate recognizes a variety of characters as 'separators' between the three elements of the date. In addition to the slash character (/), the function accepts periods, hyphens, or spaces.

InDate is also flexible about reading the individual portions of the date. You can enter the year as a two- or four-digit number, as in this example:

1/12/1988

In response to any of the above input values, the *InDate* function returns the number 31788, the scalar-date equivalent of January 12, 1988.

The function rejects date values that do not follow the required input format. For example, let's say you accidentally use separator characters that *InDate* does not recognize:

Invoice date? **1 = 12 = 88**

InDate responds to this mistake by erasing your input and keeping the input prompt on the screen:

Invoice date? _

The *InDate* function continues eliciting a date until it has received valid input.

Significantly, *InDate* also rejects dates for reasons other than format problems. If you enter a date that does not actually exist on the calendar, *InDate* will recognize your mistake. Here are some examples of input dates that the function will reject:

- A date containing a month element that is greater than 12, such as 14-2-88. (Note that *InDate* does *not* recognize this as a date in the European format, 14 February 1988.)

- A date containing a day that is greater than the actual number of days in the specified month, such as 6-31-88.

- An input of February 29 in a date that is not a leap year, such as 2-29-89. (The month of February 1989 has only 28 days, since 1989 is not a leap year.)

In all of these cases, *InDate* rejects the input and keeps the input prompt on the screen.

Let's look briefly at the listing of the *InDate* function.

Inside the *InDate* Function

As we have seen, *InDate* accepts a single string argument; inside the routine, this value is stored in the string parameter *prompt:*

FUNCTION InDate (prompt: STRING): LONGINT;

InDate controls the input and validation process within one large REPEAT/UNTIL loop. Each iteration of this loop accepts an input of one date value and determines whether the input is valid. In response to an invalid date, the routine stores a value of false in the BOOLEAN variable *good* and another iteration ensues. When the user enters a valid date, *good* becomes true and the iterations stop.

The first actions performed inside the loop record the current cursor position, display the prompt on the screen, and accept the date input as a string:

```
xSave : = WHEREX;
ySave : = WHEREY;
WRITE (prompt);
READLN (inDateString);
```

Recording the cursor position allows *InDate* to redisplay the prompt at the same location if necessary.

Inside the main input loop, a nested REPEAT/UNTIL loop searches through the input string for acceptable separator characters. The built-in POS function is used to find the positions, *firstDiv* and *secondDiv*, of the two required separators in the date string. Assuming the date string is properly formatted, the function then uses the COPY function to isolate the three elements of the date and the VAL procedure to convert these elements to integers—*month*, *day*, and *year*, respectively.

To be accepted as a legal date, these three values must then pass a series of validation tests. First, *month* must be within the range from 1 to 12, and *year* must be greater than 0:

```
good : = (1 < = month) AND (month < = 12);
good : = good AND (year > 0);
```

Finally, the day element, *day*, must be within the correct range of days indicated by the given month and year. To perform this test, *InDate* calls on another function, *DaysInMonth:*

```
good : = good AND
          (day < = DaysInMonth (month, year))
```

As you can see, *DaysInMonth* takes both a month and a year as arguments. This important *ChrnUnit* function is used by several of the routines in the date library. Its central structure is a CASE statement that determines how many days are contained in a given month. Eleven of the months contain either 31 or 30 days each:

```
CASE month OF
```

```
1, 3, 5, 7, 8, 10, 12:
   temp : = 31;

4, 6, 9, 11:
   temp : = 30;
```

February is a special case, containing 29 days in a leap year and 28 in any other year:

```
2:
  IF ((year MOD 4) = 0) THEN
     temp : = 29
  ELSE
     temp : = 28
```

The MOD operation determines whether *year* represents a leap year, a number evenly divisible by 4. (This is why *DaysInMonth* requires the year value as an argument.) The selected number of days is returned as the value of the function:

```
DaysInMonth : = temp
```

Back in the *InDate* routine, if any one of the validation tests fails, the function sends the cursor back to its original position, erases the line, and loops back for another input value:

```
IF NOT good THEN

   BEGIN
      GOTOXY (xSave, ySave);
      CLREOL
   END
UNTIL good;
```

Once the function determines that an input date is valid, it calls on the *ScalarDate* routine to convert the date to a scalar value; *InDate* returns this scalar value as its result:

```
InDate : = ScalarDate (month, day, year)
```

We'll examine the *ScalarDate* function in the next section.

A Scalar-Date Conversion Routine: The *ScalarDate* Function

ScalarDate receives the three integer components of a date as its arguments, and returns the corresponding scalar date as a LONGINT value:

```
FUNCTION ScalarDate (month,
                     day,
                     year: WORD): LONGINT;
```

Calculating the scalar date is a straightforward process of counting the days forward from January 1, 1901 up to the target date. This count is accumulated in the variable *temp*.

First the function adds up all the whole years up to the year just before the target date:

```
FOR i : = 1 TO (year − 1) DO
   INC (temp, DaysInYear (i));
```

A call to the *DaysInYear* function returns a value of 366 for a leap year and 365 for any other year.

The next step is to add the days of all the months in the target year, up to but not including the target month. To find the correct number of days in each month, *ScalarDate* calls the *DaysInMonth* function, which we looked at in the previous section:

```
FOR i : = 1 TO (month − 1) DO
   INC (temp, DaysInMonth (i, year));
```

Finally, the last step is to add on the number of days that have elapsed in the target month itself:

```
INC (temp, day);
```

The value *temp* is returned as the result of *ScalarDate:*

```
ScalarDate : = temp
```

Given the *ScalarDate* function, the following general expression yields the difference in days between the two dates *mo1/da1/yr1* and *mo2/da2/yr2:*

ScalarDate (*mo1,da1,yr1*) − ScalarDate (*mo2,da2,yr2*)

You can also use the built-in ABS function to make sure that the result of a subtraction operation will be a positive number, regardless of the order of the two dates. For example, imagine that you want to calculate the elapsed time between an invoice date (3/24/88) and the date the invoice was paid (6/11/88). The following expression performs the calculation:

ABS (ScalarDate (3,24,88) − ScalarDate (6,11,88))

The numeric result of this expression is 79, the number of days between the two dates. Note that this particular example would not be successful if the two scalar dates were stored as WORD values. The subtraction itself produces a negative number, which is undefined in the range of the WORD type. This is why the date library uses LONGINT-type values to represent scalar dates.

We frequently need to determine the number of days between the current date and another date; the *TodaysDate* function is designed to perform this calculation. We'll look at the *TodaysDate* function in the next section.

The Current Date: The *TodaysDate* Function

TodaysDate takes no arguments; it supplies a long integer value representing the current system date, as in the following statement:

systemDate : = TodaysDate

The following general expression yields the number of days between today's date and another date in the past or future, represented by *mo/da/yr:*

ABS (TodaysDate − ScalarDate(*mo,da,yr*))

For example, imagine that you want to know how long a certain employee has worked for your company; the employee started working for you on September 22, 1986. The following expression yields the number of days that have elapsed since that starting point:

    TodaysDate − ScalarDate(9,22,86)

If today's date were April 15, 1988, the result of this expression would be 571. Notice that in this case the ABS function is not required, since the scalar equivalent of today's date is larger than a scalar date in the past.

The *TodaysDate* function is a very simple one. The function begins by reading the current system date from the GETDATE procedure:

    GETDATE (year, month, day, weekday);

Then, the final result is determined by a call to the *ScalarDate* function:

    TodaysDate : = ScalarDate(month, day, (year MOD 100))

Since *ScalarDate* expects the year to be between 1 and 99, this statement uses the MOD operation to produce a value in the correct range.

We have examined functions that produce scalar dates; now let's look at a function that converts a scalar date into a displayable date string.

A Date Display Routine: The *ScalarToString* Function

ScalarToString takes a single long-integer argument, representing a scalar date. The result of the function is a string that supplies the day of the week, the month, the day, and the year corresponding to the specified scalar date. For example, consider the following statement:

    WRITELN (ScalarToString (31882))

This statement displays the following date string on the screen:

    Fri., Apr. 15, 1988

The *ScalarToString* function has many applications, but perhaps the most common one is to convert the result of a date-arithmetic operation into a displayable date. For example, let's say you want to display the date that is 15 days into the future from the current date. You know that the following operation supplies the scalar value for the target date:

```
TodaysDate + 15
```

To display this date in a readable form on the screen, you could use the following statement:

```
WRITELN (ScalarToString (TodaysDate + 15))
```

For example, if today's date were April 15, 1988, this statement would display the following string:

```
Sat., Apr. 30, 1988
```

ScalarToString is one of the more complicated routines in our date library; let's see how it works.

Inside the *ScalarToString* Function

ScalarToString receives its scalar date argument in the long-integer parameter variable *scDate:*

```
FUNCTION ScalarToString (scDate: LONGINT): STRING;
```

The function's first task is to convert *scDate* into four integer components representing the year, month, day, and day of the week of the target date. To accomplish this task, *ScalarToString* progressively subtracts representative numeric values from *scDate*, always storing the current remainder in a variable named *remainder*. This variable starts out with the value of *scDate:*

```
remainder : = scDate
```

The first part of the task is to find the year represented by *scDate*. Inside a WHILE loop, the routine subtracts whole years from *scDate* until the remainder is less than a year:

```
year : = 1;
```

```
WHILE (remainder > DaysInYear(year)) DO
  BEGIN
    DEC (remainder, DaysInYear(year));
    INC (year)
  END;
```

Notice that this sequence uses the *DaysInYear* function to determine the correct amount to deduct for each year. When the iterations of this loop stop, the variable *year* contains the target year, and *remainder* contains the number of days that have elapsed since the beginning of this target year.

The next step is to determine the target month from the remainder of the scalar date. Again, a WHILE loop subtracts whole months from *remainder* until there are fewer than a month's worth of days left:

```
month : = 1;
WHILE (remainder > DaysInMonth(month, year)) DO
  BEGIN
    DEC (remainder, DaysInMonth(month, year));
    INC (month)
  END;
```

This loop uses the *DaysInMonth* function to determine the correct number of days to subtract for each month. When the process is complete, *month* contains the number of the target month and *remainder* contains the target day inside this month.

The final step is simply to assign *remainder* to the variable *day:*

```
day : = remainder;
```

This assignment statement performs an implicit data type conversion from the long integer *remainder* to the WORD-type integer *day*. Since the remainder will be a value of 31 or less at this point, the routine can safely assign the value to a regular integer variable.

Next, the *ScalarToString* function must determine the day of the week of the date represented by *scDate*. A call to the *DayOfWeek* function supplies this value:

```
weekday : = DayOfWeek (scDate);
```

We'll examine the *DayOfWeek* function a little later. For now, notice that the function takes a scalar date as its argument. (This is why *ScalarToString* copies the value of *scDate* into *remainder* before beginning the process of calculating the components of the date; *scDate* itself must be retained for the eventual call to *DayOfWeek*.) The result of the *DayOfWeek* function is an integer from 0 to 6.

Finally, *ScalarToString* makes a call to the *ChronString* function to produce the string date from the four numeric date components:

```
ScalarToString : =
   ChronString ((year  +  1900), month, day, weekday)
```

ChronString uses a variety of string operations to build the appropriate string. You might notice that the new version of the *DateString* function also calls *ChronString* to convert the components of the current date to a string:

```
GETDATE (year, month, day, weekday);
DateString : =  ChronString (year, month, day, weekday)
```

As we have seen, most of the code for *ChronString* was part of the original *DateString* function.

The last date routine we'll examine is *DayOfWeek*.

The *DayOfWeek* Function

DayOfWeek receives a scalar date, *scDate*. The function uses the MOD operation to find an integer from 0 to 6, representing the weekday of *scDate:*

```
DayOfWeek : =  ((scDate  +  1) MOD 7)
```

This short function is deceptively simple; its one-line algorithm is based on the fact that the starting point of the scalar date system—January 1, 1901—is a Tuesday. (For example, you can see that a scalar-date argument of 1 results in a return value of 2, representing Tuesday.)

DayOfWeek is intentionally presented as an independent function rather than as a part of the *ScalarToString* function. In some applications you may find special uses for the day-of-the-week value. For example, let's say you are working on a scheduling application that adds a certain number of days to the current system date. If the result of this operation happens to fall on a weekend, you want to adjust the scheduled date backward or forward to a business day—specifically, to the previous Friday or the following Monday.

The following passage illustrates how you might accomplish this task:

```
scheduleDate : = TodaysDate + 75;
day : = DayOfWeek(scheduleDate);
IF day = 6 THEN
   DEC (scheduleDate)
ELSE
   IF day = 0 THEN
      INC (scheduleDate);
WRITELN (ScalarToString (scheduleDate))
```

In this passage, the scheduled date is decreased by one day if the initial calculation happens to fall on a Saturday, or increased by one day if the calculation falls on a Sunday.

This completes our discussion of the functions included in the date library. In the next section of this chapter we'll examine a sample application that demonstrates these routines in action—the *LateCli* program.

Printing Late-Payment Notices: The *LateCli* Program

The *LateCli* program is an application designed for an imaginary software company named Custom Solutions, Inc. The program generates late-payment notices to be sent to certain recalcitrant clients of the firm, in an attempt to collect payment on aging and delinquent invoices.

Imagine that Custom Solutions produces customized software for particular business applications; at various stages during the work in progress for a given client, the company sends out an invoice for the work completed to date. The invoices specify that payment should be made in full within 30 days. In response to unpaid invoices, the *Late-Cli* program follows a fixed schedule for producing late-payment notices:

- For an invoice that is from 61 to 90 days old (that is, 31 to 60 days overdue), the program prints a reasonably polite reminder notice. An example of this notice appears in Figure 14.3.

- For an invoice that is more than 90 days old (that is, more than 60 days overdue), the program generates a more strongly worded reminder notice, an example of which is shown in Figure 14.4.

To elicit the information required for either one of these notices, the program conducts a short and simple input dialog. The program needs only three data items to determine the appropriate output: the client's name, the date of the late invoice, and the amount of the invoice. Here is an example of the complete input dialog:

Print a late payment notice

―――― ― ――― ――――― ―――

Client's name? **TechCo, Inc.**
Invoice date? **12/24/87**
Invoice amount? **4500**

Given the invoice date, *LateCli* computes the number of days since billing. If fewer than 60 days have elapsed, the program does not print a late notice; instead, a message like the following appears on the screen:

* * * No late message is necessary yet.
    Invoice is only 38 days old.

On the other hand, if the invoice falls into one of the two scheduled categories for late payment notices, the program alerts the user to turn on the printer, and then prints the appropriate notice.

The listing of the *LateCli* program appears in Figure 14.5. The program uses the new version of *ChrnUnit* that we have developed in this chapter. In the next section we'll examine the listing of the *LateCli* program, concentrating in particular on how the program uses the

```
                    Late Payment Notice
                    ---- ------- ------

    Notice Date:    Fri., Apr.  8, 1988

    To:             XYZ Corporation
    From:           Custom Solutions, Inc.

    Invoice Date:   Tue., Jan. 12, 1988
    Invoice Amount: $2,300.00
    Terms:          Full payment within 30 days.


    Your payment for this invoice is now 57
    days overdue. To avoid any delays in our
    current work-in-progress on your account, we
    would appreciate your immediate action on this
    matter. If we do not receive full payment by:

            Fri., Apr. 22, 1988

    we will be forced to stop work on your project.
```

Figure 14.3: A warning notice produced by the *LateCli* program

```
                    Late Payment Notice
                    ---- ------- ------

    Notice Date:    Fri., Apr.  8, 1988

    To:             TechCo, Inc.
    From:           Custom Solutions, Inc.

    Invoice Date:   Thu., Dec. 24, 1987
    Invoice Amount: $4,500.00
    Terms:          Full payment within 30 days.


    Your payment for this invoice is now 76
    days overdue. We are stopping all work on
    your project immediately. If we do not
    receive full payment by:

            Fri., Apr. 15, 1988

    we will be forced to take further action.
```

Figure 14.4: A delinquent notice produced by the *LateCli* program

```
PROGRAM LateCli;

   USES CRT, PRINTER, InUnit, StrUnit, ChrnUnit;

   CONST
     company = 'Custom Solutions, Inc.';
     formFeed = #12;

   VAR
     clientName:    STRING;
     invoiceDate:   LONGINT;
     inVoiceAmount: REAL;


   PROCEDURE InData;

      { The InData procedure elicits three items of information
        from the user: the client's name, the invoice date, and
        the amount of the invoice. }

      BEGIN    { InData }

        WRITELN ('Print a late payment notice');
        WRITELN ('----- - ---- ------- ------');
        WRITELN;

        WRITE ('Client''s name? ');
        READLN (clientName);

        { Store the invoice date as a scalar date. }

        invoiceDate := InDate ('Invoice date? ');
        invoiceAmount := InReal ('Invoice amount? ');
        WRITELN;
        WRITELN

      END;    { InData }


   PROCEDURE Heading;

      { The Heading procedure prints the heading information on
        both types of printed reports produced by this program. }

      BEGIN    { Heading }

        WRITELN (LST);
        WRITELN (LST, RightJustify ('Late Payment Notice', 36));
        WRITELN (LST, RightJustify ('---- ------- ------', 36));
        WRITELN (LST);

        WRITELN (LST, LeftAlign ('Notice Date:', 17), DateString);
        WRITELN (LST);
        WRITELN (LST, LeftAlign ('To:', 17), clientName);
        WRITELN (LST, LeftAlign ('From:', 17), company);
        WRITELN (LST);

        WRITELN (LST, LeftAlign ('Invoice Date:', 17),
                      ScalarToString (invoiceDate));

        WRITELN (LST, 'Invoice Amount:   ,
                      DollarDisplay (ROUND (invoiceAmount * 100), 9));
```

Figure 14.5: The listing of the *LateCli* program

```
                WRITELN (LST, LeftAlign ('Terms:', 17),
                              'Full payment within 30 days.');

            WRITELN (LST); WRITELN (LST)

        END;    { Heading }


    PROCEDURE Warning (daysOld: LONGINT);

        { The Warning procedure prints a warning message for
          an invoice that is from 61 to 90 days old (that is,
          from 31 to 60 days overdue). }

        CONST
          message: ARRAY [1..6] OF STRING =
            ('Your payment for this invoice is now ',
             'days overdue. To avoid any delays in our',
             'current work-in-progress on your account, we',
             'would appreciate your immediate action on this',
             'matter. If we do not receive full payment by:',
             'we will be forced to stop work on your project.');

        VAR
          i: BYTE;

        BEGIN    { Warning }

          Heading;
          WRITELN (LST, message[1], daysOld - 30);
          FOR i := 2 TO 5 DO
            WRITELN (LST, message[i]);

          WRITELN (LST);
          WRITELN (LST, Spaces (10),
                        ScalarToString (TodaysDate + 14));

          WRITELN (LST);
          WRITELN (LST, message [6]);
          WRITELN (LST, formFeed)

        END;    { Warning }


    PROCEDURE Serious (daysOld: LONGINT);

        { The Serious procedure prints a message for a
          delinquent invoice that is over 90 days old
          (that is, over 60 days overdue). }

        CONST
          message: ARRAY [1..5] OF STRING =
            ('Your payment for this invoice is now ',
             'days overdue. We are stopping all work on',
             'your project immediately. If we do not',
             'receive full payment by:',
             'we will be forced to take further action.');

        VAR
          i: BYTE;
```

Figure 14.5: The listing of the *LateCli* program (continued)

```
      BEGIN    { Serious }

        Heading;
        WRITELN (LST, message[1], daysOld - 30);
        FOR i := 2 TO 4 DO
          WRITELN (LST, message[i]);

        WRITELN (LST);
        WRITELN (LST, Spaces (10),
                      ScalarToString (TodaysDate + 7));

        WRITELN (LST);
        WRITELN (LST, message [5]);
        WRITELN (LST, formFeed)

      END;    { Serious }


  PROCEDURE TakeAction;

    { The TakeAction procedure examines the age of the
      invoice, and decides whether or not to print a
      warning letter. }

    VAR
      age: LONGINT;


    FUNCTION Continue: BOOLEAN;

      { The Continue function accepts a signal from
        the user to indicate the next action: space bar
        to print the list, escape to return to the menu. }

      CONST
        spaceBar = ' ';
        escKey   = #27;
        prompt   =
          '<Space Bar> to print letter. <Escape> to cancel.';

      VAR
        inKey: CHAR;

      BEGIN    { Continue }

        inKey    :=
          InChar (prompt, [spaceBar, escKey]);
        Continue := (inKey = spaceBar)

      END;    { Continue }


    BEGIN    { TakeAction }

      age := TodaysDate - invoiceDate;
      IF age < 60 THEN
        BEGIN
          WRITELN ('*** No late message is necessary yet.');
          WRITELN ('   Invoice is only ', age, ' days old.')
        END
      ELSE
```

Figure 14.5: The listing of the *LateCli* program (continued)

```
        IF Continue THEN
          IF age > 90 THEN
            Serious (age)
          ELSE
            Warning (age)

    END;      { TakeAction }


  BEGIN     { LateCli }

    CLRSCR;
    InData;
    TakeAction;

  END.      { LateCli }
```

Figure 14.5: The listing of the *LateCli* program (continued)

various date routines in *ChrnUnit*. We will find that the program performs a number of interesting date operations in the process of printing a late-payment notice.

Inside the *LateCli* Program

The main program section controls the action by making calls to two major procedures:

```
InData;
TakeAction
```

The first of these, *InData*, is the program's input procedure; the second, *TakeAction*, is the routine that decides how to react to the input.

The *InData* routine elicits the three required input values and stores them in the global variables *clientName*, *invoiceDate*, and *invoiceAmount*. The procedure uses the *InDate* function from *ChrnUnit* to elicit the invoice date:

```
invoiceDate : = InDate ('Invoice date? ');
```

As we have seen, *InDate* displays the input prompt on the screen, accepts the date input in any one of a variety of formats, and returns a LONGINT value representing the scalar equivalent of the date.

The *TakeAction* routine subsequently uses the following statement to compute the age of the invoice:

```
age : = TodaysDate - invoiceDate;
```

This statement performs one of the two essential date-arithmetic operations that we outlined at the beginning of this chapter—finding the difference in days between two dates. In this case, the first date is the current system date, supplied in scalar form by a call to the *ToaysDate* function. The second date is the invoice date originally returned from the *InDate* function.

The program's subsequent action depends on this calculated value *age*. A series of nested IF statements determine the nature of the output. First, if the invoice age is less than or equal to 60, no notice is printed; instead the program displays a notice on the screen:

```
IF age < 60 THEN
   BEGIN
      WRITELN ('* * * No late message is necessary yet.');
      WRITELN ('    Invoice is only ', age, ' days old.')
   END
```

On the other hand, if the invoice is older than 60 days, one of the two notices is printed. The printing itself is performed by either the *Serious* procedure or the *Warning* procedure:

```
IF age > 90 THEN
   Serious (age)
ELSE
   Warning (age)
```

Both of these routines begin with a call to a procedure named *Heading*, which prints the first part of the late-payment notice. As we look briefly at the *Heading*, *Warning*, and *Serious* routines, we'll find that all three of these routines make calls to the *ScalarToString* function to produce appropriate display dates for the printed reports.

Among other items of information, the *Heading* procedure prints two dates—the date of the notice and the date of the invoice. The notice date is produced by a call to the *DateString* function:

```
WRITELN (LST, LeftAlign ('Notice Date:', 17), DateString);
```

This statement yields an output line such as

```
Notice Date:      Fri., Apr.   8, 1988
```

In a second date operation, the *Heading* procedure calls the *Scalar-ToString* function to display the invoice date:

```
WRITELN (LST, LeftAlign ('Invoice Date:', 17),
              ScalarToString (invoiceDate));
```

The *Warning* and *Serious* procedures each print lines of text from an array of strings named *message*. (A CONST declaration located at the top of each procedure serves to initialize this array.) Incorporated within the printed text are two calculated items of information. On the first line of text, each of the routines prints the number of days by which a given invoice is overdue. This number is 30 days less than the actual age of the invoice, stored in the parameter variable *daysOld:*

```
WRITELN (LST, message[1], daysOld – 30)
```

Finally, near the end of the late notices, each routine prints a new due date for the payment in question. In effect, the *Warning* routine offers the client a two-week grace period:

```
WRITELN (LST, Spaces (10),
              ScalarToString (TodaysDate + 14));
```

The *Serious* routine gives a one-week grace period:

```
WRITELN (LST, Spaces (10),
              ScalarToString (TodaysDate + 7));
```

These statements illustrate another one of the essential date arithmetic operations—adding a number of days to a reference date to produce a new date in the future. In this case, a call to *TodaysDate* gives the reference date, and *ScalarToString* converts the calculated date into a displayable string.

Summary

The new version of *ChrnUnit* contains several important date functions:

- The *InDate* function reads and validates a date entered from the keyboard, and returns the scalar equivalent of the date.

- The *ScalarDate* function performs the necessary calculations to determine the scalar equivalent of a date.

- The *TodaysDate* function gives the scalar equivalent of the current system date.

- The *ScalarToString* function converts a scalar date to a displayable date string.

- The *DaysInMonth* function supplies the number of days in a given month of a given year.

- The *DaysInYear* function gives the number of days in a given year.

- The *DayOfWeek* function produces a string representing the day of the week corresponding to a given scalar date.

As we have seen, these functions together form a convenient collection of date-handling routines, designed for use in any business application that performs chronological operations.

C H A P T E R

15
Recursion

Our final programming topic in this book is a short but interesting one. *Recursion* is the technique by which a structured routine makes calls to itself in the process of accomplishing a repetitive task. You can use recursion in both procedures and functions in Turbo Pascal. However, this technique is not meant as a solution for just any programming task. Recursion often appears to be a somewhat esoteric trick and can result in algorithms that are difficult to grasp. Nonetheless, in certain special situations recursion can accomplish tasks much faster and more elegantly than other approaches.

Undoubtedly the best way to learn about recursion is to study examples of its use in programs. There are several classic examples of recursive algorithms; one of the most interesting and useful is a sorting algorithm called the *quick sort*. This procedure uses recursion to alphabetize a list of strings or to arrange a list of numbers in ascending or descending order. The quick sort is generally even faster than the Shell sort, the algorithm that we discussed and used in the programs presented earlier in this book. For this reason, the quick-sort algorithm is a rather dramatic example of the speed and efficiency of recursion.

One potential problem that you may have to allow for when you write recursive algorithms in Turbo Pascal is the amount of memory set aside for the stack. The stack is the memory space where Pascal keeps track of the return addresses associated with procedure calls and function calls. During a recursive process, a routine may call itself many times; for this reason, Turbo Pascal may need more than the usual amount of stack space to keep track of the calls.

While you are developing a program that contains a recursive routine, you should be sure to turn on the Stack checking option in the Options menu's Compiler command:

```
Stack checking          ON
```

With this option activated, Turbo Pascal will be on guard for stack problems that might occur during the performance of your program. If there is not enough stack space, the program will terminate with an appropriate run-time error message.

Ultimately, you may have to allocate more than the default amount of stack space in order to perform a recursive routine successfully. By default, Turbo Pascal provides 16K bytes of stack memory at run time. You can use the $M compiler directive within a program to increase this amount if you need extra stack memory for that program. For example, this directive increases the stack space to 32K:

```
{$M 32768, 0, 0}
```

In other words, this directive doubles the default stack space.

Demonstrating the Quick Sort: The *ShowOff* Program

To test the quick-sort algorithm—and to show off its remarkable speed—this chapter presents a simple demonstration program called *ShowOff*. The program generates a list of 200 randomly generated strings of uppercase letters, and then submits the list to the quick-sort procedure for alphabetization. (To create the list, the program makes use of a function included in *RandUnit—the RandStr* function. See Chapter 9 for a review of this unit.)

The program first displays the unsorted list on the screen, and then presents the sorted list when you signal that you are ready. Figures

15.1 and 15.2 show examples of an unsorted and sorted list, respectively. When you run the program, you'll see that the sorting process occurs almost instantaneously. The program alphabetizes the list in the short time interval between the appearance of the unsorted list and the display of the following message:

Press <Enter> to see sorted list.

```
XUJBVZX FYPPOYK CJXTBIE PRYFHGQ IRZBLHQ JVVQZNO FRTADUA JXUDAOD VHHZBNZ KLMGEAS
FWKJHDA OZSMLLX PBHUOIH ZFMRZHS TQHRPSB BAHJURT PQAFKEO VENGGOX NKYQEDM LIQEBIO
GUTKDBW CZSUOJV DOMYEPU AEPFYZJ PBGGPZP JYQDPMA EXAEMQI GQSAEJV FILKCDS TOXEISL
BQGKLTF DXNNSVV OTLOSQF WKJSFYO NIGHFDT LAHAYSV JLMAUVI YPGTKAQ DOHHMRF DTYNNWW
FDPGDOT LKRXFAC BAPOGRC QGILGES CAMRCFD NDSKLSF EXSJSXM JCJUJEQ HBUCPXH BBXLXFH
MUMDOHU PVVLOWE PLXELZC ULHXGYM MHMYZDF LMTVZUQ XUFVQCY SLFJYHM UMWBESO LHRRNDC
XZEYOIU HPYQBNJ INVJSUG LURMZTF XFIDWEC DARYTDQ YGWXUJA YDNLMOV RYFCXPZ IMTLRWE
ZXXANMI XLWFMUU CGZQEEK SNUIKJK CUDKHLL NNBGOTT DVDNSEB ZYHLQIV CVZZUTS LRCEOKN
YYAGYBB MIGUFDN EEKZELM TAOFXAW OBICVSS XCTSFQS ZHMCEYZ HISKYAE HFMIRTH BSLTZRB
NUFEKHE JJKFWXE BIXUZXY YDMKQYJ LQEOMLH VXLJGJT NPYWYZD DTJZTHO EZMVBHX VCGLBLQ
NUIAAKD GUADTGT OVFCQYD WADAQDO QUYMISV VRCYNIY OEOPVHZ PQHHPLX MLUQYHR HTLVPIC
VWAOCTG QMHVPGB IUWKOER GHPBQFD PAOHZRB QRQKWLV XCTRCER TZJGFVA IUPIXLB NAYWANG
DZPLBUD LQEHNOJ IVIJBOT KRTCKMN HOCOUDJ EOYGYHE XPLHQZQ KZEZSAG VTXSQGF WTHSTHX
KLHDBJV LACKBYT RLHGNVJ PHGOEBM NCFPRWP MQYVMNU BVUEODC UWZFTBG MEBGGOR EGUCVKT
BXDKNGE ESXUTOE GRXUIJP SHRTZIA KVBXSCZ AOQKHVK JFLWLIK IFTTZHU CQPHZSO UZBBZRO
HAEJUPM ATIBYFN VGEINCP NGQTBCI OYVAHRP EZNDJNL USYOOIO MYWWSDI KUJVGRA LNUPNIK
CIVCGJG IVVCZWH UOFTUAA MQSZKHD GHEBGTI YYECUGE CSRCMNY TZVCXRR USFDOVO SERLHVW
IHKHIEH OKQMYZK QLNKOHI IWSQIMU YYOAPBE RYDFFLP UEWWJRW KJRURTA FIUGSIY ORXWKZN
NKVRVOF IDDSNZS HHRWUTN UVRMHJM DSYXLYL HDLOIYN ZMUMSZL IRJDDRH HQUJCPG BDEHEBO
NLUVESW FFYQCNJ CMIBUGJ CVDWQXV KFXHSEO PNSDIAW LBKAHEY WTHYMCM NDVZVRB IKGGXIM
```

Figure 15.1: An unsorted list of randomly generated strings

```
AEPFYZJ CVDWQXV FDPGDOT HPYQBNJ JVVQZNO LQEOMLH NNBGOTT PRYFHGQ ULHXGYM XCTRCER
AOQKHVK CVZZUTS FFYQCNJ HQUJCPG JXUDAOD LRCEOKN NPYWYZD PVVLOWE UMWBESO XCTSFQS
ATIBYFN CZSUOJV FILKCDS HTLVPIC JYQDPMA LURMZTF NUFEKHE QGILGES UOFTUAA XFIDWEC
BAHJURT DARYTDQ FIUGSIY IDDSNZS KFXHSEO MEBGGOR NUIAAKD QLNKOHI USFDOVO XLWFMUU
BAPOGRC DOHHMRF FRTADUA IFTTZHU KJRURTA MHMYZDF OBICVSS QMHVPGB USYOOIO XPLHQZQ
BBXLXFH DOMYEPU FWKJHDA IHKHIEH KLHDBJV MIGUFDN OEOPVHZ QRQKWLV UVRMHJM XUFVQCY
BDEHEBO DSYXLYL FYPPOYK IKGGXIM KLMGEAS MLUQYHR OKQMYZK QUYMISV UWZFTBG XUJBVZX
BIXUZXY DTJZTHO GHEBGTI IMTLRWE KRTCKMN MQSZKHD ORXWKZN RLHGNVJ UZBBZRO XZEYOIU
BQGKLTF DTYNNWW GHPBQFD INVJSUG KUJVGRA MQYVMNU OTLOSQF RYDFFLP VCGLBLQ YDMKQYJ
BSLTZRB DVDNSEB GQSAEJV IRJDDRH KVBXSCZ MUMDOHU OVFCQYD RYFCXPZ VENGGOX YDNLMOV
BVUEODC DXNNSVV GRXUIJP IRZBLHQ KZEZSAG MYWWSDI OYVAHRP SERLHVW VGEINCP YGWXUJA
BXDKNGE DZPLBUD GUADTGT IUPIXLB LACKBYT NAYWANG OZSMLLX SHRTZIA VHHZBNZ YPGTKAQ
CAMRCFD EEKZELM GUTKDBW IUWKOER LAHAYSV NCFPRWP PAOHZRB SLFJYHM VRCYNIY YYAGYBB
CGZQEEK EGUCVKT HAEJUPM IVIJBOT LBKAHEY NDSKLSF PBGGPZP SNUIKJK VTXSQGF YYECUGE
CIVCGJG EOYGYHE HBUCPXH IVVCZWH LHRRNDC NDVZVRB PBHUOIH TAOFXAW VWAOCTG YYOAPBE
CJXTBIE ESXUTOE HDLOIYN IWSQIMU LIQEBIO NGQTBCI PHGOEBM TOXEISL VXLJGJT ZFMRZHS
CMIBUGJ EXAEMQI HFMIRTH JCJUJEQ LKRXFAC NIGHFDT PLXELZC TQHRPSB WADAQDO ZHMCEYZ
CQPHZSO EXSJSXM HHRWUTN JFLWLIK LMTVZUQ NKVRVOF PNSDIAW TZJGFVA WKJSFYO ZMUMSZL
CSRCMNY EZMVBHX HISKYAE JJKFWXE LNUPNIK NKYQEDM PQAFKEO TZVCXRR WTHSTHX ZXXANMI
CUDKHLL EZNDJNL HOCOUDJ JLMAUVI LQEHNOJ NLUVESW PQHHPLX UEWWJRW WTHYMCM ZYHLQIV
```

Figure 15.2: The sorted list

You will find the listing for the *ShowOff* program in Figure 15.3. The main program section makes four procedure calls in sequence:

- The *FillList* procedure creates the list of 200 randomly generated strings.

- The *PrintList* procedure displays the unsorted list on the screen.

- The *QuickSort* procedure sorts the list.

- A second call to *PrintList* displays the sorted list on the screen.

```
PROGRAM ShowOff;

  { The ShowOff program is a simple test program designed to
    demonstrate the speed of the QuickSort procedure. }

USES RandUnit;

CONST
  listLength = 200;

TYPE
  arrayType = ARRAY [1..listLength] OF STRING[7];

VAR
  nameList: arrayType;
  continue: STRING;


PROCEDURE PrintList;

  { The PrintList procedure displays the table of 200
    randomly generated strings, both before and after
    the sort. }

  VAR
    i,
    j: BYTE;

  BEGIN    { PrinList }

    FOR i := 1 TO 20 DO
      FOR j := 1 TO 10 DO
        BEGIN
          WRITE (nameList [(j - 1) * 20 + i], ' ')
        END

  END;     { PrintList }


PROCEDURE FillList;

  { The FillList procedure generates the list itself,
    making 200 calls to the RandStr function to produce
    the string elements. }
```

Figure 15.3: The listing of the *ShowOff* program, containing the *QuickSort* procedure

```
    VAR
      i: BYTE;

    BEGIN    { FillList }

      FOR i := 1 TO listLength DO
        nameList [i] := RandStr(7)

PROCEDURE QuickSort (VAR stringList:   arrayType;
                         firstElement,
                         lastElement:  INTEGER);

  { The QuickSort procedure is a recursive sort. It
    makes repeated calls to DivideList to separate
    sections of the list into two parts. Following each
    call to DivideList, QuickSort calls itself twice
    to sort the two parts of the list. }

  VAR
    newFirst,
    newLast:  INTEGER;

    PROCEDURE DivideList (VAR workList: arrayType;
                          VAR begin1,
                              final1:   INTEGER;
                              begin2,
                              final2:   INTEGER);

      { The DivideList procedure divides the current portion
        of the list into two parts and swaps pairs of elements
        between the two parts when they are found to be out
        of order. }

      VAR
        reference,
        tempStr:   STRING[7];

      BEGIN    { DivideList }

        reference := workList [(begin2 + final2) DIV 2];
        begin1 := begin2;
        final1 := final2;

        WHILE begin1 < final1 DO
          BEGIN
            WHILE workList [begin1] < reference DO
              INC (begin1);
            WHILE reference < workList [final1] DO
              DEC (final1);

            IF begin1 <= final1 THEN
              BEGIN
                tempStr             := workList [begin1];
                workList [begin1] := workList [final1];
                workList [final1] := tempStr;
                INC (begin1);
                DEC (final1)
              END
          END
      END;    { DivideList }
```

Figure 15.3: The listing of the *ShowOff* program, containing the *QuickSort* procedure (continued)

```
      BEGIN    { QuickSort }

        IF firstElement < lastElement THEN

          BEGIN
            DivideList (stringList, newFirst, newLast,
                        firstElement, lastElement);
            QuickSort (stringList, firstElement, newLast);
            QuickSort (stringList, newFirst, lastElement)
          END

      END;    { QuickSort }

BEGIN    { ShowOff }

  { Set the seed of the random-number generator. }

  RANDOMIZE;

  { Set up the array of strings, display it on the
    screen, and then alphabetize the list. }

  FillList;
  PrintList;
  QuickSort (nameList, 1, listLength);

  WRITELN; WRITELN;
  WRITE ('Press <Enter> to see the sorted list.');
  READLN (continue);
  WRITELN; WRITELN;

  { Display the sorted list. }

  PrintList;
  WRITELN; WRITELN

END.    { ShowOff }
```

Figure 15.3: The listing of the *ShowOff* program, containing the *QuickSort* procedure (continued)

The main focus of our attention in this chapter is the *QuickSort* procedure itself, along with a local routine named *DivideList*. We'll discuss these two procedures in the next section.

Recursion in the *QuickSort* Procedure

The *ShowOff* program stores its list of random strings in a one-dimensional array called *nameList*. The named constant *listLength* contains the length of the list, 200. Given these two identifiers, a call to the *QuickSort* procedure appears as follows:

QuickSort (nameList, 1, listLength%)

QuickSort receives these three arguments in the parameters *stringList*, *firstElement*, and *lastElement*, respectively:

```
PROCEDURE QuickSort (VAR stringList:    arrayType;
                         firstElement,
                         lastElement: INTEGER);
```

The *QuickSort* procedure consists of three procedure calls inside a decision structure. The calls are made only if *firstElement* is less than *lastElement:*

```
IF firstElement < lastElement THEN
```

The first procedure call is to *DivideList*. As its name implies, this procedure divides the list it receives into two sections:

```
DivideList (stringList, newFirst, newLast,
            firstElement, lastElement);
```

While dividing the list in two, this procedure also makes sure that all elements in the second part of the list are alphabetically "greater than" the elements in the first part of the list. In other words, *DivideList* rearranges any pairs of elements that do not conform to this condition.

When its task is complete, *DivideList* returns two integer values to *QuickSort* via VAR parameters: *newFirst*, the beginning element of the second part of the list; and *newLast*, the final element of the first part of the list. *QuickSort* uses these two values in two subsequent recursive calls. The following call submits the first half of the divided list for further sorting:

```
QuickSort (stringList, firstElement, newLast);
```

The next call works on the second half:

```
QuickSort (stringList, newFirst, lastElement)
```

Each recursive call starts the entire process over again. The designated portion of the list is sent to *DivideList*, to be subdivided yet again and to have its elements rearranged appropriately. Then the first and second portions of the new list are each dealt with separately in yet another level of recursive calls.

This recursive process continues as the target portions of the list become smaller and smaller. Finally, the list portions consist of pairs of adjacent elements; when these pairs have been arranged correctly, the sorting process is complete. (Thanks to the condition *firstElement < lastElement*, the *QuickSort* procedure stops making recursive calls when it receives lists consisting of single elements.)

Before ending our discussion of this sorting algorithm, let's look briefly at how the *DivideList* routine works. This procedure has five parameters, as follows:

```
PROCEDURE DivideList (VAR workList: arrayType;
                      VAR begin1,
                          final1:    INTEGER;
                          begin2,
                          final2:    INTEGER);
```

The variables *begin2* and *final2* represent the actual first and last elements of the current *workList*. *DivideList* ultimately determines beginning and ending markers for further subdividing this list and uses *begin1* and *final1* to return these markers back to the *QuickSort* routine.

DivideList begins by finding the string element located in the approximate middle of the list it receives. This element is stored in the variable *reference:*

```
reference : = workList [(begin2 + final2) DIV 2];
```

The markers *begin1* and *final1* start out with the same values as *begin2* and *final2:*

```
begin1% = begin2%
final1% = final2%
```

Then, inside a WHILE loop, the routine works forward from the beginning of the list and backward from the end, checking to see if any elements are located in the wrong section of the list. Two nested WHILE loops compare each element with the middle string, *reference:*

```
WHILE workList [begin1] < reference DO
   INC (begin1);
WHILE reference < workList [final1] DO
   DEC (final1);
```

Any elements that are already located in the correct section are left alone. But any time two distant elements are found to be out of order, they are exchanged:

```
tempStr           : = workList [begin1];
workList [begin1] : = workList [final1];
workList [final1]  : = tempStr;
```

Meanwhile, the routine continually increments the value of *begin1* and decrements the value of *final1:*

```
INC (begin1);
DEC (final1)
```

The process of comparing and exchanging continues until *begin1* is no longer smaller than *final1*, as expressed in the condition of the outer loop:

```
WHILE begin1 < final1 DO
```

When the iterations of this outer loop finally stop, the new values of *begin1* and *final1* are sent back to *QuickSort* as the markers for the next level of recursive calls.

To get some experience with the *QuickSort* routine, you might want to try incorporating it into the various modules of the billable-hours application, replacing the Shell-sort routine.

Another interesting exercise is to use Turbo Pascal's *Trace into* single-step debugging mode to step through part of the performance of the *QuickSort* routine. Establish the four marker variables— *begin1, begin2, final1*, and *final2*—as watch variables, and notice how their values change during a given call to the *DivideList* procedure.

Summary

Recursion is yet another technique that you can add to your programming repertory in Turbo Pascal. Recursion is the process by which a routine makes calls to itself to accomplish a job. Turbo Pascal allows recursion in both procedures and functions.

The recursive technique can prove difficult to conceptualize. However, when you translate a recursive algorithm into actual code, the resulting program often appears simpler and shorter than an equivalent nonrecursive routine. For example, if you compare the quick-sort routine with the Shell sort, you will see that the former is logically and structurally more straightforward than the latter.

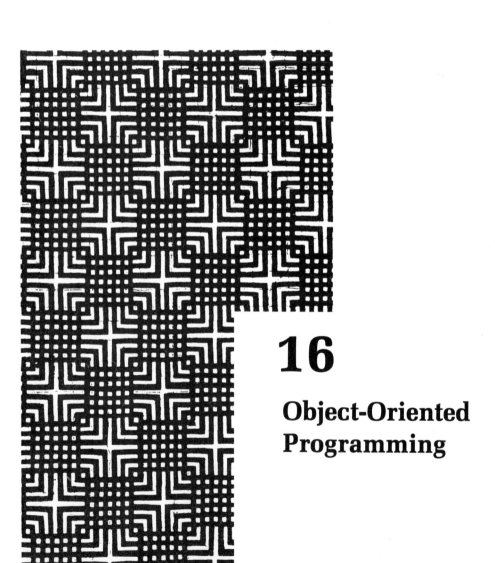

C H A P T E R

16

Object-Oriented Programming

Version 5.5 of Turbo Pascal introduces a new way of thinking about and structuring computer programs: *object-oriented programming*. With the tools that Turbo Pascal offers for this powerful approach, you can create better structured, more flexible, and easier-to-modify programs in less time. You don't have to use Turbo Pascal's object-oriented features if you don't want to (and for simple programs, they're not always appropriate), but they are there when you need them.

Object-oriented programming originally came out of ideas in the Simula programming language of the 1960s. Most of the research work that developed the object-oriented approach, however, was done at Xerox Corp.'s Palo Alto Research Center (PARC) in a 10 year project that developed Smalltalk, the first truly object-oriented programming language. Xerox PARC is perhaps most famous for developing the "Xerox Star" microcomputer and its icon-based screen interface, which provided the inspiration for the Apple Macintosh. The difficulty of creating such a screen interface, and making it work exactly the same from one application program to another, was a key motivation in the development of object-oriented programming techniques.

It's important to realize, however, that object-oriented programming has no necessary connection with icon-based screen displays. A widespread misconception on this point has discouraged many people, who don't work with icon-based programs, from learning about OOP techniques. Object-oriented programming is used to create icon-based screen interfaces because it's a highly efficient approach—and the same efficiency can be put to work in other kinds of applications.

Turbo Pascal 5.5 traces its object-oriented heritage from Xerox PARC's original work on Smalltalk through Apple's Object Pascal and AT&T's C++ programming languages. It takes the best features of each, prunes out what is redundant or of questionable value, and builds them into standard Turbo Pascal as added features that you can use or ignore as you wish.

Consider the following problems:

- You have a customer billing system and want to create several different customer types. They are all basically the same, but each differs from the others in some minor detail.

- You are creating a program with on-screen windows and menus. Although there are several different types of each, you want them all to perform certain operations in the same ways.

- You create a library of Turbo Pascal routines and distribute a compiled version, but want users to be able to extend and modify your routines without having the source code.

Object-oriented programming has a clean, logical solution to all of these problems. In the customer billing system, it lets you create a single *parent* customer type that contains basic customer characteristics such as name, address, and account number. Based on this parent type, you can then create as many specialized customer types as you need—*without* repeating any code from the parent type or using complex CASE statements. Each specialized type—called a *child* of the parent type—*inherits* all the features of the parent type and can add its own new features. It can even cancel out parent features that don't apply to it. Extending the parent-child metaphor, a type that is derived from an earlier type is called its *descendant*, while the earlier type, likewise, is referred to as the descendant type's *ancestor*.

Because these types—called *objects*—inherit the characteristics of their ancestor types, you can extend the capabilities of already compiled units of library routines, even if you don't have the source code. You simply create descendant objects of already existing object types, and then add new features or cancel inherited features as needed. Procedures designed to work on ancestor objects will work on their descendant objects as well.

But objects are more than just a new, highly customizable data type. They also contain their own *methods* (internal procedures and functions) that tell them how to behave in response to various program commands. If you have five customer types, each with its own billing procedure, you can send a single command *SendBill* to any of them, and it will carry out the correct billing procedure. This ability of objects to respond to the same command in different ways is called *polymorphism*, and with inheritance, is one of the most powerful tools in the object-oriented arsenal.

Turbo Pascal Objects

Object-oriented programming introduces several new concepts:

- *Objects*, which look similar to records
- *Object types*, which define particular objects and their powers
- *Encapsulation*, which binds data together inside an object with the methods that process it
- *Inheritance*, by which the characteristics of an object type are passed along to its descendant object types
- *Polymorphism*, the ability of different objects to respond in their own unique ways to the same program command
- *Extensibility of code*, by which already compiled units can be used as a basis for creating and using new objects that were unknown at compile time

Appropriately enough, the fundamental concept in object-oriented programming is that of an *object*. An object is very much like a Pascal record with a lot of new powers built right in. For example, you could (as in Chapter 6) create a Pascal customer record as follows:

```
TYPE
  addressRecord = RECORD
    name:        STRING[30];
    phone:       STRING[20];
```

```
refNo:        BYTE;
HeadOffice:   BOOLEAN;

street:       STRING[30];
city:         STRING[20];

CASE usa:     BOOLEAN OF
   TRUE:
     (state:  STRING[2];
      zip:    STRING[5]);
   FALSE:
     (otherLoc,
      country: STRING[15]);
END;
```

This works fine, but there are two problems. First, suppose you want to create a new record type that is similar to *addressRecord* but differs in some minor ways. You can either copy the original source code into your new record type and modify it, or you can code the original record type again with a more complicated CASE statement. Either way, your program is more complex, harder to modify, and takes longer to write.

The other problem is that this is a messy way of doing things. Using the CASE field to determine if the client is American or foreign is a good solution in the context of traditional Pascal programming, but with object-oriented Turbo Pascal, it can be done better. Let's see how this would be done with Turbo Pascal's new *object* type instead of the traditional record type.

Creating Objects and Object Types

An object has data fields just like a record and is declared in the same way; its methods are declared after the data fields. Let's simplify the *addressRecord* example and define an object type (called a "class" in Smalltalk and Object Pascal):

```
TYPE
  address = OBJECT
    name:   STRING[20];
    street: STRING[20]
```

```
    city:      STRING[10];
    balance:   REAL;
    FUNCTION PaidUp (acctBal: REAL): BOOLEAN
END;
```

Of course, this does not create an object, any more than declaring a record type creates any records. To create an object, you declare a variable of the particular object type:

```
VAR
  cust : address;
```

You can refer to an object's fields and methods in the same way as you refer to those in a record, by prefacing the field or method name with the name of the object:

```
cust.name : = 'Frank Borland';
cust.paidUp : = TRUE;
```

You can also use Pascal's WITH notation, just as you would with a record:

```
WITH cust DO
  BEGIN
    name : = 'Antony Hoare';
    paidUp : = TRUE
  END;
```

Our *address* object type is pretty Spartan, of course, but *address* is only an *abstract* type that contains fields and methods which are shared by all the different object types we want to create. An abstract object type serves merely as a template for the creation of descendant object types with specialized features. Now, we can create some descendant types:

```
USAaddress = OBJECT (address)
  state:   STRING[2];
  zip:     STRING[5];
  PROCEDURE SendBill
END;

IntlAddress = OBJECT (address)
  otherLoc,
```

```
  country:    STRING[15];
  PROCEDURE SendBill
END;
```

There are several things to notice here. First, when we declared the descendant object types, we put the name of their parent type, *address*, in parentheses after the new reserved word OBJECT. This tells Turbo Pascal that the new types are children of the already created object type. They will automatically inherit all of *address*'s data fields and methods.

Because of this, *address*'s fields and methods do not need to be declared again when we define descendant object types. Instead, we can simply add in the features that are special for each child type. U.S. customers, for example, have slightly different address information and billing procedures from those of overseas customers. Therefore, *USAaddress* and *IntlAddress* have different added data fields and *SendBill* procedures.

But suppose that you need to create a new type of American customer object with its own *SendBill* method? For example, orders from within the same state are usually subject to sales tax, while out-of-state purchases are not. If the *SendBill* method in *USAaddress* does not add in sales tax to the amount due, then you would want to create a descendant of *USAaddress* but define a new *SendBill* method. And it's really as simple as that:

```
InStateAddr = OBJECT (USAaddress)
  PROCEDURE SendBill
END;
```

InStateAddr is a descendant object type of *USAaddress*, and as such inherits all of *USAaddress*'s data fields and methods. However, *InStateAddr* also declares its own *SendBill* method, which *overrides* any methods that are inherited from parent object types. This means that when you tell an object of type *InStateAddr* to "SendBill," it carries out its own version of the procedure—not the one it inherits from *USAaddress*.

Thus, to override an inherited method in a Turbo Pascal object, you simply declare a new method with the same name as the inherited method. When a method call is made to a particular object, it first looks inside its own object type to see if the method is defined there. If the method isn't there, it then looks for the method in its parent object type, then in its grandparent, all the way up to the end of the line.

One important point: *only methods can be overridden; data fields cannot.* If you define an ancestor object type with a certain set of data fields, those are carried forward to *all* of that object type's descendants. This is because any descendant of an object type is type-compatible with the ancestor type. If a procedure or function takes an object of a certain type as a parameter, then the object it receives can also be any descendant of that object type. If data fields could be overridden, this would not be possible.

We've been declaring *SendBill* all over the place, but so far haven't said anything about where to spell out its details. While the declaration of the object type itself is made in the TYPE section of the program, each object type's methods are declared in the procedures and functions section later on. An example might be:

```
TYPE
  ...
  InStateAddr = OBJECT (USAaddress)
    PROCEDURE SendBill
  END;
  ...
  ...

PROCEDURE InStateAddr.SendBill;
  VAR ...
  BEGIN
  ...
  END;
```

When you're defining the object type itself in the TYPE section, you simply give the name, formal parameters, and type (for functions) of each method, and give the details in a separate procedure or function declaration. The declaration, of course, must begin with the name of the object, a period, and then the name of the procedure or function.

If you're creating object types in a Turbo Pascal unit rather than in a program, you declare the object type in the INTERFACE section of the unit and the details of the object's methods in the IMPLEMEN-TATION section. You can also create local objects that are "private" to the unit by putting both their TYPE declaration and their details in the IMPLEMENTATION section.

Objects and Encapsulation

Almost all introductory programming courses now sing the praises of "information hiding" and modular program design. All this really means is that how one module in a program interacts with the rest of the program should not depend on any internal details of the module. That way, you can make changes inside a program module without having to change anything else in the program. That makes the program easier to understand and maintain.

Objects are a logical extension of this principle. Although Turbo Pascal permits you to access an object's fields directly (as discussed above), it's a bad programming practice because it violates the principles of information hiding and modularity. Instead, you should give the object type enough internal methods to do whatever is needed, and access an object's data fields by sending commands to activate its methods. This keeps the internal details of how the object is implemented from becoming entangled with the rest of your program.

The *Clibil_1* Program

Let's see how these principles would apply in a simplified example program. The unit *Customer*, listed in Figure 16.1, creates three object types that are used by the program *CliBil_1* (listed in Figure 16.2):

- *Cust*, an abstract object type
- *AmerCust*, which represents U.S. customers
- *IntlCust*, which represents non-U.S. customers

However, the author of the *CliBil_1* program found that he needed a new object type to represent in-state customers, who are required to

```
Unit Customer;
   (* Creates customer object types *)



INTERFACE

USES PRINTER, CRT, DOS;

TYPE

   Cust = OBJECT
            name:       STRING[20];
            street:     STRING[20];
            city:       STRING[20];
            balanceDue:  REAL;
            FUNCTION PaidUp:BOOLEAN;
   END;

   AmerCust = OBJECT (Cust)
            state:      STRING[2];
            zip:        STRING[5];
            PROCEDURE PrintBill;
            PROCEDURE SendBill
   END;

   IntlCust = OBJECT (Cust)
            otherLoc:   STRING[25];
            country:    STRING[15];
            PROCEDURE PrintBill;
            PROCEDURE SendBill
    END;



IMPLEMENTATION

{ -------------------------- }
{ Cust methods              }
{ -------------------------- }

FUNCTION Cust.PaidUp : BOOLEAN;

   BEGIN
      IF balanceDue = 0 THEN
         PaidUp := TRUE
      ELSE
         PaidUp := FALSE
   END;

{ -------------------------- }
{ AmerCust methods          }
{ -------------------------- }

PROCEDURE AmerCust.PrintBill;

   CONST
      formFeed = #12;
      months : ARRAY[1..12] OF STRING[3] =
            ('Jan', 'Feb', 'Mar', 'Apr', 'May', 'Jun',
             'Jul', 'Aug', 'Sep', 'Oct', 'Nov', 'Dec');

   VAR
      y, m, d, dow : WORD;
```

Figure 16.1: The Listing of the *Customer* unit

```
    BEGIN    { Procedure PrintBill }
      GetDate(y, m, d, dow);
      WRITELN(lst, '                         DINGMAN BROTHERS FOUNDRIES');
      WRITELN(lst, '                            - Invoice -        ');
      WRITELN(lst, '                         -------------------------');
      WRITELN(lst); WRITELN(lst);
      WRITELN(lst, 'TO: ', name);
      WRITELN(lst, '     ', street);
      WRITELN(lst, '     ', city, ', ', state, ' ', zip);
      WRITELN(lst); WRITELN(lst);
      WRITELN(lst, 'Date: ', months[m], ' ', d, ', ', y);
      WRITELN(lst);
      WRITELN(lst, 'Dear Customer: ');
      WRITELN(lst);
      WRITELN(lst, 'As of the date of this invoice, your current');
      WRITELN(lst, 'balance due is $', balanceDue:3:2, '.');
      WRITELN(lst);
      WRITELN(lst, 'The Dingman Brothers appreciate your business.');
      WRITELN(lst, 'Please pay within 30 days unless you have made');
      WRITELN(lst, 'other arrangements with us.');
      WRITELN(lst);
      WRITELN(lst, 'Sincerely,');
      WRITELN(lst);
      WRITELN(lst, 'THE DINGMAN BROTHERS');
      WRITELN(lst, formFeed):
    END;                       { Procedure PrintBill }




PROCEDURE AmerCust.SendBill;

    VAR
       Continue      : BOOLEAN;
       yesNo,
       SendToPrinter : CHAR;

    BEGIN                          { Procedure SendBill }
       Continue := TRUE;
       WHILE continue = TRUE DO
       BEGIN
          CLRSCR;
          WRITELN('Send bill to a customer in the United States.');

          WRITE('Enter the customer''s name: ');
          READLN(name);
          WRITE('Street address: ');
          READLN(street);
          WRITE('City: ');
          READLN(city);

          WRITE('State: ');
          READLN(state);
          WRITE('Zip code: ');
          READLN(zip);

          WRITE('Balance due: ');
          READLN(balanceDue);

          IF paidUp = TRUE THEN
             BEGIN
                WRITELN('This customer has a zero balance.');
                WRITELN('Do not send out an invoice.')
             END;
```

Figure 16.1: The Listing of the *Customer* unit (Continued)

```
            WRITELN('Send the bill to the printer? (Y/N): ');
            READLN(SendToPrinter);

            IF (SendToPrinter = 'Y') OR (SendToPrinter = 'y') THEN
              PrintBill;
            WRITELN;
            WRITELN('Do you wish to continue? (Y/N): ');
            READLN(yesNo);
            IF (yesNo = 'N') OR (yesNo = 'n') THEN
              continue := FALSE
        END
    END;                        { Procedure SendBill }




{ ------------------------- }
{ IntlCust Methods          }
{ ------------------------- }

PROCEDURE IntlCust.PrintBill;

    CONST
        formFeed = #12;
        months : ARRAY[1..12] OF STRING[3] =
              ('Jan', 'Feb', 'Mar', 'Apr', 'May', 'Jun',
               'Jul', 'Aug', 'Sep', 'Oct', 'Nov', 'Dec');

    VAR
        y, m, d, dow : WORD;

    BEGIN    { Procedure PrintBill }
        GetDate(y, m, d, dow);
        WRITELN(lst, '                    DINGMAN BROTHERS FOUNDRIES');
        WRITELN(lst, '                         - Invoice -        ');
        WRITELN(lst, '                    -------------------------');
        WRITELN(lst); WRITELN(lst);
        WRITELN(lst, 'TO: ', name);
        WRITELN(lst, '    ', street);
        WRITELN(lst, '    ', city, ', ', otherLoc, ' ', country);
        WRITELN(lst); WRITELN(lst);
        WRITELN(lst, 'Date: ', months[m], ' ', d, ', ', y);
        WRITELN(lst);
        WRITELN(lst, 'Dear Customer: ');
        WRITELN(lst);
        WRITELN(lst, 'As of the date of this invoice, your current');
        WRITELN(lst, 'balance due is $', balanceDue:3:2, '.');
        WRITELN(lst);
        WRITELN(lst, 'The Dingman Brothers appreciate your business.');
        WRITELN(lst, 'Please pay within 30 days unless you have made');
        WRITELN(lst, 'other arrangements with us.');
        WRITELN(lst);
        WRITELN(lst, 'Sincerely,');
        WRITELN(lst);
        WRITELN(lst, 'THE DINGMAN BROTHERS');
        WRITELN(lst, formFeed);
    END;                          { Procedure PrintBill }




PROCEDURE IntlCust.SendBill;
```

Figure 16.1: The Listing of the *Customer* unit (Continued)

```
    VAR
        Continue     : BOOLEAN;
        yesNo,
        SendToPrinter : CHAR;


BEGIN                              { Procedure SendBill }
    Continue := TRUE;
    WHILE continue = TRUE DO
        BEGIN
            CLRSCR;
            WRITELN('Send bill to a customer outside the United States.');

            WRITE('Enter the customer''s name: ');
            READLN(name);
            WRITE('Street address: ');
            READLN(street);
            WRITE('City: ');
            READLN(city);

            WRITE('Province and mail code: ');
            READLN(otherLoc);
            WRITE('Country: ');
            READLN(country);

            WRITE('Balance due: ');
            READLN(balanceDue);

            IF paidUp = TRUE THEN
                BEGIN
                    WRITELN('This customer has a zero balance.');
                    WRITELN('Do not send out an invoice.')
                END;

            WRITELN('Send the bill to the printer? (Y/N): ');
            READLN(SendToPrinter);

            IF (SendToPrinter = 'Y') OR (SendToPrinter = 'y') THEN
                PrintBill;
            WRITELN;
            WRITE('Do you wish to continue? (Y/N): ');
            READLN(yesNo);
            IF (yesNo = 'N') OR (yesNo = 'n') THEN
                continue := FALSE
        END
    END;                           { Procedure SendBill }


END.    { Unit Customer }
```

Figure 16.1: The Listing of the *Customer* unit (Continued)

pay sales tax on their purchases. The amount due is calculated by the *PrintBill* method, which in turn is called by another method, *SendBill* (separating the two functions for program modularity).

Here, however, it gets a little sticky. You might think that if the only change is in the *PrintBill* method, then only the *PrintBill* method needs to be overridden with a new method declaration. However, consider what

```
      { Shows how a descendant object is created and polymorphism is
      achieved -- less efficiently -- without the use of virtual methods. }


    PROGRAM CliBil_1;

    USES customer, CRT, DOS, PRINTER;


    TYPE
       StateCust = OBJECT (AmerCust)
                 PROCEDURE PrintBill;
                 PROCEDURE SendBill
          END;

    VAR
       USCust  : AmerCust;
       FRCust  : IntlCust;
       STCust  : StateCust;
       yesNo,
       InState : CHAR;



    PROCEDURE StateCust.PrintBill;

       CONST
          formFeed = #12;
          months : ARRAY[1..12] of STRING[3] =
                 ('Jan', 'Feb', 'Mar', 'Apr', 'May', 'Jun',
                  'Jul', 'Aug', 'Sep', 'Oct', 'Nov', 'Dec');
          SalesTax = 0.05;

       VAR
          y, m, d, dow : WORD;
          totalBalance : REAL;

       BEGIN    { Procedure PrintBill }
          totalBalance := BalanceDue + (BalanceDue * SalesTax);
          GetDate(y, m, d, dow);
          WRITELN(1st, '                        DINGMAN BROTHERS FOUNDRIES');
          WRITELN(1st, '                            - Invoice -      ');
          WRITELN(1st, '                        -------------------------');
          WRITELN(1st); WRITELN(1st);
          WRITELN(1st, 'TO: ', name);
          WRITELN(1st, '      ', street);
          WRITELN(1st, '      ', city, ', ', state, ' ', zip);
          WRITELN(1st); WRITELN(1st);
          WRITELN(1st, 'Date: ', months[m], ' ', d, ', ', y);
          WRITELN(1st);
          WRITELN(1st, 'Dear Customer: ');
          WRITELN(1st);
          WRITELN(1st, 'As of the date of this invoice, your current');
          WRITELN(1st, 'balance due is $', totalBalance:3:2, '.');
          WRITELN(1st);
          WRITELN(1st, 'The Dingman Brothers apprcciate your business.');
          WRITELN(1st, 'Please pay within 30 days unless you have made');
          WRITELN(1st, 'other arrangements with us.');
          WRITELN(1st);
          WRITELN(1st, 'Sincerely,');
          WRITELN(1st);
          WRITELN(1st, 'THE DINGMAN BROTHERS');
          WRITELN(1st, formFeed);             { Procedure PrintBill }
       END;
```

Figure 16.2: The listing of the *Clibil_1* program

```
PROCEDURE StateCust.SendBill;

    VAR
        Continue     : BOOLEAN;
        yesNo,
        SendToPrinter : CHAR;

    BEGIN                          { Procedure SendBill }
        Continue := TRUE;
        WHILE continue = TRUE DO
        BEGIN
            CLRSCR;
            WRITELN('Send bill to a customer in the United States.');

            WRITE('Enter the customer''s name: ');
            READLN(name);
            WRITE('Street address: ');
            READLN(street);
            WRITE('City: ');
            READLN(city);

            WRITE('State: ');
            READLN(state);
            WRITE('Zip code: ');
            READLN(zip);

            WRITE('Balance due: ');
            READLN(balanceDue);

            IF paidUp = TRUE THEN
                BEGIN
                    WRITELN('This customer has a zero balance.');
                    WRITELN('Do not send out an invoice.')
                END;

            WRITELN('Send the bill to the printer? (Y/N): ');
            READLN(SendToPrinter);

            IF (SendToPrinter = 'Y') OR (SendToPrinter = 'y') THEN
                PrintBill;
            WRITELN;
            WRITELN('Do you wish to continue? (Y/N): ');

            READLN(yesNo);
            IF (yesNo = 'N') OR (yesNo = 'n') THEN
                continue := FALSE
        END
    END;                            { Procedure SendBill }




BEGIN
    CLRSCR;
    WRITELN('Do you want to send a bill to a customer in');
    WRITE('the United States? (Y/N): ');
    READLN(yesNo);
```

Figure 16.2: The listing of the *Clibil_1* program (Continued)

```
        IF (yesNo = 'Y') OR (yesNo = 'y') THEN
            BEGIN
                WRITE('Is this an in-state customer? (Y/N): ');
                READLN(InState);
                IF (InState = 'Y') OR (InState = 'y') THEN
                    STCust.SendBill
                ELSE
                    USCust.SendBill
            END
        ELSE
            FRCust.Sendbill
    END.
```

Figure 16.2: The listing of the *Clibil_1* program (Continued)

will happen when you send the command *SendBill* to a *StateCust* object in which only the *PrintBill* method has been overridden.

First, Turbo Pascal looks inside the *StateCust* object type and tries to find the *SendBill* method there. Since it isn't there, Turbo Pascal moves up to *StateCust*'s parent object type, *AmerCust*, to look there for the *SendBill* method. It finds the method there, and executes it.

So far, so good? Hardly. Even though the wording of the *SendBill* procedure doesn't need to change from *AmerCust* to *StateCust*, the *copy* of *SendBill* that's in *AmerCust* will call the nearest copy of *Print-Bill* that it can find. Since the closest copy of *PrintBill* is in the *Amer-Cust* object type, *SendBill* will execute that *PrintBill* method instead of the one in the *StateCust* object type. If you want *SendBill* to call the correct *PrintBill* method, then you must also declare the *SendBill* procedure inside of the *StateCust* object—even though its wording is exactly the same.

Virtual methods provide a way around this problem and are discussed in the next section. Figure 16.2 shows how it works with what we've learned so far.

Virtual Methods and Late Binding

The *CliBil_1* program works fine. However, part of the benefit of object-oriented programming is supposed to be that it reduces the amount of code you have to write. If a method doesn't change at all between a parent object type and its descendants, then it doesn't make sense that you should have to keep redeclaring it at each new level. That kind of redundancy violates the spirit, if not the letter, of object-oriented programming.

Fortunately, there is a simple solution. Let's return to the question of why *SendBill* calls the "closest" copy of *PrintBill*. When the *Customer* unit and the *CliBil_1* program are compiled, each copy of *SendBill* is given the address of any other methods it calls. Since *SendBill* and *Print-Bill* are in the same object type, *SendBill* is *bound* at compile time to one and only one version of *PrintBill*—the one whose address it received. When you run the program and *SendBill* executes, it will always call that *PrintBill* routine—even if *SendBill* is invoked by a descendant object that overrides *PrintBill*.

The problem arises because we have been using "static" methods, i.e., methods that are fully determined when the program is compiled. Object-oriented Turbo Pascal, however, gives us another option: *virtual methods*, which let us postpone any decision on which methods to call until the program is actually running.

Because static method calls are bound to the methods they call at compile time, this process is called *early binding*. With virtual methods, on the other hand, the connection is not made until the program is running and the call is actually sent; therefore, this is called *late binding*.

Turbo Pascal's default setting is for static methods and early binding, which results in slightly faster performance than virtual methods and late binding. To make a method virtual, you simply follow its heading in the object type declaration with the new reserved word VIRTUAL, as in:

```
AmerCust = OBJECT (Cust)
  state:  STRING[2];
  zip:    STRING[5];
  constructor Init;
  PROCEDURE PrintBill; VIRTUAL;
  PROCEDURE SendBill
END;
```

Notice that we have made one other change in the static-method definition of the *AmerCust* object type: we have added a new line with a *constructor* method. The constructor is a special method that initializes an object's data fields and creates a link to the object type's *virtual method table* (VMT) that tells the program at run-time where to find the object's virtual methods. You don't have to do anything yourself to create the link to the VMT; calling a method that is defined with the reserved word CONSTRUCTOR does it automatically.

All objects that include virtual methods must have a constructor routine that is invoked in the program before any of their methods are called. With static methods, the program is told at compile time where to find the methods it needs; but with virtual methods, it doesn't find out until run-time—and it's the constructor's job to tell it. If an object with virtual methods doesn't have a constructor routine, or the constructor routine isn't invoked before its methods are called, your program will head straight into the Twilight Zone.

Apart from creating the virtual method table and initializing the object's data fields, the constructor can do whatever other housekeeping chores are appropriate. The main thing is that it has to be called before you use the object and its methods.

Once a method has been declared as virtual, then it must remain a virtual method in any descendants of the original object type. Hence, they, too, must have the constructor routine.

What happens when we use virtual methods in the *Customer* unit and the *CliBil_1* program, as we have in the *CustomV* unit and *CliBil_2* program of Figures 16.3 and 16.4? The major benefit is that we do not have to repeat the *SendBill* method in the *StateCust* object type, thus eliminating redundant code, saving programmer time, and—let's admit it— creating a more elegant and satisfying program.

Now that *PrintBill* is a virtual method, none of its versions are bound to *SendBill* when the program is compiled. When *SendBill* is called by a *StateCust*-type object, it looks in *StateCust*'s virtual method table for the address of the appropriate *PrintBill* method; if it had been called by an *AmerCust*-type object, it would have looked in *AmerCust*'s VMT. Now, instead of having to use the closest *PrintBill* method, it can find the correct *PrintBill* method—and we don't need to put an extra copy of *SendBill* inside the *StateCust* object type to make it all work. Once again, inheritance is doing its job and making our program easier to write.

The tradeoff between static and virtual methods is that static methods are slightly faster. When a call is made to a virtual method, the

```
Unit CustomV;
   { Creates customer object types with virtual methods }

{$R+}            { Range checking turned on: this makes
                 sure, among other things, that objects
                 with virtual methods have been properly
                 initialized by invoking a constructor. }

INTERFACE

USES PRINTER, CRT, DOS;

TYPE

   Cust = OBJECT
            name:        STRING[20];
            street:      STRING[20];
            city:        STRING[20];
            balanceDue:  REAL;
            PROCEDURE Init;
            FUNCTION PaidUp:BOOLEAN;
   END;

   AmerCust = OBJECT (Cust)
            state:       STRING[2];
            zip:         STRING[5];
            CONSTRUCTOR Init;
            PROCEDURE PrintBill; VIRTUAL;
            PROCEDURE SendBill
   END;

   IntlCust = OBJECT (Cust)
         otherLoc:     STRING[25];
            country:STRING[15];
            PROCEDURE PrintBill;
            PROCEDURE SendBill
   END;


IMPLEMENTATION

{ --------------------------- }
{ Cust methods               }
{ --------------------------- }


PROCEDURE Cust.Init;
   BEGIN
      name   := '                    ';
      street := '                    ';
      city   := '                    ';
      balanceDue := 0.0
   END;


FUNCTION Cust.PaidUp : BOOLEAN;

   BEGIN
      IF balanceDue = 0 THEN
         PaidUp := TRUE
      ELSE
         PaidUp := FALSE
   END;
```

Figure 16.3: The listing of the *CustomV* unit

```
{ -------------------------- }
{ AmerCust methods          }
{ -------------------------- }
CONSTRUCTOR AmerCust.Init;
   BEGIN
      Cust.Init;
      state := '  ';
      zip := '     '
   END;


PROCEDURE AmerCust.PrintBill;

   CONST
      formFeed = #12;
      months : ARRAY[1..12] OF STRING[3] =
             ('Jan', 'Feb', 'Mar', 'Apr', 'May', 'Jun',
              'Jul', 'Aug', 'Sep', 'Oct', 'Nov', 'Dec');

   VAR
      y, m, d, dow : WORD;

   BEGIN    { Procedure PrintBill }
      GetDate(y, m, d, dow);
      WRITELN(lst, '                    DINGMAN BROTHERS FOUNDRIES');
      WRITELN(lst, '                          - Invoice -        ');
      WRITELN(lst, '                    -------------------------');
      WRITELN(lst); WRITELN(lst);
      WRITELN(lst, 'TO: ', name);
      WRITELN(lst, '    ', street);
      WRITELN(lst, '    ', city, ', ', state, ' ', zip);
      WRITELN(lst); WRITELN(lst);
      WRITELN(lst, 'Date: ', months[m], ' ', d, ', ', y);
      WRITELN(lst);
      WRITELN(lst, 'Dear Customer: ');
      WRITELN(lst);
      WRITELN(lst, 'As of the date of this invoice, your current');
      WRITELN(lst, 'balance due is $', balanceDue:3:2, '.');
      WRITELN(lst);
      WRITELN(lst, 'The Dingman Brothers appreciate your business.');
      WRITELN(lst, 'Please pay within 30 days unless you have made');
      WRITELN(lst, 'other arrangements with us.');
      WRITELN(lst);
      WRITELN(lst, 'Sincerely,');
      WRITELN(lst);
      WRITELN(lst, 'THE DINGMAN BROTHERS');
      WRITELN(lst, formFeed);
   END;                        { Procedure PrintBill }




PROCEDURE AmerCust.SendBill;

   VAR
      Continue     : BOOLEAN;
      yesNo,
      SendToPrinter : CHAR;
```

Figure 16.3: The listing of the *CustomV* unit (Continued)

```
BEGIN                           { Procedure SendBill }
  Continue := TRUE;
  WHILE continue = TRUE DO
  BEGIN
    CLRSCR;
    WRITELN('Send bill to a customer in the United States.');

    WRITE('Enter the customer''s name: ');
    READLN(name);
    WRITE('Street address: ');
    READLN(street);
    WRITE('City: ');
    READLN(city);

    WRITE('State: ');
    READLN(state);
    WRITE('Zip code: ');
    READLN(zip);

    WRITE('Balance due: ');
    READLN(balanceDue);

    IF paidUp = TRUE THEN
      BEGIN
        WRITELN('This customer has a zero balance.');
        WRITELN('Do not send out an invoice.')
      END;

    WRITELN('Send the bill to the printer? (Y/N): ');
    READLN(SendToPrinter);

    IF (SendToPrinter = 'Y') OR (SendToPrinter = 'y') THEN
      PrintBill;

        WRITELN;
        WRITELN('Do you wish to continue? (Y/N): ');
        READLN(yesNo);
        IF (yesNo = 'N') OR (yesNo = 'n') THEN
          continue := FALSE
    END
  END;                          { Procedure SendBill }



{ -------------------------- }
{ Int1Cust Methods          }
{ -------------------------- }

PROCEDURE Int1Cust.PrintBill;

  CONST
    formFeed = #12;
    months : ARRAY[1..12] OF STRING[3] =
            ('Jan', 'Feb', 'Mar', 'Apr', 'May', 'Jun',
             'Jul', 'Aug', 'Sep', 'Oct', 'Nov', 'Dec');

  VAR
    y, m, d, dow : WORD;

  BEGIN    { Procedure PrintBill }
    GetDate(y, m, d, dow);
```

Figure 16.3: The listing of the *CustomV* unit (Continued)

```
          WRITELN(lst, '                    DINGMAN BROTHERS FOUNDRIES');
          WRITELN(lst, '                       - Invoice -      ');
          WRITELN(lst, '                       ------------------------');
          WRITELN(lst); WRITELN(lst);
          WRITELN(lst, 'TO: ', name);
          WRITELN(lst, '    ', street);
          WRITELN(lst, '    ', city, ', ', otherLoc, ' ', country);
          WRITELN(lst); WRITELN(lst);
          WRITELN(lst, 'Date: ', months[m], ' ', d, ', ', y);
          WRITELN(lst);
          WRITELN(lst, 'Dear Customer: ');
          WRITELN(lst);
          WRITELN(lst, 'As of the date of this invoice, your current');
          WRITELN(lst, 'balance due is $', balanceDue:3:2, '.');
          WRITELN(lst);
          WRITELN(lst, 'The Dingman Brothers appreciate your business.');
          WRITELN(lst, 'Please pay within 30 days unless you have made');
          WRITELN(lst, 'other arrangements with us.');
          WRITELN(lst);
          WRITELN(lst, 'Sincerely,');
          WRITELN(lst);
          WRITELN(lst, 'THE DINGMAN BROTHERS');
          WRITELN(lst, formFeed);
     END;                          { Procedure PrintBill }

PROCEDURE IntlCust.SendBill;


     VAR
        Continue      : BOOLEAN;
        yesNo,
        SendToPrinter : CHAR;



     BEGIN                         { Procedure SendBill }
        Continue := TRUE;
        WHILE continue = TRUE DO
           BEGIN
              CLRSCR;
              WRITELN('Send bill to a customer outside the United States.');

              WRITE('Enter the customer''s name: ');
              READLN(name);
              WRITE('Street address: ');
              READLN(street);
              WRITE('City: ');
              READLN(city);

              WRITE('Province and mail code: ');
              READLN(otherLoc);
              WRITE('Country: ');
              READLN(country);

              WRITE('Balance due: ');
              READLN(balanceDue);

              IF paidUp = TRUE THEN
                 BEGIN
                    WRITELN('This customer has a zero balance.');
                    WRITELN('Do not send out an invoice.')
                 END;

              WRITELN('Send the bill to the printer? (Y/N): ');
              READLN(SendToPrinter);
```

Figure 16.3: The listing of the *CustomV* unit (Continued)

```
              IF (SendToPrinter = 'Y') OR (SendToPrinter = 'y') THEN
                 PrintBill;
              WRITELN;
              WRITE('Do you wish to continue? (Y/N): ');
              READLN(yesNo);
              IF (yesNo = 'N') OR (yesNo = 'n') THEN
                 continue := FALSE
          END
      END;                              { Procedure SendBill }


  END.   { Unit CustomV }
```

Figure 16.3: The listing of the *CustomV* unit (Continued)

```
  PROGRAM CliBil_2;

  {$R+}              { Range checking turned on }


  USES CRT, CustomV, DOS, PRINTER;


  TYPE
     StateCust = OBJECT (AmerCust)
              CONSTRUCTOR Init;
              PROCEDURE PrintBill; VIRTUAL;
     END;

  VAR
     USCust  : AmerCust;
     FRCust  : IntlCust;
     STCust  : StateCust;
     yesNo,
     InState : CHAR;



  CONSTRUCTOR StateCust.Init;
     BEGIN
        AmerCust.Init;
     END;


  PROCEDURE StateCust.PrintBill;

     CONST
        formFeed = #12;
        months : ARRAY[1..12] OF STRING[3] =
              ('Jan', 'Feb', 'Mar', 'Apr', 'May', 'Jun',
               'Jul', 'Aug', 'Sep', 'Oct', 'Nov', 'Dec');
        SalesTax = 0.05;

     VAR
        y, m, d, dow : WORD;
        totalBalance : REAL;

     BEGIN   { Procedure PrintBill }
        totalBalance := BalanceDue + (BalanceDue * SalesTax);
        GetDate(y, m, d, dow);
        WRITELN(lst, '                         DINGMAN BROTHERS FOUNDRIES');
        WRITELN(lst, '                             - Invoice -        ');
        WRITELN(lst, '                         -------------------------');
```

Figure 16.4: The listing of the *Clibil_2* program

```
        WRITELN(lst); WRITELN(lst);
        WRITELN(lst, 'TO: ', name);
        WRITELN(lst, '    ', street);
        WRITELN(lst, '    ', city, ', ', state, ' ', zip);
        WRITELN(lst); WRITELN(lst);
        WRITELN(lst, 'Date: ', months[m], ' ', d, ', ', y);
        WRITELN(lst);
        WRITELN(lst, 'Dear Customer: ');
        WRITELN(lst);
        WRITELN(lst, 'As of the date of this invoice, your current');
        WRITELN(lst, 'balance due is $', totalBalance:3:2, '.');
        WRITELN(lst);
        WRITELN(lst, 'The Dingman Brothers appreciate your business.');
        WRITELN(lst, 'Please pay within 30 days unless you have made');
        WRITELN(lst, 'other arrangements with us.');
        WRITELN(lst);
        WRITELN(lst, 'Sincerely,');
        WRITELN(lst);
        WRITELN(lst, 'THE DINGMAN BROTHERS');
        WRITELN(lst, formFeed);
    END;                            { Procedure PrintBill }



BEGIN
    STCust.Init;
    USCust.Init;
    FRCust.Init;
    ClrScr;
    WRITELN('Do you want to send a bill to a customer in');
    WRITE('the United States? (Y/N): ');
    READLN(yesNo);
    IF (yesNo = 'Y') OR (yesNo = 'y') THEN
        BEGIN
            WRITE('Is this an in-state customer? (Y/N): ');
            READLN(InState);
            IF (InState = 'Y') OR (InState = 'y') THEN
                STCust.SendBill
            ELSE
                USCust.SendBill
        END
    ELSE
        FRCust.Sendbill
END.
```

Figure 16.4: The listing of the *Clibil_2* program (Continued)

program does not already know where to find it, and has to look up the address in the object type's virtual method table. This doesn't take much time, but it is still a bit slower than calling a static method. Therefore, if you are sure a method won't need to be overridden, you should make it static; if you're not sure, make it virtual. Turbo Pascal, unlike most other object-oriented languages, gives you that choice.

Note that we did not have to make the *PrintBill* method virtual in the *IntlCust* object type. This is because the "once virtual, always virtual" rule only applies to a parent object type and its descendants. Since *Print-Bill* was defined as a virtual method in the *AmerCust* object type, any other object types descended from *AmerCust* must have *PrintBill* as a virtual method. However, *IntlCust* is not a descendant but rather a sibling of *AmerCust*, since they are both children of the *Cust* object type. Therefore, *PrintBill* can still be a static method in *IntlCust*.

There's one other item in the code listings that you may have noticed: each has the {$R + } compiler directive at the top to turn on range checking. Turbo Pascal's range checking features in version 5.5 have been enhanced to check for uninitialized virtual methods, i.e., to check if you forgot to include or invoke a constructor routine. While you're writing and debugging your program, it's a good idea to include this.

Dynamic Allocation with Objects

Although it's a little more complicated, objects can be used with pointers just like any other variables:

```
VAR
  AmerCustPtr : ^AmerCust;
  ...

  ...
BEGIN
  ...
  NEW(AmerCustPtr);
```

If a newly created object uses virtual methods, of course, it has to be initialized before any of its methods are used. You can still do this in a separate step, but Turbo Pascal's NEW command has been extended to do the allocation and initialization in a single step. Thus,

```
NEW(AmerCustPtr);
AmerCustPtr^.Init;
```

is equivalent to

```
NEW(AmerCustPtr, Init);
```

The extensions of NEW are purely optional, of course, and NEW will still work just fine with other variable types, the same as before.

Turbo Pascal's DISPOSE command, which deallocates the memory space of dynamic variables that are no longer needed, has also been extended to work with object variables. Because objects are more complex than traditional variable types, DISPOSE now works with a new method called a *destructor* whose job is to clean up after a dynamically-allocated object variable. The destructor method can be either static or virtual, and is declared like any other method:

```
AmerCust = OBJECT (Cust)
  state:  STRING[2];
  zip:    STRING[5];
  CONSTRUCTOR Init;
  DESTRUCTOR Done;
  PROCEDURE PrintBill; VIRTUAL;
  PROCEDURE SendBill
END;
```

The specific cleanup activities needed will naturally vary from object to object, and are defined in the implementation of each destructor method. The destructor is called with DISPOSE when you are deallocating a dynamic object variable:

```
DISPOSE(AmerCustPtr, Done);
```

As with a constructor method, Turbo Pascal performs certain activities automatically when a method called DESTRUCTOR is invoked by the DISPOSE command, so that even if the implementation of the destructor method is empty, it can still work:

```
DESTRUCTOR AmerCust.Done;
  BEGIN
  END;
```

Object-Oriented Debugging in Turbo Pascal

Turbo Pascal's integrated debugging features in version 5.5 have also been enhanced to handle object-oriented programs. Methods are treated just like any other procedures and functions; you can step through them with the F7 key or jump over them with the F8 key. To get a list of each object's methods, you can look in the Call Stack window. Object variables can be added to the Watch and Evaluate windows.

Summary

The OBJECT data type introduces a powerful new dimension to Turbo Pascal programming. By providing for inheritance of ancestor data fields and methods, objects reduce the amount of code needed to implement an application. By encapsulating data and methods together, objects simplify program structure and make them easier to debug and maintain.

Polymorphism and virtual methods give you a way to create library units that can be extended by users without any need for the source code. And because Turbo Pascal's object-oriented extensions are optional, you can do as little or as much object-oriented programming as you wish.

Object-oriented programming is not a "magic bullet" that can solve any programming problem with no effort. However, properly used, it is another valuable arrow in the quiver of the Turbo Pascal programmer.

A P P E N D I X

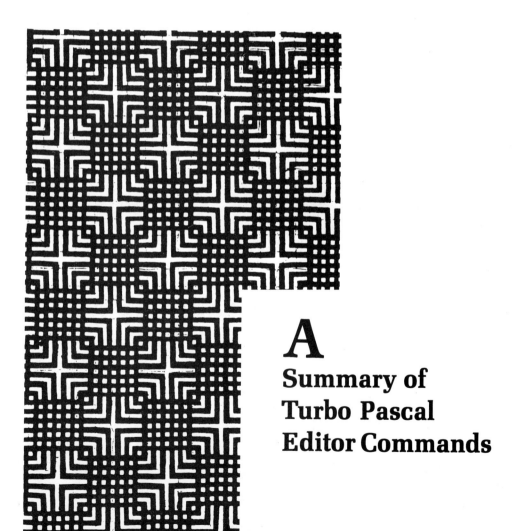

A
Summary of
Turbo Pascal
Editor Commands

Command	Keystroke

Cursor Movement Commands

Single-position moves

Up	↑ *or* Ctrl-E
Down	↓ *or* Ctrl-X
Right	→ *or* Ctrl-D
Left	← *or* Ctrl-S

Whole-word moves

Right	Ctrl-→ *or* Ctrl-F
Left	Ctrl-← *or* Ctrl-A

Moves within the current line

Beginning of line	Ctrl-Q-S
End of line	Ctrl-Q-D

Moves within the current screen

Top of screen	Ctrl-Home *or* Ctrl-Q-E
Bottom of screen	Ctrl-End *or* Ctrl-Q-X

Scrolling and page moves

Scroll up	Ctrl-W
Scroll down	Ctrl-X
Page up	PgUp *or* Ctrl-R
Page down	PgDn *or* Ctrl-C

Moves within a file

Top of file	Ctrl-PgUp *or* Ctrl-Q-R
Bottom of file	Ctrl-PgDn *or* Ctrl-Q-C

Command	Keystroke
Moves within a block	
Beginning of block	Ctrl-Q-B
End of block	Ctrl-Q-K
Marker moves	
To marker 0	Ctrl-Q-0
To marker 1	Ctrl-Q-1
To marker 2	Ctrl-Q-2
To marker 3	Ctrl-Q-3
To previous position	Ctrl-Q-P

Insert and Delete Commands

Inserting	
Toggle on/off	Ins *or* Ctrl-V
Insert a line	Enter *or* Ctrl-N

Deleting	
Character to the right	Del *or* Ctrl-G
Character to the left	Backspace *or* Ctrl-H
Word to the right	Ctrl-T
To the end of current line	Ctrl-Q-Y
Entire line	Ctrl-Y

Block Operations

Setting block markers	
Beginning marker	Ctrl-K-B
Ending marker	Ctrl-K-K
Mark one word	Ctrl-K-T
Hide/restore the block	Ctrl-K-H

Command	Keystroke

Copying, moving, and deleting a block

Copy to cursor position	Ctrl-K-C
Move to cursor position	Ctrl-K-V
Delete block	Ctrl-K-Y

Block file operations

Read a block from a disk file	Ctrl-K-R
Write current block to a file	Ctrl-K-W
Print the current block	Ctrl-K-P

Search and Replace Commands

Search for a target string	Ctrl-Q-F
Replace a target string	Ctrl-Q-A
Repeat previous search or replace	Ctrl-L

Marker Commands

Set marker n (0 to 3)	Ctrl-K-n
Move cursor to marker n	Ctrl-Q-n

Miscellaneous Commands

Tab	Tab *or* Ctrl-I
Toggle tab	Ctrl-O-T
Toggle automatic indent	Ctrl-O-I
Undo work on current line	Ctrl-Q-L

A P P E N D I X

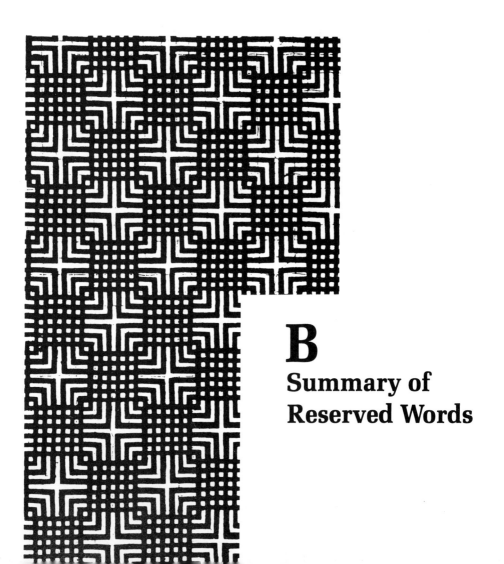

B
Summary of Reserved Words

This appendix gives brief descriptions and examples of all the reserved words in Turbo Pascal, version 5.5. (Where appropriate, each entry supplies a chapter reference indicating where you can read more about a given reserved word.)

ABSOLUTE

A clause that specifies the memory address where an absolute variable will reside:

```
VAR
  testVar: BYTE ABSOLUTE $B000:$0100;
```

(Turbo Pascal normally takes control of determining appropriate storage locations for variables. Use ABSOLUTE only where there is a specific reason for doing so.)

AND

A logical operator that connects two BOOLEAN expressions. The expression *a AND b* is true only if both *a* and *b* are true (Chapter 5).

ARRAY

A data structure designed to store lists or tables of indexed components:

```
VAR
  clientFiles: ARRAY [1..100] OF STRING;
```

(Chapter 6)

BEGIN

A marker for the beginning of a compound statement:

```
IF OIRESULT < > 0 THEN
  BEGIN
    WRITELN;
    WRITELN ('     * * * Can't open file.');
  END;
```

(Chapter 1)

CASE

(1) A decision structure that selects one of a list of statements for performance:

```
CASE sortSelection OF
nameAtoZ:       firstAddress : = firstName;
nameZtoA:       firstAddress : = lastName;
refNoAscend:   firstAddress : = firstRefNo;
refNoDescend: firstAddress : = lastRefNo;
   END;
```

(Chapter 5)

(2) A variant clause in a RECORD-type structure definition:

```
TYPE
   addressRecord =  RECORD
      name:           STRING[30];
      street:         STRING[30];
      city:           STRING[20];

      CASE usa:       BOOLEAN OF
         TRUE:        (state:  STRING[2];
                       zip:     STRING[5]);
         FALSE:       (otherLoc,
                       country:STRING[15])
   END;
```

(Chapter 6)

CONST

A declaration section for declaring named constants or for assigning initial values to typed variables or data structures:

```
CONST
   optionDisplay  = 'U B L P Q ';
   nullChar       = #0;
   enter          = #13;

   menuChars: SET OF CHAR =
      ['U', 'B', 'L', 'P', 'Q', nullChar, enter];
```

(Chapters 4 and 7)

CONSTRUCTOR

A special procedure to initialize an object that contains virtual methods.

```
AmerCust = OBJECT (Cust)
  state:   STRING[2];
  zip:     STRING[5];
  CONSTRUCTOR Init;
  PROCEDURE PrintBill; VIRTUAL;
  PROCEDURE SendBill
END;
```

(Chapter 16)

DESTRUCTOR

A special procedure that is used with DISPOSE to free up the memory used by a dynamically-allocated object.

```
AmerCust = OBJECT (Cust)
  state:   STRING[2];
  zip:     STRING[5];
  CONSTRUCTOR Init;
  DESTRUCTOR Done;
  PROCEDURE PrintBill; VIRTUAL;
  PROCEDURE SendBill
END;
```

(Chapter 16)

DIV

An arithmetic operation that gives the whole result from the division of two integers. The result of the expression *7 DIV 2* is 3 (Chapter 4).

DO

(1) A word that appears in the syntax of FOR and WHILE loop structures:

```
WHILE listJump > 1 DO
FOR j : = 1 TO sortLength − listJump DO
```

(Chapter 5)

(2) A word that appears in the syntax of the WITH structure:

```
WITH addresses [currentRecord] DO
```

(Chapter 6)

DOWNTO

A word that directs a FOR loop to decrement the control variable after each iteration of the loop:

```
FOR i : = 10 DOWNTO 1 DO
```

In the performance of this loop, the value of the control variable *i* will take on values from 10 down to 1 (Chapter 5).

ELSE

A clause in an IF decision structure:

```
IF currentRecord > 1 THEN
  APPEND (addressFile)
ELSE
  REWRITE (addressFile);
```

The ELSE clause is performed if the expression *currentRecord > 1* is false (Chapter 5).

END

A marker for the end of a compound statement:

```
IF OIRESULT < > 0 THEN
  BEGIN
    WRITELN;
    WRITELN ('     * * * Can''t open file.');
  END;
```

(Chapter 1)

EXTERNAL

A declaration for an external procedure or function written in assembly language:

```
FUNCTION GetAddr (inStr: STRING); EXTERNAL;
```

FILE

A structured variable that represents a typed or untyped disk file:

```
VAR
   profileFile: FILE OF profileRecord;
```

(Chapter 12)

FOR

A loop structure that employs a control variable to determine the number of iterations:

```
FOR j : = 1 TO sortLength – listJump DO
```

(Chapter 5)

FORWARD

A declaration for a procedure or function that is actually defined later in the program:

```
FUNCTION SampleFun (a, b: BYTE); FORWARD;
```

A FORWARD declaration is necessary when two routines make circular calls to each other.

FUNCTION

The heading section for a function definition:

```
FUNCTION LowerCase (inString: STRING): STRING;
```

(Chapter 4)

GOTO

A statement that transfers control to a defined label inside the current procedure or function block:

```
LABEL
  jumpLabel1,
  jumpLabel2;

BEGIN
  RANDOMIZE;
  IF RANDOM (10) > 5 THEN
    GOTO jumpLabel1;

  WRITELN ('Less than or equal to 5.');
  GOTO jumpLabel2;

  jumpLabel1:
    WRITELN ('More than 5.');

  jumpLabel2:
END.
```

IF

A decision structure that selects between two courses of action:

```
IF currentRecord > 1 THEN
  APPEND (addressFile)
ELSE
  REWRITE (addressFile);
```

(Chapter 5)

IMPLEMENTATION

The second section in a UNIT, where procedures and functions are actually defined after being declared in the INTERFACE section (Chapter 3).

IN

An operator that determines membership in a defined SET. The expression

inChar IN menuChars

results in a value of TRUE if *inChar* is a member of the *menuChars* set (Chapter 7).

INLINE

A statement that contains machine-level code in a procedure or function.

INTERFACE

The first section of a UNIT, where public procedures and functions are declared. These routines are actually defined later in the IMPLEMENTA-TION section (Chapter 3).

INTERRUPT

A declaration for an interrupt procedure.

LABEL

A declaration section that declares labels for GOTO statements:

```
LABEL
    jumpLabel1,
    jumpLabel2;
```

MOD

An arithmetic operation that supplies the remainder from the division of two integers. The expression *7 MOD 2* returns a value of 1 (Chapter 4).

NIL

A value assigned to a pointer variable to indicate that the pointer does not currently point to another variable:

```
newRecord ^ .nextName : = NIL;
```

(Chapter 7)

NOT

A unary logical operation that supplies the opposite of a logical value. The expression *NOT a* is TRUE if *a* is FALSE, or FALSE if *a* is TRUE (Chapter 4).

OBJECT

A structured data type similar to the record type, but which inherits features from ancestor objects and includes its own procedures and functions.

```
USAaddress = OBJECT (address)
```

```
     state:    STRING[2];
     zip:      STRING[5];
     PROCEDURE SendBill
END;
```

(Chapter 16)

OF

(1) A word that appears in the syntax of a CASE decision structure:

```
CASE sortSelection OF
```

(Chapter 5)

(2) A word that appears in the syntax of ARRAY, FILE, and SET type definitions or variable declarations:

```
VAR
   clientFiles: ARRAY [1..100] OF STRING;
menuChars: SET OF CHAR;
   profileFile: FILE OF profileRecord;
```

(Chapters 6, 7, and 12)

OR

A logical operator that connects two BOOLEAN expressions. The expression *a OR b* is true if *a* is true or *b* is true or both *a* and *b* are true (Chapter 5).

PACKED

In Standard Pascal, a qualifier for the definition of a structured data type, resulting in compressed data storage. PACKED has no special effect in Turbo Pascal, which automatically compresses storage when possible.

PROCEDURE

The heading for a procedure definition:

```
PROCEDURE GraphTitle (inTitle: STRING);
```

(Chapter 4)

PROGRAM

The optional heading for a program, supplying the program's name:

```
PROGRAM GraphDemo;
```

(Chapter 4)

RECORD

A structured data type, consisting of a sequence of named field components:

```
TYPE
  addressRecord = RECORD
    name:           STRING[30];
    street:         STRING[30];
    city:           STRING[20];

    CASE usa: BOOLEAN OF
      TRUE:  (state:   STRING[2];
              zip:     STRING[5]);
      FALSE: (otherLoc,
              country: STRING[15])
  END;
```

(Chapter 6)

REPEAT

A loop structure that performs iterations until a specified condition becomes true. The end of the loop block is marked by an UNTIL clause:

```
REPEAT
  inSignal : = READKEY
UNTIL inSignal = ' ';
```

A REPEAT/UNTIL loop always performs at least one iteration (Chapter 5).

SET

A data structure that contains a collection of values:

```
VAR
  menuChars: SET OF CHAR;
```

```
BEGIN
  menuChars : = ['U', 'B', 'L', 'P', 'Q'];
  { ... }
END.
```

Turbo Pascal supports a variety of set operations, the most useful of which is IN, for set membership (Chapter 7).

SHL

The *shift-left* operation, available for integer operands. The expression *int1 SHL int2* shifts the bits of *int1* to the left by *int2* places.

SHR

The *shift-right* operation, available for integer operands. The expression *int1 SHR int2* shifts the bits of *int1* to the right by *int2* places.

STRING

A standard data type that stores a sequence of characters:

```
VAR
  clientName: STRING;
```

(Chapter 4)

THEN

The first block in an IF decision structure, performed if the condition evaluates to true:

```
IF dirRequest THEN
  Directory (inName)
```

(Chapter 5)

TO

A word that appears in the syntax of a FOR loop. The TO clause indicates the beginning and ending value of the control variable:

```
FOR j : = 1 TO sortLength  − listJump DO
```

(Chapter 5)

TYPE

A declaration section for declaring user-defined type identifiers:

```
TYPE
  activities = (updateClient, billClient,
                listClients, listAddresses, quit);
  activityRange = updateClient..quit;
  activityRecord = RECORD
    fileName: STRING[8];
    row, column: BYTE;
    menuString: STRING[25]
  END;
```

(Chapters 4, 6, 7, 8, 11, 12)

UNIT

The heading of a Turbo Pascal unit, supplying the unit's name:

```
UNIT ChrnUnit;
```

A unit has two required sections, INTERFACE and IMPLEMENTATION. Optionally, a unit may also have an initialization section (Chapter 3).

UNTIL

The final clause of a REPEAT/UNTIL repetition loop, marking the end of the loop and supplying the condition that controls the loop's iterations:

```
REPEAT
  inSignal : = READKEY
UNTIL inSignal = ' ';
```

(Chapter 5)

USES

The statement that identifies the precompiled units that a program uses, including both standard units and units that you have written yourself:

```
PROGRAM PtrAddr;
  USES CRT, PRINTER, InUnit, StrUnit;
```

(Chapter 3)

VAR

A declaration section for global or local variables in a program, procedure, or function:

```
VAR
  newRecord: addressPointer;
  done:      BOOLEAN;
  addressFile: VAR;
```

(Chapters 4, 6, 7, 8, 11, 12)

VIRTUAL

Denotes an object's method to which program calls must not be bound until run-time.

```
AmerCust = OBJECT (Cust)
  state:   STRING[2];
  zip:     STRING[5];
  CONSTRUCTOR Init;
  DESTRUCTOR Done;
  PROCEDURE PrintBill; VIRTUAL;
  PROCEDURE SendBill
END;
```

(Chapter 16)

WHILE

A loop structure that performs repeated iterations as long as a specified condition is true:

```
WHILE NOT EOF (targetFile) DO
  BEGIN
    READLN (targetFile, chronStr, hours);
    total : = total + hours)
  END;
```

If the condition of a WHILE loop is false at the outset, the loop will perform no iterations (Chapter 5).

WITH

A control structure that allows you to abbreviate the notation for referring to the fields of a specified record:

```
WITH addresses [currentRecord] DO
  BEGIN
    WRITE ('State:   ');
    READLN (state);
    WRITE ('Zip code:   ');
    READLN (zip);
  END
```

(Chapters 6 and 8)

XOR

A logical operator that connects two BOOLEAN expressions. The expression *a XOR b* is true if either *a* is true or *b* is true, but not if both are true (Chapter 5).

INDEX

, (commas), 163, 177
− (minus sign), 171, 284–286
/ (slashes), 171
* *See* asterisks
{} (curly brackets), 29
$ (dollar sign), 74
# (number sign), 221
() *See* parentheses
. *See* periods
? (question marks), 57
' (single quotes), 151, 179
[] (square brackets), 250–252, 281
_ (underscore character), 147, 150
+ *See* plus sign
: (colons), 159, 247
; *See* semicolons
< (less than sign), 200, 286–287
= *See* equal sign
> (greater than sign), 200, 286–287
^ (caret character), 318, 321–322

A

$A compiler directive, 80
ABS function, 366
ABSOLUTE clause, 598
abstract object types, 571
actual parameters, 162
adapters, graphics, 492, 499
Add watch command (Break/watch
    menu), 14, 47–48, 102
AddClient procedure (CliProf),
    481–484
addition, 171
AddrCom program, 401–416
alignment, compiler directive for, 80
alphabetic case, 30
    functions for, 391–392
    for identifiers, 150

with set membership, 287
Alt key, 15–16, 307
ancestors of objects, 274, 568, 572–574
AND logical operator, 201–202, 598
appending records
    to random access files, 482–484
    to sequential files, 424, 426–427, 431
ARCTAN function, 364
arguments, 162–163
    arrays as, 254–256
    See also parameters
arithmetic functions, 365–366
ARRAY structure and arrays, 153–154,
    235, 598
    as arguments, 254–256
    definition of, 249–256
    initialization of, 295–296
    of records, 267–271
    of strings, 199
arrow keys, 307–308
    with Edit window, 7, 33–34
    with menus, 5, 11–12
ASCII codes, 157, 307–308
    comparison of, 201
    representation of, 221
ASSIGN procedure
    with random access files, 448, 458
    with sequential access files, 424–425,
        431
    with untyped files, 441
assignment statements, 159–160
asterisks (*)
    for changed files, 31
    for comments, 29
    as file wild-card characters, 57
    for multiplication, 171
    for set intersection, 284, 286
ATT.BGI file, 492
auto-detect mode, 500, 503

B

$B compiler directive, 81–82, 205
backspace key for deletion, 33, 35
.BAK and backup files, 33, 61, 90
BAR and BAR3D procedures for bar
      charts, 513–515
base type, pointer, 314, 318
BEGIN statement, 145–146, 598
      for blocks, 28
      with CASE, 210
      errors involving, 40
      with FOR, 212
      with IF, 206–207
bell character, 306
.BGI files, 492
BillTime program, 182–193
binary operations, 171
binary searches, 481
binding of objects, 352, 581–583,
      589–590
bitwise operators, 202
blank lines
      insertion of, 36, 178
      for readability, 30
BLOCKREAD procedure, 440, 442
blocks
      edit commands for, 596
      operations for, 104–105
      separation of, 28
BLOCKWRITE procedure, 440
BOOLEAN data type, 154, 159
      as array index, 251
      compiler directive for, 81–82, 205
      and decisions, 196
      and READLN, 271–272
      writing of, to files, 428
BOTTOMTEXT constant, 506
Break/watch menu, 14, 16, 47–50,
      101–103
breakpoints, 14, 47–50, 103
      and Go to cursor command, 66

      and Integrated debugging command,
            99
      and Program reset command, 65–66
Build command (Compile menu), 13,
      68–70
bullets with Watch window, 102
byte, alignment by, 80
BYTE data type, 155

C

Call stack command (Debug menu), 95,
      97–98
calls
      of functions and procedures, 19,
            160, 163–165
      near and far, 79
caret character (^) with pointers, 318,
      321–322
carriage returns as delimiters, 430
case and case sensitivity, 30
      functions for, 391–392
      for identifiers, 150
      with set membership, 287
CASE decision structure, 19, 195–196,
      208–212, 599
CENTERTEXT constant, 506, 508
CGA (Color/Graphics Adapter), 492,
      499, 501
CGA.BGI file, 492
Change dir command (File menu), 62
CHAR data type and characters, 154,
      157–158
      as array indexes, 251
      as control variables, 213
      deletion of, in Edit window, 33,
            35–36
      repeated, function for, 174, 394–395
      See also STRING data type and
            strings
CheckArguments function (AddrCom),
      413–415

child object types, 568, 572
.CHR files, 498, 507
ChrnUnit unit, 126–128, 522–543
CHRONINC.PAS file, 126
ChronString function (ChrnUnit),
        524–525
CIRCLE procedure, 508–510
Clear all breakpoints command
        (Break/watch menu), 50, 103
CliAddr program, 236–240, 256–272
CliBil_1 program, 574–581
CliBil_2 program, 588–589
CliChart program, 421–423, 431–439
ClientStatus function (CliList), 225
CliList program, 197–200, 224–232
CliMenu program, 278–280, 297–310
CliProf program, 450–456, 464–485
CLOSE procedure
        with random access files, 449
        with sequential files, 425, 431
CLREOL procedure, 125
CLRSCR procedure, 10, 125
Col message (Edit window), 31–32
colons (:)
        in assignment operator (:=), 159
        for variant fields, 247
color, 11, 113, 492, 499
Color/Graphics Adapter, 492, 499, 501
command-line parameters, 397–403,
        412–415
commas (,)
        in argument lists, 163
        in WRITE statements, 177
comments, 28–29, 74
COMP data type, 155–156
comparisons
        of sets, 286–287
        of strings, 201
compilation and compilers, 8–9, 39–41
        conditional, 75, 84–87
        directives for, 68, 74–76
        menu for, 13–16, 50–51, 67–73

and object binding, 352, 581–583,
        589–590
options for, 74–88
with Run command, 64
See also units
Compile command (Compile menu),
        14–15, 50–51, 68 ·
Compile menu, 13–16, 50–51, 67–73
compile-time errors, 40–41
complete evaluation of Boolean
        expressions, 81–82, 205
compound statements, 206
CONCAT function and concatenation
        of strings, 173
conditional compilation, 75, 84–87
Config auto save option, 89–90
configuration file commands, 93–94
CONST declarations and constants,
        144–145, 151, 294–297, 599
CONSTRUCTOR procedure, 583, 600
constructors for objects, 352–353
context-sensitive help, 8, 16–18
control commands for Edit window,
        34–35
control structures, 18–19, 146
See also decision structures; loops
control variables in FOR loops, 196,
        212–213
conversions
        of data types, 271–272, 366–368,
        396–397
        of dates, 537–542
coordinates, graphic, 501
coprocessor, 20
        COMP data type for, 155–156
        compiler directive for, 82–83
        conditional compilation symbol for,
        87
COPY function, 387
copying of blocks, 105
COS function, 364
cpu86 and cpu87 conditional

compilation symbols, 87
CreateAddressPointers procedure
    (RandAddr), 380–381
CreateChart (CliChart), 431
CRT standard unit, 124–125, 149
Ctrl key, 34–35, 105, 307
curly brackets ({ }) for comments, 29
cursor, 31
    in Edit window, 33–35, 594–595
    procedures for, 125, 304
customization of editor, 112–113
CustomV unit, 583–588

D

$D compiler directive, 83–84
data structures, 19, 146, 154
data types
    array, 249–256
    for functions, 161
    object, 570–574
    record, 241–243
    standard, 153–160
    user-defined, 20
database program, 450–456
date-arithmetic procedures, 521–551
DateString function (ChrnUnit), 525,
    550
DateString function (Today), 23, 45–49,
    126
DayOfWeek function (ChrnUnit), 532,
    541–543
DaysInMonth function (ChrnUnit),
    532, 535–537, 541
DaysInYear function (ChrnUnit), 532,
    537, 541
Debug menu, 13–14, 16, 94–101
debugging and debugger, 45–50
    compiler directive for, 83–84
    and map files, 88
    menu for, 13–14, 16, 94–101
    of objects, 592

and Program reset command, 64–66
of run-time errors, 42–45, 71–72
tools for, in Run menu, 13
and Trace into command, 66
and Watch window, 10
DEC procedure, 169
decimal places in formatted output,
    178–179
decision structures, 19, 195–196
    CASE, 208–212, 599
    IF, 206–208, 603
DEFAULTFONT constant, 507
$DEFINE compiler directive, 85
definitions
    for arrays, 249–256
    for records, 241–243
    for typed files, 457–459
    for variables and procedures, 19
Del key for deletion of characters, 35
DELETE procedure, 392–393
Delete watch command (Break/watch
    menu), 102
deletion
    of blocks, 105
    of characters, 33, 35–36, 595
    of current program file, 59–60
    of lines, 596
    of words, 36, 595
delimiters in text files, 430
descendants of objects, 274, 568,
    572–574
Destination command (Compile menu),
    13, 16–17, 51, 70–71
DESTRUCTOR procedure, 600
destructors for objects, 353–354, 591
development of programs, Parameters
    command for, 92–93
difference of sets, 285–286
dimensions, array, 235, 250
direct access files. *See* random access
    files
direction keys. *See* arrow keys

directives, compiler, 68, 74–76
directories option, 91–92
directory, listing of, 58, 61–62
Directory command (File menu), 61–62, 91
disk
   compilation to, 71
   files on, 8, 420
display screen
   and CRT unit, 125
   and Display swapping command, 100–101
   output to, 176–179, 419
   and Refresh display command, 101
   resolution of, 499
   writing to, 10
Display swapping command (Debug menu), 100–101
DisplayClient procedure (CliProf), 481
DISPOSE procedure, 321, 350–354, 591
DIV operator, 171, 600
DivideList procedure (ShowOff), 561–562
division, 171, 600
DO statement, 212, 217–218, 600–601
DoCommand procedure (AddrCom), 415–416
dollar sign ($) for compiler directives, 74
DollarDisplay function (StrUnit), 174, 185, 191, 393–394
DOS commands, execution of, 62–63, 231–232, 310
DOS standard unit, 107–108, 124, 149
DOUBLE data type, 156
double-linked lists. *See* linked lists
DOWNTO clauses, 213–214, 601
DrawBar procedure (GrphDemo), 513–515
DrawPie procedure (GrphDemo), 509–512

DRAWPOLY procedure, 516–517
DrawShapes procedure (GrphDemo), 515–517
DrawSine procedure (GrphDemo), 503–505
drop-down menus, 11
dynamic allocation of objects, 352–354, 590–591
dynamic variables, 313–314, 320–322
   strings as, 154, 158

E

$E compiler directive, 83, 156
early binding of objects, 582
Edit auto save option, 90
Edit watch command (Break/watch menu), 102–103
Edit window and editor, 5–9, 11, 31–39
   block operations in, 104–105, 596
   cursor movement in, 33–35, 594–595
   customization of, 112–113
   and Find-and-replace command, 108–112
   and include files, 105–108
   insert and delete, 595–596
   search and replace, 596
EGA (Enhanced Graphics Adapter), 492, 499
EGAVGA.BGI file, 492
elements, array, 199, 250–253, 268
ELLIPSE procedure, 516
ELSE clauses, 601
   with CASE, 209–211
   with IF, 206–208
$ELSE compiler directive, 85
empty sets, 282
empty strings, 158
emulation of math coprocessor, 83, 156
encapsulation of objects, 569, 574
end of file function, 218–219, 425, 430–431, 460, 463

END statement, 145–146, 601
  for blocks, 28
  with CASE, 209–210
  errors involving, 40
  with FOR, 212
  with IF, 206–207
  with units, 119–120
$ENDIF compiler directive, 85
Enhanced Graphics Adapter, 492, 499
enumerated data type, 288–293
  as array indexes, 251
  as control variables, 213
environment options, 89–91
EOF function, 218–219, 425, 430–431,
    460, 463
equal sign (=)
  in assignment operator (: =), 159
  as relational operator, 200
  for set equality, 286
equality of sets, 286
errors
  compile-time, 40–41
  input, 77–78, 181–182, 425, 427
  run-time, 42–45, 71–72
escape key, 15
Evaluate command (Debug menu),
    95–97
.EXE files, 13, 39, 50–51, 71, 92
EXEC procedure, 124, 231–232, 310
executable program files, 13, 39, 50–51,
    71, 92
EXIT with OS shell command, 62
EXP function, 358, 362–363
exponents for floating-point numbers,
    156
extended ASCII codes, 307–308
EXTENDED data type, 156–157
extensions
  .BAK, 33, 61, 90
  .BGI, 492
  .CHR, 498, 507
  .EXE, 13, 39, 50–51, 71, 92

.PAS, 32–33, 57, 106
.TP, 93
.TPU, 92, 120
EXTERNAL declaration, 601–602

F

$F compiler directive, 79
FALSE value, 159, 196, 200
far calls, 79
fields of records, 235, 240–245
  variant, 245–249
File menu, 12, 16, 50–51, 56–63
FILE structure and files, 419–421, 602
  backup, 33, 61, 90
  closing of, 431
  definition for, 457–459
  disk, 8, 420
  include, 68–69, 78, 92, 105–108, 117
  loading of, 8, 57–59
  menu for, 12, 16, 50–51, 56–63
  opening of, 426–427, 457–459
  random. *See* random access files
  reading from, 429–431, 462–463
  sequential, 130, 419–431
  TEXT, 130, 419–421
  typed, 420, 457–459
  untyped, 420, 439–443
  writing to, 427–428, 460–462
FILEPOS function, 460
FILESIZE function, 458–459
FillList procedure (ShowOff), 558
Find-and-replace command, 108–112
Find error command (Compile menu),
    71–72
Find function command (Debug
    menu), 95, 99
FindNamePointers procedure
    (PtrAddr), 344–348
FindNamePointers procedure
    (RandAddr), 380–381
FindRefNoPointers procedure

(PtrAddr), 344–348
FindRefNoPointers procedure
    (RandAddr), 380–381
FirstChar function (StrUnit), 387–391
floating-point numbers, 156
font files, 498, 505, 507
FOR loops, 19, 196, 212–217, 602
Force far calls, directive for, 79
formal parameters, 162
format notations for WRITE and
    WRITELN, 178–179
FORWARD and forward-referenced
    declarations, 318, 602
function keys, 8, 307
functions, 144–145, 160–161
    and Call stack command, 97–98
    calls to, 19, 160, 163–165
    in CRT unit, 149
    definition for, 19
    in DOS unit, 149
    and Find function command, 99
    global and local declarations in,
      165–167
    in GRAPH unit, 493–517
    headings for, 23, 602
    parameters for, 162–163, 167–170
    and Step over command, 67
    in SYSTEM unit, 148
    and Trace into command, 66
    See also methods

G

Get info command (Compile menu),
    72–73
GetClient procedure (CliProf), 481
GETDATE procedure, 124, 522
GetFileName function (BillTime), 186,
    192
GetFiles procedure (CliChart),
    431–432, 435–439
GetFiles procedure (CliList), 224

GETMAXX function, 501–502
GETMAXY function, 501–502
GetSelection procedure (CliMenu),
    305–308
GetSelection procedure (CliProf),
    480–481
GETTIME procedure, 124
global declarations, 165–167
global variables, 19
Go to cursor command (Run menu), 66
Gothic font, 498, 505, 507
GOTO statement, 19, 144, 602–603
GOTOXY procedure, 10, 125, 304, 492
GRAPH standard unit, 124, 491,
    493–517
GRAPH3 standard unit, 124, 147, 491
GraphContinue procedure
    (GrphDemo), 508
graphics, 491–497
    bar charts, 513–515
    circles, 508–509
    initialization of, 498–502
    pie charts, 509–512
    points and lines, 502–505
    shapes, 515–517
    text with, 505–508
GRAPH.TPU file, 498
greater than sign (>)
    as relational operator, 200
    for supersets, 286–287
GrphDemo program, 493–498, 503–517

H

Heading procedure (LateCli), 550–551
headings
    for function, 23, 602
    for procedures, 27, 605
    for programs, 144–145
    for units, 118–120
heap
    compiler directive for, 75, 87

management of, 320–322, 350–352
help facility, 8, 16–18
HERC.BGI file, 492
highlighting of menu items, 11
HighlightSelection procedure
    (CliMenu), 304–305, 307, 309
HORIZDIR constant, 507
hot keys, 7
Hours program, 129–138

I

$I compiler directive
    for include files, 78, 92, 105–108,
       117
    for I/O checking, 77–78, 182, 425,
       427
IBM8514.BGI file, 492
identifiers
    standard, 146–147
    user-defined, 147–151
    variables as, 152
IF decision structure, 19, 195–196,
    206–208, 603
$IFDEF compiler directive, 85–86
$IFNDEF compiler directive, 85–86
$IFOPT compiler directive, 85
IMPLEMENTATION section of units,
    119–122, 221–222, 603
IN operator with sets, 280, 287–288,
    603
InByte function (CliAddr), 256–258
INC procedure, 169
InChar function (CliAddr), 256–258
include files, 68–69, 78, 92, 105–108,
    117
InData procedure (LateCli), 549–551
InDate function (ChrnUnit), 524,
    533–536, 549–550
Indent message (Edit window), 31, 38
indentation, 30–31, 37–39

indexes
    for arrays, 199, 250–253
    in help facility, 17
    for random access files, 449
inheritance by objects, 273–274,
    568–569, 572–574
INITGRAPH procedure, 500–501
InitialCap function (StrUnit), 222–223,
    391–392
initialization
    of graphics, 498–502
    of virtual methods, 352–353
initialization section of units, 120
InitializeMenu procedure (CliMenu),
    303–305
InitializeMenu procedure (CliProf),
    480–481
INLINE statement, 604
INPUT file, 419
InReal function (CliAddr), 257
Insert message (Edit window), 31
insert mode in Edit window, 36, 595
INSERT procedure, 392–393
Installation menu, 112–113
INT function, 364
INTEGER and integer data types,
    154–155
    division with, 171
    functions for, 364–365
Integrated debugging command (Debug
    menu), 99
interactive programming, 176
    BillTime, 182–193
    and READ, 180–182
INTERFACE section of units, 119–121,
    221, 604
intersection of sets, 284, 286
InUnit unit, 184, 256–258
InvoiceHeading procedure (BillTime),
    186, 191–192
IORESULT function, 77, 182, 427

iterations of loops, 196

J

justification of strings, 174, 222, 224, 393

K

keyboard input, 180–182, 419
    for menu selection, 12
    and Output window, 9
    and READKEY, 220

L

$L compiler directive, 84
LABEL declarations, 144–145, 604
late binding of objects, 352, 581–583, 589–590
LateCli program, 543–551
Left function (StrUnit), 388–390
LeftAlign function (StrUnit), 222, 224, 393
LEFTTEXT constant, 506
LENGTH function and length of strings, 157–158, 395
less than sign (<)
    as relational operator, 200
    for subsets, 286–287
Line message (Edit window), 31
LINE procedure, 502, 504
LineOfChars procedure (Today), 27
lines
    drawing of, 502–505
    insertion of, into programs, 30, 36, 178
Link buffer option, 88–89
linked lists, 313–318
    accessing values in, 327–329
    creation of, 322–326
    insertion of records into, 344–348

moving through, 348–350
linking, 51
    options for, 88–89
    of units, 123
lists. *See* linked lists
LITT.CHR file, 498
LN function, 362–363
Load command (File menu), 57–58
Load options command, 93
loading of files, 8, 57–59
local procedures, 27, 165–167
Local symbols command, 84
local variables, 19, 84, 165–167
logarithms, 358, 362–363
logical values and operations, 159, 195, 200–205
LONGINT data type, 155, 522–523
loops, 19, 195–196
    FOR, 212–217, 602
    REPEAT/UNTIL, 219–221, 606
    WHILE, 217–219, 609
LowerCase function (StrUnit), 222–223, 391–392
LST text file, 125, 147, 177

M

$M compiler directive, 75, 87, 232, 320, 556
Main menu, 10–15, 55–56
Make command (Compile menu), 8, 13, 68–70
mantissas for floating-point numbers, 156
Map file option, 88
marking of blocks, 104–105, 596
masks for file names, 58
math coprocessor, 20
    COMP data type for, 155–156
    compiler directive for, 82–83
    conditional compilation symbol for, 87

MaxReal function (CliChart), 438
MCGA (Multicolor Graphics Array)
        adapter, 492, 499
membership, set, 280, 287–288
memory
    compilation to, 39–40, 71
    compiler directives for, 75, 87, 232,
        320, 556
    management of, 320–322, 350–352
    and objects, 352–354
    and recursion, 555
    and stack, 76–77
Menu procedure (CliAddr), 258–259,
        269
menu system
    Break/watch, 14, 16, 47–50,
        101–103
    Compile, 13–16, 50–51, 67–73
    Debug, 13–14, 16, 94–101
    File, 12, 16, 50–51, 56–63
    help for, 16–18
    Main, 10–15, 55
    Options, 13, 16, 73–94
    Run, 12–13, 16, 49, 63–67
    techniques for using, 14–16
Message program, 20–31
methods, 272–274, 569–570
    overriding of, 573
    virtual, 352, 581–583, 589–590
minus sign (−)
    for sets, 284–286
    for subtraction, 171
MOD and modulo operation, 171, 604
modular organization of Pascal, 18
modular programming and objects, 574
moving of blocks, 105
msdos conditional compilation symbol,
        87
Multicolor Graphics Array adapter,
        492, 499
multidimensional arrays, 251
multiplication, 171

N

$N compiler directive, 82–83, 156
named constants, 151
natural logarithms, 358, 362–363
near calls, 79
nesting
    of blocks, 28
    of loops, 215–217
    of parentheses, 172–173
    of procedures and functions,
        165–166
New command (File menu), 50, 59–60
NEW procedure, 321, 351
    for objects, 353, 590–591
New value box, 95
NewAddress procedure (CliAddr), 259,
        269
NewAddress procedure (PtrAddr),
        350–351
NIL for pointers, 324–325, 604
NOT logical operator, 201–202, 604
null character, 307
null sets, 282
null strings, 158
number sign (#) with ASCII codes, 221
NumDemo program, 358–362
numeric functions, 358–369
numeric operations, 171–173
Numeric processing option, 82–83, 156

O

$O compiler directive, 79–80
object code and files, 9, 92
objects and object-oriented
        programming, xxi-xxii, 20,
        567–569, 604–605
    creation of, 570–574
    dynamic allocation with, 352–354,
        590–591
    programs using, 574–590

structure of, 272–274
OF statement, 208–209, 605
OpenFiles procedure (CliProf), 479–480
opening
    of sequential files, 426–427
    of typed files, 457–459
operations, 146, 170–176
    bitwise, 202
    logical, 200–205
    relational, 200–201
    set, 282–284
Options menu, 13, 16, 73–94
OR logical operator, 201–202, 204, 605
ORD function, 290–292
order
    with enumerated types, 288
    of program sections, 146
ordinal data types, 154
    functions for, 290–293
origin, coordinate, 501
OS shell command (File menu), 42, 62–63
OUTPUT file, 419
output screen. *See* display screen
Output window, 6–10, 67
OUTTEXTXY procedure, 505–508
overflow, 367–368
OVERLAY standard unit, 124–125, 147
overlays, compiler directive for, 79–80

P

PACKED qualifier, 605
pages, graphic, 499–500
PARAMCOUNT function, 399–401
parameters, 19, 162–163
    command-line, 397–403, 412–415
    for compiler directives, 75
    and PARAMSTR function, 93, 397–401
    value and variable, 167–170

See also arguments
Parameters command, 92–93
parent object types, 568, 572
parentheses ( )
    for arguments, 163
    with array initialization, 296
    for comments, 29
    for logical expressions, 204
    with objects, 274, 572
    and operator precedence, 172–173
    for type casting, 271
.PAS extension, 32–33, 57, 106
PC3270.BGI file, 492
periods (.)
    with END, 28, 119
    with record fields, 243
    with subranges, 293
PgUp and PgDn keys for Edit window, 35
Pick command (File menu), 59
Pick file name option, 92
PIESLICE procedure, 509–512
pixels, 492
plus sign (+)
    for addition, 171
    for concatenation of strings, 173
    for set union, 284
pointers, 313–315
    declaration of variables for, 318–320
    and dynamic variables, 320–322
    with objects, 590–591
    See also linked lists
points, plotting of, 502–505
polymorphism, 569
pop-up menus, 14–15
POS function, 292, 395
powers, program to find, 363
precedence of operators, 172–173, 204
precision of data types, 155–157
PRED function, 290–291, 293
Primary file command (Compile menu), 68–70

PrintAddresses procedure (CliAddr), 269

PrintAddresses procedure (PtrAddr), 349–350

PrintBackward procedure (PtrTest), 315, 327–329

PrintBill procedure (BillTime), 186, 191–192

PrintClientList procedure (CliList), 224

PRINTER standard unit, 124–125, 147, 177

PrintExplanations procedure (CliList), 225

PrintForward procedure (PtrTest), 315, 327–329

printing of blocks, 105

PrintList procedure (CliAddr), 259, 269–270

PrintList procedure (PtrAddr), 348–350

PrintList procedure (RandAddr), 380–381

PrintList procedure (ShowOff), 558

PrintPhones procedure (CliAddr), 269

PrintPhones procedure (PtrAddr), 349–350

private elements of units, 119

private objects, 574

procedures, 144–145, 160–161
and Call stack command, 99
calls to, 19, 160, 163–165
in CRT unit, 149
definitions for, 19
in DOS unit, 149
and Find function command, 97–98
global and local declarations in, 165–167
in GRAPH unit, 493–517
headings for, 27, 605
parameters for, 162–163, 167–170
and Step over command, 67
in SYSTEM unit, 148
and Trace into command, 66

See also methods

Program reset command (Run menu), 49, 64–66

PROGRAM statement, 144–145, 606

programs
compilation of, 39–41
renaming of, 61
running of, 41–45
saving of, 8, 41, 60–61, 90
stand-alone, 397–399
structure of, 23, 144–153

PtrAddr program, 328–352
See also RandAddr program

PtrTest program, 314–320, 323–328

public elements of units, 119

punctuation of programs, 28

PUTPIXEL procedure, 502–503

Q

question marks (?) as file wild card characters, 57

Quicksort procedure (ShowOff), 558, 560–563

Quit command (File menu), 51, 63

R

$R compiler directive, 75–76

RandAddr program, 372–382

RandBoolean function (RandUnit), 371

RandFile program, 453–463

RandInt function (RandUnit), 370

random access files, 237, 420, 447–450
appending records to, 482–484
management of, 456–463
revising records in, 484–485

RANDOM function, 368–369

RANDOMIZE procedure, 369

RandStr function (RandUnit), 370

RandUnit unit, 369–372

ranges

compiler directive for checking, 75–76
of data types, 155–157
with objects, 590
with sets, 281
READ procedure, 180–182
  with INPUT, 419
  with random access files, 449, 462–463
  with sequential files, 429–431
readability of program code, 30, 37
  constants for, 151
  and identifiers, 150
ReadAddresses procedure (PtrAddr), 344
READKEY function, 125, 220, 305, 307–309
READLN procedure, 180–182
  with BOOLEAN types, 271–272
  with sequential files, 429–431
REAL data type and real numbers, 154, 156
records and RECORD structure, 153–154, 235, 240, 606
  arrays of, 267–271
  definition for, 241–243
  field values of, 243–245
  pointers for, 459–461
  and random access files, 447, 449, 459–460
  See also linked lists; objects and object-oriented programming
RECTANGLE procedure, 516
recursion, 20, 555–564
reference, passing parameters by, 81, 167
Refresh display command (Debug menu), 101
relational operators, 200–201
Remove all watches command (Break/watch menu), 49, 103
RemoveHighlight procedure (CliMenu), 306

renaming of program files, 61
REPEAT/UNTIL loops, 19, 196, 217, 219–221, 606
repeating-character functions, 174, 394–395
reports, program to generate, 182–193
reserved words, 30, 146–147, 150, 598–610
RESET procedure
  with random access files, 448, 458
  with sequential files, 424, 426–427, 431
  with untyped files, 441–442
resolution, screen, 499
Result box, 95
Retrieve options command, 94
reverse video for menu highlighting, 11
ReverseVideo procedure (CliMenu), 303–304
ReviseClient procedure (CliProf), 481, 484–485
REWRITE statement
  with random access files, 448, 458
  with sequential files, 424, 426, 431
  with untyped files, 442
Right function (StrUnit), 388–390
RightJustify function (StrUnit), 174, 393
RIGHTTEXT constant, 506
roots, program to find, 363
ROUND function, 365
Run command (Run menu), 64
Run menu, 12–13, 16, 49, 63–67
run-time errors, 42–45
  and Find error command, 71–72
running of programs, 8, 41–45
  menu for, 12–13, 16, 49, 63–67

S

$S compiler directive, 76–77
SalesTax program, 215–216
sans-serif font, 498, 507

Save-and-continue operation, 32–33
Save command (File menu), 60–61
Save options command, 93–94
SaveAddress procedure (PtrAddr), 351
SaveIndex procedure (CliProf), 480
saving
    of configuration, 89–90
    of programs, 8, 41, 60–61, 90
scalar data types, 154
    range checking for, 76
ScalarDate function (ChrnUnit), 524, 536–539
ScalarToString function (ChrnUnit), 532, 539–542, 550–551
Screen size option, 91
    See also display screen
search and replace commands, 596
SearchIndex function (CliProf), 481–484
searching algorithms, 481
SEEK procedure, 448–449, 459–460, 463
SelectNextActivity procedure (CliMenu), 308–309
selector expression with CASE, 209
SelectPreviousActivity procedure (CliMenu), 308–309
semicolons (;)
    with END, 28
    errors involving, 40
    in IF structures, 207
    as separators, 28, 30
sequential access files, 130, 419–431
Serious procedure (LateCli), 550–551
Set colors command, 113
SET structure and sets, 154, 280–281, 305–306, 606–607
    arithmetic operations with, 282–286
    comparison operations with, 286–287
    membership in, 287–288
SETDATE procedure, 522

SETFILLSTYLE procedure, 509–512, 515
SetLetterPointers procedure (PtrTest), 315, 323–326
SetPointers procedure (PtrAddr), 344–345, 351
SetPointers procedure (RandAddr), 380–382
sets. *See* SET structure and sets
SetTest program, 283–285
SETTEXTJUSTIFY procedure, 505–508
SETTEXTSTYLE procedure, 505–507
Shell sort algorithm, 230–232
SHL bitwise operator, 202, 607
short circuit mode for Boolean evaluation, 81–82, 204–205
SHORTINT data type, 155
ShowOff program, 556–563
SHR bitwise operator, 202, 607
simple data type, 154
SIN function, 364
    procedure to display, 503–505
SINGLE data type, 156
single quotes (')
    for strings, 151
    in strings, 179
slashes (/) for division, 171
small font, 498, 507
Smalltalk language, 567–568
SortAddresses procedure (CliAddr), 269–270
SortClientFiles procedure (CliChart), 431
SortClientFiles procedure (CliList), 224, 230–232
SortIndex procedure (CliProf), 480
sorting, 230–232
    with quick sort, 555–563
source code, 9
    in Edit window, 6
    and include files, 106, 117

spaces as delimiters, 430
Spaces function (StrUnit), 222–223, 394–395
SQR function, 366
SQRT function, 366
square brackets ([ ])
    for array elements, 250–252
    with sets, 281
stack
    compiler directives for, 75–77, 87
    and recursion, 555–556
stand-alone programs, 397–399
Standalone debugging command (Debug menu), 100
standard data types, 153–160
standard identifiers, 146–147
standard units, 20, 107–108, 118, 124–126, 137
statements, separation of, 28
Step over command (Run Menu), 67
STR function, 396–397
STRING data type and strings, 154, 157–158, 607
    as arguments, 255
    arrays of, 199
    comparison of, 201
    constants, 151
    functions for, 386–397
    operations for, 173–176
    passing of, by reference, 81
    POS function for, 292
StringOfChars function (StrUnit), 174, 394–395
structure of programs, 23, 144–153
structured data types, 19, 146, 154
structured language, Pascal as, 18
StrUnit unit, 173–176, 221–224, 387–395
subdirectories, 62, 91–92
subprograms, 160
subrange types, 268, 293–294
subroutines, 160

subscripts for arrays, 250
    range checking for, 76
subsets, 286–287
substring functions, 387–392
subtraction, 171
    of sets, 284–286
SUCC function, 290–291
supersets, 286–287
symbolic constants, 151
syntax, help screens for, 17
SYSTEM standard unit, 124, 148, 357, 385

T

Tab fill message (Edit window), 38
Tab key in Edit window, 38
Tab size command, 38, 90
tabs as delimiters, 430
tag fields, 246
TakeAction procedure (LateCli), 549–551
Testing of programs, Parameters command for, 92–93
TestUnit program, 121–123
TEXT files, 130, 419–421
text on graphics screen, 505–508
text screen, 491
TEXTBACKGROUND procedure, 304
TEXTCOLOR procedure, 304
THEN statement, 206–208, 607
three-dimensional arrays, 251
three-dimensional bar charts, 513–515
TimeString function (Today), 23, 27, 126
TINST utility program, 35–36, 92, 112–113
TO clauses, 212–214, 607
Today program, 20–31, 41–45
TodaysDate function (ChrnUnit), 524, 538–539, 550–551
TodaysMessage procedure (Today), 27

Toggle breakpoint command (Break/watch menu), 47, 103
TOPTEXT constant, 506, 508
TotalAccount function (CliChart), 437–438
TotalAccount function (CliList), 224–225
TotalLine procedure (BillTime), 186
.TP extensions, 93
.TPU files, 92, 120
TPUMOVER.EXE file, 126
tracing and Trace into command (Run menu), 8, 48, 66
    and Integrated debugging command, 99
trigonometric functions, 364
Triplex font, 498, 505, 507
TRUE value, 159, 196, 200
TRUNC function, 365
TruthTbl program, 202–204
Turbo Debugger, 100
Turbo directory, 92
TURBO.TP file, 93
TURBO.TPL file, 118, 125–126
TURBO3 standard unit, 124, 147
turtle graphics, 491
two-dimensional arrays, 251
type casting, 271–272, 292–293
    and numeric conversions, 366–368
type conversion functions, 396–397
TYPE declarations, 144–145, 152, 608
typed constants, 294–297
typed files, 420, 457–459
typeover mode in Edit window, 36
types. *See* data types

U

unary operations, 171
$UNDEF compiler directive, 85
underscore character (_) in variable names, 147, 150

Undo command, 36
unindent feature, 31, 38
union of sets, 284–285
units, 20, 68–69, 106–108, 117
    ChrnUnit, 126–128
    creation of, 118–122
    directories for, 92
    expansion of, 221–224
    heading for, 118–119, 608
    and objects, 568
    standard, 2, 18, 107–108, 124–126, 137
    and USES statement, 122–124
UNTIL clauses, 219–221, 608
untyped files, 420, 439–443
UPCASE function, 305
UPCHAR function, 391
UpperCase function (StrUnit), 174, 391–392
user-defined data types, 20, 152
user-defined identifiers, 147–151
user-defined units, 118, 137
user interface, design of, 398
User screen command (Run menu), 67
USES statement, 69, 107, 122–124, 137, 144–145, 608

V

$V compiler directive, 80–81
VAL function, 396–397
value parameters, 167–170
VAR declarations, 144, 152–153, 609
    with text files, 423
Var-string checking, compiler directive for, 80–81
variable parameters, 167–170
variables
    and Add watch command, 102
    array, 249–256
    definitions for, 19
    and Evaluate command, 95–97

for objects, 571
record, 241–243
See also pointers
variant fields, 245–249
ver50 conditional compilation symbol, 87
VERTDIR constant, 507
VGA (Video Graphics Array) adapter, 492, 499
View next breakpoint command (Break/watch menu), 103
VIRTUAL keyword, 582–583, 609
virtual method table, 583
virtual methods, 352, 581–583, 589–590
VMT (virtual method table), 583

W

WaitForEnter procedure (Today), 27
Warning procedure (LateCli), 550–551
Watch window, 5–8, 10, 47–48
watches
and Break/watch menu, 14, 16, 47–50, 101–103
and Program reset command, 65–66
wedges, drawing of, 509–512
WHEREX procedure, 125
WHEREY procedure, 125
WHILE loop structure, 19, 196, 217–219, 221, 609
width in formatted output, 178
wild-card characters with files, 57

windows
Edit, 5–9, 11, 31
Output, 6–10, 67
Watch, 5–8, 10, 47–48
WITH control structure, 235, 244–245, 248, 268, 610
with objects, 571
word, alignment by, 80
WORD data type, 155
words, deletion of, in Edit window, 36
WordStar commands, 8, 15
work-hour records, program for, 129–138
Write to command (File menu), 61, 105
WRITE procedure, 10, 27, 176–179
and LST, 125, 177
with OUTPUT, 419
with random access files, 449, 461–462
with sequential files, 427–428
WRITELN procedure, 10, 27, 176–179
help screen for, 17–18
and LST, 125, 177
with sequential files, 427–428
writing of blocks, 105

X

XOR logical operator, 201–202, 610

Z

zooming of windows, 7, 9, 31, 90

TO JOIN THE SYBEX MAILING LIST OR ORDER BOOKS
PLEASE COMPLETE THIS FORM

NAME _____ COMPANY _____

STREET _____ CITY _____

STATE _____ ZIP _____

☐ PLEASE MAIL ME MORE INFORMATION ABOUT **SYBEX** TITLES

ORDER FORM (There is no obligation to order)

PLEASE SEND ME THE FOLLOWING:

TITLE	QTY	PRICE
_____	____	____
_____	____	____
_____	____	____
_____	____	____

TOTAL BOOK ORDER   ____ $____

CUSTOMER SIGNATURE _____

SHIPPING AND HANDLING PLEASE ADD $2.00
PER BOOK VIA UPS   _____

FOR OVERSEAS SURFACE ADD $5.25 PER
BOOK PLUS $4.40 REGISTRATION FEE   _____

FOR OVERSEAS AIRMAIL ADD $18.25 PER
BOOK PLUS $4.40 REGISTRATION FEE   _____

CALIFORNIA RESIDENTS PLEASE ADD
APPLICABLE SALES TAX   _____

TOTAL AMOUNT PAYABLE   _____

☐ CHECK ENCLOSED   ☐ VISA
☐ MASTERCARD   ☐ AMERICAN EXPRESS

ACCOUNT NUMBER _____

EXPIR. DATE _____ DAYTIME PHONE _____

CHECK AREA OF COMPUTER INTEREST:

☐ BUSINESS SOFTWARE

☐ TECHNICAL PROGRAMMING

☐ OTHER: _____

THE FACTOR THAT WAS MOST IMPORTANT IN YOUR SELECTION:

☐ THE SYBEX NAME

☐ QUALITY

☐ PRICE

☐ EXTRA FEATURES

☐ COMPREHENSIVENESS

☐ CLEAR WRITING

☐ OTHER _____

OTHER COMPUTER TITLES YOU WOULD LIKE TO SEE IN PRINT:

_____

_____

OCCUPATION

☐ PROGRAMMER   ☐ TEACHER

☐ SENIOR EXECUTIVE   ☐ HOMEMAKER

☐ COMPUTER CONSULTANT   ☐ RETIRED

☐ SUPERVISOR   ☐ STUDENT

☐ MIDDLE MANAGEMENT   ☐ OTHER:

☐ ENGINEER/TECHNICAL   _____

☐ CLERICAL/SERVICE

☐ BUSINESS OWNER/SELF EMPLOYED

CHECK YOUR LEVEL OF COMPUTER USE

☐ NEW TO COMPUTERS

☐ INFREQUENT COMPUTER USER

☐ FREQUENT USER OF ONE SOFTWARE

   PACKAGE:

   NAME _____

☐ FREQUENT USER OF MANY SOFTWARE

   PACKAGES

☐ PROFESSIONAL PROGRAMMER

OTHER COMMENTS:

_____

_____

_____

_____

_____

_____

_____

PLEASE FOLD, SEAL, AND MAIL TO SYBEX

SYBEX, INC.
2021 CHALLENGER DR. #100
ALAMEDA, CALIFORNIA USA
94501